Happiness Rules

Happiness Rules

Mark Hebwood

First published in Great Britain in 2018 by Mark Hebwood

A CIP catalogue record for this book is available from the British Library.

ISBN 978-0-9956509-0-9

Printed and bound in Great Britain by Clays Ltd, St Ives plc.

MIX
Paper from
responsible sources
FSC® C018072

Cover design by
Isaac Tobin

You cannot teach a man anything, you can only help him find it within himself

Galileo Galilei

Contents

INTRODUCTION
This book is not promising anything

It worked for me . . .

A few years ago, I was on a business trip to the US. I was there for a week and on Friday I had arrived in Los Angeles. My afternoon meetings were cancelled and I got to my hotel early. Once settled into my room, I got myself a drink from the mini-bar and sat down on the balcony to relax from the week. It had been a busy week, with a lot of travelling and a lot of meetings, and I was looking forward to a Saturday in LA before going back to London. I settled back into my chair and looked out over the city in the afternoon sun. I remember thinking, 'This is nice'. And then something hit me. I realised that I was happy!

I lived in a place I loved, I had a job I liked and I had a partner who loved me for who I was. I felt I had nothing to prove and I could be myself. Sure, it would be nice to make more money, find a few new challenges at work, have more time to do sports, go out with friends . . . But there would always be *some*thing that could improve. Basically, I realised that there was nothing much missing. Life was OK.

But how did this come about? Did this just happen, or did I have a hand in it? Was I merely lucky, or had I done something to deserve this?

I thought about this over dinner, and during the next day spent by the hotel pool. When it was time to go home I had my answer. Yes, I *did* have something to do with it. I *had* made decisions in my life consciously, and deliberately. I *had* gradually shaped my life into something that made me fundamentally happy. And it was *not* down to luck. When I arrived in London, I thought my story could actually be of interest for others too. Several months later, I had written it all down.

No reason why it should not work for you

And this is why this book may differ from other accounts which have a similar gist, and which you can pick up under the heading self-improvement or self-help. I am not a trained psychologist, I have not run thousands of seminars which I am condensing into a book and I do not promise anything. This is my story, and the experiences I am discussing are all taken from my life and those of friends and acquaintances.

And yet, the methods and tricks I used to build a happy life for myself translate easily into methods and tricks that you can employ in your own life. The ideas, maxims, tools and recipes that I am going to share with you are the result of a lifelong thought process, and they have proven to work for me. None of them are special or private, anybody can apply them and there is no reason to believe that they would not work for you too.

Who am I to say this?

Let me introduce myself. My name is Mark Hebwood, but that is a pen name chosen to protect the innocent. I was born in Germany and came to the UK for business school after completing a Masters in Literature and History at a German university. Fresh out of business school, I started my professional life in the insurance industry. After a few years, I changed my career and joined a firm of stockbrokers in the City of London as a research analyst. And that is what I still do today.

I am not saying that this is more of a journey than others have completed; in fact, it is quite possibly less. What I *am* saying is that I have taken many *conscious* steps on the way. As I was progressing through life, I gained ever more insights into my personality, into my likes and dislikes, into the reasons I preferred certain choices to others.

In short, I was finding out *who I was*. And knowing who I was, I discovered what I wanted in life. And knowing what I wanted, I found out how to get it.

That, in brief, is the reason why I feel well adjusted – and happy – today.

Upside and downside

I said earlier that I cannot think of a compelling reason why the methods I am discussing in this book should not work for you as well as they have worked for me. But there is a catch, and it would be churlish not to tell you. I did not start out in life as balanced and happy as I am now. It took a lifetime of application to get there, and I do not believe there are quick fixes in the pursuit of happiness. With this caveat out of the way, I cannot see a huge downside to reading this book, but I can see a lot of upside.

The downside is you may get bored with me and chuck the book in the bin.

The upside is you may learn more about who you are, find out what really matters to you, care less about what others expect of you, make decisions more confidently, control your life more efficiently, develop internal balance by letting go of the urge to judge others, learn how to take advice, how to find a partner who loves you for who you are, assemble a toolkit to shape your world, and develop a positive attitude towards yourself. Anything else? Oh yes, and learn how to tell 'right' from 'wrong'.

'Yeah right,' I hear you say, 'come off it, mate.' Granted, this sounds like a lot. And yet, I am going to discuss all these things in the book. In each chapter I give you lots of stories and then bring them together with what I hope is some analytical rigour. I guess some of my stories will make you frown and invite contradiction and debate. Others may make you smile, or even laugh. Some of the analysis you may find intuitive and some more esoteric.

But at the end of the day, after all the stories and the analysis and the thoughts and the suggestions, what I think will remain are a few insights, tricks and methods for how to build a happier life.

Guess I *am* promising something after all.

Mark Hebwood
London 2018

Part I

Know yourself

RULE 1

Know who you are

Know whom?

So let us jump right in at the deep end. The hardest step, and by far the most important one, is to understand who we are.

What is it that I want in life? And why do I want it? What do I think gives meaning to things? Why do I think that? What makes me sad, angry and, dare I say it this early on, happy? And why? Why am I backing away from some challenges and why am I embracing others? Why have I fallen in love with Peter? Why do I dislike Joan? Why do I like the colour blue, hate cooking, love gardening, like to ride a bicycle? Why do I not worry about my weight? Why am I religious? Why am I not?

I contend that I would know the answers to all those questions with certainty if I could perfectly know myself. And if I did, I would never again make a decision that was wrong for me. And if I made the right decisions, I would end up in a good place. I would have a meaningful job. I would be with the right person. I would live in the right place. I would *like* myself. I would be happy.

We have started the journey – no turning back now. Three steps lie between us and the goal:

(1) Know who you are.
(2) Know what you need.
(3) Get it.

These steps need to be taken in sequence. I cannot know what I need before I know who I am. I cannot go after what I need before I know what I need.

A pragmatic principle

The idea that self-knowledge is important is not new. Here is how Pausanias, a Greek geographer who lived in the second century AD, describes the forecourt of Apollo's temple at Delphi:

> In the fore-temple at Delphi are written maxims useful for the life of men, inscribed by those whom the Greeks say were sages . . . These sages, then, came to Delphi and dedicated to Apollo the celebrated maxims, 'Know thyself' and 'Nothing in excess'.[1]

The ancient Greeks clearly regarded the principle as sufficiently important to give it pride of place in the temple dedicated to one of their highest gods. But not important enough to reside there on its own – 'gnothi seauton'[2] was inscribed next to 'meden agan'.[3]

Although the pragmatic Greeks may not have elevated self-knowledge to the highest principle, the maxim nevertheless rings out through the ancient world. In one of his dialogues, Plato, widely acclaimed as one of antiquity's most prolific thinkers, shows the fictional Socrates in conversation with Phaedrus, an intellectual and aristocrat. In one passage, Phaedrus asks whether a particular event in mythology should

---

[1] Pausanias. *Description of Greece*. Translated by WHS Jones, Theoi Texts Library http://www.theoi.com/Text/Pausanias5A.html, 10.24.1.

[2] 'Know yourself', in modern English.

[3] You guessed it – 'Nothing in excess'.

be conceded as true. Socrates responds that many learned men give rational explanations of why it should not be considered so. But, he says, he declines to join the debate on either side:

> ... shall I tell you why? I must first know myself, as the Delphian inscription says; to be curious about that which is not my concern, while I am still in ignorance of my own self, would be ridiculous ... I want to know not about this, but about myself: am I a monster more complicated and swollen with passion than the serpent Typho, or a creature of a gentler and simpler sort, to whom Nature has given a diviner and lowlier destiny?[4]

To Socrates at least, self-knowledge took precedence over subjects as elevated even as mythology. And he is not alone in his view. The idea that self-knowledge is an object worthy of study reverberates through the ages:

> Knowing others is intelligence; knowing yourself is true wisdom. (Lao-Tzu, *The Way of Life*, 6th century BC)

> Knowing yourself is the beginning of all wisdom. (Aristotle, 4th century BC)

> A man who finds no satisfaction in himself will seek for it in vain elsewhere. (La Rochefoucauld, 17th century)

> There are three things extremely hard. Steel, a Diamond, and to know one's self. (Benjamin Franklin, *Poor Richard's Almanack*, 1750)

> If most of us remain ignorant of ourselves, it is because self-knowledge is painful and we prefer the pleasures of illusion. (Aldous Huxley, 1945)[5]

I could easily fill a whole book with aphorisms about self-knowledge, but of course there would be no point in doing so.

---

[4] *Plato, Phaedrus.* Translated by Benjamin Jowett. The Internet Classics Archive. http://classics.mit.edu/phaedrus.html.

[5] Huxley, Aldous. *The Perennial Philosophy.* Copyright © 1945 by Aldous Huxley. Reprinted by Georges Borchardt, Inc. for the Estate of Aldous Huxley.

The only point I am making here is that the pursuit of self-knowledge has been recognised as important by many eminent men and women throughout the ages. So we find ourselves in good company when we identify self-knowledge as the first goal on a journey to greater contentment in life.

Know yourself I

A photo album of life snapshots
Again, why do I think self-knowledge is so important?

I think Socrates made an excellent point. Self-knowledge needs to come first; other pursuits can only be meaningful if it precedes them.

If I do not know myself, I do not know what I need. If I do not know what I need, I risk making the wrong decisions, following the wrong advice, giving in to peer-group pressure, acting to please others.

But if I *do* know myself, I have a good chance of making decisions that are right for me, surrounding myself with people who like me for who I am, developing a feeling of self-worth and moulding life into a shape that is good for me.

The problem, of course, is how to develop self-knowledge. It certainly sounds like an elusive object and does not appear to lend itself to direct scrutiny. Still, I believe it is perfectly possible to develop an in-depth understanding of our own personality.

In fact, I would like to propose a formal method of how to get there. But I am not going to reveal it just yet. Indeed, I think most of us will have a reasonable idea of what it is we want to achieve, how we would react in a given situation, what we like, what we dislike. What we may not know is *why* we like what we like, want what we want, act as we do.

So before I get to the how, let us talk about the what. To find out what we may already know about ourselves, I suggest looking through past life experiences. Nothing big or, necessarily, fundamental. Just things we remember. That party we went to when we were teenagers. That boss who drove us crazy. That friend who always made us laugh. I suppose you could say I am inviting you to look at your life as if it was a photo album full of snapshots, where each snapshot stands for a story. Each story will reveal something about you, will show you a glimpse of your personality. I suggest we let a stream of consciousness take over. Let us not censor anything, suppress certain stories or favour others. Let us just relax in that hot bath, lose ourselves in music, sit back in that armchair and look out over the sea, the rolling hills, the city.

And let the stories come.

Normative behaviour

The first story that pops into my mind takes me back to school, to a time when I was 17 years old.

I was sitting in the Social Sciences class waiting for the arrival of Mr Byass, our teacher. The door opened and Mr Byass walked in. Without a word he strode across the room, arrived at his desk, climbed onto his chair and then got onto the desk itself. He remained standing on his desk, arms folded behind his back, for a good two minutes.

Excellent! At least this lesson was not going to be dull! We all stared at him in expectation of further antics. But nothing happened. Byass was just standing there, staring at the wall. After a while the silence gave way to soft chattering. 'What the hell is he doing?', 'He looks taller that way – good thinking', 'Shall we chuck something at him?' Some of us started to giggle. The class was getting more unruly, beginning to lose interest in him, when he climbed down from his desk and announced that he was engaged in a social experiment in normative behaviour. He was studying how people behave when somebody deliberately acts in a way that breaks the mould.

Hearing that, I had an idea. I leaned over to my best mate and told him what I had in mind. Not surprisingly, he was immediately up for it. We needed a third guy and we asked Matti Schröder, who happened to sit next to us, whether he was in. He was, and the stage was set.

My mate Pete and I were passable gymnasts, so we got up from our chairs and started walking slowly into the aisle between the students' desks. Pete called out to Matti: 'Mr Schröder, would you mind?' Matti got up and opened the classroom door, then stood next to it ramrod straight, like a butler. Pete and I got down on the floor and each of us pressed into a handstand. Then, in measured steps, we walked out of the door on our hands. Matti shut the door and that was that.

We were outside the classroom in the corridor, laughing. Then we realised something. We were outside the classroom in the corridor! There was an open window at the end of the corridor. We were on the second floor but we knew there was a high wall running outside that window. Surely we could jump down and, from there, drop to the ground outside? Turned out we could, so we did. Once outside, we legged it and were gone.

I heard later that our teacher was absolutely livid at what we had done. We both got a citation to see the dean about it. Next time in class I pointed out to Mr Byass that he had behaved like any other teacher when confronted with students displaying 'non-normative' behaviour. Indeed, the social experiment Pete and I conducted demonstrated that people seek refuge in normative actions when confronted with behavioural patterns that 'break the mould' and are therefore interpreted as a threat. I also remember demanding a good mark for our contribution and my analysis, and arguing with Mr Byass for half an hour or so over it.

And now for a little interpretation.

When I was at school I never liked Mr Byass much. I did not think he was a good teacher, and I rarely gained any intriguing insights in his classes. Still, he fancied himself as a left-wing intellectual with a station above the middle classes, whom he clearly held in low esteem.

On the day I remembered, something rubbed me up the wrong way about the experiment he was conducting. It seemed to me that he was using us as guinea pigs and, in so doing, trying to set himself apart from the students in his care.

My own little stunt was meant to expose what I saw as arrogance, and it reveals several nuggets of insight into my personality. I have little time for people I regard as pseudo-intellectuals. I do not respect authority if I do not believe it has been earned. And the fact that I was arguing with him to give me a good mark? I am irreverent and I can be stroppy. To give Mr Byass credit, he did give me a good mark for my overall performance at the end of the course. In spite of my little stunt, not because of it. But still.

Ballsed that one up . . .

The next story I remember also plays out at school, only three years earlier.

I was 14 years old and at a school athletics day. I hated athletics. I was not useless at sports, but I was never particularly competitive. Sports I liked all involved an element of balance, like gymnastics, skateboarding or rollerblading. I also tended to think sports activities were for playing around and having fun. I certainly did not think they were something to be taken seriously.

Yet here I was, forced into an environment of competitive athletics. The event I was told I needed to engage in was the shot-put. I found myself standing in a longish line of kids, waiting for my turn to chuck a ball of iron into a sandpit. It was a slightly cold day, it had been drizzling, the ground was wet, it was early in the morning. I did not want to be there and I was shivering in my shorts and T-shirt.

Me next. I tried to remember the technique. Take the ball, nestle it in the side of your neck, toss your leg up and sort of shuffle backwards on one foot, turn half way and shove the ball as far as possible into the sand. So that is what I did. The ball was quite heavy, plus it was dirty. I smeared the wet sand that was clinging to it all over my neck in an attempt to lodge it properly, then turned and explosively discharged all the energy coiled up in my arm.

With a lacklustre thud, the ball dropped onto the grass, not even making it into the pit. But it rolled down a slight incline and came to rest just inside the sandpit, at the edge closest to me. My official distance was recorded as 10 centimetres.

Well, whatever. I was glad it was over. I proceeded to shuffle back to the end of the line, preparing for a repeat performance in a best of three type of sportive ordeal. After taking a few steps, a long-drawn, deafening snarl stopped me in my tracks. I looked up from my feet and saw that the noise appeared to emanate from the mouth of Mr Kaptin, one of the teachers tasked with supervising these events.

Mr Kaptin was a former army officer turned teacher. I was not taking any classes with him, and I did not know him particularly well. What I *did* know was that he had a reputation for shouting. And clearly he was living up to this reputation at that moment.

It was clear he believed that he was communicating something to me. I remembered that we were supposed to pick the ball up and hand it over to the next aspiring athlete, in this way contributing to the smooth execution of the sports event. 'PICK THE SHOT UP!!' was what I was able to make out.

Fine. So I did. With another thud, the ball hit the grass again, this time in front of Mr Kaptin's feet. 'Pick up your own ball', I heard myself say, before walking away, having stopped caring.

Hmm. This one was beyond stroppy really. Picture the scene: by the time Mr Kaptin had caught up with me, I had already passed a few students and was standing next to somebody about three kids up the line. Then I walked all the way back to the sandpit and picked up the ball. But instead of delivering it to the student whose turn it was to compete next, I covered the *longer* distance to the spot where Mr Kaptin was standing and chucked the ball at his feet. This was an open and unmistakable act of provocation. There was no possible way my action could have been misunderstood, or interpreted in any other way.

And interestingly, this is surprising. Contrary to what my behaviour suggests, my default attitude to adults was one of respect. I would never have dreamed of acting in an impolite, disrespectful or bad-mannered way towards an adult, or indeed towards any person of any age. Quite the contrary; my normal attitude, at least at that age, would have been to accept members of the teaching body unquestioningly as persons of authority.

And yet, my reaction to Mr Kaptin's action was instantaneous and entirely natural. What I felt was indignation. Who was Mr Kaptin to shout at me? Shouting demonstrated a lack of empathy, a lack of control. The response also felt disproportionate to the minor infraction of the rules I had committed. It was as if the shouting had pushed open a hidden door inside me. Behind that door lay an uncompromising defence mechanism, a machine that would not allow me to be treated in a way that I regarded as inappropriate and unfair. Indeed, I think the insight I can draw from this goes even deeper than that. It was not just that I defended myself. It was what I was defending. In that instant, I was defending my integrity and my pride. In doing what I did, I was keeping face. But not in front of the other students. I was keeping face in front of *me*.

What – no mistakes?

The next story that drifts up from my subconscious takes place in the army.

As I said in the introduction, I grew up in Germany. At the time, Germany had a conscript army and male citizens had to do a stint in the armed forces.

Basic army training included a lot of things: weapons training, choreographed walking in groups, formal tuition and – class tests. The class tests were designed to check whether we had all been paying attention in the various sessions where the instructors tried to back up practice with theory.

I remember sitting a test concluding a module called citizenship. The class taught basic things about the German political system, how the state worked, what rights and duties came with German citizenship and things like that.

We sat the test and a few hours later the drill instructor of our platoon entered the barracks to reveal the test results.

Hebwood!
Yes, Sir!
Zero mistakes!

Before I continue I need to give you a taste of how difficult this test was, otherwise you will not be able to put this result into perspective. Let me quote a question from the test that is representative of its overall quality: 'Name the colours of the German flag.'

Well. Let us assume that it is somehow possible *not* to know the design of the national flag used by the country in which you have been living for some two decades since birth. Not to worry, help is at hand. The test was printed on official Bundeswehr[6] stationery. This had headers and footers. In the footer it said: 'This stationery is the property of the Federal Republic of Germany.' And next to this statement was printed ... you guessed it, the German flag. And yes, it was printed in colour.

Yes, Sir. Thank you, Sir!
Well, it is **impossible** not to make any mistakes!
Yes, Sir!
In the next test, there will be more mistakes!
Yes, Sir! I will perform worse in future, Sir!

At that, our drill instructor looked at me as if I had spilt his pint, clearly debating with himself whether I was worth further bother. It lasted two seconds, then his head snapped to the right. 'Kaufmann!' He moved on to reveal the next recruit's test results.

I hope you found this story as amusing as I did when it happened to me. There is no huge insight here, other than to record what I felt at the time. I remember thinking that these 'tests' were a complete waste

---

[6] The official name of the German forces. Literally, this means something like Federal Guard.

of time and the interchange with my instructor a fine example of a charade. Did grown men really not have anything better to do than that? And of course, even in an environment characterised by rigid hierarchies, I was not able to keep my mouth shut entirely. I clearly dislike environments where form prevails over substance.

I am done!

I was still in the army. I wished I was not. Why did I wish that? Because I was engaged in one of the many strenuous activities the army held in store for its soldiers. This one was a 10-mile march. It was drawing to a close and I was absolutely exhausted.

What? No biggie, you are saying? You regularly run more than that distance and it's a doddle?

Well, maybe you have a point. I am not claiming that I was the fittest in our platoon, not by a long shot. But the army had a habit of spicing things up. This was no ordinary march. For starters, there was a backpack involved, which we had to carry around for the distance. That backpack was filled with weights to achieve uniform ballast of 20 kg[7] for everybody. And that made it awkward to carry.

Worse than that, the last few miles of the march had to be completed in full ABC warfare gear. ABC is the German acronym for 'atomic, biological, chemical' and involved putting on a number of unpleasant items of equipment, such as the poncho, a sort of all-body rubber cape designed to shelter the body and most of the equipment from fallout. Or the gloves, a pair of oversized mittens that transformed the handling of any kind of object into a challenge of dexterity.

But the worst accessory was the gas mask. A tight-fitting rubber hood with oversized bug-eyes and a filter sticking out in front. The problem with the mask was that it filtered most of the moisture out of the air and hence made normal breathing difficult. Wearing it for a long time while marching around carrying heavy equipment made for a very unpleasant experience.

---

[7] About 3 stone.

So there I was, panting through some wood in the middle of nowhere, looking like an oversized lampshade in a gimp mask. I was getting close to the limit of what was physically possible for me, but I knew the march was almost over, and that knowledge somehow gave me the mental discipline to soldier on, no pun intended.

I was rounding a bend in the fire-track and prepared to tackle the last mile or so. But hang on. Was that one of us, slumped against a tree, looking as if he had passed out? I was getting closer and recognised Kaufmann, slouched on the grass next to the path. He had not passed out, but his gas mask was off, his rifle discarded on the wet ground and he was clearly not intending to go anywhere.

I knew this would not end well for Kaufmann. The drill instructors were tailing us and, if they found him like this, he would be in serious trouble. He was already on the blacklist because he had panicked the day before in the ABC test chamber and had knocked somebody's mask off while the room was being flooded with tear gas.

I forced myself to interrupt my trance-like plodding and came to a stop next to him. 'Kaufmann! The fuck you doing? If the drills see you like that, you're history! This time, they'll throw you in jail or something . . .' I was not sure how much of this he was getting. The gas mask did not exactly enhance my ability to enunciate clearly. So I took it off and asked him again. This time I got an answer: 'Gand go on. Wond . . . wheva. Inzdrugder gan stuffimself.'

Great. Kaufmann was clearly in a complete state. But I could not leave him there like that. Shit. This was the last thing I needed. OK then. I called out to my mate Chris and together we pulled Kaufmann up and sort of bundled him along for the remainder of the march, carrying his pack between us. One hundred yards outside the barracks we forced the mask back on him, made him wear his backpack and kind of kicked him down the road so that he walked through the gate on his own, completing the march as required.

Oh wow. Kaufmann. There's a name from the past. For the entire time we were in basic training, Kaufmann managed to be the odd one out. Granted, most of his fellow conscripts were constantly picking on him and that was not nice, but he had a clumsy manner that tended to make him the butt of the jokes. When a drill instructor bellows 'eyes right' and, after executing this command, I am staring Kaufmann in the face, something's not right. That sort of thing – and yes, I may not be the practical sort myself, but I can tell left from right.

Yet, when I saw Kaufmann in distress on that day, there was no way I could have simply continued on and left him to his fate. I helped him grudgingly, but help him I did. This was no act of heroism – I was merely helping out a fellow recruit. Nor was it noble – Chris immediately came to the rescue too, just as much as I did. But there was something in my action I approve of, now that I look back on it for the first time in years. I like the fact that I helped somebody else when it was in my power to do so. Especially because, at the time, I felt as if I had no physical strength left in my body. I also like this because I have no keenly developed *abstract* sense of social justice. I donate small sums of money to charities of my choice, but I never tell anybody about it.[8] I would certainly not make myself the visible champion of a charitable cause, nor do I feel the need to make the world a better place.

'Mark is good at the things he wants to do'

A decade later, I found myself in London. I was six months into a job as a credit analyst with a German commercial bank. I liked the job but it was becoming obvious to me that the bank was not making a lot of money on counterparty loans to financial institutions. The reason for the low margins was that we were required to put up a lot of capital against these loans to cushion the credit risk we were accepting. But the interest income we received on these loans, when measured in per cent of this capital, was woefully low.

However, I was aware of more complex transactions that increased the margin the bank received on its economic capital.

---

[8] Until now.

So I started researching how these deals were structured, and after a few weeks I had developed a good understanding of their financial dynamics. I pitched my idea to Pierre, my immediate boss, and he told me to write up a formal proposal. We began the process of selling the idea internally, and my big bosses in Frankfurt were interested and wished to explore the idea further. I started working closely with one of them, Mick, who was a client relationship manager. We came up with a presentation (a pitch book), and the plan was that we would go out and market the idea to several institutions in Europe.

But I had not counted on the realities that prevailed in the hierarchical structure of a German commercial bank. Over the previous few months, I had been busy developing my idea and had somewhat neglected the job I was employed to do – which was credit analysis.

Pierre must have been keenly aware of this fact, since he appeared at my desk and informed me of a 'business decision' that had been made. 'We have decided that the German department will handle the presentations. You have done excellent work but need to refocus on credit analysis.'

Now, from my point of view, there was a flaw in this strategy. There was no doubt that everybody had been supportive of my idea, and I had been allowed to develop something that was outside the remit of a credit analyst. But it was still *my* initiative! And the potential profitability to the department vastly exceeded counterparty credit loans – of course, only if we actually *did* these deals. I could not allow this to be taken off me at this critical juncture. If these deals turned out to be a success for the department, the credit would be associated with those who brought the deals in. And that would be those who pitched the idea and saw the execution through – not some guy sitting in London who claimed to have had the idea in the first place. Something needed to be done.

Luckily, Mick and I had started working together very closely, and our co-operation was not just purely professional – we got on privately as well. So I gave him a call and explained the situation. I expressed my conviction that Pierre was likely to listen to an explanation from a 'bigger boss' and that such an explanation might wish to focus on the necessity to place the right people at the centre of the pitching process.

Next thing I saw was Pierre, my immediate boss, picking up his telephone. There was a 15-minute discussion. He put the phone down. He got up and came over to my desk. 'Mark, that was Mick on the phone just now.' *No surprises there . . .* 'He specifically requested you for the pitches in Europe.' *Good man. Nicely done.* 'So I guess you will need to go.' *Sorted!* 'But you must ensure that you do not fall behind in your credit analysis.' *OK, fair enough.*

However, a year later we had a similar conversation. The bank had struggled to execute these deals, and in my annual appraisal Pierre told me that I could not continue to treat credit analysis, my primary responsibility, as an afterthought. But, at the time of that chat, I had already accepted a job with a firm of stockbrokers, and within two weeks of my appraisal I had resigned. Pierre told me years later that he was asked for a reference by my new employer and to this day I think what he wrote showed good insight into my personality.

It said: 'Mark is good at the things he *wants* to do.'

Well . . . I am beginning to see some consistent personality traits shining through. During my time at the commercial bank, I did not seem to care very much what my job description was. I had discovered a type of deal that fell into the purview of my department, and which would be many times more profitable than the other products we were selling there. I did not understand why I should be forced to write internal credit reports and withdraw from the development of the product for the benefit of the centre in Frankfurt. I was not opposed to *sharing* credit – we were developing the idea as a team – but I was opposed to leaving a deal team that only existed because I had had the idea in the first place. And I reacted in a way that appears to be typical of me: I disregarded hierarchical structures, refused to see reason or accept my place in the organisation. In fact, this time I even used hierarchical structures to my advantage – I knew Mick was higher up than Pierre, and I knew that Pierre would be inclined to listen to views from the top.

So again I am encountering a sense of irreverence, defiance and an inability to accept what I see as form over substance. This has made it difficult for me to 'exist' in environments with a rigidly defined structure – for example, in organisations with a clear hierarchy, like the military or the commercial bank. But the principle also occurs, I believe, in a wider context. I have always felt uneasy in groups that promote a defined common culture, such as sports clubs, ideological groups, organised religions, even the wider context of my extended family. And yet the label 'does not play well with others' does not apply – I am very sociable, easy-going and love to laugh. But I love to do it with people who are right for me, whom *I* select and whom are not selected *for* me by others.

Blimey. I think I just had an insight into my personality that goes beyond the story at the commercial bank. Seems that this method is working! Most of what I have learned about myself so far I sort of knew before I started. But this one is a nugget of insight I did not have before. Let us see what else I can find.

Bazookas in the classroom

The next story transports me back into the army.

I had successfully completed basic training and the HR people transferred me to army headquarters in Cologne for the remainder of my stint in the forces. The department in which I worked administered the database recording personnel and equipment of the army. For example, an entry might look something like this:

- Panzeraufklärungslehrbataillon 11, Münster. 1. Kompanie, 3. Zug. 1 Pz Faust Le.

- Fallschirmjägerbataillon 261, Lebach. 3. Kompanie, 1. Zug. 8 Stu Gew m Zielfernrohr.

Yes, this confirms something you have always known. German words can be long. Even German native speakers think they are long. This meant that the army referred to the different units by way of abbreviations. The first one, which translates roughly into armoured reconnaissance training battalion, was PzAufklLehrBtl 11, the second one, the paratroopers, FschJgBtl 261.

However, by removing those helpful vowels from the words, the abbreviations only served to make things even less accessible. The confusion was further heightened by the fact that the equipment listed in the records was identifiable by way of a unique code. For example, the light bazooka listed in the third group of the first company in PzAufklLehrBtl 11 had a code denoting portable, anti-tank, rocket-launching, light. The scope-mounted rifles in FschJgBtl 261 had another code, and before you knew it, you were drowning in bristly acronyms and meaningless alphanumerical codes.

Why is this important? Because it was my job to update the databases recording all this stuff. The army was constantly shuffling equipment and people around between units, transferring things temporarily for the duration of an exercise and was generally meddling with things for no apparent reason. Inch-thick printouts were arriving on my desk on a daily basis. They were marked up all over, the edits indicating that these tanks needed to be moved, those trucks decommissioned, this personnel relocated.

All this had to be done manually by inputting codes into a database running on the army mainframe.

After a month in the department, I had discovered the following facts:

(1) The software was basic, user-unfriendly and clunky.
(2) The work was mind-numbingly boring.
(3) It was possible to copy smaller units across, but there was a read–write protection for units larger than a company. This protection was put into place as a safeguard to prevent large-scale errors.

(4) Equipment and personnel had codes. These codes uniquely identified the piece of equipment, but they were not mapped to a specific army unit.

(5) The codes did not map stuff to a specific army unit! If they had done, the army could not have moved their kit around all the time.

(6) This was the reason for the read–write protection on larger units. Otherwise somebody could have simply copied whole regiments across, potentially making a huge mess.

(7) The read–write protection on the larger units could be disabled.

I walked into the department on a fine Wednesday morning in May. On my desk was a particularly bulky wad of paper. It was a brigade with four battalions. Somebody high up had decided that it needed to be a brigade with five battalions. My boss revealed to me that it was my task to input the entire new battalion from scratch: 'Yes, this is a lot of work but unfortunately it has to be done and there is no other way to input this since, as you know, Mark, we cannot copy battalions.'

A battalion has between two and seven companies. A company has two to six platoons and these have two to six sections each. The battalion I had to create had five companies, a total number of 24 platoons and 123 sections. It was more than 1,000 men strong and had countless positions of equipment.

My heart sank. This was a lot of stuff to put in. Sure, I did not have anything else to do, but this was no longer merely boring. This was tedium on an unprecedented scale.

Luckily I was a smart guy. I remembered fact number 7 and decided to use a creative solution to break the problem down.

First, I took note of the brigade I had to enhance. It was a PzLehrBrig. The army wanted to expand the armoured training brigade and establish an additional training battalion to complement the brigade's other four battalions and two companies.[9]

---

[9] I cannot remember the actual units that were involved in this story. The examples I use here are made up, but illustrative.

Second, I tried to identify a battalion that was similar to the armoured infantry training battalion I was asked to set up. But I could not find one that was identical. After a bit of searching I found an armoured infantry battalion with five companies and 1,000 strength, close to the six companies I needed to create. It was an intervention unit but, apart from the missing specifics that would make it a *training* unit, it was basically identical to the training battalion I had to establish. Good. That would do.

Third, I disabled the read–write protection for large units. This was not expressly prohibited, but certainly highly discouraged. I copied the battalion across, inserted it into the hierarchical structure of the PzLehrBrig and my new training battalion was born. Or very nearly, anyway. To complete the job, I copied one of its companies to create a sixth one, changed the designations of the various sub-units, saved it, re-enabled the read–write protection and that was that. I spent the rest of the day pretending to be really busy whenever my boss was in the room, and flirting with Hannah, our female civil employee, whenever he was not.

Fast forward two weeks. For the past fortnight I had congratulated myself on my resourcefulness; a victory of brilliance over mediocrity, of irreverence over obedience, of inventiveness over regulations. I was sitting at my desk, entering codes, when I heard a commotion from the anteroom where my boss sat. Loud voices, rising to shouts.

> Why are there bazookas in the classrooms of the training battalion? This was JUST set up by YOUR department! This is completely UNACCEPTABLE!

The voices stopped. A door banged. Then the one to our room burst open and my boss entered in a state of heightened agitation.

CORPORAL HEBWOOD!!

I had never seen the Sergeant Major like this. I jumped out of my chair. Now was not the time to be flippant.

> Yes, Sir!
> How is this possible? You created this battalion from scratch!
> Yes, Sir. I did not pay enough attention. I will correct the errors immediately. SIR!
> See to it. This goes past the Colonel. I've got the Major General on my back!

He stormed out. A door banged again.

> . . . immediately. SIR!

Hannah was all smirks and I was standing there blushing, looking like an idiot to the rest of the department.

Hmm. There it is again. This deeply ingrained sentiment of irreverence. This time it made me do something that I explicitly knew was discouraged by best practice, simply because it was in my power to do it. OK, the barriers were quite low in this case – conscripts do not tend to take the army they are forced to join temporarily very seriously. But my sergeant's reaction on that day taught me a good lesson. The fact that something looks unimportant to me does not mean that it is unimportant to others. That day I created a problem for my boss, a man who had always respected me and shown me kindness during my stint in his department. I remember correcting my 'mistake' and delivering a pristine battalion to him within the day, including my apologies for acting like an arrogant prat who believes he is above the rules.[10] I am afraid the irreverence is natural, though. It is part of my DNA and I cannot change it. But, as my discussion of other topics later in the book will show, I have learned to use it 'responsibly'.

In terms of the exercise in self-discovery, I think I may be getting somewhere. Certain things tend to show up repeatedly, and that may

---

[10] I think he had a good idea what had happened, though, even without the apology.

be significant. Plus I am having a good time remembering these episodes from my life. If you are doing the same exercise, I hope you are having fun as well. Just a few more and then we are done.

Three interviews
School's out! Business school, that is. I was starting the interview process that would eventually lead to a meaningful career and a fulfilled professional life.

Interview 1
I was in Germany and at an assessment day conducted by a market-leading, US-based manufacturer of consumer goods in the field of household cleaning, drugs and disposable nappies. I had had three interviews, an IQ test, a chaperoned lunch and I was facing my last hurdle in the form of a chat with Cheryl, the head of the household care division. After predictable questions seeking to explore my strengths and weaknesses, and inviting insights into my reasons for wishing to work for this company and no other, Cheryl came out with a novel one. We had the following chat:

> Mark, what would you do if you won a million euros in the lottery?
> Ah. Well. Never thought about that. Invest it, probably.
> Invest in what?
> Well ... gosh. This is a wide field. Currently, we are in a boom phase, and I guess interest rates are gonna rise further. So bonds are out. Equity – but I'm not sure which sector. US sounds good in general – they're growing faster over there so the chances are I am going to get some tailwind from the exchange r—
> Would you not start a venture? Build something of your own?
> Erm ... no, probably not ... No, don't think so. I'd invest in the markets.
> Ah. Well, I was just asking. You know, we are all small entrepreneurs here.
> Oh really? Is that why you are a salaried employee working for the man?

They did not offer me anything. Disappointing.

Interview 2

I was in England being interviewed for a graduate trainee programme with a life assurance company based in the southeast. After a chat with the department head, I was talking to the chap who headed up the section in which I would be working. He had just asked me what I think of life assurance, which was basically the only product the company manufactured.

I don't know. I would never buy it.

Oh really? Why ever not?

Well, for starters the life office accepts an obligation to pay out a guaranteed sum of money at the end of the term of the contract. Because the office accepts a fixed liability, it needs to invest in assets that are secure and liquid. That's basically government bonds.

Good work. But why should that matter?

It matters because the returns offered by the contracts are commensurately low. And then you also have a component that is just there to pay out money if you die. I do not really need that, but this benefit is priced into the premium so I am forced to buy something I don't want.

Ha, ha! You don't have family, do you, Mark?

No. How did you know?

Oh, wild stab in the dark. You could buy unit-linked, though . . .

What's unit-linked?

Not heard of that one? No worries, I won't hold it against you. Cheers for coming in, Mark. We'll be in touch.

A few days later, they called and told me I could start next week.

Interview 3

It was years later. I was being interviewed by a firm of stockbrokers in London. It was an iconic firm, highly regarded in the City,[11] and recognised for its standing in society.

They were not making the process easy. I had already had a pre-screening chat with the headhunter, four internal interviews

---

[11] The City of London, the capital's financial district.

and a written exam. After that, they *still* asked me to give a presentation to a selection of salespeople. Well, at least today was the final interview. I arrived at their premises, slightly apprehensive because the headhunter advised me to reserve the whole afternoon for this event, and a secretary kindly ushered me into a large conference room. In it there were a large number of tables that had been arranged into a square. She asked me to sit down at one side and said somebody would soon be with me.

And somebody was. The door opened and a long procession of people filed in, all identifying themselves as senior brokers and partners in the business. After a few minutes, I was facing a U-shape of 15 senior partners in the firm.

And then the questions started. I was subjected to a constant flow of questions, covering current affairs, points of financial theory, my motivation, stocks, my background, the firm. Sometimes two questions were fired off at the same time, coming from different locations in the U. Sometimes people were challenging, sometimes bantering, but there was always a point, and I needed to be alert, think on my feet and remain in control. Still, I found that I was enjoying the event, and there was a sense that I did not have to be careful *how* I said things, that I could be myself. Then I faced the firm's version of the strengths and weaknesses question.

> Mark, when you had your annual appraisals at the insurer, what were the good and bad points your boss said about you?
> Oh, I was in the graduate training programme. Progress was driven by the rate at which you passed exams . . . there was never much in terms of a classical assessment in my appraisals, I'm afraid.
> OK. Let me put it a different way. If your friends were here now, what good and bad things would they say about you?
> Oh dear. You did see my CV, didn't you? I am German – I don't have any friends!

The room erupted with laughter. Fifteen senior partners, looking at me, laughing and nodding. I was sure I saw some of them wiping their eyes. It lasted for about a minute.

After that, the firm was on my side. The atmosphere had noticeably shifted. *Yes, he'll fit in,* was what people appeared to be thinking. The event continued for another hour or so and then I was back in the real world.

The following morning, I was at my desk when the phone rang. It was the headhunter. 'They loved you. When can you start?'

This interview triplet is telling, actually. In brief, it shows that I do not feel at ease in environments in which I have to be perceived as some-body who takes himself very seriously. Cheryl's comment rankled because I thought she was seeking to project an image of herself that was at odds with her actual status. I thought she was taking herself too seriously and was not able to laugh at herself. As a consequence, she forced me to take myself overtly seriously, and that made me ill at ease with our discussion.

On a subconscious level at least, my response to the question in my insurance interview was to test how seriously I would have to take myself in the culture of the company. And immediately, I got on splen-didly with my interviewer, who had the same self-deprecating streak as I have. In my responses, I actually made serious points about the finan-cial dynamics present in an insurance contract, but I was allowed to make them with my tongue slightly in my cheek, and that is how I like it.

Clearly, my interview at the stockbroker got hugely easier after my comment broke the ice. Looking back, I actually think that there was a tinge of relief in the laughter. I guess I must have been doing all right in the events that preceded the final interview, but there may have been reservations about whether I would fit into the culture of the firm, whether I would be at ease with the banter on the dealing floor. From my point of view, I liked the dynamics that were developing in the interview and I was simply being myself.

Looking back at these three discussions, I am rediscovering a core aspect of my personality. I am naturally irreverent, as by now we know, but I am also irreverent in relation to myself. Self-deprecation comes naturally to me, and I feel at ease in environments where that is understood for what it is: self-irony, but not flippancy.

Cow, dog and horse

I grew up in a big city in Germany, but my grandparents had a working farm in the north and so I spent many weekends on their farm in the country.

This was such a weekend. I woke early to a cacophony of sound. Our cockerel started crowing as if Grandma had hidden all his chickens. But she had not. Quite the contrary. I heard some fifty chickens making squawking and clucking noises as Grandma was entering the shed where they were kept, presumably to feed them. Pigs were squealing. From inside the farm, I heard cows mooing. And it was only 6 am. Blimey.

Later on, Grandma took me to see the cows. I was 10 years old at the time and I was one and a half metres tall. I was standing in front of a cow. It was a huge animal, almost half as tall as I was again, and it was looking down at me from an even greater height. It also had huge horns and a glistening snout. Grandma was moving between the cows to start the milking process. She was deftly shoving them out of the way to position herself properly. The cows did not mind but they still expressed a mild preference not to be treated in this way. 'MOOOOOOOO.' The stables echoed with the sound of their protest. And the cow which was staring down at me started nodding, as if to make a point, lowering the frightening horns on its head towards me threateningly. I was out of the stables in a flash.

Fast forward to a scene years later. I was taking a walk in the countryside with Mary, my girlfriend at the time. We were approaching a farmhouse and the dogs resident on the premises must have interpreted this innocent action as a threat, since they came rushing up the path, blocking further progress. I stood rooted to the spot, resigning myself to an early death. Mary picked up a rock from the ground and made a swerving motion backwards with her arm, pretending to throw it at one of them. The dogs looked at her uncertainly and retreated back into the farm. 'Always pretend to throw stones at dogs who have an attitude,' Mary advised. 'Yeah sure,' I responded, feeling a bit flat, 'that may work for you, but in my case they would sense immediately that I am kidding, rush forward and eat me.' Mary laughed good-naturedly, as if this incident had amused her greatly.

A bit later, we got to a field with horses. Mary tore some high grass from the kerb and held out her arm. Miraculously, the horses stopped feeding and came over to where Mary was standing. One of them started eating the grass out of her hand and Mary patted the horse on the nose. Both of them seemed to be enjoying themselves enormously. Mary clearly wished to include me in the rural bliss, and she invited me to do the same. Of course, I declined vigorously, but Mary could be very insistent. Eventually, I gave in and cautiously held out a tuft of grass. Mary's horse started nibbling, and then it snapped at my hand viciously.

'You've got to be careful when they bite,' Mary pointed out helpfully. I was incredulous. 'Mary! The fact that horses sometimes bite would have been useful information to have *before* I tried to feed one!' Mary chuckled, clearly amused at my misfortune. It was obvious she was having a good time, and I am sure the horse was grinning too.

The insight I draw from these little stories is clear. I do not like the countryside, and the countryside does not like me. And my dislike is genetic; it is nature, not nurture, which keeps me from the country. I have been exposed to farm life ever since I was little, but I never felt drawn to a farmer's lifestyle, and never had any affinity with the animals. Animals sense immediately that I am out of my comfort zone, which in turn makes *them* nervous and heightens exactly the defensive behaviour which I expect to find in the first place. Hence, there has always been an uncomfortable dynamic between animals and me, and that is the reason that I tend to get impaled by cows, eaten by dogs and maimed by horses. Plus I have hay fever. My natural habitat is the big city. It is not the countryside.

Self-insights, anybody?

Well, by now I think you know me better than I know myself. Let us remember why I was suggesting this exercise. My guess is that we all know ourselves reasonably well already, deep down. But that is exactly the issue. Our insights are deep down; they are rarely at the surface, rarely *conscious*.

By revisiting a few life experiences and briefly thinking about them, we can make some of what lies deep down drift to the surface. And, if we feel so inclined, we can analyse the stories that come to us in more depth, or discuss them with friends and family. If we do this regularly, we can develop a deeper insight into our personality, and consequently into what is good for us and what is not. This process reminds me of digging out minerals from the ground and so I will refer to this method as EXPERIENCE MINING.

So let me see what I have learned from my mining session. To sift through the evidence, I made a table. Here it is.

Story	Dominant trait	Like?	Secondary traits	Like?
Normative behaviour	Irreverence	♂	Academic interest	♂
Ballsed that one up...	Sense of justice, pride	♂	Light-hearted, playful	♂
What - no mistakes?	Substance over form	♂		
I am done!	Some regard for others	♂		
Mark is good at what he *wants* to do	Substance over form	♂	Manipulation	♀
Bazookas in the classroom	Irreverence	♀	Resourcefulness	♂
Three interviews	Self-deprecation	♂	Irreverence	♂
Cow, dog and horse	City dweller	♂		

Fig. 1.1 A list of character traits, derived from a session of **EXPERIENCE MINING**. Personality traits are categorised into dominant and secondary classes within the context of each life story. Evaluations are added which denote approval or disapproval of a character trait discovered.

A word in advance: the likes and dislikes are first impressions only – they are not meant to represent results of in-depth investigations into our personality. Also they are only relevant in the context of a specific story. For example, my 'like' in 'Normative behaviour' does not mean that I approve of irreverent behaviour as a general rule in life. It only means that, with hindsight, I think it was appropriate for me to behave in a particular way at the moment the story refers to.

So looking through the list, what can I learn? The first point that strikes me is that one personality trait keeps popping up. There are three cases of irreverence, twice as a dominant trait and once as a secondary one. But it was also there when I chucked the shot-put at the feet of my teacher, and to some extent at the commercial bank. This personality trait appears to be always present. It seems to be part of my genetic make-up. This is significant and I should not ignore it in planning my life.

Looking at the table, I see a few other traits that come up repeatedly. They are substance over form and self-deprecation. Again, I need to take note of this fact. It would be a mistake if I allowed life to push me in a direction in which I would need to act against these natural parts of my personality.

The second thing I notice is that there are more likes than dislikes. That is a good sign. In the main, I seem to approve of my behaviour in relation to others. It follows that I like myself, that I have a positive view of myself, indeed of my 'self'. But now that I think about this, something makes me pause. Is it really a good thing to be stroppy, to consciously provoke my teacher because he was shouting at me? How can I possibly like that about myself?

Well, I do not actually like the fact that I am stroppy. To be honest, this is something I need to control as I go through life. But I like the motivation that stands behind the act. I will not allow somebody to act inappropriately towards me. I will stand up to figures of authority if I believe they are wielding their power irresponsibly. Deeper down, I seem to have an innate defence mechanism that will protect me against the tendency of some to take advantage of me or to treat me unfairly. So that is the part I like. But there is another side of this coin and it looks dark, I am afraid to say.

Clearly, my defence engine is good for me, but it needs to be operated responsibly. I need to make sure that I do not take things too far, that I do not subject others to exaggerated pushback. I need to keep things in perspective, and any defence needs to be proportionate to the 'attack'.

I will stop here with the interpretation of my mining session. I could continue, but I just wanted to give you a flavour of how we might think about the stories that come to us in this little exercise. I must admit I find it extraordinary how much the random selection of stories taken from my life reveals about my personality, so I think this method works. We get valuable insights into our personality.

But why should this be so important? Why should we care so much? Is this not idle navel-gazing? Are there any real-world lessons to be learned here?

Signposts

Oh yes there are. I think these insights can act like signposts indicating the right direction to take at the many crossroads we come to in our lives.

Let me give you a few examples of what I mean:

- As discussed, I have a natural streak of irreverence. One aspect of this is that I do not accept authority before I think it has been earned. It follows, for example, that I should not seek employment in organisations that are innately hierar-chical in nature. I am afraid the military, public service and hierarchically structured companies are all out. I need a flat structure. Maybe a start-up? Maybe a boutique?

- I am also self-deprecating and ill at ease if I have to create the impression that I am taking myself very seriously all the time. That means I need to seek out others who also have the same self-deprecating streak. In the UK not many people seem to have a problem with me on that level. Indeed, many seem to share a similar disposition. Maybe I should live in the UK?

- I do not like the countryside. This is innate in me and appears to be reciprocated by the countryside. This one is easy. I should not live in the countryside. Actually, it is a bit more than that. If I am honest with myself, I need to realise that I can only live in a big city. And by big I mean several million people. It needs to be one of the cosmopolitan centres of this world. I can combine this insight with the previous bullet point. Maybe I should live in London?

Of course, I could spin this further. But I do not think I have to – the point is clear. If you act against your better knowledge of yourself, the chances are that you will create an environment that is wrong for you, that does not bring out your strengths, that affects your well-being and eventually your sense of self-worth. But if you *do* act in accordance with what you know about yourself, you stand a good chance of creating a life in which your natural strengths are encouraged, a life in which you do not have to play a role and in which you can be yourself.

But, before we move on, I feel I have to tie up three loose ends.

Loose end 1: 20–20 hindsight
I am conducting my session of EXPERIENCE MINING from hindsight, with the wealth of a few decades of life experience to draw on. By now I know myself reasonably well. But do I not need to know these things about myself early in life? Early enough, in fact, to make the right decisions when they matter? Which job to go for. Whether to have kids. Where to live.

The answer is yes. In an ideal world. But nothing is perfect. We need to go through life and learn our lessons as they arise. What I am advocating is that we recognise these life experiences as episodes from which we *can* learn. Each experience will teach us something about ourselves. The insight is there for the taking – but we *have* to take it. And we can only do that if we think about our life experiences and ask ourselves what they might teach us. Not *all* the time, but regularly.

Eventually, a coherent picture will emerge that helps us to make our next decision more competently. And it *may* take time! Although I know today, for example, that I am not good in hierarchical organisations, I did not always recognise the nature of organisations *as* hierarchical. Fresh out of university, I applied for a position in the diplomatic service. I did not get in and the feedback I received from the Foreign Office was telling: 'Mr Hebwood is insufficiently diplomatic.' It took me a few years to understand what this meant and to harness the insight from this lesson, but harness it I did. Eventually.

Loose end 2: Yin and yang

Remember the likes and dislikes in my EXPERIENCE MINING table? The purpose of these is to 'take the temperature' and provide a first indication of how much we like a particular character trait in a specific situation.

But these seemingly innocuous evaluations hide a more difficult issue, as serious as it is thorny. It is serious because we need to learn how to treat discoveries of something we may *not* like about ourselves. It is easy to embrace positive things we might learn, but not so easy to accept negative traits.

And the issue is thorny because it is hard to tell positives from negatives. When are personality traits 'good' and when are they 'bad'? What is the benchmark? Who decides? More to the point, what does bad even *mean*? Is it something that I will need to correct? Or is it something that I may not like about myself in all circumstances but which nevertheless forms part of my personality? Something that is like darkness to light, like a yin to a yang?

I think it is still too early for us to discuss these difficult questions. Still, at some stage we will need to find answers to these deepest of issues. I will attempt to tackle these questions in Rule 9, which I grandly name 'Know what's right. How to tell right from wrong'. In that chapter, I will try to develop a method that allows us to distinguish between two types of dislike. The good dislikes are those that complement other aspects of our personality and are therefore an important part of our DNA. The bad dislikes represent infractions of some ethical standard that we believe is important enough to uphold and therefore represent traits that we need to watch, control or change.

For example, a good dislike for me is irreverence if it is a defence mechanism that protects my world. A bad dislike is irreverence if it leads to actions that disregard, and perhaps endanger, the integrity of the worlds of others. The good dislike therefore becomes a like, and the bad dislike ideally becomes extinct.

Whatever our personal answers might be, I believe it is most important that we do not sit in judgement of ourselves. We need to strive for a balanced, well-adjusted blend of personality traits. A blend that we are consciously aware of and whose components we have examined. If we get there we will be able to like ourselves. And if we like ourselves, happiness will be in our grasp.

Loose end 3: Courage of conviction

And finally, just a brief comment on an obvious problem. Even if I *do* find something out about myself, and even if it *does* represent a fundamental personality trait, I will still need to act on my insight if I wish to generate a real-world benefit from what I learn.

And to do so I need to be *convinced* that my self-insight is true. If I am not convinced, I will not be able to act in accordance with what I know about myself. I will not be able to defend my insight against obstacles I might encounter. Against parents who learn that I may not wish to get married. Against teachers who disapprove of my choice of career. Against friends who urge me not to join the military. Against friends who urge me *to* join the military. So many decisions. So many opinions. So much advice. So easy to go with the flow. So easy to please others.

But in the end, there is only one person who will be able to decide what is right for you and that is *you*. These decisions are difficult to make, and I will discuss later how we may develop the tools to select between choices ('Rule 2: Know what you need') or sift through the advice of others ('Rule 6: Seek advice').

However, if we wish to stand a chance of making right decisions more often than wrong ones, we need to develop the courage of our convictions. Courage that the insights into the nature of our personalities are *right* and that acting upon them will bring benefits and eventually happiness.

To do this, I believe we need a more refined method than the exercise we were engaged in earlier. Before I present it, I would like to illustrate why it is so important to act in accordance with the insights we gain about ourselves. I will do this by telling you three real-life stories.

The first is a story in which the characters act *with* self-knowledge; in the second, they act *against* it; and in the third one, they fail to act at all.

Courage of conviction – some examples

A painful choice
More than 10 years ago, I was in a relationship that lasted two years. It is important to say outright that this was a good relationship; I was in love with Mary and she was in love with me. We respected each other, we liked ourselves, possibly as individuals more than as a couple, but we got on well and enjoyed each other's company.

Despite this, ultimately we each wanted different things from life. Indeed, there were several fundamental aspects that did not go together, things that over the course of two years made the relationship unworkable. I am going to list just a few:

- I need to live in the big city. I live in central London and when I leave town, I go either to other cities or on outdoor sports holidays. It is no exaggeration to say that I have spent maybe 15 days in the English countryside in the past 10 years. In other words, I hardly ever leave town.

Mary was exactly the opposite. She liked to spend as much time in the countryside as possible. She was working in London at the time, but she saw the city in a completely different light. When I heard the buzz, she heard noise; when I saw rich ethnic variety, she saw overcrowding; what I thought was cool, she thought lacked warmth; when I saw style, she saw pricey. Hence, in an attempt to keep her sanity, she took every chance to escape to the countryside. Eventually, she bought a cottage in Oxfordshire and I there-fore found myself in a rural setting far more often than I would have liked (a low benchmark since, as we established above, this was basically never).

- I am rather private and she enjoyed being part of a large set of friends and acquaintances. I often found myself attending parties with her, meeting people with whom I had little in common, when in fact I would have preferred to stay at home and read a book.

- Which brings me to the final and most important point I need to mention. She wanted children and I did not. This is a fundamental, and insurmountable, difference of intention. If both parties know themselves sufficiently to understand their expectations, such a gulf cannot be bridged.

And of course, it was not bridged. When we eventually broke up, we did so in the mutually shared understanding that it was 'because of the kids'. And we did so even though at the time we both still felt in love with each other.

So what has this got to do with courage of conviction? To illustrate this, I think you might benefit from a more intimate insight into the quality of my sentiments:

- You know by now that I cannot live in the country. But let me share some deeper reasons with you why that is: I feel claustrophobic in the countryside – I feel constantly over-looked by others, my neighbours observe me when I get home and they know when I leave the house. Cultural pursuits are few and far between, there is nobody on the village streets after 9 pm and often not even at noon.

  As life is more sheltered than in the city, small decisions appear to matter more. Should the village build a car park or a playground on the disused space next to the commons? Should there be another roundabout on the A5050 'to slow everything down a little'? Would we like to contribute to this year's village fair? Acceptable neighbourly responses to these considerations include 'A playground would be lovely', 'Yes, very reasonable' and 'We would be delighted', rather than my favoured 'I don't care', 'Whatever' and 'No'.

  Needless to say, this does not mean that country life *is* awful. It only means it is wrong for *me*. Equally, the considerations listed before are of course not in themselves petty, unreasonable or imposing. And I hope my responses do not illustrate that I am indifferent, juvenile or rude. But they do illustrate that country life brings out the worst in me, makes me grumpy and, eventually, makes me unhappy. This is as true for me as the opposite was true for Mary.

- I do not want children. I know this with a certainty that eclipses everything else I may know about myself. The reasons for this are complex, but ultimately come down to the fact that I wish to keep my life free of responsibilities that I do not enjoy having.

  The desire not to have children is second only to my need for self-preservation. And Mary may have felt the opposite desire with equal intensity.

The point of the story is that I made a conscious decision to end the relationship at a time that I was still in love, and so did Mary. I knew with certainty that I would have to become a different person had I wanted to stay with her. I knew that, in a continued relationship with Mary, I would have become fundamentally unhappy.

So I knew that splitting up was the right thing to do. But that did not make actually *doing* so any easier. I still went through a time of intense emotional distress, turmoil and sadness. How easy would it have been to go with the flow, to convince myself that a life that is right for many can also be right for me and that I was merely scared of the commitment?

Looking back on the experience now, I think I can say that I did two things:

(1) I knew key traits of my personality so well that they stood out consciously in my mind.
(2) I found the courage of my conviction to act in accordance with what I knew about myself.

And did that make me happy? Not at the time. But in the long run? Emphatically so. I am now in a relationship that is natural for me. A relationship in which I do not have to turn into somebody I am not in order to stay in it. A relationship in which I can be myself, which brings out the best in me and in which I am loved for who I am. I love Ursina for who she is, we are in love, we like each other, we are independent and we are friends.

But what would have happened had I ignored what I know about myself? Who knows? We can only live one life, and we do not know what the alternative would have been.

However, I *do* know that it is dangerous to act against self-knowledge that is felt with conviction. My next story shows why.

An insight ignored
One of my acquaintances is a doctor. Bob was never particularly fond of children, but he developed a dislike of kids so

intense that he had to give up treating them as a GP. Clearly, his attitude went beyond a simple dislike, and he was consciously aware, beyond all doubt, that he was unable to tolerate children around him, at least those of a younger age.

He met Nicola through his work and, after a short period of dating, they got married. She knew about his aversion and they married on the clear and explicit understanding that they would not have children together. However, after a few years, Nicola developed an increasing desire to have kids.

Eventually, Bob agreed to try. They had a child and, six weeks after the birth, Bob left his wife, finding himself unable to deal with the experience. Nicola went through a period of intense emotional distress and has since brought up her child as a single mother.

So interpretation, please . . .

- Bob clearly acted against self-knowledge. He may not have known *why* he disliked young children with the intensity he undoubtedly felt, but he was certainly aware *that* he did.

- If you have a psychological condition so severe that it affects your professional conduct, I would think it is reasonable to expect this condition to prevail also in your private life.

- Nicola knew of his aversion as clearly as Bob. At best, her decision to have a child with him was high risk. At worst, she acted against her self-knowledge as much as Bob did.

It seems that neither Bob nor Nicola were, in the end, determined enough to make the painful decisions self-knowledge would have dictated – Bob not to have children with anybody and Nicola not to have children with Bob.

Clearly, therefore, acting *against* what you know about yourself can be dangerous. But so can acting without self-knowledge, as my final story illustrates.

A stand not taken

One of my friends is a high-flying executive. Jemima is extremely bright and graduated with honours from a top university in Germany. She is driven and her professional goal is to run her own company. She is married to Josh, an individual of similar stature, a professional as driven and successful as she is and no less accomplished. Both of them are delightful company, well balanced and life competent.

He always wanted children and she never did. Or perhaps more to the point, she never admitted to herself that she did not want them.

Jem's family is rather traditional and does not really accept childless marriages as a viable life choice. During the early years of her marriage, Jem was subjected to a fair amount of pressure, both from members of her own family and from those of her husband's. Josh, meanwhile, was adding to this pressure. Conversations that focussed on his desire for kids grew increasingly frequent, and as a result their marriage increasingly strained.

So let us consider the evidence:

- A highly intelligent, highly driven woman in her 40s.

- A woman who is an independent professional, but certainly in no way rejects her parents' values or rebels against them.

- A woman with no kids.

I believe that somebody who truly wants children, and is conscious of this desire as a tangible goal, rather than a vague possibility at some later stage in life, will start a family a lot earlier than in their 40s. And I believe that somebody who does not naturally rebel against the expectations of her parents would not be in a childless marriage unless she does not want to have kids.

In short, I do not believe that Jem truly knew herself. I believe that she *suspected* she did not want children, but did not analyse her feelings deeply enough to be certain. And not being certain, she never developed the courage of her conviction that *not* having children was the right life choice for her. That conviction failing, she proved ill-equipped to defend her natural lifestyle against steady (and probably well-meaning) persuasion to accept another. And not being of a rebellious disposition, she had no natural means to defend herself. Eventually, she acquiesced and the marriage has now produced one child.

But how would I know that the arrival of their child did not herald a change in mindset, did not make Jem embrace the prospect of children as a positive life choice, after decades of professional success? How do I know that the experience of having a child did not change her? How do I know that she is not ecstatically happy now?

Well, let us see:

- Following the birth of her child, Jem continued working at the high level of responsibility she had enjoyed before. As a consequence, most of the burden of juggling everyday necessities for the family was compressed into the short time span left at the end of a long work day. Despite the help of a full-time nanny.

- Josh did his best to pick up the slack, but his extensive business travels did not allow him to lighten Jem's workload materially.

- Jem and Josh are now considering marriage counselling and Jem is seeing a psychologist.

I think it is safe to say that Jem is currently unhappy – and so is Josh. She is uncertain of how to pursue her professional goals, her marriage is severely strained, she has difficulty adapting to a life that has changed; indeed, she finds it hard to accept that it has changed in the first place.

I believe Jem's story is a cautionary tale of what might happen when we act without sufficient self-knowledge:

(1) Jem should have been able to read the signs. It should have been clear to her that, at the very least, she was not strongly motivated to have kids.

(2) Jem did not trust what she knew about herself enough to develop the courage of conviction she needed to withstand peer-group pressure.

(3) She allowed herself to be cajoled into a life choice that is turning out to have been wrong for her.

So what would have happened had she known herself sufficiently well to resist the demands on her? Would she have been happier? Again, probably not in the short term. She may still have had marriage counselling. She may even have had a divorce. But I believe ultimately the answer is yes. I believe she would have been able to lead an authentic life.

Would that have been an easy choice? Decidedly not. Getting to know ourselves, accepting who we are and then acting in accordance with our insights can be difficult, and it can be painful. But, acting without knowing ourselves, or even consciously ignoring what we *do* know, is likely to be a recipe for unhappiness.

Know yourself II

Fine. So self-knowledge is important – we are getting it. This is all very well, but how do you get to know who you are? Sure, we had that little exercise with the life experiences, but you promised us a more thorough method. Well, get on with it, Mark. Where is it?

This, or something similar, is what I can imagine you may be thinking right now. So I *am* going to get on with it and discuss my formal method to generate self-insights. And actually, this method is very similar to the photo album of life snapshots we were looking at earlier. The only difference is that now I am proposing to subject each story to in-depth scrutiny and as penetrating an analysis as is within our grasp.

I am proposing that we enter into a question-and-answer conversation with ourselves, a conversation that asks why at every step of the way. Why did I behave in a particular way? What did I feel in a particular situation? Was my behaviour consistent with how I behaved in other similar situations? If not, why not? And so on. I am proposing not to give in and not to accept initial insights as sufficient. I am proposing to probe the depths of an experience with as much perseverance as we can and to dig out some nuggets of self-insight.

Let me give you an example of how I think EXPERIENCE MINING could work.

'Ello, 'ello, 'ello!

The other night, I was driving back from an evening with friends. I stopped at a red traffic light at the T-junction of Bond Street and Piccadilly. A police van squeezed into the space next to me, almost touching my wing mirror. The driver started talking to me and we had the following conversation:

'Ello, 'ello, 'ello!

OK, so he did not actually say that. What he *did* say was:

Did you see us earlier, when you were pulling out in front of us?
Pulling out in front of you? Oh . . . at the police station? Yes, I saw you.
You saw us and still cut us off? That's even worse . . .

With that, he pulled out into Piccadilly, traffic lights now green, and left me behind. He never gave me the chance to explain. Surely it had been my right of way at the crossroads of Burlington Street and Clifford Street? I was still thinking about this conversation half an hour later, almost home, feeling self-righteous about it. Only now, as I write this incident down, does it occur to me that it was actually not my right of way and I *did* cut him off. A little bit. Maybe.

So that was the incident. Now for how to use it:

- The incident was innocuous. It is an example of countless small things of a similar nature that happen to us every day. One option open to me is to tell myself that the guy was being an idiot and forget all about it instantly.

Life vs Self-knowledge: *1–nil.*

- Another option I have is not to forget about it. The incident was indeed innocuous so why did it churn me up so much? Thirty minutes later I was still thinking about it, and of course I am remembering it now, writing it down . . . Why?

Life vs Self-knowledge: *no score yet–but the match is on!*

At this stage, I have taken conscious note of my reaction to a petty incident. I am not letting this go and instead I am trying to get to the bottom of it. Here is how I may be thinking about it:

- Was the policeman aggressive? Decidedly not. Condescending? No. Did he lecture me? Not exactly . . . Did he give me the chance to respond? No. *Ah!*

- In fact, he passed his verdict and drove off, leaving me behind. Like a scolded schoolboy. I did not like that.

- Also I was in the right, wasn't I? He cut *me* off, not the other way round. Can't believe it! He's the police. If he doesn't know the traffic code then who does? I hate police bullies. Next thing we know we'll have a police state – they should protect citizens not hassle them. *OH!* Now here I am on to something. Where did that come from?

Life vs Self-knowledge: *1–catching up.*

- Was it the fact that he was a policeman? That is part of it. Was it the fact that I felt unjustly reprimanded? Certainly. I also had a problem at school with teachers telling me what to do. With bosses at work demanding respect.

- I think I am getting to an insight here. I have a problem with figures of authority. I also have a problem with people treating me unfairly. Nicely done. Score?

Life vs Self-knowledge: *still laughing, solidly at 1–a little bit.*

Why only a little bit? Surely I have gained a self-insight?

Maybe. But it is no more than a glimpse. There is more here and it is deeper down. The next questions are, 'Why do I not like authority, then?', 'Is this really true?' and 'Why do I feel so strongly about being treated (un)fairly?'

- What did I really resent here? The fact that the guy drove off without giving me a chance to explain that I was in the right. I seem to dislike authority if I think it is being abused. *Ah – interesting.*

- In fact, I only had problems with my teachers if they told me what to do without explaining why they wanted it. Like Mr Kaptin, who was shouting at me. Or Mr Byass, who I thought treated us cynically. I actually got on brilliantly with teachers who involved me in dialogue and treated me as if I was their equal.

- Indeed, I only had problems with bosses at work if they demanded respect before I felt they had earned it. When I saw obvious substance, I was usually glad to be mentored by an individual more experienced, knowledgeable, capable or intelligent. In those cases it never seemed to matter to me if the person was, for example, younger than I, or had spent less time in the business, or had somehow failed to score on another superficial measure that may be deemed relevant by some.

- Interestingly, when I was a conscript in the army, I never had a problem with my superiors at all. How odd though. Surely the military embodies rigid hierarchies which, from the point of view of the new recruit, are by definition never based on substance? But in the army I never felt that being shouted at reflected disrespect. It represented merely a means of teaching new recruits the discipline needed to function within a rigidly hierarchical framework. As such, it was a tool, and never personal.

- Had it occurred to me at the time that I had been wrong and that indeed I *had* cut off the police van, I probably would have listened and apologised.

Finally, I think I am able to filter out a proper self-insight from my emotional muddle. I dislike authority if it is not based on substance and therefore appears an abuse. I dislike being treated unfairly because it goes against my feeling of self-worth. But I do not have a problem with authority if I think it is earned or fairly wielded, nor with being criticised if I think it is justified. At the deepest level I have been able to penetrate so far, I seem to value substance over form.

Life vs Self-knowledge: *nil–1. Thank you very much.*

Is this the end of the quest? Hardly. Questions now worth asking include, 'Have I developed an inflated view of myself?' and 'Am I getting too big for my boots?' These questions are worth exploring and my running answer would be: 'I do not think so, but it is a tendency worth watching and, if need be, correcting.'

But, even without exploring these further questions, I need to pause and realise that I managed to pan a nugget from the sediment of my experience. It is important for me to realise that my insight is valuable.

We have already seen that insights such as this one can be used in the real world. I should avoid situations in which rigid hierarchies are important. It is unlikely that I would thrive in the army or the police force; careers in public office, or as a public servant, seem unadvisable, but so do managerial careers in businesses that value corporate ethos more than individual personality. Away from my professional life, I may wish to seek out the company of those who are naturally confident in themselves as individuals, rather than taking pride in a particular lifestyle or ideological persuasion.

A recipe for self-insights

You have heard me speak about these insights and these real-world results before. Of course, I did not get all of these ideas from this little incident alone. The investigation I described merely exemplifies how the raw material life provides can be processed, refined and distilled into useable insights. I am not suggesting that every little thing is subjected to intense navel-gazing all the time.

What I *am* suggesting is that we go through life consciously, take note of small things and try to understand why we react to them in the way we do.

Not every incident needs to be processed, and not every processed incident needs to lead to an insight. We file most of our experiences away in the subconscious for later use and are able to call upon them when needed. Or rather, they will bubble up when the time is right, like they did in the example above. The policeman reminded me of incidents at school, at work, in the army. Incidents I may have noted and filed away at the time, or may have noted and half processed, but importantly did not ignore and forget about. In my case, the incident with the police reminded me of many similar incidents which, although unimportant in themselves, formed a pattern leading to a self-insight when considered together.

Therefore, what I am suggesting is that we make EXPERIENCE MINING a habit:

- The cashier at the supermarket checkout made me angry. *Take note!* Why was this? She was snappy with me. For no reason. I value professionalism. Because I strive to deliver it in my own job. I set demanding standards for myself and I tend to hold others to these. *File away.*

- The window display at the retailer looks really arty and I like that. *Take note!* How interesting that I think that. I am not normally arty. But this design had clean lines. This is what I seem to like. Maybe this is also what the house is missing? I might redecorate, get rid of clutter everywhere. *File away.*

- I can see the sun rising over London from my offices. How romantic. Me – romantic? No way. *Take note!* The way the sun filters through the mist, reflecting off the glass and steel . . . I seem to like the big city. Maybe I should spend more private time in town? *File away.*

- I cannot believe how rude that switchboard person was on the phone. What a plonker. I did nothing to deserve this. No wonder I gave him an earful. *Take note!* Well, maybe my reaction was a bit sharp. I tend to lose my temper a lot lately. Especially when I am on the phone. Why is this? *File away and return to it later.*

- What a great atmosphere in this bar. A throwback to the 20s. Almost looks like a sepia photograph. Not normally my cup of tea. My mates would take the mickey big time if they saw me here. *Take note!* Maybe I am artier than I think? Perhaps I should go to a jazz club once in a while? I tend to go along with what my mates want to do. Perhaps too often? *File away.*

And so on. Over time, we discover that the things we like and dislike tend to have something in common, that we like or dislike people for consistent reasons, that we get angry when certain things happen and that we feel at our most contented, elated, relaxed or happy when certain other circumstances prevail.

Eventually, nuggets of self-insight may lead us to a vein of self-knowledge and, perhaps, an even more profound understanding of our personality. Is this goal elusive or somehow esoteric? Certainly not. EXPERIENCE MINING, the processing of small experiences, is a pragmatic method, a tool that I can use like a pan to extract gold from a river.

Is it an easy tool to use? Basically, yes. Is it easy to achieve results? Absolutely not. Useable insights will be the result of years spent 'panning', by consistent habit. It takes skill to use a gold pan expertly, and we get better through practice.

RULE 2

Know what you need

How to make decisions

The second step

As we become better acquainted with ourselves, we notice that we understand better what we want in life. Some things seem rather obvious. I like skiing because I enjoy adrenalin sports and have a good sense of balance. I like football because I like the team spirit and the strategic aspect of the game. Other things are more difficult and perhaps we are less certain about them. I would like kids some time because I like the idea of starting a family. I would like to study journalism because writing about world affairs would give me a sense of purpose.

If we know ourselves quite well, we may even have deeper insights into why we want what we want. I am ambitious and an individualist – I like skiing because it is a competitive sport and is not played in a team. I have a social conscience and words come easily to me – I wish to be a journalist because I can use my talent to empower people through information.

But, even if we know these things about ourselves, we still need to make the actual decisions that steer our lives in a particular direction and, over time, shape our personal worlds. How do we make these decisions? How do we know at any given time what is right for us and what is not?

Well, I would suggest that there are several tricks and devices that can aid us in our decision making. None of them replaces self-knowledge; indeed, they would not work particularly well if we did not know ourselves. But they are useful tools to use as we discover more about who we are.

Some decisions in life are less important than others. Consequently, decision tools that enable them are simple and can be applied without great effort. As decisions get more complex, the methods that aid making them get more complex too, and we need to apply ourselves more when we use them. And finally, there are decisions of potentially life-changing magnitude. I am afraid I have found no formal tool that will help us making those – we need to hope that we have achieved a self-knowledge so profound that it will allow us to make these decisions well, if – or when – they arrive.

But simple things first. Let us start with decisions that are relatively easy to make.

Basic decision making – the dice test

Decisions that fall into this category are everyday decisions. Nothing much will happen if we get them wrong, what happens as a consequence is entirely reversible and we are faced with choices of this nature many times in our lives. Here are a few examples of the most innocuous ones in this class:

- Should I have tiramisu or apple pie for dessert?

- Shall I buy this shirt in pink or in blue?

- Shall we watch this movie or that one?

Other decisions of this type can be a bit more involved:

- Shall we buy the more expensive car or the one that does not cost that much? The more expensive one has a better build quality and would offer far better safety for the kids. But if we buy the cheaper one, we could use the money left over to go on holiday this year.

- It is our anniversary coming up. Shall we treat ourselves and go for a long weekend in this really swanky spa hotel, or should we opt for a week away and stay somewhere nice, but more affordable?

Others seem more involved still, but nevertheless belong in this first category:

- Shall I go out with this bloke on a second date? He was nice enough but somehow uninspiring. Would I get his expectations up if I did? But maybe he was just having an off-day on our first date?

Decisions of this nature will not matter hugely. Still, if we got the answers to these types of question right every time, we would probably be happier people than if we constantly got the answers wrong.

But how do we know what is the best answer? Sure, pink shirt or blue shirt is not hard. But the car question may be slightly more difficult to decide, and possibly also whether to go on a second date. To help with decisions of moderate complexity such as these, I suggest the use of a simple tool. I call this tool the DICE TEST.

> . . . if that die has a one face up, I thought, I'm going downstairs and rape Arlene. 'If it's a one, I'll rape Arlene,' kept blinking on and off in my mind like a huge neon light and my terror increased. But when I thought if it's not a one I'll go to bed, the terror was boiled away by a pleasant excitement . . . a one

means rape, the other numbers mean bed, the die is cast. Who am I to question the die?

I picked [it] up and saw staring at me a cyclopean eye: a one.[12]

There are those who might suggest that Dr Rhinehart, the main character in Luke Rhinehart's novel *The Dice Man*, is taking it a bit far. Fair enough. I am not suggesting that it is reasonable to give life decisions over to the throw of a die. In fact, and you know I would say this, I am suggesting exactly the opposite.

But there is an analogy between the fictional Rhinehart and the test I am about to introduce. In my test, the person casting the die needs to develop a mindset that the decision mandated by chance is irrevocable and *must* be followed. The DICE TEST is unlikely to unfold its full potential if the person using it does not accept this condition in her mind.[13]

So what is the DICE TEST? Let me use an example to illustrate:

By now you may be asking yourself whether you should continue reading this book or stop and get on with something more productive. Let us use the DICE TEST to make this decision. You will need a fair die to conduct this experiment.

Got one? Good. Now follow these steps:

(1) **Calibration.** If you throw a 1–3, you will throw this book in the rubbish. If you throw a 4–6, you will continue reading this book.

---

[12] Rhinehart, Luke. *The Dice Man.* Harper Collins, 1972, London, p. 69. Reprinted by permission of HarperCollins Publishers Ltd © George Cockcroft 1971.

[13] A note on the use of gender: I tried to avoid gender bias as much as possible. In cases where nouns do not denote a specific gender, I have assigned one arbitrarily. I would therefore refer to a person or individual arbitrarily as 'he' or 'she'. I am treating nouns denoting professions similarly, and carpenters, doctors or nurses are sometimes male and sometimes female in the text. In addition, I use third person plural pronouns ('they', 'their' etc.) to keep expressions such as 'somebody' or 'someone' gender-neutral.

(2) **Brainwash.** Accept unconditionally that you *will* do what the outcome of the throw tells you to do.

(3) No really. Do it again. You *must* be clear in your mind that there is no other choice. If you leave the option open to ignore the die, this will not work.

(4) So no other option exists. You will do what the die dictates.

(5) **Execution.** Throw the die. It shows a 1.

(6) Quick! *Immediately* take note of your first reaction.

(7) Was it relief? Or disappointment?

(8) If it was the former, chuck this book away. If it was the latter, continue reading.

The dice test – critique

Oh good! You are still here. Thank you very much!

Step 2 basically conditions you to obey an order. The throw of the die represents this order and in step 6 you simply record your emotional reaction to this order. At no point during this process did you actually *make* a decision. You had already made the decision before you started the process, in your subconscious mind.

I assure you this works for things we naturally know about ourselves. We are merely unaware of this knowledge and it tends to apply to the smaller things in life.

However, all this test does is to make unconscious knowledge conscious. It is as if a window briefly opens in the black box that is our subconscious mind, one piece of insight flies out and then the window slams shut again before we are able to take a good look inside.

As such, the DICE TEST is only helpful with binary decisions of a yes or no type, but is not really appropriate for complex choices. Those depend on several interacting factors and they have a higher potential impact on our lives. They are things like, 'What career path should I choose?', 'Which company should I join?', 'Public school or state for our child?'

For those more heavyweight decisions, I suggest a more advanced version of the DICE TEST. I call it the ABACUS TEST, and I am afraid it involves a spreadsheet.

Advanced decision making – the abacus test

Ten years ago, I was faced with a difficult decision. I was clear in my mind that I needed a change professionally, but had absolutely no idea which one of two job offers I should accept.

I called all my friends. I talked to those among my professional contacts whom I could trust to keep the situation secret. I talked to my parents. No breakthrough.

Basic salary is better at Company B, but benefits are not obviously better. The team at Company A is not as good as Company B's, but the level of marketing support is clearly better at A. Job security seems better at A, but then A is a takeover target[14] and what happens if the company disappears? B is a bit at the periphery of the City and slightly more difficult to get to. The hierarchy at A is really steep and I liked people better at B . . .

So what to do? It was driving me crazy. I just *could not* weigh up all the conflicting factors and get to a clear preference. All I knew was that I *had* to leave my current job.

In the end, I decided to sit down and sift through my thoughts in a systematic way. I wrote down all the things that mattered to me on a piece of paper. Salary, bonus scheme, location, people, level of responsibility, and so on. Just as an unstructured list, whatever came to mind. Next, I assigned a number from 1 to 5 to each item, denoting whether the company would score poorly (1) or highly (5) on the matter in question. Last, I assigned a weighting to each item, depending

---

[14] Company A was widely expected to be acquired by another company at the time they made me an offer.

on whether I thought the matter was unimportant (1), interesting (2) or vital (3). I then calculated a weighted score for each company and observed the result. I would join the company with the higher score.

Oh no! Shock. Company A comes out with the higher score? I thought Company B would win out. Oh dear. I don't really like Company A ...

Ah! Result. I seem to favour Company B in my subconscious mind. This phase in the process is exactly the same as in the DICE TEST.

But this problem is a little bit more complicated and more is riding on the decision I will ultimately make. This problem cannot be solved simply by following the result of the test.

I decided to transfer my piece of paper to a spreadsheet and study the result. Here is what my decision model looked like:

Criterion	Company A		Company B		Weights
	Score	Weighted score	Score	Weighted score	
Basic salary	2	4	4	8	2
Potential bonus	5	15	5	15	3
Benefits	4	8	5	10	2
Location	3	3	2	2	1
Seniority in team	4	4	4	4	1
Level of responsibility	4	12	3	9	3
Travel to work	4	4	3	3	1
Marketing support	5	15	1	3	3
Quality of team	2	6	4	12	3
Hierarchical structure	3	6	2	4	2
Job security	4	4	2	2	1
Takeover target?	2	6	2	6	3
Financial soundness	4	12	3	9	3
Culture, atmosphere	3	6	5	10	2
Total score		**105**		**97**	

Fig. 2.1 An unstructured list, with scores (*Score*) assigned to each criterion on a range from 1 (poor) to 5 (excellent). Weighting factors are shown in light grey in the final column (*Weights*), indicating whether the aspect is unimportant (1), interesting (2) or vital (3). The product of the weights and the score is the *Weighted score*, shown separately for the two companies. Company A wins on a higher *Total score*, although subconsciously I preferred Company B.

Next, I ordered the criteria into groups of a common nature. This gave my loose original listing more structure. This is what I got:

Criterion	Company A		Company B		Weights
	Score	Weighted score	Score	Weighted score	
Basic salary	2	4	4	8	2
Potential bonus	5	15	5	15	3
Benefits	4	8	5	10	2
Compensation		27		33	
Level of responsibility	4	12	3	9	3
Marketing support	5	15	1	3	3
Quality of team	2	6	4	12	3
Professionalism		33		24	
Job security	4	4	2	2	1
Takeover target?	2	6	2	6	3
Financial soundness	4	12	3	9	3
Company health		22		17	
Location	3	3	2	2	1
Travel to work	4	4	3	3	1
Seniority in team	4	4	4	4	1
Hierarchical structure	3	6	2	4	2
Culture, atmosphere	3	6	5	10	2
Soft factors		23		23	
Total score		105		97	

Fig. 2.2 The same list as shown in fig. 2.1, but with criteria structured into four subgroups and with subtotals shown for each.

Based on my table, I was now in a position to analyse the results and gain some clear insights:

• Compensation looks similar, but is actually better at B. Basic is a lot higher and benefits are better too.

• Company A seems to be in better financial health. It certainly looks sounder on the balance sheet, and that drives better job security. But both are takeover targets, so there is no telling what might happen to either of them.

• Soft factors are identical. Looks like I am actually neutral on that one. Although I did like people better at B . . .

• But professionalism. Wow! *Much* better at A. Still, the quality of the team is actually *worse*, and I am broadly neutral on the responsibility I would have in either job.

- Marketing support stands out. It looks as though I feel a lot stronger about that one than I thought! And I know why. It was that one person in marketing who I would have to work with – I just did not get a good feeling about him from the interview.

- Hmmm. Let us see. What if that problem did not exist? If I could assign a 5 to marketing support, the same as for A, what would the outcome be? Now the total score is 109 and B wins. Even on a 4, B wins.

So I had my answer! It basically boiled down to one problem with one individual at Company B. What I did next was to ask for another meeting with the department head and a meeting with the marketing chap to get to the bottom of the issue. I now knew exactly the questions I wanted to ask, and the meetings went well enough for me to think that I would be able to deal with the specific problem in marketing.

I accepted the offer from B and was relieved to finally make a decision that felt right.

But was it, in fact, the right decision? In the end, it did not work out as I would have hoped. The guy I was sceptical about did turn out to be a major problem and was sacked six months in. Fifteen months later I moved on to join the company I still work for as I am writing this. Company A was taken over a year later by a different company and the team I would have joined disappeared in the restructuring.

Was it the right decision or not? I would say that the ABACUS TEST helped me make the decision, and this was valuable in itself. It was clearly a better decision than joining A, and also better than doing nothing. Ultimately, Company B did not work out, but by the time that became obvious I had made another decision, and I have been with my current employer for a long time. Looking back, I think the decision I made was the best, given the set of choices I had at the time. And I would not have been able to make it had I not had a certain level of self-knowledge and had I not employed the ABACUS TEST to examine that knowledge.

Abacus or dice?

Basically, the ABACUS TEST is a more elaborate version of the DICE TEST. Both rely on the same premise – that on a subconscious level we have already formed a preference. But the ABACUS TEST differs from the DICE TEST in two ways:

(1) It is flexible and transparent. The DICE TEST only offers an unqualified glimpse into the subconscious mind. The window opens, then it shuts.

   The ABACUS TEST allows us to analyse the drivers of our subconscious preference. It clearly highlights all components of the problem, and also the weight with which these components enter into the equation. More than that, it enables us to do scenario analyses – how would the result change if isolated components carried a different weight or a different score? It is as if part of the black box becomes transparent, revealing the clockwork within, allowing us to examine and understand how the levers and cogs work together to produce the result.

(2) However, the ABACUS TEST requires self-awareness. Anybody can do the DICE TEST; it is not necessary to know yourself particularly well, or at all. But the ABACUS TEST requires personal insights as input. Without self-knowledge, we would not be able to define the weights (see figs 2.1 and 2.2). Neither would we be able to analyse the problem exhaustively and write down all the relevant components.

   Without self-knowledge, we would not be able to build the right model; without the right model, we would not arrive at valuable answers.

   The ABACUS TEST is an advanced tool. It is best suited to people with advanced self-knowledge who are facing problems of some complexity and importance.

But what about a third class of problem? What about decisions that are truly life-changing, irrevocable or even existential? It is to these that I am turning next.

Expert decision making – no simple test

Decisions in this category concern potentially life-changing problems such as, 'Shall I buy a property with my partner?', 'Shall we have children?', 'Shall I quit my job and start out again?'[15]

I am afraid some of these decisions are so critical that no simple test can aid us in finding the answer. In some of the examples I gave, we are not making decisions that will impact only our lives; they will have an impact on the lives of others as well. Problems in this category can truly challenge us at a fundamental level.

We cannot find the right answers to these questions without a highly advanced degree of self-knowledge. As an example, let me examine a popular issue.

Shall we have children? This is a life-changing decision which most of us will wrestle with at some point in our lives. According to the Office for National Statistics, more than 80 per cent of couples in their 30s have children.[16] In this case, statistics support something we intuitively know – that we are genetically programmed to have kids. The question of whether to have kids is therefore quite an ordinary one after all.

Ordinary the question may be. But trivial it is not.

Let us not pretend that having children will not change our lives. It will mean an end to nights of uninterrupted sleep. Nipping down the pub for a quick one with your mates? Girls'

---

[15] There is also a class of even more weighty problems of an existential nature, but I will leave discussion of these until the last section.
[16] Office for National Statistics. *Focus on Families*. 2007. In fact, 81% of adults aged 35–39 have dependent children, only 2% have independent children and the rest are DINKs. If you must know.

night out? These are still possible but will require military-style precision planning and forward thinking. Nannies have to be organised, spare-time quotas have to be negotiated and allocated between partners, mobiles have to be switched on at all times. Sleeping in at the weekend? You must be, pardon the pun, kidding.

But these are the easy ones. What really matters is that you are no longer on your own. You willingly take responsibility for another person, somebody who is entirely dependent on you. On your maturity, on your level of responsibility, on your caring, on your love. On your ability to provide a home, protection, clothes . . . On your ability to make the right decisions on their behalf. On your luck in avoiding too many of the wrong ones. On your ability to show them what is right, and what is wrong.

Which means that you need to *want* the responsibility they bring. That you do not mourn the days where you had freedom as an individual, but embrace the days where you experience such freedom as a family. You may not be able to nip down the pub at short notice, but the family can have a picnic in the garden without huge planning, for example. In short, you need to be happier *with* children than without.

So how do you decide whether you are cut out for it? How do you know whether you want children for the right reasons? Indeed, what *are* the right reasons to have children? The answer is, of course, through self-knowledge. However, this time your self-knowledge needs to be conscious. And, most importantly, you need to be sufficiently self-aware to understand that you need to examine yourself *before* you go ahead.

As I discussed earlier in the stories 'A stand not taken' and 'An insight ignored', the decision to have kids is not an easy one. If it is made as an unexamined choice, the consequences to your emotional well-being, and to that of others, may be dire. But if the choice is both examined and right, the chances are that you may become more, or differently, fulfilled, happy and content. As ever, there is no right way in absolute terms. But there is a right way that applies uniquely to you.

I am afraid my tests may not work in this scenario.[17] The reason is that if you need a decision tool for this, it is clear that you are still actively working through the issues, that you see pros and cons and that you need to weigh up the evidence. My feeling is that if you see the need to use a tool for the weightier decisions in bucket number three, you are not ready to make them yet. The more you are wavering, the less you should attempt decisions of this severity.[18]

But what to do? Of course, it is always possible to spend another few years EXPERIENCE MINING and hope that you will develop sufficient self-knowledge to make such a decision with confidence. But this may take years and the outcome would still be uncertain. What if you do not wish to wait?

Then, I believe, you will need to seek the advice of others. If you do not know yourself well enough to make the important life decisions contained in bucket number three, you need to know people who do. But how do you know whether they do? Do you have people in your life whom you can trust to give you wise counsel? Why do you think that? What are these people like – do you know them sufficiently to understand why they are advising you in a particular way? Do *they* know *you* sufficiently to give you good advice? Do they have your well-being at heart? Or do they merely tell you what would be right for them? These questions are important, but this is not the place to discuss them. We will chat about these issues in Rule 6, 'Seek advice'.

---

[17] I would certainly not suggest the DICE TEST. 'OK honey, on 1–3 we have kids, on 4–6 we won't. Yes?' Your partner may be bewildered, to say the least, by this apparent display of flippancy.

[18] For example, I felt the desire to move in with Ursina about a year later than she did. I did not get out my abacus, and I did not force myself to make the decision before I felt the desire. And neither did she.

Existential decision making – the final frontier

I must admit I would prefer not to discuss this category of decisions at all. It contains problems such as these. 'My parents suffer from acute dementia, so shall I arrange for them to be put into long-term care? Shall I care for them myself?'; 'My partner named me the executor in his living will and I agreed, so am I now ethically bound to switch off life support for my clinically dead husband of 40 years?'

The reason I would prefer not to discuss these is obvious. They represent dilemmas of the gravest kind, problems that test our ethical, religious and ideological convictions to break-ing point, and problems which may well prove too much for us to handle. I certainly feel ill-equipped to do them justice, having little life experience that comes close. Nevertheless, I ask your indulgence to follow one more example from my life, and I apologise to those who may be facing grave decisions of this nature. I am not suggesting my experience is adequate. It is merely the best I have to offer.

When I was a conscript in the army, duties included guard-ing the barracks at night. Mostly, being a conscript was more like playing at cowboys and Indians – I could never quite take it seriously; the guns were firing blanks, our time in the forces was limited, we would never see real action in the event of conflict anyway.

Standing guard, however, was the exception. Standing guard involved handling live ammunition. Standing guard meant that you were under orders to fire your gun if the situa-tion demanded it. And if the situation demanded it and you did *not* fire your gun, there would be real-world consequences. Convictions under military law and sentences served in a mili-tary jail would not give you the cleanest start in civilian life after they let you out. So here was something not to be made light of.

I still remember when I was first briefed for guard duties. The sergeant was explaining again how the gun we would be given worked and what sort of ammunition it fired. He was identifying the situations that demanded firing the gun. These generally involved unidentified individuals moving around within the barracks grounds. As you see in the cop shows on telly, we were programmed to follow a clear procedure. First, you would ask the person to identify themselves. If they failed to do that and ran from you instead, you would order them to stop. You would do that twice. If they kept running, you would fire your gun, aiming to incapacitate them. In short, you were ordered to shoot.

When I first heard that, I said to myself, 'Yeah right. As if. Whatever. Just give me that gun so we can get this over with. Nothing's going to happen anyway. I certainly will not be shooting anybody in the back.'

But then, after a while, something was beginning to niggle. Yes, the chances that I would be confronted with a situation were slim. But what if it *did* happen? What would I do? I decided I needed to be mentally prepared. I needed to know what I would do *before* it happened, not start questioning myself when it did.

This is how I worked through this issue – it looks like a dialogue but all the thoughts are mine:

> OK, I am ordered to shoot so I shoot. But I'll shoot into the air and nobody will ever know. After all, I am not a trained marksman so nobody will expect me to hit anybody anyway.
>
> But what if the person running away from me has a reason to run away? What if they broke into the ammunition room and were making off with an armful of hand grenades or plastic explosives?
>
> Whatever. Still not my business. I won't shoot a human being in the back, whether ordered to do so or not.
>
> But what if the person used the plastic explosive to make a bomb? And what if the bomb went off in a supermarket, or another public place? Could I live with the responsibility of not having intervened when I had the chance?
>
> OK, so I try to incapacitate but I won't kill. I'll aim at the legs.

But that won't work. It will be dark. I will be full of adrenalin. The gun's aim is hardly going to be true, given the treatment they receive in the gun room – it only takes a light knock and the barrel is slightly off target. And I am not a trained marksman. There is no chance I will hit legs moving away from me 50 yards out into the dark. So, if I shoot, I'd better do it right and aim at the centre of the body, like they taught us to do.

But then I may kill the guy, or he may end up paralysed for life. What if he is not carrying a sack with plastic explosives and a bazooka strapped to his back? What if he is just a teenager on a dare?

The point is, I do not know either way. If I knew, with certainty, that the guy was a terrorist stealing explosives, the decision might be slightly easier. In that case, I would choose to save the lives of the many against an unprovoked attack by the few.

So I shall execute the order that was given. I shall stick religiously to the script, but if the situation escalates, I shall aim to incapacitate the person by firing my gun at the centre of the body, maximising the chance of a hit. If I kill or paralyse a teenager on a dare, ultimately that was his risk to take. If I kill a terrorist, that would potentially save innocent lives.

But, teenager or terrorist, in both cases I would have to live with the consequences of my action. And, make no mistake, it would be irrelevant to me that I had been obeying lawful orders. I might not be able to handle the psychological aftermath. What if I develop severe post-traumatic stress?

That, I think, would be the price I would have to pay. If the responsibility is forced upon me, I will not shirk it. If that is the price, I will pay it.

I am lucky that the worst challenge I ever faced on guard duty was to stay awake in the presence of extreme boredom. Nothing ever happened that tested my ethics in the way they could have been tested.

What was the point of my story, then? Is it not easy for me to say I would pay the price? Not quite. It took some hard, uncomfortable thinking to work through the issues. So it was hard to *say*. And it would be harder still to actually *do*. But the point of my story is that I tried to work through the existential implications of a situation that might be forced upon me, before it came to the test and not after. As a result, I was mentally resolved to follow a certain course of action, and conscious that it might have consequences for my well-being afterwards.

The analogy with the existential decisions I mentioned at the start of this section may still be poor. People put into extreme scenarios such as these will need to find an inner strength eclipsing any they may have had to muster before. Switching off the life support of a loved one, caring for the incapacitated, saving lives at conscious risk of personal well-being – all these are acts of altruism. Not of pseudo-altruism – if I help others because it makes me feel noble, that is still a commendable act, but it is not truly altruistic.[19] Helping others when doing so brings emotional distress is.

Existential choices, therefore, rest on a sense of self that surpasses mere self-knowledge. This final frontier of self-penetration demands that we put the fate of others above our own – and know what such an action would do to us. This level of insight will reveal whether we are strong enough to live with the consequences. If we are, the decision will go one way and we will know what to do. If we are not, the decision may need to go another way.

If it is the latter, do not sit in judgement of yourself. Not everybody is cut out to perform acts of (true) altruism. Not everybody has the strength to live a life in care of someone else. This does not mean that we excuse ourselves from our responsibilities. But it *does* mean that we find a mode that we

---

[19] Here is a quote from a source nearly 2000 years old. In it, we find the following statement: 'So when you give to the needy, do not announce it with trumpets . . . so that your giving may be in secret. Then your Father, who sees what is done in secret, will reward you.' (Matt 6:2–4). I am not making a religious statement with this quote. I merely wish to illustrate that the idea of altruism as giving without seeking reward has a long history. (The Bible, New International Version. Hodder & Stoughton 2005)

know we can handle. By transferring the decision to switch off life support to a neutral party *before* the incapacitating event occurs. By moving our parents to a care home close to our home, enabling us to do as much as we are able to and perhaps discussing this in good time.

These are the true heavyweights as far as decisions are concerned. I believe they require the highest level of self-knowledge possible. And I believe we will be best prepared to deal with them if we know what our response will be *before* the test occurs and not *after*.

The decision wall

Dare I say it but I believe we may have some answers by now. When we started the quest, we had three challenges to over-come on the way to happiness:

(1) Know who you are.
(2) Know what you need.
(3) Get it.

We discussed the first one. It is vital to know who you are since everything else will flow from self-knowledge. EXPERIENCE MINING is one method we can use to gather insights about ourselves. No doubt this is not the only way, but it strikes me as a common sense, real-world tool to go after something that may otherwise remain elusive, even esoteric.

We can only make inroads into the second challenge if we have mastered the first. Happiness is essentially a state in which we are content with the life choices we have made. It brings us emotional balance and a sense of control. We get there by making the right decisions, and we make the right decisions by knowing ourselves.

I have made up a simple chart to show how the various life decisions relate to each other.

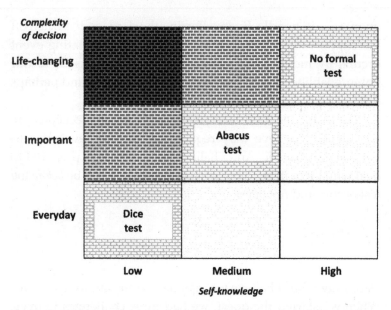

Fig. 2.3 The wall shows no-go areas as a black obstacle and more easily accessible regions in lighter shades. Increasingly important decisions in life can be made more easily as self-knowledge grows. Decisions involving everyday choices and those of some importance may be aided by formal decision methods, but there is no simple model for existential decisions.

On the vertical axis we find the severity of the decisions we need to make, and on the horizontal axis the level of self-knowledge required to make them.

If our self-knowledge is low (either because we have only recently started to seek it or because we are indifferent), we can only hope to get everyday, simple decisions right. This is the domain of the DICE TEST – it may help us with some of the challenges. There is a risk that we may get important decisions (such as which job to take) wrong – they are solidly bricked up (the middle square in the first and second columns respectively). And it would be risky, not to say reckless, to attempt decisions of a life-changing nature with low self-knowledge – problems such as whether to leave school, quit your job or have kids are better left alone. They reside behind the black no-go zone on the map.

As we develop self-knowledge, everyday decisions become a doddle and we are less likely to buy DVDs we do not like or go out on a date with that weird bloke for a second time. Important decisions are now firmly in our grasp, although they may continue to be bewildering – the ABACUS TEST may ease some of the pain. Life-changing decisions remain a challenge and there is a risk that we may get them wrong . . .

At the most advanced level of self-knowledge, we never watch movies that we do not like – ever. Career changes are made with confidence, and if they turn out to go astray they are corrected. Joining the Red Cross or not is still a challenge, but we are now likely to know what we want and more often than not will make a choice which will enrich our lives. We no longer need simple tests and we have left the realms where they would help.

Existential decisions are not on the map. These are singularities – they define the extreme points at which any structural analysis is strained to breaking point. The best we can do is to be prepared for the tests when, or if, they arrive.

So what happened to point (3) Get It? Well, we have not touched upon that yet. We are now well along the road towards knowing who we are and understanding what we need. The next challenge is to develop the courage of our conviction to act in accordance with our insights and to make things happen.

But it will not be easy to get it. It will take courage, like that of Ursina's sister, who swapped a steady job for four years of training as a nurse. Or intense frustration with the confines of life, like mine when I decided to leave the country of my birth and live permanently abroad. Or clear understanding, like Ursina's when she left the world of business to work for not-for-profit organisations.

We shall explore the mindsets that aid getting it throughout the remainder of the book. But the foundation is clear: self-knowledge is the key. If we work responsibly to achieve it, happiness will be within our grasp.

Part II

Get it!

RULE 3

Everything is your fault!

How to control your life

Really? I mean – really?

This is the first chapter on getting it? This will help me achieve what is right for me? A sense that I constantly need to blame myself for everything? Last week this guy drove into my car then took off – £2,000 damage. Jumped a red light. How's that my fault? And my brother's house was burgled when he was on holiday. He didn't exactly arrange for that one to happen, did he? There's a £500 excess on my policy. I just don't need that sort of thing happening right now. And now you come along suggesting that this was somehow my fault? First injury, now insult!

This was not exactly a reader's letter in response to the title of the chapter, but I can imagine some of you may be having thoughts along those lines at the moment.

The key to understanding what I mean is to appreciate that I am talking about a *mindset*. I am not suggesting that we are to blame for everything that is happening to us. But I *am* suggesting that we should look at things *as if* we were. Why am I suggesting this? Because if we believe that we are the authors of the things that happen to us, we are in charge. If we blame circumstances, however, we give away control, whether we are responsible or not. If we blame others, we turn ourselves into powerless victims. If we blame ourselves, we remain empowered agents.

But, as ever, I can talk. So let me tell you a story from my life that may illustrate what I mean. This one falls into the category of times when I *was* responsible for something that happened but did not realise it.

Can't believe it!

A few years ago, I did an advanced driving course. This involved driving a car around the English countryside[20] in the presence of Tom, my tutor. Tom was an ex-Met[21] police driver and said things like: 'Remember *TOT* – tyres on tarmac!', 'Always have an escape route!', 'At the humpback bridges, accelerate as you get to the top to generate downforce' or 'Gently accelerate in the bends to keep your overall speed constant'. When he was driving, the car seemed to obey different physical laws – it was rock solid and glued to the road. When I was driving . . . well, here is not the proper place to go into that.

So there I was in the fast lane of a dual carriageway trying to execute all the different tricks that would make the car move like a train. Thumbs out, not in, on the steering wheel? *Check.* Changing down while leaving the foot on the accelerator? *Check.* Keeping the speed constant? *Check.*

A clap of thunder. A green flash in the corner of my eye. A Lamborghini overtaking furiously in the slow lane, accelerating like a fighter jet.

I could not believe it. What an idiot! The speed limit marks the *top* speed, not the minimum! And overtaking in the slow lane? I did not see that coming. Would not have dreamed that anybody would do that.

I expressed my sentiments to my tutor, firm in my moral indignation, confident of his support. Here is what I got:

---

[20] This actually accounts for one of the 15 days in the countryside I mentioned earlier.
[21] London Metropolitan Police.

Always be aware of what's going on around you!

Sure, but he overtook in the slow lane. That's illegal.

You made him do that. Do not provoke other drivers.

I'm sorry? Provoke? That dude came tearing down the road like a moron! He broke at least two laws here – how is that my fault?

Because you were tootling around in the fast lane at the speed limit, blocking it for faster drivers. It's irrelevant that he was breaking the limit – if that's what he wants to do, that's his business, not yours.

. . .?

That last bit was me, not believing what I was hearing.

You should have seen him tailgaiting. Should have moved over to the slow lane and let him pass. That way, you would always have been in control. Any worse than this, we would have been looking at an accident. Be in control, know how your actions affect other drivers and take responsibility for your own driving, not that of others.

Be the agent, not the victim

I still remember that exchange to this day. Tom taught me an important lesson that day, and it had very little to do with driving.[22] What others do may be directly or indirectly caused by our own actions. Sometimes we are aware that our actions, directly or indirectly, have led to another action, but sometimes we are not. And when we are not, we tend to think that something that happens to us is *done* to us, that we did nothing to provoke it, that we were powerless to prevent it and that we are innocent victims of circumstance.

The problem with this mindset is that we give away control. We let somebody else be the agent and we become the victim. I

---

[22] Although it was a good driving tip as intended, too. It works. For one thing, you get less worked up. As another aside, this episode also shows that no setting is too mundane for life to teach us a lesson.

allowed the Lambo-guy to shock me, whereas I could easily have remained in command of the situation. I reacted, rather than acted.

Once we have given away control, we can no longer act. And when we do not act, we cannot bring about change or go after what we need. This statement works for almost all situations in life. Of course, the fictional reader's brother in my introductory thought did not invite the burglar into his home. But perhaps the financial impact of the situation would be less severe if adequate insurance had been bought. Perhaps the burglary could have been prevented if security had been arranged with a neighbour or security equipment had been installed. The emotional aftermath of having your privacy invaded may be handled by managing your attitude and by choosing not to let it take hold of you, choosing not to let it control you.

I realise that there is a real risk here of sounding glib. But my essential point remains simple. A mindset that blames circumstance for a personal predicament relinquishes control. A mindset that searches for reasons in our own actions remains in control. It is important to realise that I am talking about *mindset*. This mindset is a deliberate choice to look at things in a specific light and not in another. It is a *choice*, like a game of pretence.

Of course, it may not always be the case that my own actions set things in motion that affect me in turn. But it will often be the case. And even when it is not the case, even when I *am* the innocent victim of a burglary or a car accident, a mindset of MOCK SELF-INCRIMINATION may empower me to act and deal more competently with the problems life throws at me.

May. Not will. As ever, there are no guarantees. If I adopt the mindset, I *may* take control. If I do not adopt the mindset, I *cannot* take control. Choose to be the agent, not the victim.

Slow motion

Before I turn to a discussion of how these mindsets may work in practice, I should like to get out a magnifying glass and analyse my Lamborghini experience in some more detail. What I would like to achieve is some insight into the sequence of cause and effect and understand how this interaction led to my state of shock. Of course, the analysis remains illustrative, but here is what the sequence may have looked like.

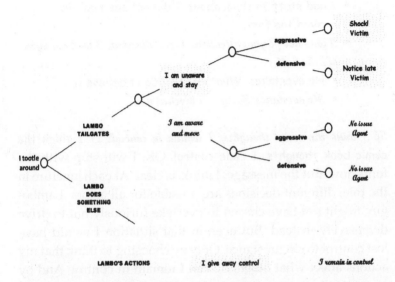

Fig. 3.1 The tree illustrates two possible scenarios that may unfold after an event. The scenario shown in **comic book font** corresponds to behaviour that does not control circumstances. In this case, the individual feels dominated by external factors. The scenario shown in *script font* illustrates the opposite case. The individual acts to control circumstances and as a consequence sees himself as empowered to make choices.

First, let us see what actually happened.

❖ I tootle around. OK, I was at the speed limit, but that was clearly too slow for Lambo-guy.
  ➢ Lambo tailgates.
    ▪ I do not pay attention.
      • He overtakes 'energetically' in the slow lane.
        ◆ I am shocked. Victim.

Now, let us see how I could interpret the sequence with hindsight. I can blame circumstances (**comic book font**) or choose to blame myself (*script font*).

- ❖ I tootle around.
  - ➢ Lambo tailgates.
  - ➢ *I make Lambo tailgate.*
    - ▪ I had stuff to think about. I did not see him. He arrived too fast.
    - ▪ *I was not paying attention. I was diverted. I took my eyes off the ball.*
      - • He overtakes. What an idiot! Can't believe it.
      - • *He overtakes. Sorry – I blocked you.*

If I think the script thoughts, I remain in control. If I think the comic book thoughts, I cede control. OK, I will stop with the fonts now. But the message, I think, is clear. At each juncture in the tree, different decisions are possible for all actors. Lambo-guy might not have chosen to overtake furiously but to drive defensively instead. But even in that situation I would have lost control to circumstance. Only by choosing to think that my actions affect what others do can I remain in control. And by remaining in control, I can change a situation to my advantage. Like, in this instance, by learning from the experience and paying attention next time I am on the road. The sequence would then be the script path in the tree:

- ❖ I tootle around.
  - ➢ Lambo tailgates.
    - ▪ I am aware. I made him do that. I move to the slow lane.
      - • He makes his choice, driving either defensively or aggressively.
        - ◆ I am indifferent to his choice. I made mine and remained in control.

My analysis of this experience also demonstrates that any action is nested in a complex flux of action and reaction. An omnipotent researcher might stop the clock at any time and would then be able to isolate a given action as the final point in a long chain of preceding actions and reactions – like connecting yourself to your predecessors on a family tree. After retracing a few steps (generations), the impact of a cause (predecessor) on its longer-term effect (descendant) becomes so diluted that we may think it loses all practical meaning. This may sometimes, or even often, be the case, but it is not necessarily *always* the case.

My point remains the same: if I choose to believe that my actions will generate a noticeable effect on others now, or might have a noticeable effect on things happening in the future, then it will be increasingly difficult for me to think of circumstance as a space that is somehow divorced from me. It will be hard to think that others exclusively act on me, and not I on them. It will be hard to think that my actions somehow dilute in impact immediately and never have consequences that come back to me. But if I *choose* to think the opposite, I will less often think of myself as the victim and I will preserve a measure of control over my destiny.

How large a measure? Well, that tends to depend on two things: how bad the problem that we are facing is and how much we manage not to blame circumstance for its existence. We need to develop a feeling for the nature of situations and how to think about them to take control of the ball.

But enough theory. Let me share some stories with you that will illustrate these points. I will deal with the easy problems first and then work up to more difficult ones.

Basic ball control – shooting

A slap in the face
When I came to the City as a young analyst, I started my career at one of the iconic English stockbrokers. This was before the

time of close regulation, before the time of political correctness and before the time of the firm's IPO.[23] It was the height of the equity market boom, the firm dominated its UK niche and its partners were 'God'.

As a consequence, conversations were sometimes held in a style that nowadays would simply be impossible. I was witness to many of these but the following short exchange still looms large in my mind.

My boss had just finished a note on the UK sector and was waiting for our editorial department to sign it off. This is what we did – we were equity analysts so we analysed companies quoted on a stock exchange. We wrote our insights up as a report, known as a note, added a recommendation and a paragraph outlining actionable advice to investors and passed the note to the editorial department. The editors would then look through it, correct typos, amend spelling mistakes and polish up the presentation. The analyst would finally sign off the edited note and out it went to all of the firm's clients.

The chap from the editing department entered the dealing floor and approached my boss. He opened his mouth and said this: 'Sorry, you put the note in the wrong template. Could you use the UK sector template and send it up again please?'

My boss was a partner. The editor was support staff. I was leaning back, knowing what would happen next.

My boss looked up from his desk and studied the editor for a moment as if he had discovered a hitherto unrecorded species of beetle. Then he said: 'Do you understand the concept of a

---

[23] An Initial Public Offering, or IPO, is a process during which a business changes its ownership status from a private company or partnership into a public company. This is done by selling shares in its value to investors. The price of the shares is quoted real-time on a securities exchange and the public nature of the company typically attracts a higher level of regulatory scrutiny than applies to private companies.

fucking cost base?'[24] The chap from editorial stood as if he had been slapped in the face. 'Get back up to wherever it is you came from and put it in the right fucking format yourself. Don't come here again unless it's done.'

Well, polite this was not. Did this convey a sentiment that all employees of the firm were equally valued? Not really. But this is not about Harry Gordon-Vaughan (my boss had a name). It is about the chap from editorial.

Ethan (he had a name too) was distraught by this exchange. I ran into him later that day in the pub; he had taken the comment very hard and had several uncompromising things to say about Harry. From his point of view the scolding had been entirely unprovoked. He had done nothing to deserve this and how dare the — (this is me censoring an expression) speak to him like that?

He did not see it coming, and yet I did. Why? Let us consider the evidence:

- Ethan had walked up to Harry and spoken to him without addressing him first. My boss had been concentrating on a piece of work and felt interrupted.

- Butting in on anybody in this way would have been slightly impolite, whoever it was.

- But Harry was not whoever. Harry was a partner. You did not address one of the firm's partners like that. Or only if you were a more senior partner. But not if you were not a partner. And certainly not if you were support.

- Ethan bothered Harry with a simple bureaucratic issue of which template to choose. He could have called on the

---

[24] In the jargon used in the markets, a corporate department that does not directly bring in any revenues is often referred to as a cost base, while a department that does is known as a profit centre (unless its expenses exceed its revenues). Which corporate functions constitute a cost base depends on the type of company. In an investment bank, the editorial function is a cost base; in a publishing house, it is not.

phone to address this if he had felt compelled to do so. He could have simply corrected the error quietly, as can be argued was his job to do. But he chose to come over in person.

So who is to blame? Ethan is. He could have avoided this situation very easily simply by acquainting himself with the culture of the business in which he chose to work and then by acting in accordance with this knowledge. Does this mean he should have been obsequious? No. But observing basic rules of politeness would have done the trick. Perhaps quietly correcting Harry's procedural error and getting on with it would have been better still – very few people in a secretarial function would try to address board members of the company they work in directly, so why should a similar action be welcomed merely because hierarchies in a broking house are flat?

But was Harry's response not disproportionate to the mild offence caused? Undoubtedly. I cannot think of any benchmark against which Harry's behaviour would be acceptable conduct. And is this social pecking order not silly, entrenched, feudal even? Yes, totally. But guess what? This is not about Harry, nor is it about the firm. Just as with Lambo-guy, it is irrelevant whether Harry was at fault or whether his conduct was acceptable. Ethan provoked it, and he was *not* the victim of circumstance, whatever he may have thought.

Had Ethan analysed the dynamics of the exchange in this way, it would have enabled him to take control of the situation. Not *while* he was speaking to Harry, but afterwards. He could have taken a disinterested look at his situation and he could have asked himself whether the firm offered a culture in which he could thrive and be happy.

But he did not. He chose to be petulant instead and, during the time I was with the firm, remained quite a bitter individual, a person who saw himself as a member of a disenfranchised underclass of employees, a person who developed a sense of us against them. He allowed himself to be the victim and never emancipated himself to be the agent.[25]

Change your shoes!

The exchange above happened about two years into my employment at the firm. Here is an anecdote that happened after a week of being there.

At the time, I was very much trying to get my feet under my desk and cope with the culture shock of moving from a small commercial bank to one of the City's most fabled institutions. One day I found myself in conversation with one of the partners. Well, it was more that he was holding forth and I was nodding and making generally affirmative noises when a pause in his speech indicated that such a response was called for. Truth be told, I felt well pleased with myself – here I was, a junior analyst one week in, standing up for everyone to see, chatting to a partner! And he was saying good things too about how the firm was confident that I would help roll out the European franchise, about how the firm was changing and about how I would be among those that are key to that change.

Yes, yes, absolutely, I thought, *I speak two European languages, I have a background in business and applied maths and I want this. They are inviting me in and they love me. I am going to be one of the boys.* 'And another thing,' he said, now walking away, 'change your shoes.'

---

[25] I feel the need to quote an expert on social dynamics in the corporate world: '. . . different [corporate] cultures call for differing psychological contracts . . . certain types of people will be happy and successful in one culture, not in another. A match between organization, culture and an individual's psychological contract should lead to a satisfied individual.' Handy, Charles B. *Understanding Organizations.* Penguin 1985, p. 204. Reproduced by permission of Penguin Books Ltd © Charles B Handy 1976, by permission of Oxford University Press and by permission of Oxford University Press, USA © Charles B Handy 1993.

Poof. Bubble gone. Back in the room. I would never be one of the boys. They may think I could be an asset to this firm if I proved myself, but they are certainly not going to welcome me into the clan.

Now I had a choice. I could have thought of the partner as a blasé toff and dismissed the comment with a sentiment of no one tells me what to wear. In fact, that would have been quite like me and would have been my natural response.

But I also had another choice. I could observe the culture of the business and wear lace-ups rather than loafers. What exactly would be the cost of that choice? I did not have a particular preference for loafers. In fact, I was only wearing them because I did not own any other pair of black shoes.

So I made a conscious choice to pick my battles wisely and to demonstrate independence in substance rather than form. I changed my shoes. Next time I was chatting to the partner, I glanced meaningfully down at my feet, the gesture meant to send him a message. He got the message, and I got the very small satisfaction of subtly manipulating a partner in the firm into thinking that I wanted to be one of the boys and that I had what it took.

As it turned out, I did not. In the end, the feudal culture got the better of me and I left after four happy years. But on that day I remained in control. I remained the agent and did not become the victim.[26]

Read the FT!

Back then my normal day in the firm would start like this:

5.00 Alarm clock makes sleep impossible.
5.30 I am on the platform, reading the FT[27] and waiting for the tube.
6.00 I am at Bank, getting off. Finished reading the FT.

---

[26] By the way, I am still wearing lace-ups and love them . . .
[27] *Financial Times.*

6.15 I am at my desk, scanning the Reuters screens for over-
        night newsflow, checking my inbox for press releases of
        my companies.
7.00 Morning meeting starts.

Actually, this is how it used to work after about a year or so.
When I first started there was one memorable day that began
like this:

5.00 Alarm clock makes sleep impossible.
5.30 I am on the platform, waiting for the tube.
6.00 I am at Bank, getting off.
6.15 I am at my desk, scanning the Reuters scr— 'Mark, what
        in God's name is that article on Bank Wonga all about?
        Why are they saying it's about to run out of liquidity?'
        HGV (everybody on the floor called my boss this, presum-
        ably because of his girth) was wading in, holding up his
        copy of the FT.
6.16 'Uh dunno. What's it say there?' This was me, responding.
6.16 'What do you mean "What's it say"? You did see this,
        didn't you?'
6.17 'Well no, actually. I don't get the FT in the morning.'
6.17 'What? Why not? What do you do in the morning?'
6.18 'Erm well . . . I don't pass a newsagent on my way to the
        tube . . . and where I live they are all closed that early
        anyway . . .'
6.18 'No they're not. I don't give a shit if they're closed. Break
        in! Move house! Get a preview copy the night before! But
        you won't come to work without reading the FT!'

Blimey! This was not good. But it was, of course, also completely
unreasonable. It is absolutely not my fault that no newsagents are
open that early where I live. What can I do about that? None of
the three suggestions HGV had made were remotely helpful . . .
     Was it my fault that those lazy layabouts of shopkeepers
did not throw open their doors for me at 5 o'clock in the

morning? No. Was it my fault that they chose to build their establishments in inaccessible and remote corners of the borough where normal people would not go? NO.

Was it my fault that I lived where I lived? No. Well. Of course, nobody *forced* me to live there . . . But money does not exactly come in by the truckload if you work in commercial banking, and I had just joined this firm so my small flat was all I could afford. So NO.

OK, so I chose to live there. Maybe it was a little bit my fault then. But what could I do? I suppose I *could* move, as in it was within my power, but that would be an extreme response to the situation . . . On the other hand, I really did not want HGV getting heavy on me again . . .

In the end, I spotted a new delivery service that the *FT* was about to start. They would deliver your copy of the paper by 6 am guaranteed. Good idea but still useless if they could not make it 5 am. I called them up and got nowhere. But after a bit of chat the *FT* guy told me that they were picking up the consignments at 4.30 am from their warehouse, they were just not *guaranteeing* delivery for before 6 am. I pointed out that my flat was not far from their delivery route from the warehouse so why not start their day with my postcode then move on? I sensed that the terms of the new service were still slightly in flux, and chose that moment to offer to subscribe to the *FT* for two years fixed if they guaranteed it for 5 am. He said 'Yes, fine. Done', and so did I, and the service turned out to work beautifully.

Now for the interpretation of this story:

- I believe this is a classic example of a moment when you could think you are at the mercy of circumstance. It may sound like a trivial thing, but actually it is not. If you are starting out in a career and want to prove yourself, it does come as a bit of a downer that an action as simple as buying the morning paper could lead to an issue with your boss and yet seemingly there is nothing to be done about it.

- When I looked through the reasons for my predicament, the first 'generation' of factors, in terms of my analysis in figure 3.1, was indeed not my fault. Business hours and location of newsagents are not within my sphere of influence.

- But it can be argued that the factors one generation removed were. *I* moved to that area, nobody forced me to. Admittedly, I moved there when I came to London to work in commercial banking, when money was tight, the flat was affordable and I certainly never anticipated a logistical bottleneck with the morning paper.

- The important point is that I *chose* to look at it as if it had been my fault. And that choice immediately empowered me to look for a solution. I was the agent. I did not sulk and say to myself 'HGV is an idiot – nothing *I* can do'. I did not become the victim.

- Yes, the fact that the *FT* was about to introduce the new service just at the time I needed it was luck. But even that did not turn out to be that easy – it took some negotiation and quick thinking to make the guy on the phone promise me the paper for 5 am.

- And if that had not worked, I would have found another solution. I would have got up even earlier and accepted a detour via Victoria station, where the newsagents *are* open that early. It would have meant getting up at 4 am but I *would* have done it.

- Or there may have been hotels in the area who got the *FT* earlier. I may have been able to arrange a delivery to my door from them or pay a cab driver to bring them from Victoria every morning.

- Or, all else failing, move house. This probably would have been overkill, but I *would* have been prepared to do it. There was no chance that I would have allowed circumstances to triumph.

In the end there was one reason that I was able to do what I did, and would have been prepared to do the other things to solve it. I *chose* to look at the situation as if it *was* in my sphere of influence and not forced on me. In other words, as if it was my fault.

That enabled me to act and to change a potentially sticky situation at work into one of professional routine. I chose to be the agent, not the victim.

Did that make me happy? Well, of course not in itself. But I avoided constant run-ins with HGV on this issue. A small thing in itself but, seen in conjunction with many others of a similar nature, an important component in building confidence and creating happiness.

We lost (re)direction

After a year or two in the firm, I was able to buy a slightly larger flat in a nicer part of town. In London, nice and not-so-nice areas can be quite close together, and are often just separated by a minor road which forms a border between the two. In my case, moving to the nicer area involved crossing the river from south to north and travelling perhaps one mile as the crow flies.

It also involved making sure that I continued receiving my mail, and to this end I organised a redirection order. But after two weeks I had not received any mail with a redirection label on it. Luckily, I had not moved far and so I popped in at my old address to ask whether any mail had arrived for me. Balancing the 30 or so items of different size and shape in my arms was a major test of agility on the tube back . . .

I called the postal company to find out why the service seemed to have teething problems. I waited for 10 minutes before somebody picked up my call, repeated my personal details a few times and soon we were getting down to business. New redirection orders, I heard, can sometimes take a little time to get going.

A week later I was still self-executing my redirection order. I got through to the company after 15 minutes. I told them my name and found, to my surprise, that I had to explain the nature of my problem again, since the customer service software did not allow the customer service specialist to take notes of customer-related issues.

After two months of regular interactions of this nature, I finally decided to write a letter to the complaints department. After two weeks I received a response. I was informed that they did not have sufficient evidence to investigate the problem. If, however, I could forward copies of unreceived letters, they would be able to look into it further.[28]

This suggestion did not make sense to me. If I could get hold of a letter that I had not received, and send them this letter that I did not have, they could then sort the problem?

It was at this stage that I realised something. The company had mucked up my redirection order, for whatever reason, and were unable to fix it. I resigned myself to this fact and gave up on the matter. As far as I recall I did not even make an attempt to ask for a refund. All I wanted was to push past the matter and forget about the whole issue.

But that, it turned out, was not as easy as I expected it to be. I am relating this story in a deliberately light-hearted manner, since essentially we are talking about a trivial matter and certainly I can see the comical side of the story now, looking back almost a decade later.

At the time it was happening, however, I did not see the comical side. Far from it. All in all, I must have explained the problem five or six times to the customer services people. They remained uninformed, unengaged and unhelpful throughout our conversations. I remember this left me trembling with irritation every time I needed to call them up. The farcical response I received from the complaints department only served to make me feel even more abandoned as a customer. And the requirement to handle the mail collection from my old place

---

[28] This really happened. I am not inventing this.

myself made me feel indignant and angry. But more than anything else, I felt that I was losing control over a tiny portion of my life and that this lack of control was beginning to affect other parts of my life – I certainly argued more frequently with Mary and generally had a shorter fuse.

I told you this story because we all recognise it for something similar we have experienced. Something which, in itself, may be trivial but which grows beyond its natural boundaries and affects us more than it should. And if a few things of this nature happen at the same time, we feel that we are losing control and that the world is coming down on us.

In the redirection incident there was nothing I could do. It was not my fault and no degree of creative thinking would have revealed an alternative course of action. There was no way in which I could have empowered myself to become the agent.

But . . . There is always a but, and here it is. I still allowed myself to be the victim. How so? By proving unable to shield myself emotionally from the fallout. By becoming irritated beyond what might be regarded as reasonable. And by allowing my irritation to seep into other areas of my life.

I could have handled the situation better, and if there is something to learn here it is this: it is OK to be irritated, indignant even, in situations such as this, but only to a point. Even as we are righteously angry, we need to remain in control, we need to keep our balance, we need to contain the frustration we feel. This may not be an easy thing to do, and I certainly did not accomplish it at the time. But in situations similar to the redirection incident, a change of attitude is often the only course of action that prevents us from becoming the victim.

The choice to be made is whether we deal with an issue of this nature indignantly or pragmatically. The choice I had was to collect my mail as a bitter individual consumed with a sense of injustice (that is what I did – victim) or to collect my mail as a life-competent individual feeling irritated by the incompetence of the service provider (agent as much as possible under the circumstances).

Hence, the choice open to us is similar to the invocation by the American theologian and religious leader Reinhold Niebuhr in a sermon given in 1943, widely known as the serenity sermon:

> God, give us grace to accept with serenity the things that cannot be changed, courage to change the things that should be changed, and the wisdom to distinguish the one from the other.[29]

A wise insight. However, scars may remain. I recently moved house again. Guess what service I did not use.

What's the point?

Let us pause here for a moment. The four stories I told you represent experiences of a relatively trivial nature, and similar things have no doubt happened to all of us. Yet, they all have something in common. Each of them tells a story where something challenging is happening to us. Each time it appears as if we are victims of circumstance. Each time we can decide how we want to look at the situation.

If we choose to believe that circumstances are to blame, we lose there and then. If we do that, we allow circumstances to control us, and we may feel that life is treating us unfairly. If we make a habit of thinking that, we may eventually develop the idea that somehow we have been denied the success we are entitled to and that circumstances conspired against us. Worse, we may even start believing that others, who we presume are enjoying the success we ought to have, are merely luckier than we are. These sentiments are recipes for bitterness, and their main ingredient is the idea that it is not my fault.

---

[29] Reinhold Niebuhr. Reprinted by permission of the Reinhold Niebuhr estate.

But if we choose to believe that – somehow, somewhere deep down in the chain of events – it *is* our fault, the opposite happens. Then we do not allow circumstance to drive the situation; instead we take over and we are then in a position to deal with the challenge. The chances are we will find a solution. The solution will often be a compromise – it will rarely be perfect – but it will be a solution nonetheless. The more often we find a solution, the more we develop confidence that we might do so again. This type of confidence is an important ingredient in the recipe for happiness. It is not the only ingredient, but it is a crucial one.

Fine. But what if we are facing more difficult challenges than the relatively trivial problems we were discussing here?

I think we can already guess the answer – it takes energy, determination and emotional tenacity to take on circumstance and wrest back control. How much energy? This depends on the severity of the challenge.

Let us discuss this next and look at some of the more fundamental issues life can throw at us.

Intermediate ball control – dribbling

Now what?

After A-levels and national service,[30] I went straight to university. I spent five years at university, including a term abroad in England, and six months completing my Masters thesis. I found studying for my degree enormously rewarding. Subjects were taught in depth, my horizons were broadened and worlds of learning opened up which I did not even know existed when I was at school. As I became more senior, I was starting to fall in love with the world of academia. After two years I got a small job at the university as an undergraduate researcher and

---

[30] At the time I left school it was obligatory to spend 15 months in the military. At the time of writing, national service has been abolished in Germany.

was beginning to set my mind on gaining tenure myself and teaching at university. So I decided not to hang around, and graduated in good time.

But why am I telling you this? Because I believe it helps you appreciate why I was intensely frustrated when I was unable to secure an offer of employment following graduation. The reason I did not find a job was not because I had spent decades at university and was looking for an entry-level job at the age of 30. Or because the degree class I obtained would not have passed the normal hurdles.

The reason I could not find a job was because I had chosen to read English Lit., Modern History and Publishing rather than a numbers-based or business-oriented subject. It was also because there just were not any graduate researcher positions available at my university that would have provided funding for a PhD thesis, the next rung on the ladder that eventually just *might* lead to tenure.

After graduation I managed to secure a teaching position with a commercial language school, so at least money was not proving an immediate problem. What followed was a year of interviews with institutions in the private and the public sectors, with not-for-profit organisations and with charities. The year was also rich with rejection and commensurate frustration.

What had happened to me? Let us again list the evidence:

- My bubble had burst. I had felt at home in the realm of academia and thought that I had *earned* a place at university. Now I was teaching German to foreign businessmen and repatriates from the ex-German parts of CEE countries. There was nothing wrong with this job *per se*, but it was not university. I felt as if I had been ejected from my natural habitat, like a fish washed up on shore.

- And it was not my fault! It was certainly not my fault that arts faculties at universities were massively underfunded and no public money was available to support the research position I needed.

- And it was also not my fault that the German corporate sector was so infuriatingly inflexible that companies would not even entertain the idea of employing an arts graduate.

Or so I thought. But of course I had that wrong. It *was* my fault. It was *all* my fault.

I had not listened to my teachers at school, who variously suggested medicine, mathematics or economics as academic pursuits. I had not listened to my dad, who had suggested law. And if my mum had a voice in these pages, she would tell you that it was not really in my nature to listen to anybody on anything and that I would only welcome suggestions that happened to support whatever decisions I had already made.

I *chose* to study humanities; nobody forced me to. I was of course aware that employment opportunities for arts graduates were extremely thin on the ground in Germany, but I somehow managed to convince myself that these limitations would not apply to me. Even if I had somehow been able to remain ignorant of this, I could have attended the career information service on campus and they would have told me. Actually, I did, and they did. But I ignored them as well.

So I certainly started my course in the full knowledge of the practical difficulties it might have in store for me after graduation.

But was it my fault that there was no position available at university?

With hindsight I can say this: on graduation I had already lost the courage and motivation to embark on the long and winding road that eventually just *might* lead to tenure at university. If I had really craved academia as a career, I would have applied to every university in the German- and English-speaking world, and to every single scholarship-giving institution. So, sure, it may have been inconvenient that a position was not handed to me at my university, but *I* was the one who failed to muster up the energy and determination to secure a position somewhere. So again: my fault.

But surely the German corporate world was inflexible and unwilling to think outside the box?

To be fair, not really. Of course, I was not courted by companies as business graduates or engineers were. But I did have 20 interviews or so, which is not bad, considering that I did not have a relevant degree. Interviewers turned me down because I was unable to demonstrate a skillset they thought they could build on and develop in house, and because I was (still) too young to know what I wanted. Not, as I thought at the time, because I failed to say what they wanted to hear in the interviews. So my fault again, I am afraid.

And finally, something was beginning to dawn on me.

The fact that I was unable to secure permanent employment was not somebody else's fault. If I wanted to develop my life, I needed an additional, relevant qualification.

Once I had come to that realisation, I had already won. I just did not know it yet. This may sound like a bland cliché, but I am convinced it is true. The moment I consciously understood that point, I stopped being the victim and became the agent. I started a systematic search for institutions that would offer postgraduate business degrees. Eventually, I had three opportunities and chose the one that entailed relocating to the UK.

I think my experience demonstrates three things that I hope are valuable:

- It can sometimes take a long time before you develop the maturity required to understand that circumstances may not be responsible for the particular predicament you find yourself in.

- No matter how much you may feel that you are being treated unfairly, fairness does not come into it. Fairness is not a benchmark by which to measure life. Life is neither fair nor unfair. The reason? Because *you* make the rules by which life plays.

• I believe experiences like mine are classic illustrations of victim and agent. As long as I was blaming others, I allowed circumstances to control me. As soon as I blamed myself, I became empowered to act.

And then? Was it easy to change my life? Certainly not. Business school was hard work and relocating to the UK represented a fundamental change, a change that had to be managed. Turning your life around is not easy. You need to know who you are, you need to know what you need and then you need to get it.

But does my experience represent a radical or exceptionally difficult choice? Not even remotely. Many people change careers or relocate to a different country. What I did is nothing special. But it is still a relevant example that illustrates how you can reboot your life.

And yet, I shall never tire of saying this: wresting back control requires determination and it is no walk in the park. When I arrived at business school I felt motivated and empowered. I also felt overwhelmed and apprehensive. But no longer did I feel frustrated or disillusioned.

My home is my castle
The story of John and Ruby
Meet 43-year-old mum of three Ruby Oldham from Slough.

In 1996 Ruby and her husband John bought a three-bed semi in Salt Hill. It was not huge but was big enough for them and for Steve and Tom, their two boys, aged 3 and 5. It was the start of the property boom and in 2001 their property was worth £90,000, almost two thirds more than what they bought it for in 1994. They decided to spend another £20,000 on a conservatory and some other home improvements. The chap at the bank had no problem with this amount and so they remortgaged the house for £30,000, using the £10K extra to buy a better car.

One year later John left Ruby. Ruby worked part-time and therefore had trouble keeping up with the mortgage payments. The high street bank would not accommodate her, so there was really no choice but to go with a subprime lender. This institution kept raising mortgage rates and eventually Ruby started falling behind on her payments, adding late payment penalties to an ever-increasing burden of housing costs.

Fast forward to 2007. The UK and Europe are on the verge of the worst economic downturn since WWII. In a year's time the UK stock market will have fallen by 40 per cent and Ruby's mother will have been forced to sell her property and move in with her daughter to make ends meet. Ruby's new interest-only mortgage consumes all her cash, and her mum's pension goes on buying food.

Dramatic? All too real, I'm afraid. I changed the details of the story slightly to protect the innocent, but this is a real-life story that was reported in a local newspaper a few years ago. Nor is it an isolated occurrence – experiences similar to Ruby's have been the hallmark of the financial crisis that has been gripping the Western world since 2008.

Whose fault? Public sentiment

So who is to blame? Let us first see what the general public thinks. To take the temperature of public opinion at the time we will turn to the papers. Four years into the crisis, the author of an article in a free paper widely circulated in London was discussing the moral justification of senior bankers to accept bonuses:

> So we will have to wait until next month to find out if Bob Diamond[31] got £3 million, £1 million – or nothing – for his 2011

---

[31] At the time, the CEO of Barclays Bank.

bonus. [...] But perhaps we should not get too fixated on an element of his remuneration that will soon fall into the 'more trouble than it's worth' category. Mr Diamond has options on 13 million Barclays shares as part of an 'incentive' scheme and owns 12 million outright, earning him a dividend of about £762,000 last year. All that on top of his base salary of £1.35 million 'for turning up'.[32]

This commentary conveys a strong sense of us and them. On the one hand, there are most of us, who are regular sorts of people with 'real' jobs. On the other hand, there is the class of the mega-rich, of people who live in a different world.

But the article conveys a lot more than just that:

- 'We' – whoever that is, exactly – are entitled to judge whether bonuses, and salaries, of this magnitude are justified. The article does not mention the benchmark that we would apply, but the choice of words certainly identifies us as a self-appointed panel of judges.

- The language also implies that Mr Diamond's compensation package is undeserved. The word incentive is printed in quotation marks. This suggests that the incentivisation somehow fails to be proper, that it may not be based on merit but be awarded regardless of measurable achievement.

- The tacit suggestion of impropriety pervades the article and gets even stronger when the author suggests that Mr Diamond earns his basic salary without making a valuable contribution to the business. Granted, the phrase 'for turning up' is a colloquial term and may not always carry this connotation, but it does so in the context that the author deliberately creates in his article.

---

[32] Prynn, Jonathan. 'City still hasn't grasped the nettle'. *Evening Standard*, 10 February 2012, p. 2.

It is not within the purview of this book to decide whether bonuses in banking reward a commensurate service to society, whether Mr Diamond conducted his tenure at Barclays within the bounds of propriety or whether the *Standard*'s journalism in this instance met professional quality standards.

The only point relevant for us is to take note of the distinctly critical tone of the article. It is a tone that mirrors a near-hostile attitude towards UK banks that was pervading society in the heyday of the financial crisis. Even Mr Prynn conceded in his article that '. . . Mr Diamond is a skilled financier who has done a good job turning Barclays Capital into a world-class investment bank "made in Britain" '. But he continues with a warning that '. . . until the City . . . rethinks the way it rewards top executives, these achievements will be overshadowed by a furore that is simply not going to go away'.[33]

A furore that is not going to go away. An evocative phrase. But why does this anger exist?

Is it because we dislike capitalism in this country? Come on. This is the country of Adam Smith, of low regulation and *laissez faire* capitalism.

So no.

Is it because we have a strong sense of social justice and care for an equitable distribution of income? Top footballers have estimated net worth in the region of tens of millions of pounds and are reported to earn £100,000 a week. That is about £5m a year, 'just for turning up', and is equivalent to four times what Bob Diamond used to make. I have yet to see a protest urging footballers to redistribute their fortunes to the less fortunate.

So no.

Is it because we believe the bankers do not *deserve* the spoils? That they are responsible for countless stories of personal misery like Ruby's? That they put what we may see as their own personal greed above care for their customers?

Yes. That is what we think.

---

[33] Prynn 2012.

And it is not only what we think. In the worst years of the crisis, social activism was on the rise. There were people queuing outside branches of Barclays bank waiting to close their accounts. They were doing so as part of a campaign promoted as Move Your Money, in protest against bankers' bonuses. For most of the spring in 2012, there were people camping outside St Paul's Cathedral staging a protest branded as Occupy London.[34] The protesters published their ideas on banners with slogans such as 'Capitalism means war', 'Rich beware – your days are numbered' and 'Governments must serve people, not banks'.

But the most revealing slogan, the one which captures the essence of public sentiment like no other, is this one: 'We are the 99%.' This one is not an expression of powerless, and essentially immature, anger. This one conveys the idea that the vast majority of people do not make much money, and carries a clear sense of us and them, the same sentiment Mr Prynn evoked in his article in the *Standard*, the same sentiment that contributed to the public vote for the UK to leave the EU four years later.

Whose fault? Consider the evidence!
So now we know whom the public appears to blame. We have found another clear case of blaming circumstances, of feeling at the mercy of fate, of allowing others to treat us as victims.

Or so I contend.

If I am right, should I not provide evidence that we *are* responsible? Should I not be able to showcase at least a few instances where our actions have led to the predicament that followed?

Well, let us see whether I can. Let us sift through Ruby's story in search of such evidence:

---

[34] Also note the branding. A few months in, this had evolved beyond the initial Occupy London Stock Exchange movement, which was essentially a copy of the original Occupy Wall Street protest.

It is 1994. Ruby and John are buying their house for £54,000. The UK is in an economic boom phase, the property market looks set to rise and the high street bank gives them a mortgage for 95 per cent of the property's value.

What does this mean?
- Family income is £21,375[35]. John brings home some £18K as a graphic designer, and Ruby chips in for the balance as a part-time council worker. Their mortgage is £51,300[36], equivalent to 2.4 times family income.

- The country is in an economic boom phase, and interest rates are high. The Oldhams are paying an annual mortgage rate of 7 per cent, which means that £3,591 a year is consumed by mortgage payments. That is equivalent to about one sixth of gross family income.[37]

- After tax and expenditure on food, clothing and other necessities, the Oldhams are left with about £5,823 before mortgage costs (sometimes called discretionary income). The mortgage is taking up 62 per cent of their discretionary income, but still leaves them with savings of more than £2,000 every year.

Every year? Well, *that* year, certainly... But what if interest rates were to increase? Over the previous few years they had not gone down, and the papers predicted such an increase.

So yes, there were certainly risks. If interest rates were 100 basis points[38] higher, mortgage costs would have eaten up 70 per cent of discretionary income, 80 per cent if they had been 200 basis points higher.

---

[35] Numbers in the text can be found in figure 3.2.
[36] 95% of the value of their property.
[37] The exact percentage is 16.78%.
[38] A basis point is 0.01%; 100 basis points represent 1 percentage point.

On to 2001. In the past few years there has been a phenom-
enal boom in the property market. The house is now worth
£88,352. The Oldhams remortgage and add another £30,000 to
their debt.

Was this prudent?

- The Oldhams have paid back some debt. Their mortgage,
  without remortgaging, is now down to £47,709. Family
  income has increased to £24,553. The proportion of mortgage to income has decreased from 2.4x to 1.9x.

- But interest rates have gone up to curb inflation. The mortgage rate is now 8 per cent. This means that mortgage
  payments are now £3,817 a year, before remortgaging. This
  represents 16 per cent of gross family income and 58 per
  cent of discretionary income.

- This leaves them with about £2,800 savings.

Although the Oldhams may think their financial situation
has improved over the years, it really has not. They are paying
slightly more in mortgage costs in absolute terms, and mortgage costs still represent nearly 60 per cent of net family
income after expenditure, just as they did in 1994. Their
potential savings are less than in 1994 if we take inflation into
account.

- Encouraged by the property boom, the Oldhams remortgage. Now the total amount of mortgage is £77,709. The
  proportion of mortgage to income is 3.2x. This is more than
  it was in 1994 (when it was 2.4x), although the family's
  underlying financial situation has not changed.

- The Oldhams are not using the entire remortgage amount to
  improve the value of their home. One third of the new debt
  is spent on a wasting asset (they buy a car).

- Mortgage costs are now £6,217 a year. This represents 25 per cent of gross family income and 95 per cent of discretionary income.

- This leaves them with £361 savings a year.

Let me summarise the various numbers in a table:

	1994	2001 (before remortgaging)	2001 (after remortgaging)	Scenario 1: 50bps increase	Scenario 2: 100bps increase
Family income	21,375	24,553	24,553		
Value of property	54,000	88,352	108,352		
Mortgage	51,300	47,709	47,709		
Remortgage	-	-	30,000		
Total mortgage	**51,300**	**47,709**	**77,709**	**77,709**	**77,709**
Income before cost of mortgage	5,823	6,578	6,578	6,578	6,578
Mortgage rate	*7.0%*	*8.0%*	*8.0%*	*8.5%*	*9.0%*
Mortgage cost	**3,591**	**3,817**	**6,217**	**6,605**	**6,994**
Savings	2,232	2,761	361	-27	-416
Mortgage amount in % of income	*240%*	*194%*	*316%*		
Cost of mortgage in % of income	*62%*	*58%*	*95%*	*100%*	*106%*

Fig. 3.2 The table illustrates how the Oldhams allowed their financial gearing to increase. Before they chose to remortgage, their financial situation had improved moderately but remained essentially unchanged. Their mortgage represented a lower percentage of family income (their gearing reduced) but interest rates had gone up in the seven years since they bought their property, and their mortgage cost still consumed the same proportion of their income. Remortgaging added £30,000 to their mortgage, but only £20,000 to the value of their property (as they used £10,000 to buy a car), and increased their mortgage cost to a level that eroded their annual saving capacity to virtually zero. Now the Oldhams are uncomfortably exposed to further rises in interest rates. If they increased by 50 bps (scenario 1), their savings would actually *be* zero; if by 100 bps, their outgoings would exceed their income.

I believe that something is becoming clear. Remortgaging was imprudent, to say the least. After remortgaging, mortgage costs consumed 95 per cent of family income after expenditure – virtually all of their money. The mortgage-to-income ratio was higher than it had ever been.

And what would happen if interest rates increased and the cost of the mortgage went *even* higher? If interest rates rose by 50 basis points, the Oldhams would not have enough money to pay their mortgage and would need to start cutting back on expenditure. The chart demonstrates this sensitivity.

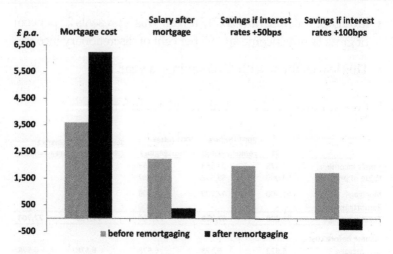

Fig. 3.3 The chart illustrates the sensitivity of household income to a rise in mortgage rates. The grey bars show this sensitivity in a scenario in which the family does not remortgage, the black bars in a scenario in which they do. The chart shows two things: (1) household savings after mortgage payments are much higher if they do not remortgage; (2) the sensitivity to rising mortgage rates is much lower if they do not remortgage. Were mortgage rates to rise by 100 bps (the set of columns on the far right), the family would suffer a household *deficit* if they remortgaged. If they did not remortgage, household income would still fall by more than a fifth in this scenario but would remain positive.

The decision to remortgage materially exposed the Oldhams to the risk that interest rates would rise. Ruby depended on her husband financially and knew she would not be able to handle the mortgage payments on her own. Ruby as an individual therefore became even more dependent on her husband.

It's 2002. John leaves Ruby. They live apart but do not get divorced.
Well, there it is. We do not have to go through the calculations to understand Ruby's predicament and why her mother eventually decided to sell her house to help.

So whose fault is it?
I think we are now able to take a disinterested look at Ruby's situation. It is clear that at various stages in Ruby's family life, the writing was on the wall. Not, probably, in 1994 when the risks appeared manageable. But certainly in 2001 when a simple calculation would have revealed that remortgaging

made the Oldhams more vulnerable to the risk that interest rates might rise.

But hold on. Surely the Oldhams are not financial specialists? How could they have known this?

By going through the simple calculations we presented above. And, let us not kid ourselves, the calculations *are* simple. Anybody would be able to perform them. But not many – indeed, probably very few – actually *do* perform them. And, if the Oldhams had been confused, they could have sought advice.

*But hold on again! Surely that is what they did, sort of? After all, the bank approved the remortgaging? They **are** financial specialists so should have been able to assess the credit risk they were taking on?*

Yes, absolutely. It is clear, certainly with hindsight, that the high street banks have been selling credit too cheaply for years and that lending criteria were insufficiently stringent. And it is also true that if you go to a household name for a mortgage, you expect that name to stand for something. For a seal of quality. For some duty of care.

But remember Lambo-guy? And HGV leaning into the poor chap from editorial? And the postal redirection issue? The extent to which others may be the authors of our problems is actually irrelevant. What matters is how we *choose* to look at it.

There is a legal concept in contract law called *caveat emptor*. It means *let the buyer beware*. It is checked by another concept, this one enshrined in the Sale of Goods Act, which determines that goods sold have to be fit and proper for purpose.

The mortgage *was* fit and proper for purpose. The bank's lending criteria may have been too lax, but that does not exonerate Ruby from her responsibility to check herself whether she can afford the burden of debt. Also nobody forced the family to remortgage. They did so because they wanted a conservatory and a car, not because they were in dire need of money.

I believe that most of us *do* use caution when we buy stuff. Who would buy a second-hand car, indeed any car, without test driving it? Without checking miles to the gallon? Insurance costs? Boot space? Who would buy a house without a survey-or's opinion? Without checking the amenities? How far away from the town centre? Is it safe for the kids to get to school? Council tax? Approximate bills for gas and electricity?

But, when it comes to a mortgage, we are not even *checking* whether we can afford the interest payments? We are unaware of whether they represent 95 per cent of our realistic net income, and indifferent to the risk that they may start exceed-ing it? Really? *Really*?

Again. Who is to blame?
Ruby is. Her husband John is. The banks are. We *all* are. Remember, this is not about shifting blame around. This is about how to take charge of our lives so that we may remain in control and able to act. This is about *mindset*, not actual guilt.

Had Ruby chosen to believe that she was the agent, rather than John or the banks, she might have empowered herself to check the family's financial situation in 2001. She might have acted with caution and, as a family, they might have decided against gearing up, and certainly against buying an asset that deteriorates in value with funds secured on their main residence.

Of course, this realisation will not help Ruby now. Her experience is a cautionary tale that demonstrates how impor-tant it is to think of ourselves as agents as we go through life. How important it is that we do not trust circumstances to provide, or blame circumstances when they do not.

What have we learned?

I have come to the end of my first two batches of stories. The first five were experiences taken from everyday life. Some were trivial (Lambo-guy, 'Change your shoes!'), some had the potential to turn into a bit of an issue ('Read the *FT*!', 'We lost (re)direction') and one was a source of genuine discontent ('A slap in the face').

The experiences are my own, but they are hardly unique. We will all have been confronted with similar problems at some point in our lives, and we all recognise them as a specific type of event. They are nothing huge or life-changing, but we cannot simply ignore them and hope they will sort themselves out.

In each of these five stories, the main 'character' had a choice. She could blame circumstances, pass responsibility on to some other party and see herself as the victim. Or she could look for responsibility in her own actions, apply the mindset of MOCK SELF-INCRIMINATION as a tool and understand that she may ultimately be the author of her own predicament. Invariably, the former choice would leave the person impotent and serve to prolong a state of anger, stress, disorientation or unhappiness. Conversely, the latter choice would empower the person to take charge, to improve the degree of control she was able to exert, to assert herself and become the agent.

The second batch of stories contained problems that were more fundamental. The problems discussed *did* have the potential to be life-changing, but they are not unique either. Many of us, at some point, will have found ourselves in predicaments of similar severity. Again, as in the more innocuous stories in batch number one, salvation comes with the realisation that *we*, and not others, may be the authors of our problems. Tragically, Ruby's story shows that if we leave it too late, if we do not develop a sense of responsibility for our actions early enough, we may allow issues to grow into obstacles that are much harder to deal with.

In the end, I believe what we can learn from the stories is a relatively simple truth. We can only act if we accept responsibility for our actions. Things we do today may have little bearing on things that happen in the distant future, but it is likely that there is *some* impact, however diluted it may be. If we accept this as *conceptually* true, we will find it harder to see circumstance as something divorced from us. And as we accept this idea more readily, as it becomes second nature for us to think that way, we will increasingly think of ourselves as in charge.

If we get to that last stage we have cracked it. We will never again see ourselves as powerless victims, and will always be able to act as agents. Of course, we may not get to apply this level of control consistently in all situations in life. Indeed, it is highly unlikely that we will. But we cannot hope to attain perfection in anything we do. As before though, when we were discussing how to get to know who we are, this restriction is not an issue. We can still try to get as close as we can.

With self-knowledge, my tool was EXPERIENCE MINING. With decision making, I suggested two tests to aid us. And to aid taking control of our lives, I propose MOCK SELF-INCRIMINATION as a tool.

Of course, success is not guaranteed. But the cost of improving control is a simple switch in mindset. A mindset that focusses on us as the agent.

On *us*. Not on circumstance.

RULE 4

Conquer circumstance

How to control fate

No simple method

But what if the decks are *really* stacked against you? What if you were born into degrading poverty? What if you were sold into slavery or prostitution? What if you were the child of abusive parents?

Clearly, the methods I described in the previous chapter will not help in those cases. A mindset that finds reasons for a predicament in personal involvement will empower a person only if circumstances are *potentially* within his sphere of influence. These circumstances do not need to be trivial; indeed, they can be quite fundamental to a person's life. But they are not to be confused with situations in which somebody finds himself the powerless victim of abusive torment or existential threat.

So does that mean that nothing can be done? If you got dealt a poor hand in life, is it game over? Does it mean you can never become the agent, never take charge, never be the master of your destiny?

No. It does not mean that. But, just as we did towards the end of Rule 2, we are now leaving a realm in which the application of simple methods yields results. We are entering one in which it takes emotional strength and psychological tenacity to survive. Even in this realm, however, we will see that those who eventually triumph over circumstance do so because they refuse to be the victim. Or more to the point perhaps, those who realise that it is in their power to make a conscious choice between the *mindset* of agent and victim will triumph.

I will discuss a real-life story of child abuse at length in the hope of developing an understanding of what it may take to triumph over circumstances in the face of extreme adversity. In addition, I will from time to time refer to one other story, which I will not present in detail but 'consult' when the analysis benefits from an additional view. Our consultant is Senait Mehari, who was abandoned by her parents into the horrors of the Eritrean civil war by the time she was 6 years old.[39] Our expert is Dave Pelzer, who endured unspeakable physical and psychological torment at the hands of his mother.

How did he succeed? What are the qualities that helped him triumph over circumstance? What was it that made him prevail where others might have faltered?

And, most importantly, *would* others have faltered? Are we in the presence of an exceptional individual or do we *all* have the potential to rise to a challenge of this magnitude if it was forced on us? In short, are we reading about exceptional individuals or exceptional circumstances? We will look at this thorny question after we get to know our expert on the panel of one a bit better.

It

Dave's story

Dave's early childhood from the age of 4 to 12 is a tragic tapestry of abuse at the hands of his mother, both physical and

---

[39] Mehari, Senait G. *Feuerherz*. Knaur 2004. Published in the UK as Mehari, Senait. *Heart of Fire: From Child Soldier to Soul Singer*. Profile Books 2006.

psychological, and has been classified as one of the worst cases of child abuse in California's history.[40]

His mother's physical transgressions started with treatments that look relatively innocuous. She made Dave stand in the corner of the bedroom for prolonged periods of time from as early an age as 4. This may not have been physically abusive treatment in itself but was typically administered as punishment for alleged wrongdoing of some type. His mother would enforce the treatment draconically, and Dave recalls that her emotional coldness changed his attitude towards her entirely, even at that early age:

> I ... had the unfortunate luck of getting caught at mischief, even though my brothers and I were often committing the same 'crime'. In the beginning, I was put in a corner of our bedroom. By this time, I had become afraid of Mom. Very afraid. I never asked her to let me come out. I would sit and wait for one of my brothers to come into our bedroom, and have him ask if David could come out now and play.[41]

Dave recalls that at this time his mother was beginning to show signs of depression; he describes her as spending entire days on the sofa, dressed only in her bathrobe, watching television, drinking and yelling at her sons.

Soon she was beginning to single Dave out more directly, and to seek satisfaction in a more abusive version of the corner punishment:

---

[40] Pelzer, Dave. *A Child Called 'It'*. Orion Books 1995, p. 168. 'It' is the first in a series of three books in which Dave narrates his life story. It covers events in Dave's life from ages 4 to 12. The second book in the series covers events from ages 12 to 18, and the conclusion in the series focusses on his adult life. I restrict my discussion to events from his early life, as told in the first book. Reprinted by permission of The Orion Publishing Group, London © Dave Pelzer 1995. Dave Pelzer, excerpts from *A Child Called 'It': One Child's Courage to Survive*. Copyright © 1995 by Dave Pelzer. Reprinted with the permission of The Permissions Company, Inc., for Health Communications, Inc., www.hcibooks.com.

[41] Pelzer 1995, p. 29.

Mother would ... grab me and smash my face against the
mirror ... Then she would order me to say over and over again,
'I'm a bad boy! I'm a bad boy! I'm a bad boy!' I was then forced
to stand, staring into the mirror.[42]

As frustration and alcohol were increasingly taking hold of
Dave's mother, violence and emotional cruelty in the Pelzer
household escalated. His mother banned him from watching
television, he was sent to bed without dinner, forced to
complete long lists of chores, or ordered to stand in the garage
until he was sent to bed, all because of having allegedly
'shamed the family'.[43] He was denied the family holiday and
instead abandoned at his aunt's house, without prior warning
or notice of any kind. In an episode of early violence, his
mother dislocated Dave's shoulder while administering a beating under the influence of alcohol.[44]

As severe as these transgressions were, his mother's actions
would soon take on a different, more sinister quality. Although
emotionally and physically cruel, up to this point the beatings
perhaps seem no more than off-the-cuff abuse, fuelled by anger
and alcohol.

This was to change in an incident a few months after the
summer holidays, when his mother ordered Dave to stand
naked in the kitchen while she turned on the gas burners on
the stove. This is how Dave remembers what happened next:

Mother told me that she had read an article about a mother who
had her son lie on top of a hot stove. I instantly became terrified.
My brain became numb, and my legs wobbled ... My brain
locked up when I felt Mother's hand clamp my arm as if it were
in a vice grip.

'You've made my life a living hell!' she sneered. 'Now it's time
I showed *you* what hell is like!' Gripping my arm, Mother held

[42] Pelzer 1995, pp. 30–1.
[43] Pelzer 1995, p. 36.
[44] Pelzer 1995, pp. 36–7.

it in the orange-blue flame. My skin seemed to explode from the heat. I could smell the scorched hairs from my burnt arm. As hard as I fought, I could not force Mother to let go of my arm . . . Mother then ordered me to climb up onto the stove and lie on the flames so she could watch me burn.[45]

'. . . so she could watch me burn.' These words stay with us. In that moment, it seems that Dave's treatment at the hand of his mother moved from drunken abuse to targeted, undisguised torture. We feel that, in that instance, his mother crossed a line, opened the door to abuse of a darker quality, passed from abuser to tormentor.

We gain the impression that Dave's mother wished him gone, wanted him removed from her life, and this impression grows to near certainty as Dave continues his account. Only by delaying his mother's attempt long enough for one of his brothers to return home was Dave able to escape serious injury that day.

The summer following this incident, Dave's mother began to starve him systematically. She would not feed him dinner, and often not breakfast either. For Dave, this started a continuing battle against starvation. Finding a means to feed himself would dominate his waking hours, and his mother would attempt to thwart any strategy he could devise.

At first, he started stealing food from his classmates at school. When found out, which he invariably was, the principal's report home would bring beatings and further food withdrawal. He was often not fed at weekends, while at the same time his mother had started a process of depersonalisation by referring to him in the third person as 'the boy', and later on, in a particularly cruel episode, as 'It'.[46] By then, he had been banned from the house proper and would be ordered to stand in the garage before being summoned to conduct chores.

After a while it had become too difficult to steal food from his classmates, so Dave started to eat leftovers, picked out of

---

[45] Pelzer 1995, p. 41.
[46] Pelzer 1995, p. 140.

the rubbish which he took out daily as part of his chores. When his mother became aware of this, she purposefully left meat to go off before she threw it away, giving Dave severe diarrhoea from ingesting spoiled food. He countered by wrapping food in paper towels and putting them at the bottom of the rubbish bin, but his mother thwarted this ploy by sprinkling ammonia into the bin.[47]

Again, we get the impression that his mother's actions are more than physical abuse. We feel reminded of the behaviour somebody may adopt when trying to eradicate a pest. A gardener, for example, may at first trample on molehills in the garden to collapse the mole's habitat. That failing, water may be poured down the holes, followed by perhaps even more drastic methods if deemed necessary. Dave's mother did not use food starvation as a cruel, sadistic even, form of punishment. It seems that she sought to actually *starve* Dave, devising ever more elaborate methods in a calculated pursuit of a practical goal.

And yet, she seemed sufficiently vindictive to punctuate this ongoing campaign with actions that do appear purely sadistic, have no obvious purpose and remind us of the incident with the kitchen stove.

During a family holiday, his mother ordered Dave to remain behind in the house as his father and brothers were going out for an afternoon's enjoyment. By that time, his mother had given birth to another child, Russell, and nappies had again become a fixture in the household. Dave recalls what happened when one day he found himself alone with his mother:

> I knew Mother had something hideous on her mind. As soon as they [his father and two brothers] left, she brought out one of Russell's soiled diapers. She smeared the diaper on my face . . . After what seemed like an hour, Mother knelt down beside me and in a soft voice said, 'Eat it.'[48]

---

[47] Pelzer 1995, p. 63.
[48] Pelzer 1995, p. 55.

Not long after this incident Dave managed to steal frozen lunches from the truck delivering food to the school cafeteria. After wolfing them down in the restroom, he ran home, recalling that he felt proud for successfully feeding himself.[49] However, in a new twisted turn of events, his mother forced him to vomit up his stomach contents to check whether she would be able to find evidence of food intake, an action that would demonstrate defiance of her orders not to steal food.

Later that day, a confrontation with her husband escalated into perhaps the most repulsive violation of Dave's dignity we hear about in his account.

'Look at this, Steve', Mother barked, thrusting her finger in the direction of the bowl [containing Steve's vomit]. 'So you think The Boy is through stealing food, do you?'

... 'Well Roerva, if you would just let The Boy have *something* to eat.'

A heated battle of words broke out in front of me, and as always, Mother won. 'EAT? You want The Boy to eat, Stephen? Well, The Boy is going to EAT! He can eat this!' Mother yelled at the top of her lungs, shoving the bowl towards me ...

I sat on a chair and picked the clumps of hot dogs out of the bowl with my hand. Globs of thick saliva slipped through my fingers, as I dropped it in my mouth. As I tried to swallow, I began to whimper. I turned to Father, who stood looking through me with a drink in his hand. He nodded for me to continue ...

I tried to swallow without tasting, until I felt a hand clamp on the back of my neck. 'Chew it!' Mother snarled, 'Eat it! Eat it all!' she said, pointing to the saliva.[50]

What leaves us speechless about this episode is not only the obvious violation. It is – perhaps equally so – the power Dave's

---

[49] Pelzer 1995, p. 64.
[50] Pelzer 1995, pp. 65–6.

mother evidently wielded over her husband. A power so complete that Dave's father would stand idly by while his wife stripped his son of all human dignity.

The episode had a profound impact on Dave's perception of self-worth, and on how he thought about the world.

> Sometimes at night I would wake up and try to imagine I was a real person, sleeping under a warm electric blanket, knowing I was safe and that somebody loved me. My imagination worked for a while, but the cold nights always brought me back to my reality. I knew no one could help me.[51]

These are the thoughts of a 7-year-old child.

How did he survive?
I think it is safe to say that Dave was forced to battle circumstances far tougher than the examples I have discussed in the previous chapter. So how was he able to survive? What made him keep his mental stability? How did he develop into the balanced and successful adult he grew up to be? And, perhaps most crucial for our purpose, was it an innate strength, unique to him, that made him triumph? Or did he tap into a strength we might all have if put to the test? In short, can we learn from Dave's experience or not?

For the next five years, his mother's violence was to continue unabated. She made him swallow ammonia, regularly forced him to sit by in a prisoner of war position as the family were having their meals, stabbed him in the stomach with a knife, forced him daily to vomit up his stomach contents for her inspection, even locked him in a bathroom with a bucket containing a mixture of bleach and ammonia, poisoning him with the chlorine gas generated in the chemical reaction.[52]

---

[51] Pelzer 1995, p. 68.
[52] See various accounts in Pelzer 1995, for example pp. 74–7; p. 84; pp. 86–98; p. 116; pp. 107–9; p. 4.

Eventually, his teachers intervened and notified the police, and he was admitted to a foster home. That was how Dave was removed from the immediate threat his mother represented. That was how he was saved.

But how did he *survive*?

Conscious resolve
Very early on in Dave's account, we get the first glimpse into the quality which I believe is at the heart of his ability to survive the ordeal he had to live through. Only two pages in, Dave tells us of an act of violence, commenting that 'Mother can beat me all she wants, but I haven't let her take away my will to some-how survive'.[53]

This short statement allows an important insight into Dave's personality. Yes, there is defiance, but another quality dominates. The statement reveals a *conscious* resolve not to give in, a *deliberate* choice to protect his survival instincts from the assaults of his mother. Dave is consciously aware that he has a will to survive, that this will is precious and that he needs to keep it intact.

Throughout his account, we witness his struggle to keep his will of survival undamaged, to make it prevail within the onslaught of emotional cruelty and physical violence. It asserts itself for the first time immediately after the burn incident with the stove. In that incident, Dave was able to save himself by consciously delaying his mother's attempts to burn him. He did so by provoking her into beating him, in this way diverting her attention from her primary plan. Dave was able to delay her attack long enough for his brother to return home, preventing his mother from going through with her original scheme.

We feel that his success in saving himself that day made something click in Dave's mind. We encounter a conscious resolve not to give in to circumstance:

---

[53] Pelzer 1995, p. 4.

> ... I realized that *I* had beaten her ... *I* had used my head to survive. For the first time, *I* had won!

> Standing alone in that damp, dark garage, I knew, for the first time, that I could survive. I decided that I would use any tactic I could think of to defeat Mother ... I knew if *I* wanted to live, *I* would have to think ahead. I could no longer cry like a helpless baby. In order to survive, *I* could never give in to her. That day I vowed to myself that I would never, ever again give the bitch the satisfaction of hearing me beg her to stop beating me.[54]

There are several things in this passage that I think are worthy of note. The personal pronoun is emphasised six times, by writing it in italics. This is no accident. We feel that in this passage, Dave's focus is shifting from circumstances to himself. He consciously realises that he needs to stand up to his fate, that he cannot allow circumstances to dominate him. In this instant, Dave mentally switches from victim ('helpless baby') to agent.

This switch, of course, did not mean that from then onwards he was somehow able to stand up to his mother on a regular basis. Quite the contrary; when her violence became overpowering, there were moments when his resolve weakened, when his will to survive was threatened:

> I could sense [my mother's] heightened confidence, and her new confidence made me fear for my life. I wished I could dissolve and be gone forever. I wished I would never have to face another human being again.[55]

And yet, although Dave tells us frequently of such moments of 'weakness', the reader feels that they are just this – moments. We never feel that these episodes are sufficient to crush his will to survive entirely, or severe enough to eradicate his resolve. Towards the end of Dave's account, we find a passage that powerfully conveys the strength of Dave's inner spirit. Dave

---

[54] Pelzer 1995, pp. 42–3.
[55] Pelzer 1995, p. 54.

recalls that, after years of emotional violence, he had lost all
sense of self-worth:

> At the core of my soul, I hated myself more than anybody or
> anything. I came to believe that everything that happened to
> me or around me was my own fault because I had let it go on
> for so long ... A few weeks before I started the fifth grade, I
> hated myself so much that I wished I were dead.[56]

Dave then continues to tell us about his thoughts during a
school trip to one of San Francisco's clipper ships:

> Looking back over the railing [of the boat], I stared at the cold,
> green water lapping against the wooden side of the ship. For a
> moment, I could visualize myself plunging into the water,
> knowing I would drown. It was a comforting thought that
> promised an escape from ... all that I hated in the world. But
> my better senses returned, and I looked up ...[57]

And this, I believe, is the key. Dave recalls that self-loathing
had replaced all feelings of self-respect, of self-worth, of self-
belief that he once had, to the point that he was contemplating
suicide.

But he was only contemplating it for a moment. What made
him beat the urge? What was the nature of the strength he was
able to draw on in that moment of utter despair? Was it steely
resolve? Was it a memory of his vows in the garage? Defiance?

No. It was his better senses. No heroic, unbending strength
that broke forth at the moment of tragedy. Instead, a disarmingly simple reference to mere common sense. Dave simply
knows better. Even stripped of the last remnant of self-worth, in
the face of overwhelming frustration and pain, Dave does not
seriously consider killing himself. What made Dave survive in
the end is an understanding that it was up to *him* to defy

---

[56] Pelzer 1995, p. 136.
[57] Pelzer 1995, p. 138.

circumstances. What made him survive is that he adopted the mindset of the agent, and not that of the victim.

What made him triumph?
In the epilogue, speaking from a point in the present, Dave gives clear testimony to the drivers that kept him alive:

> I'm so lucky. My dark past is behind me now. As bad as it was, I knew even back then, in the final analysis, my way of life would be up to me . . . I made sure I let go of my past, accepting the fact that that part of my life was only a small fraction of my life. I knew the black hole was out there, waiting to suck me in and forever control my destiny – but only if I let it.[58]

Dave makes three crucial points in this passage:

- **Be the agent not the victim!** Looking back, he realises that at a very young age he was forced to accept that he could not look to others for help. But Dave turned this insight into a positive choice, a choice to become the agent, a choice not to be the passive victim of circumstance.

- **Choose the future!** In a crucial insight, Dave says that he consciously chose to look into the future and not focus on the past. I believe his ability to do this was the reason that he survived the ordeals of his childhood and grew up to be a sane, well-adjusted adult.

- **You have a choice!** And this, perhaps, is the most important insight of all. In a characteristically sober statement, Dave says that the difference between psychological trauma and emotional adjustment is personal choice. This is not a glib statement, coming from him. In this statement, Dave impressively asserts that we decide whether we let circumstances control us, or emancipate ourselves to control them.

---

[58] Pelzer 1995, p. 156.

These three maxims carry in themselves the power to heal, to mature beyond mere survival and create a meaningful, authentic life. Dave knows this, and in his afterword draws the distinction between survival and living:

> This is my story and mine alone. For years I was confined to the darkness of my own mind and heart, being alone and a pitiful 'loser'. At first I wanted nothing more than to be like others, but that motivation grew. I wanted to become a 'winner' ... I believe it is important for people to know that no matter what lies in their past, they can overcome the dark side and press on to a brighter world ... It is important that the body survives, but it is more meaningful that the human spirit prevails.[59]

And this, I believe, is the final, and most powerful, insight into why Dave managed to survive the ordeal of his childhood physically, and then extricate himself from the potential psychological aftermath. Conscious resolve not to be beaten by circumstances made him survive. A refusal to accept that the past defines his future kept him sane. But the urge to become all that he could be made him live. In the end, his choice not to dwell on the past, but to focus on the future, allowed him to grow into the contented adult he became. It is not by accident that Dave concludes his account with a simple statement that in a few short words encapsulates the quality of what he feels today:

> I'm free.[60]

Tougher than the rest?

Exceptional people or exceptional fates?
We have now heard from our expert. As Dave said of himself, his story is his, and his alone. It is for him to tell it, and I refer

---

[59] Pelzer 1995, pp. 164–5.
[60] Pelzer 1995, p. 160.

you to his autobiographies for a full account of his life.[61] And yet, I felt I needed to let him speak extensively in these pages for us to share some of his pain, understand some of his ordeals, feel some of the sadness he felt.

I chose to present only one widely publicised story for our discussion. Yet, the circumstances its author was facing are not unique. Disturbing, sickening, saddening, certainly; they may even be exceptional in the severity of the ordeals suffered. But unfortunately they are not unique. When I ordered the books we are discussing, I ticked an option to list all available titles on the subject of child abuse. The search engine returned 42,835 results. Of course, not all of these will be autobiographical. The list is likely to contain many duplicates and many sociological studies on the subject. Even so, the number is staggering, and disturbing.

The retailer's website also featured a comparison engine, which offered search results from other customers (of the type 'you may also be interested in ...'). Scrolling through the results presented there, I would guess that there are currently in excess of 100 different titles of a similar nature available for purchase.

And these are still 'only' the ones where the victims went on to write their story down and found a publisher to make them widely available. Research conducted by the NSPCC suggests that currently more than 50,000 children in the UK alone are on child protection registers or are the subject of child protection plans.[62]

And finally, we are still talking specifically about child abuse. Many other fates are no lighter, but would not come under this heading – stories of abject poverty, of severe illness, of political oppression.

These thoughts are sobering. The numbers do not make the ordeals we are discussing in this chapter any less horrendous.

---

[61] As quoted in annotation 40.
[62] NSPCC website at www.nspcc.org.uk.

But they suggest that struggles of this nature may occur more often than we think.

Which brings me to the subject at hand. Is our author exceptionally tenacious, or does he have something others do not have? Did he develop a toughness that other people in similar situations would not have developed?

Or do we all carry a strength within us that we would be able to draw on if circumstances of a similar ferocity forced themselves on us? Would we all grow with the challenge? Do adverse circumstances bring out hidden strengths that we already possess?

In short, is the expert on our panel *tougher* than the rest? Or is he *as tough* as the rest?

This is an important question. If the answer is tougher than, we have a problem. In that case, we would have to concede that only those who are lucky enough to be tough enough can triumph over hostility.

Only if the answer is as tough as the rest do the rest of us stand a chance. Only if that is the answer can the life story we heard be inspirational.

How did he survive?
But how can we decide? Is this problem not like the famous chicken and egg dilemma, or the never-ending nature-or-nurture debate?

Not quite. Chicken and egg issues cannot be decided, because no empirical evidence can be gathered that could serve as the basis for a verdict. But for the question at hand, we have the evidence we need before us. 'All' we need to do is go back to our story and see whether we can find clues that would point to one conclusion or the other.

No silver bullet
The first thing that is striking is that our author seemed to have specific innate strengths that helped him survive. Dave found the strength to stay firm in his resolve to beat

circumstances in a natural level-headedness, a quality he calls his better senses.[63]

This quality cannot be learned. It is innate, and you either have it or you do not. So would this not suggest that little can be done if you are not lucky enough to have been born strong?

Not exactly. Yes, I do believe that the key survival instincts we have encountered are innate, and therefore cannot be imitated. If you are not like Dave, you cannot use level-headedness and defiance as survival tools, no matter *how* many times you read his account.

But the good news is you do not have to. Sure, if you happen to be like Dave, that may help you; but if you are not, there will be other tools at your disposal. If you have a natural belief in yourself, for instance, or feel pride or possess another quality not encountered in the accounts studied, you probably also have what it takes to prevail if push comes to shove.

Indeed, I have seen no evidence that would suggest you need one *specific* quality to prevail. If anything, the evidence points to the contrary. At this point, I should like to bring in our consultant Senait Mehari for the first time and briefly refer to her life account. Senait spent her early childhood in civil-war-torn Eritrea in the 70s, where she and her two sisters were subjected to severe domestic violence at the hands of her father. The sisters were then handed over to the Eritrean Liberation Front (ELF), one of the two armed organisations that fought for an independent Eritrea at the time.[64] After three years of unspeakable torment, hard physical labour, psychological trauma, degrading hunger and sexual abuse, the sisters were saved and lived in the care of an uncle before finally emigrating to Germany.

I cannot do justice to Senait's life story in this book and instead refer you to her biography for a full account. The point

---

[63] Pelzer 1995, p. 138.

[64] The other one was the Eritrean People's Liberation Front (EPLF), an organisation established in 1970 by members splitting from the ELF.

that is of interest to us is to ask how she, and her sisters, survived their ordeal. Senait says of herself that she derived the strength to survive from a sentiment of sheer defiance. But she also says that her sisters had personalities entirely different from her. She described one of them as intelligent and in control and the other as sensitive.[65]

So, considering the evidence, I am driven to conclude that there is no one specific quality that we *need* to have if we wish to survive exceptional hardship. Dave survived through his level-headedness, Senait's willpower was fuelled by defiance, and that of her sisters by yet other qualities rooted in their respective personality traits of intelligence and sensitiveness.

So it looks as though there are lots of bullets we may use to overcome hostile circumstances, but none of them is silver.

This is good news indeed, since it suggests that all of us may have what it takes to prevail in the face of extreme adversity, and that all of us have the potential to rise to the challenge if forced to.

Would we tap into it?
But not everybody will triumph over circumstances. We may all *potentially* have what it takes, but there are many who tragically do not survive, many who have committed suicide or suffered irreversible psychological damage and many we never hear about.

What then is it that makes the accounts we read stand out? By definition, everybody who gets to talk about an ordeal with hindsight has survived it, so there is positive selection in a group of published authors. They all survived and, I would argue, they all triumphed over circumstance. Their survival qualities are crucial but, as we have discussed, they may not be unique. So what is it that made them survive, and having survived how did they heal?

---

[65] Mehari 2004, pp. 253–4.

It may be the fact that they used their strengths consciously. We may all possess the strengths required to battle extreme circumstance. But we still need to be able to *use* them, and we need to know who we are, to recognise our personality traits for what they are and consciously harness them.

And would we harness them? Would we have the ability to be unwavering in our resolve and draw on our own source of strength, whichever form it may take?

This is an even more difficult question to answer, but luckily we can turn to Dave and Senait for guidance. Did they do this? Yes, it seems they did, since they both came out victorious. But yes is an answer that sees only the surface. 'Usually, but not always' appears to be a better answer.

Let us consider the evidence.

Even Dave's natural level-headedness turns out not to have been an infallible guide. He recalls how at one point he came to despair of his life to such an extent that he hoped his mother would kill him. 'So I began to purposefully irritate her, hoping I could provoke her enough that she would end my misery',[66] says Dave, describing his attempt at 'suicide by mother'. It is a rare occurrence where we see Dave's better senses abandoning him.

Senait recalls that when she was 6 her father tried to kill her. He ordered her to stand against a tree and threatened her with his machete. In that instance it was only luck that saved her. Her stepmother arrived on the scene and intervened. Had she not done so, the situation might have escalated and circumstances might have defeated her.[67]

Let us pause here and consider what we can conclude:

• Innate qualities are important. Both Dave and Senait were drawing strength from qualities that cannot be learned. But they were not relying on the same quality! We sense that

---

[66] Pelzer 1995, p. 141.
[67] Mehari 2004, p. 74.

each of us has innate qualities that we could tap into if confronted with extreme circumstances.

- Luck is still important. Dave and Senait were both able to do just that, to tap into their respective strengths. Both of them were able to do this with near-unwavering determination. And yet, they *still* occasionally needed luck to come to the rescue.

- We sense that their tenacity is exceptional, but also that it grew as they needed it to beat circumstances. We are beginning to see that they do not display superhuman strength and willpower. Hence, an ability to defeat circumstances, even if exceptionally adverse in nature, may be within the reach of the rest of us.

Dave and Senait may not have been tougher than the rest. They may have been as tough as the rest.

How did Dave triumph?

We discussed earlier how Dave was able to survive his ordeal *physically*. We have not yet explored how he was able to heal *emotionally* after he escaped tangible threats to his life. Physical survival is one thing, and it is intimidating enough on its own, but maturing into the well-adjusted, successful adult he has become seems a tougher challenge still. And yet, if he had failed that challenge, he would not have truly conquered circumstance.

Healing is the final test. Those unfortunate enough to fail this test are still beaten by circumstance. Senait's father, whom we have met only indirectly, is one example. Senait says in her account that he suffered his own ordeal at the hands of his mother. He survived physically but grew up to become an abusive parent. Dave's mother may be another example, whatever the nature of her personal ordeal was.

Only those who are able to become psychologically *whole*, I would argue, truly triumph. Indeed, Dave himself seems to say this: 'It is important that the body survives, but it is more meaningful that the human spirit prevails.'[68]

But how did he manage to do this? How was he able to let go of his past and move on? How did he heal?

Well, why don't I simply ask him in person? I am going to ask him four questions and then bring his views together and evaluate the results. I shall also bring in Senait's views as an independent consultant.

> Mark: How did you move on after your physical ordeal was over?
> Dave: I made sure I let go of my past . . . I knew the black hole was out there, waiting to . . . control my destiny – but only if I let it.
> Senait says in her account that it is a choice how to deal with the past, that you can suppress it, or you can work through the issues.[69]

Neither of them dwelt on the past, or allowed it to define their future development. Indeed, allowed is the operative word in this sentence – they both understood that their past would not dominate them unless they allowed it to do so, and that they were free to choose, *consciously* choose, how to live their lives.

These are not glib statements. These are insights from people who have been there, who have been to the brink and back. But knowing that you have a conscious choice is one thing. Actually *making* it is another thing.

> Mark: How did you make this choice? Did you find this easy, or was it a struggle?
> Dave: For years I was confined to the darkness of my own mind and heart, being alone and a pitiful 'loser'. At first I wanted nothing more than to be like others, but that motivation grew. I wanted to become a 'winner'.

---

[68] Pelzer 1995, pp. 164–5.
[69] Pelzer 1995, p. 156; Mehari 2004, p. 342.

Senait says she was unable to simply shake off the ordeals she
suffered in her formative years. The memories of the events
would remain vivid and ever-present in her thoughts. It took
reflection and conscious awareness to mature.[70]

Dave tells us how his motivation to succeed grew over time.
Senait admits what we all suspect, that the process of letting go
is painful and requires dedication and conscious reflection. But
both of them describe a process of finding themselves, a journey during which they discovered who they really are. They
describe how they gradually understood what the reasons for
the abuse may have been, how they were able to deal with
their past, what they needed to become whole and how to go
after it.

In short, they discovered who they are, what they need and
how to get it.

Mark: What is the decisive factor in beating circumstance?
Dave: As bad as it was, I knew even back then, in the final analy-
sis, my way of life would be up to me.
Senait actively, and consciously, rejected the role of victim.[71]

Both have a strong sense of not allowing themselves to be the
victim. Both see themselves as agents and neither accepted the
role of victim. I believe this is the key to their ultimate triumph
over circumstance.

Mark: Looking back from where you are now, is there anything
about yourself you would like to share?
Dave: I'm so blessed. The challenges of my past have made me
immensely strong inside ... I have a vast appreciation for
things that others may take for granted ... I'm free.
Senait's account ends with the conclusion that she has grown to
like herself.[72]

---

[70] Pelzer 1995, p. 165 and Mehari 2004, p. 339 respectively.
[71] Pelzer 1995, p. 156 and Mehari 2004, p. 344 respectively.
[72] Pelzer 1995, p. 157 and Mehari 2004, pp. 343, 345 respectively.

It is striking that both of them were able to develop a strong sense of positive self-worth. It is a central thesis of my book that self-knowledge and self-worth go hand in hand, and the life stories we have heard strongly support this thesis.

Command and conquer!

A summary

We have come to the end of our analysis of how to control fate. We read through the life story of Dave Pelzer. We suffered with him, felt for him, despaired when he faltered, rejoiced when he triumphed. Then we tried to get under the surface, we picked his story apart, looked at the components, analysed, evaluated, critiqued. We put the story together again and looked at it in context. We brought in a 'consultant' to lend additional viewpoints when needed. Now we are ready for conclusions.

The diagram summarises key points of our discussion.

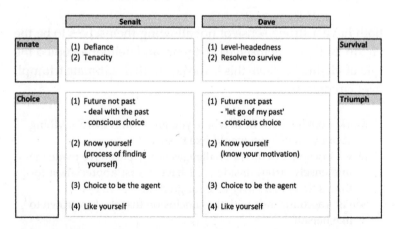

Senait	Dave	
Innate (1) Defiance (2) Tenacity	(1) Level-headedness (2) Resolve to survive	**Survival**

Choice
(1) Future not past
  - deal with the past
  - conscious choice
 	
(2) Know yourself
  (process of finding
  yourself)
 	
(3) Choice to be the agent
 	
(4) Like yourself
	(1) Future not past
	  - 'let go of my past'
	  - conscious choice
	
	(2) Know yourself
	  (know your motivation)
	
	(3) Choice to be the agent
	
	(4) Like yourself
		Triumph

Fig. 4.1 The diagram analyses the key qualities that ensured success in the face of adverse circumstances. Both individuals had a different *innate* quality. This quality helped the individual to survive physically. But each person made near-identical conscious choices. These choices ensured psychological survival. It seems reasonable to suggest that there are *many* innate qualities that can aid physical survival. However, it appears that four identical key qualities ensured psychological survival.

The building blocks in the two stories we picked are similar. Each person was facing a personal ordeal. During this period, mere physical survival was paramount, and personal qualities that made such survival possible were in focus. After surviving the physical phase, they each entered a period of healing. In this period they dealt with the psychological fallout of their predicaments. In the diagram, I labelled the successful completion of phase 1 as survival, and the completion of phase 2 as triumph.

Survival depends on personal character traits that are innate but not unique. *Triumph* over circumstance rests on *choice*. Dave and Senait were both able to heal because they made a conscious, and deliberate, choice. They chose to deal with their past, to conduct their lives in a particular manner, to ask certain questions and to work through the issues.

Several ways to survive, one way to triumph

Dave and Senait both relied on *different* strengths to survive, but they made *identical* choices to triumph:

- Both focussed on the future and refused to let the past dominate. And both of them knew that doing so was a personal choice, something that was within their power to influence.

- Both went through a period of finding themselves, a period during which they understood more about the reasons for their survival, but even more importantly during which they searched for an authentic life for themselves. For Senait, this was a life as a singer-songwriter; for Dave, first the military and then the motivational speaker circuit.

- Both made a choice to be the agent. Neither accepted the role of victim, and their refusal to do so was conscious.

Finally, both developed a strong sense of self-worth, a sense that they liked themselves as individuals, and that they approved of their own actions and choices. This feeling is not a personal choice, but it flows directly from the choices they *did* make.

In many ways it is the most important quality of all. If you get to know who you are, and go on to like yourself, you have obtained the key to happiness.

What can we learn?

I believe our discussion shows that everybody potentially has what it takes to triumph over circumstance.

True, it seems that for survival we need to rely on certain innate character traits. But the evidence we consulted suggests that there are a great many relevant survival qualities, and that each of us is likely to possess at least one. On this Dave and Senait appear to agree. Dave says: 'I believe it is important for people to know that no matter what lies in their past, they can overcome the dark side and press on to a brighter world.' Senait echoes this when she expresses conviction that anybody can take charge of their lives.[73]

But would we tap into our strengths? Now we are in the realm of conscious choice. We cannot influence whether we are born into poverty, war, an abusive household, a politically oppressive regime, or whether we suffer a million other hardships we are powerless to prevent. But we *can* influence how we handle such ordeals. Interestingly, both Dave and Senait dealt with their private hells in similar ways: by refusing to be the victim, by starting on the arduous journey of finding themselves and by *choosing* not to let their pasts define their futures.

In the end I believe they have shown themselves not to be *tougher* than the rest; they are *as* tough as the rest. But they have shown the rest of us how it is done. For that reason, their

---

[73] Pelzer 1995, p. 165; Mehari 2004, p. 348.

stories can serve as true inspiration for those who find themselves in the aftermath of similar ordeals or who are confronted with similar hardships. We all have the *potential* to prevail. Success or failure is not driven by innate traits that we cannot influence but by actions that we can.

Often these actions are merely choices to adopt a particular mindset. Perhaps the most crucial one of these is the refusal to be the victim. This is the same choice as the one we discussed in the previous chapter, a version of my mantra 'everything is your fault'.

A version of it. But not the same. My mantra will not work in circumstances of severe hardship, and we need to be careful to distinguish less severe predicaments from those that are existential in nature. In essence, though, the two choices are similar. They both rest on the refusal to accept the status of victim, and this refusal in itself is a giant step forward towards becoming the agent.

If we look at all the situations we discussed in Rules 3 and 4 in context, we see that certain qualities seem essential when taking control. If they are present, success seems assured. If they are not, we are unlikely to assert ourselves, and circumstances take over. I have listed the qualities in this table:

Situation	Be the agent!	Choose the future	Self-knowledge	I like myself	Success?
		Technique			
Lambo-guy	✗		✗		NO
A slap in the face	✗		✗	✗	NO
Change your shoes!		✓			YES
Read the FT!		✓			YES
We lost (re)direction	✗		✗	✗	NO
Now what?		✓	✓		YES
My home is my castle	✗		✗		NO
Dave	✓	✓	✓	✓	YES
Senait	✓	✓	✓	✓	YES

Severity shadings: Everyday | Life changing | Existential

Fig. 4.2 The four requirements for triumph shown in a wider context. If we examine the part they play in all the stories examined in this chapter, we find a clear correlation between their presence and success. When they are absent (denoted by a cross), a person tends to lose out to circumstance and sees himself as the victim. When at least one of them is present (denoted by a tick), a person tends to triumph over circumstance and finds empowerment as the agent.

Even in the lightest of incidents, an ability to adopt the role of agent is key. In everyday situations, but also in those of a potentially life-changing nature, this empowerment may come as we change our mindset. Self-knowledge is crucial in all but the most trivial situations. A determined refusal to let the past dominate your fate, it almost goes without saying, is not required in any context other than in life-threatening ordeals.

And there you have it. A sense that we are able to exert a measure of control over our lives is essential in achieving overall happiness. The choice to emancipate ourselves as agents emerges as the most important quality allowing us to assume this control. We need an ability to focus on the future as an additional tool to wrest back control if the challenges become life-threatening. Self-knowledge, as ever, is the foundation on which everything rests.

In the end, I may develop a feeling of positive self-worth, I may approve of what I do in life; in short, I may come to *like* myself. If I get to this stage, I will have achieved the balance that is the base of all deeply rooted states of happiness.

Humble pie, anyone?

We cannot conclude this chapter without making an important observation. Not everybody faced with predicaments of the nature just described will make it. Not everybody *did* make it. There are those who have tragically committed suicide, those who have suffered irreversible psychological damage and those whose fates we never hear about.

As crucial as it is to embrace the fact that we have a choice, and as uplifting as it is to read life stories that prove this, it is important to maintain a sense of humility, a sense of modesty. I maintain that self-knowledge and the refusal to be a victim are key ingredients in dealing with life challenges of any kind. I also maintain that there is no excuse for not trying.

But there is no guarantee that we will succeed. If we remain aware of this potential limitation, we may avoid a trap of a different kind, a risk of becoming glib, of thinking too much of those who *did* make it, or too little of those who did not. Let us remember that, even for Dave and Senait, there were moments where success or failure hung in the balance and could have gone either way.

In the end, we will find happiness only if we manage to develop into well-adjusted, balanced individuals. If taking control of our lives as agents is a yin, we need a yang in counterbalance. We need humility to complement a growing confidence as agents, we need a sense of perspective to interpret the actions of others and we need a quality that makes us benign custodians of the evidence we see around us. We need to learn how to judge what people around us do.

Even more importantly, we need to learn how *not* to judge others prematurely. This is what I will turn to next.

RULE 5

Don't judge

How not to judge

Why not judge?

The first thing you might ask yourself is why an ability not to judge is important in the context of this book at all. Why should it be the case that I get to be a happier person if I do not judge others? What does judging *others* have to do with *me* anyway? And even if there was a point to this somewhere, how could I even achieve this – is judging not a perfectly natural thing that we do all the time, even subconsciously?

Also is judging not a consequence of having personal standards of some description? If somebody falls short of these, or exceeds them, how can I not judge that person by these benchmarks? In fact, would it not follow that I am indifferent to others if I do not judge? Or worse perhaps, that I have somehow failed to develop personal standards by which I live, and the only reason that I do *not* judge is because I have no frame of reference of my own?

All good questions. As before, I will endeavour to explore the themes by looking at stories taken from my life and the lives of my friends and acquaintances. But before I do this, let me share a few thoughts with you on the questions above.

It is my belief that an individual who does not feel the need to judge others is contented, balanced and confident. I also

believe that it is possible to heighten a state of balance by training yourself not to judge. I am aware that I am deliberately
reversing the apparent sequence of cause and effect when I
advocate this. But I am convinced that if we put this cart before
the horse, we end up avoiding a lot of what, for the sake of this
discussion, I will call ambient anger.

What do I mean by this phrase? If we judge somebody, we
do so if we believe that the person falls short of personal standards to which we hold ourselves (or would like to). We get
angry at the behaviour of others, we work ourselves up about
what a brute somebody is, how a particular action shows that
this person is a liar, that person an obnoxious show-off and a
third person is just plain intolerable. Each time we get angry, it
takes time to calm down again, and each time we judge somebody, we lose our balance, if only for a moment.

So would it not be great if we could lose this ambient anger
and somehow banish it from our lives? I should think so. The
result would be a self-sufficient, happier person. Easier said
than done though – how can I not judge if somebody obviously falls short of standards I value in my own life?

I believe the answer may lie in the realisation that people
are complex and that no single trait is representative of all we
are. If we realise this, we should be able to separate an action
from the person performing the action. And having done that,
we should be able to judge the *action* and not the *person*.

But to do that we need to develop the deepest possible insight
into a person's reasons for acting in a certain way. The deeper
this understanding, the fairer the assessment of the action. There
is no danger that our value system will come under attack from
a deeper level of understanding. It is possible to understand the
reasons for an action without condoning the action.

I would like to translate these two points into a set of
maxims.

Maxim 1 *I shall strive to understand the reasons that motivated an
action or that led to a statement of opinion.*

Maxim 2 *I will remember that no single character trait defines all that a person is.*

It is perfectly safe to apply the first maxim – an attempt to explore reasons for a particular behaviour will not mean that we condone this behaviour. And it is also safe to apply the second one – we still evaluate how to interact with people, whether to avoid or build a relationship with someone, only now we may do so from an *examined* position.

As our value system remains intact in the exploration of reasons (*maxim 1*) and our perspective remains broad in the knowledge that we are complex (*maxim 2*), we are building the mindset that allows us to judge the *action* and not the *person*.

If applied consistently, and over a long time, the two maxims should therefore be a useful tool in getting to a state where we find it less necessary to judge. Less judging should increase our emotional balance, reduce ambient anger and this in turn should make us more content.

Well then. Let us see how all this might work in practice.

Hang on a second . . .

This is just semantics though, isn't it? If somebody is a plonker, why can't I call him a plonker? If somebody is a murderer, surely I can call her a murderer?

This was how a friend of mine objected to my reasoning when we were discussing this chapter over a cup of coffee. My maxims had been put to the first test! To see whether they pass, I shall first turn to a discussion of . . . gardening tools! As you do.

It is a sunny day in spring. I am walking into the garden and realise that I forgot to put the tools back into the shed the night before. Several of them are still propped up against the wall where I left them and others have fallen over and are lying on the grass in an ungainly heap.

Clearly the first job today is to tidy them away into the shed. There is only so much gardening a person can do, and I did a week's worth of it yesterday . . .

Leaning against a wall is a tool approximately 130 cm in length. It consists of three components: a handle, a shaft and a head. The shaft is a cold-rolled steel tube 80 cm in length and 30 mm in diameter. At one end of the shaft is a large D-handle with a 100 x 60 mm opening, fitted at a 17-degree angle to the shaft. Welded onto the other end of the shaft is a 20 x 30 cm steel blade with a treaded upper and a sharpened and curved lower edge.

This is a spade. It is in the full view of daylight and I can describe its components clearly. I also recognise it from yesterday, when I used it at length to slice grass tufts and mix soil. I do not think my description of the tool is missing anything material. *This is a spade and I can call it a spade.*

Lying in the grass is a tool which is partially obscured by another tool lying on top of it. It seems to be composed of a shaft, a handle and a blade, just like the spade. But I cannot see the handle, and the head is in the shadows cast by our shed. The shaft is longer than that of the spade, and the blade seems to stick out at a more acute angle.

This may be my shovel. But it could be my power-digging spade. I do not know. Better not call it a spade though. I do not know about the hierarchy of gardening tools but something tells me a shovel would not like being judged as a spade.

How does this help answer my friend's challenge? It helps by choosing a deliberately simple application for my first maxim. At the heart of Maxim 1 lies the realisation that we are never in possession of all the facts pertaining to somebody's actions or statements. That is why the first maxim urges us to make an effort and seek as much information as we can, and to use the information we have gathered to develop a deeper understanding of somebody's motives.

I have a mental image of you grinning as you are reading this. 'What does the spade say its motives are then?' I hear you snigger.

But hold on. Remember my friend's objection? She said, 'If somebody is a plonker, why can't I call him a plonker?' And the answer is a sobering 'No reason'! If somebody *is* a plonker, of course you can call him a plonker. But how do we know? Only in the most trivial of life situations may we be in possession of sufficient information to decide the nature of something beyond reasonable doubt. If something is a spade, call it a spade. But as soon as life gets just a touch more complicated than that, we are stumped. Might as well admit it. The spade lying in the shade of my shed may be a shovel.

If there are situations where I cannot even decide with certainty whether a garden tool is a spade or a shovel, how can I hope to know whether somebody *is* a plonker or *is* a murderer?

The simple point I am making here is that Maxim 1 urges us to hold off with our judgements until we have had a little more time to gather information and to understand a little bit more about motive. Once we get there, Maxim 2 crucially reminds us that one trait does not make a whole person.

So the guy who was rude to us on the bus this morning had just heard that his ex-wife had abducted their daughter and was suing him for all his money? OK then. Still, he was rude and he should have been more in control of himself, but maybe he is not a *total* bastard . . . Hmmm, so that murderer killed a guy who had raped and killed her 16-year-old daughter? Phew . . . tough one. I still cannot condone it, but I certainly understand how she could be driven to do this.

OK then. *Now* let us see how all this might work.

Innocuous stories

Complain to management!

My first few stories are light-hearted in nature. None of them are of huge consequence, but nonetheless they help to illustrate a few points, which I will bring together at the end of this section.

The first story I wish to share with you takes us to Dublin, where I was staying in a hotel for a night on a business trip. Actually, it is entirely irrelevant to the story where I was, but you might as well know.

As I was getting ready for bed, I heard loud talking from the room next to me. After a while the talking grew louder and developed into shouting. Then it stopped. There was silence. The incident faded in my mind and I was about to fall asleep when it started up again. Loud, agitated talking, like somebody was on the phone to somebody. Then shouting again, followed by silence.

Not altogether conducive to getting a good night's sleep basically. After a few repetitions of this cycle I decided to get to the bottom of it and deal with the situation. Off I went in my bathrobe into the corridor to face the authors of the disturbance. The hallway was deserted, but the voices were clearly coming from inside the room facing mine. I braced myself and knocked on the door. This is what happened next:

- The shouting stopped. There was a brief silence. The door opened.

- The doorway was filled with a huge man, probably 1.90 m tall with body mass to match.

- This man glared down at me (I am not nearly 1.90 m tall). The man barked 'Yea? What?'

- I enquired whether he would kindly consider stopping shouting.

- Instead of apologising the man snapped 'Oh, why don't you complain to management!' and slammed the door shut.

Well. Unexpected. Most people would have apologised. The man's demeanour and attitude bordered on the threatening, so my judgement of his character was quick and sound. 'What an insolent brute', I muttered under my breath before repeating this assessment to the management of the hotel, as the gentleman had suggested.

The next morning brought closure. Management formally apologised on behalf of their guest, extending his sincere regrets and adding that he had just received very bad personal news leading to the previous night's incident.

The message is as simple as it is clear. I had not been in possession of all the information but judged the guy an aggressive brute. But was this much of an issue? Not really. I did not genuinely judge his character; indeed, he was irrelevant to me, and in the instant that he briefly became relevant he *was* an aggressive brute.

The point of this story is to exonerate us from judgements such as this. They are fleeting moments, we do not really sit in judgement of others when we are briefly angry and such matters are quickly forgotten.

Still, innocuous as this story may be, even in circumstances such as these we need to remain in control of the judgements we dispense. If we are able to forget the matter after a good night's sleep, fine. But if we hold on to it, if we hold a grudge and develop a habit of constantly micro-judging others in this way, ambient anger may establish itself as a background tension that is constantly present in our lives.

Wipe out!

The second story in this category takes place in Italy in March on a ski slope.

I had just started off on the relatively steep final section of a run down to the valley lift station. It was a gloriously sunny day, I was in high spirits and I knew this run inside out. I like to go fast if circumstances permit, and at that moment there was virtually nobody ahead of me on the slope. Even so, I was keeping very close to the edge of the run, since that way I would be able to minimise the area I needed to scan for slower skiers and remain alert to the possibility of having to break sharply.

I was just speeding up nicely and getting into the swing of things (literally) when I found myself lying on the ground. Then the pain started throbbing in my left hip. And then I realised, dimly, that a noise I had been briefly aware of must have been somebody shouting. And indeed, when I cautiously sat up and looked down the slope, I spotted another skier getting up and nursing himself back to life.

At this point the adrenalin must have taken over because the next thing I knew I was standing next to the guy, shouting at him at the top of my voice. Never before had I felt so angry. The rage was pure, searing, unadulterated. After a while I calmed down sufficiently to interact in a vaguely rational way and we were able to deal with the issue.[74]

Was I judging this chap? You bet I was. I later estimated that he must have hit me at a relative speed of maybe 10 or 20 mph, luckily sideways so that we were both sliding down the slope and did not break anything. Still, to squeeze past a skier who was going at some 50 mph, through the space between me and the edge of the slope, a space which can have been no wider than a metre, was irresponsible to the point of insanity. An entirely reckless chap with no care for others.

But is that what he really *was*? Granted, in that instance he was. No excuse. But he may not act like this in all aspects of his life, and I never considered the possibility that he may not

---

[74] A by-product of the experience was that it demonstrated to me a side of my character that I approve of. Although I felt an all-encompassing rage that unleashed itself with biblical force on the poor chap who had skied into me, there was not a single instance in our interaction during which I had felt, even fleetingly, the urge to harm him physically. After the incident had passed, I consciously noticed this, and I am happy to find that an urge for physical violence appears to be absent from my personality. This is an example of EXPE-RIENCE MINING and also shows that life experiences can be used in many ways, and that they can teach us a number of things simultaneously.

have been doing this deliberately. He may simply have been going too fast for the bend and, running wide, had no other option than to squeeze past me on the left. That still makes his action irresponsible of course, but maybe not consciously reckless.

Also note how I am talking about this now, with the benefit of two years' hindsight. I am referring to his *action*. Not to *him* as a person. Granted, the incident was sufficiently severe for me to judge him as a person for a while, but I think I can honestly say that this may have lasted for no longer than a day or so.

And the point of these stories?

Of course, I could sit here and fill a whole book with stories of this nature, as we all could. The experiences I narrated do not run deep, but nevertheless they allow some observations on the nature of judging at this most superficial level:

- Judgement dispensed in situations such as these does not genuinely qualify as judging others. Even when we denounce somebody as rude or reckless, we are aware that we are not making a comprehensive assessment of somebody's character. As such, judgements of this nature are allowed. They are no more than brief comments on isolated incidents of the behaviour of others.

- However, even these micro-judgements have to be watched. If we indulge in micro-judging others all the time, and lose sight of the limitations of these assessments, we may be more prone to judging in more fundamental instances, instances where our emotional balance is more at stake.

- Even if we feel justified in micro-judgement, and believe that we are in control of the habit, there is a danger that the judgements may fuse to ambient anger, an almost subconscious strain that inserts itself into our lives and is bound to detract from our emotional well-being. The guy in the hotel *is* a brute, the dude on the slopes *is* reckless, this chap *is* a plonker, that person *is* a bitch etc.

But let me turn to more substantial instances of judging next.

Less innocuous stories

Black and white
The first two stories that I would like to share with you from this category explore the dynamics of what I am calling deep judging. What is going on when we judge? How are judgements formed? Why do we make them? What if anything does the act of judging say about the person who does the judging?

Approximately a year after Ursina and I met, we were driving to a friend's house for dinner. Our relationship was still young and we were still exploring each other's circles of friends. I was still eager to find out who was currently important in Ursina's life, and still apprehensive to hear about those who were important in her past.

We were chatting about her best friend Judeena. Judeena lives in the US and had at the time been in a relationship with Kadhi for 10 years. Judeena was not quite 40 years old, ran her own business and was white Caucasian. Kadhi was a few years younger, a lawyer by profession and black American.

Ursina and I had the following conversation.

(1) You know my friend Judeena? She was in a relationship with this chap for 10 years. She called me yesterday – they broke up!

Really? After 10 years? That is a very long time. Is your friend OK? I mean – must be difficult . . .

Well – she is devastated, obviously. Turns out they were discussing kids . . .

Let me guess. She wanted kids, he didn't?

(2) Yes. He said he would not want to have kids with a white woman.

(3) What? He said what? Has it taken him 10 years to discover that she's white? I can imagine that your friend is devastated – to find out that your boyfriend of 10 years is a racist must be hard to swallow. What a wanker.

(4) Actually, I think his point was that he did not think it wise to raise children of mixed race in the social environment where they live.

Our conversation ran on, of course, but the remainder of what was said is of little relevance for our purpose. Especially not the parts where I was chided for judging. Definitely not those parts. We have what we need.

So let us go through the conversation again with a fine-tooth comb and analyse the dynamics.

Everything in (1) is basically setting the scene: two people splitting up after a long time together over the subject of kids. My final comment in the paragraph betrays a measure of frustration drawn from my own history of relationships – remember we discussed in an earlier chapter that I choose not to have children. The relevant point for us, however, is that my comment was presumptuous, even though only mildly so. When I spoke I did not have any information that equipped me to judge who the driving force behind the split was. However, I certainly had an expectation of what the reasons might have been.

My expectation was contradicted in (2), and my vehement reaction in (3) was driven by two emotions. One was surprise and the other one indignation about what I saw as a racist comment.

I think it is important to highlight the exact way in which I said this at the time.[75] I referred to Kadhi as a racist. Literally, what I said was that he *is* a racist. My final statement then offers another succinct, and disparaging, evaluation of Kadhi's personality.

---

[75] I am not pretending that I am transcribing a tape recording of our conversation. But I know the quality of the things I said. This conversation is substantially correct as it is written.

However, Ursina's response in (4) makes clear that neither designation was appropriate. When I branded Kadhi a racist and a wanker, I did not have any information at my disposal to warrant an evaluation of his comment, much less to critique his entire personality. Ursina's statement provided more information and illustrated that Kadhi's reasons were motivated by something other than racism.

I think the episode is a perfect illustration of what is going on when we judge others:

- We often have little or no information that allows us to properly evaluate a comment or an action.

- We relate the comment or action to our personal set of ethics, preferences or otherwise defined standards.

- We evaluate the comment or action against this frame of reference. In the instant that we are doing this, our reference frame is absolute. We do not appreciate that there may be other valid frames of reference against which the comment or action would take on a different quality.

- Having made our evaluation, we then generalise our finding. In my example, this generalisation looked like this:

  ○ Kadhi made a comment. This was a racist comment. [*my* evaluation]
  ○ ⇒ Therefore, Kadhi is a racist. [generalisation]
  ○ ⇒ Therefore, he lacks ethical maturity in every other aspect of life. [even wider generalisation, expressed as an expletive]

Often there is another layer of psychology involved when we judge others. Often a tendency to judge illustrates a lack of confidence on the part of the person doing the judging. I believe the more we are discontented with our own lives, the more we may be inclined to judge. Not only does the act of judging divert frustration, it even creates the impression, albeit

short-lived, that the judging party somehow occupies a higher
ground than the person being judged. A psychology that could
be paraphrased as 'I may not be totally happy with my life, but
I would certainly never do *that*!'

Was this subtle psychology present in my conversation
with Ursina? Yes, perhaps. I may have been slightly frustrated
by the subject of kids, at the time still relatively fresh in my
mind from previous relationships. I may also still have felt
somewhat insecure as Ursina initiated me into her world. I
may therefore have taken a stronger stance in support of her
friend than I otherwise would have done.

Who knows? What I do know is this. The episode did not
make me happy. I remember getting all worked up about what
I saw as unacceptably racist behaviour. I also remember feeling
sheepish when Kadhi's motives turned out to be something
that was not racist, and defensive when Ursina accused me,
rightly, of judging before I had all the information.

All in all, not an exactly stress-free ride to our dinner party.

More spice, please!

Forward five years. I am sitting in a restaurant with one of my
best friends. It is a balmy evening in London; we are in high
spirits, laughing and having fun. We are discussing this book
and Tom gives me excellent advice on how to make it better.
He also contributes a story which he thinks could have a place
in the first chapter. The story involves our mutual friend Sean.
Both of us knew Sean well when we were studying for a professional qualification with Amélie, our first employer, but had
lost touch with him since. I agreed that the story would sit well
in the first chapter, but it seems even more appropriate in the
context of judging. Here is the story.

When we were all working together, Sean gradually started
having a 'near-affair' with Amélie, a married colleague from
another department. I am unsure about the particulars but
they grew increasingly close and eventually got married after
Amélie divorced her husband. At the time our conversation

took place, Sean was enjoying a successful career and Amélie was happy to tend to their home and manage the upbringing of their two kids.

(1) Dude, I have a story for your book. Remember Sean? Actually this is a terrible story.

Why? What happened?

He announced to Amélie that he is going to leave her and the kids.

(2) Blimey. After – what? – almost 10 years of marriage? What brought that on?

Turns out he had an affair with a colleague from work.

Oh yeah? Funny that – at least he's consistent . . . How long has that been going on for?

Almost six years.

What? Six years? Great. How is Amélie taking it?

I'm not sure. When we spoke on the phone, she seemed as composed as you would expect anybody to be under the circumstances.

(3) This is quite drastic actually. I can never understand it when I hear things like this. It's bad enough to betray the trust of his wife like that, but he is a dad as well! You would think his kids look up to him. Hard to tell what that does to a kid . . .

Apparently, he told Amélie that he felt bored in his marriage. There wasn't enough spice, enough adventure. He sort of even blamed her for making life too dull and not being a good wife to him.

(4) I am amazed. Does that kind of warped thinking come naturally, or do you have to go on a course to learn it?

I wonder. I hear the woman he had the affair with is also married.

So what's the plan now? The two of them get together, get married and then the whole thing starts again?

Something like that. This is as bad as it gets, actually.

(5) Entirely. I can't understand why you would start a serious relationship with somebody who cheats on their partner. The only thing you know for certain about them is that they cannot be trusted!

True. Clearly, Sean did not know himself when he got married and had kids. I think that's a classic example for your book.

And it is. Sean's story is a great example of somebody who has never got to know himself, somebody who never cared to find out what his motivations are in life and who remained indifferent to the weight of the responsibility taken on when he chose to enter into a marriage with children.

But there is another angle to this experience, an angle that I think is even more relevant in the context of judging. As before, I am going to go through my conversation step by step and record the dynamics.

What Tom said in (1) is the expository part – basic information on what happened is given. My reaction in (2) is one of surprise, but not of outrage or indignation. All during (2), Tom reveals more information, but my responses remain broadly unemotional. Sure, I was sarcastic and shocked, but up to this point in the conversation I had not evaluated Sean's behaviour. So far, I had not judged.

I did a bit of judging in (3), but note the difference in quality from (3) in 'Black and white' above. I am no less outspoken in my assessment than I was five years ago in my conversation with Ursina. But now I am evaluating what Sean's lack of ethical standards might do to his family and what the repercussions of his actions might be on others. Now I am judging the action, not the person!

More information comes to light in (4), revealing that Sean's conduct might have been driven by entirely selfish and untenable reasons. Even then I did not start judging Sean the person. Yes, my response was sarcastic, but again it was not indignant. My final statement in (5) displays a tinge of judgement, and of generalisation, but still remains mild by comparison with 'Black and white'.

I believe this episode illustrates how it is possible to maintain clear moral and ethical standards *without* judging the personality of others:

- Throughout the conversation my ethical position was clear. It was uncompromising and undiluted. I judged Sean's actions to be ethically unsound, hurtful and dishonest to his wife, irresponsible and potentially damaging to his children, immature and egotistical.

- But the key is that I was judging his *actions* and not the *person*. I evaluated the actions as if they were abstract examples in a textbook on ethics or practical philosophy.

- Well, OK, this is not exactly true – since I know Sean, I can never divorce the behaviour from the man. But I noticed with positive surprise during my chat with Tom that I did not feel urged to use base language in an attempt to describe Sean's personality. I was significantly more in control and less prone to judging than five years previously.

- Lastly, this did not come at the expense of ethical substance. Throughout our exchange, I knew exactly where I stood on these matters myself.

Sure, it is tempting to associate the quality of actions with the person performing the actions. But we have to remember that we are only ever in possession of incomplete information about the reasons that motivate a person to do something. Even in my chat with Tom, the information revealed in (3) was not first-hand. In fact, it was third-hand; Sean told Amélie, who told Tom, who told me. That does not mean that the information was wrong, but it had undergone multiple interpretations when passed down the line, and it was certainly incomplete. Indeed, only if I was somehow able to examine all the evidence, if I could *be* Sean for a day, or see his mind,[76] would I perhaps be able to *understand* his motivation.

But even then understand would not mean *condone*, which means that an attempt to understand somebody's actions, even if they seem anathema to us, is oddly safe. Understanding does not dilute the strength of ethical standards we have and hence

---

[76] I'd rather not, though. Sorry Sean. No offence.

they are not at risk. Because of this we can try to look for
reasons in the behaviour of others, understand their behaviour
from an intellectual vantage point, while still preserving the
ability to know what is right and what is wrong. If we do this,
we are in a position to judge the actions in isolation and not the
actors themselves. And when we judge the actions, we find
that we become much less agitated, remain in control and keep
our balance.

And this is easy, I hear you ask? No, I do not believe it is
easy. I can only speak for myself but I found it a hard skill to
learn. In the five years separating the two conversations, I got
better at it, and I can report that I do now have less ambient
anger in my life. I can also report that I feel lighter, more
balanced and happier for it.

But non-judgement is not easy. It gets harder the more critical we are of the behaviour that we hear about. My next example illustrates this.

Dave's mum
A test case
Remember Dave Pelzer? Remember the torrent of abuse he
had to endure at the hands of his mother, the often life-threatening physical attacks, the degrading humiliations?

When you were reading about Dave, were you judging his
mother? Were you incredulous at the extent of the violence?
Were you judging her as callous, cruel, sadistic, mean? Were
you judging *her* or her actions?

Hands up who was judging *her*! My hand is up. I cannot
see yours, but you know where it is. I judged her and yet I do
not know who she is. I have never met her, have no insight into
her motives, I do not know her circumstances. I have no idea
what drove her to do the things she did.

And neither it seems did Dave. In interviews the adult Mr
Pelzer admits that he does not know the reason for his mother's abusive behaviour, or why she singled him out among his
siblings. He believes that his mother herself may have been

abused, an interpretation denied by his grandmother. He also considers it a possibility that his mother may have developed a mental illness or proved unable to deal with the pressure of bringing up four boys.[77]

I am certainly in no position to shed any light on the reason for the abuse, nor is it within my purview to do so. But what I *would* like to do is look for clues in Dave's book that give us some insight into the personality of his mother and see whether I can develop a better understanding of *why* she behaved in the way she did. My goal is to see whether it is possible to get to a stage where I judge her *actions* and not *her* as a person.

It is important to remember at this point that we are merely looking for insights and that we are not putting our own value judgements at risk by doing so. If deeper understanding was within our grasp, we still would not exonerate or condone her actions. Basically, I am using this exercise as a test to see whether my approach works, and I am using an extreme case to calibrate it. If we can achieve a detached rather than an emotional judgement in the case of Dave's mum, it seems possible to do it anywhere.

A model parent

Dave includes an account of his earliest childhood in the second chapter of his book. Entitled 'Good Times', it contains Dave's earliest childhood memories.[78] He recalls a happy and intact family life. In fact, he remembers it as better than just intact. Dave describes his family as the 'Brady Bunch of the 1960s'[79] and his life as nothing short of idyllic. The family lived in Daly City, immediately south of San Francisco. His dad worked as a fireman for the SFFD, the San Francisco Fire Department. For Dave and his two brothers, their mother

---

[77] English, Ella. 'Family Feud'. *The Boston Globe*, 26 April 2006, quoted on www.boston.com. See also Kellaway, Kate. 'No pain, no gain'. *The Observer*, 15 February 2004, quoted on www.guardian.co.uk.

[78] Pelzer 1995, pp. 17–26.

[79] Pelzer 1995, p. 17.

represented the centre of family life, and Dave describes her as 'a woman who glowed with love for her children'.[80]

His mother lived her life entirely for her family. She kept the house and garden in pristine condition, prepared imaginative and expertly cooked meals for her husband and sons and generally took charge of family matters. But more than that, she created a stimulating environment for her sons, an environment where Dave recalls feeling loved and appreciated. A sightseeing trip to Chinatown, for example, would not remain merely an interesting day out for the boys. As they were walking around the district, Dave's mother would talk about the culture and history of the Chinese people. On returning home, she would play records with music from the Orient and decorate the house with Chinese lanterns. At dinner that night, she would be wearing an Oriental robe and serve a meal modelled on Chinese cuisine.

Family trips to destinations in the region were full of adventure, Christmas celebrations filled with magic, and Dave recalls that his mum made him feel safe, warm and loved. Once at Christmas he remembers his mum crying with joy. She told him she was crying because she was so happy to have a real family.[81]

Reasons – a scenario
Dave's early account of his mum could not be further from the person that we encounter during the rest of the book.

In his account, Dave never speculates on the reason his mother changed from the model parent of the early years to the abusive tormentor he remembers for most of his childhood.

What I would like to do next is offer an illustrative scenario. The point of this exercise is to test what would happen to the quality of our judgement if we *did* have a deeper understanding of the motives that drove Dave's mum.

---

[80] Pelzer 1995, p. 18.
[81] Pelzer 1995, p. 23.

Let us recall that Dave's mum was 'happy to have a *real* family'.[82] What if something had happened that destroyed this happiness, something that she saw as a destruction of the family bonds that gave her life meaning? Something that would take away the quality she described as real?

I am now inventing the following scenario:

Dave's mum found out that her husband had fathered a child with another woman. She gave birth to Dave after her husband had fathered this child out of wedlock. She projects her frustration onto Dave, whom she sees as living evidence that her family had ceased to be intact, had ceased to be 'real'. Guilt drove Dave's father to drink and prevented him from helping his son when his wife abused Dave in his presence.

Certainly, some of Dave's account does not contradict this illustration: Dave's parents fight increasingly and Dave is almost always the subject of their quarrels.[83] Dave's mother accused him of shaming the family[84] and called him a bastard child.[85] She had her husband cremated after his death, in Dave's opinion against his father's wishes.[86]

I need to make clear again that I am presenting a purely fictitious scenario. Its only purpose is to test whether we are able to judge the *action*, rather than the *actor*, if we assume it is true.

Judging the actions

So show of hands, please! Who judges Dave's mum now? I am uncertain – I can feel my hand going up, but I am pausing half way, wavering. Who judges her *actions*? My hand is up.

If we were to pretend that my scenario was real, we would understand better why Dave's mum behaved in the way she did. We would understand that something happened that took

---

[82] My emphasis.
[83] Pelzer, Dave. *The Lost Boy*. Orion Books 1997, p. 38.
[84] Pelzer 1995, p. 36.
[85] Pelzer 1995, p. 140.
[86] Pelzer, Dave. *A Man Named Dave*. Orion Books 1999, p. 112.

away her reason for living, something that 'pulled the rug from under her feet'. If this heightened level of insight was possible, it would accomplish a number of things, in my opinion:

- We would be judging the actions and not (so much) the person. We would have more intimate knowledge of Dave's mum's personality, but our value system would have survived intact! We would certainly not condone her actions, but at least we would have some understanding of what might have driven her to abuse.

- We would maintain some emotional detachment, a distance that we were unable to keep when we read Dave's account without the benefit of the scenario.

- This distance would allow us to evaluate her actions more dispassionately and explore where and how she might have gone wrong. Perhaps we would see why Dave's mother failed to shield herself from her own emotional torment. We would understand why she was unable to choose her future in defiance of her past. We would understand that she had not found the strength to move on and deal with her demons in the constructive way Dave himself proved able to do.

To repeat, this was a theoretical exercise. We have no idea why Dave's mum did the things she did. And yet I think the exercise shows that, with better understanding, we are less prone to judging the person, even in a case as extreme as Dave Pelzer's mum.

The story above illustrates that my two maxims may also work in extreme circumstances. But these were circumstances of somebody else's life. How would we fare if confronted with circumstances that challenge the very fabric of our own ethical convictions? How would we then avoid judging? Would not judging even be desirable in such a scenario? My next story illustrates the challenge.

No yoke
Dramatis personae

Before we get into the story, you must know that I have three 'best' friends in the world. My first best friend in the world is Ursina, whom you know a little bit by now. The second one is Aaron, whom you will meet later on, and the third one is Tom, whom you met earlier. All three of them are my friends, my confidants and my counsellors. We laugh together, we go on holidays together,[87] we are close, we are serious, we are juvenile, we talk, we do stuff and the world is good when we are together. You know what it's like. The bestest of friends.

You also need to know a little bit more about Tom to fully appreciate this story. Tom has a twin brother, George, and they used to be inseparable. They went to the same school, attended the same university, where they lived in the same college, were reading the same subject and went on to complete the same degree. After university they went off to buy a house together and joined the same employer.

Then Tom married Jeanine and moved out. George went off to work on a series of projects in Japan, where he met Yabuko.

An earthquake at dinner

The story I wish to share with you takes place slightly before George and Yabuko got married. This was a time during which Tom and I were asking ourselves whether they would take this step, and whether there was a risk that the twin brothers might drift apart.

Tom and I were sitting over dinner in a restaurant by the *Thames* (we went there regularly, and again the location does not really matter, but it is nice if you know) and were discussing George and Yabuko. It is a long time ago now but our conversation went pretty much like this:

---

[87] Not necessarily all at the same time.

So, Tom . . . What's happening with George and Yabuko?

Well, it looks like they're going to get hitched.

Wow . . . great for George . . . It's brilliant that he's found someone . . . but do you think there could be a problem between
you two?

Well . . . there might be actually . . .

Do you think you may actually drift apart? I mean you have
your own life with Jeanine now . . . you guys are thinking of
having kids, perhaps . . .

I don't think that would be much of a problem. We are so close
we'll never **really** drift apart. But there are some other
issues.

Like what?

Well, she's bright and has her own career – I wonder how they'll
handle this if they ever want kids . . . and she's Japanese of
course.

Yes, well that could be an issue, if she wants him to move to
Japan perhaps . . .

I am afraid this is **the** issue, Mark.

Erm . . . what? What do you mean?

She's not Christian.

I am not sure what I said next but I know that I did not say
anything for a moment.

But he **knows** that? Sorry, I don't follow.

Not an issue for **him**. An issue for **me**. And mum.

Why? What does the fact that she is not a Christian have to do
with anything?

Christians do not get married to non-Christians.

I think I must have looked confused at that point because he
went on to elaborate:

'Don't be yoked to an unbeliever', it says in the Bible.

Huh . . . and you are basing your value judgements on a brief
statement in a 2000-year-old text that has been redacted and
translated a million times? That reflects values of an ancient
society in Judea that has absolutely nothing to do with
21st-century London?

Don't get hung up on the words, Mark. It's the concept that's
important.

But the concept is deeply discriminatory! You can't judge others
on the basis of their ethnic origins or skin colour. And I know
you don't, so why are you saying this?

You're not impressed with my reason.

I am actually appalled, Tom. How about Aaron then? How can
you be friends with him – he's Jewish you know . . .

Yes, 'friends', Mark. 'Friends' is fine – but **married** . . .

The aftershock

I have to admit that I was dumbstruck by our exchange. This
was not just anybody I was talking to. This was Tom. My friend
Tom, in whose company I had always felt safe, whose opinions
and arguments always carried something like a seal of quality.
When I discussed things with Tom, I never felt that I needed to
be cautious about the motivations that led to a statement, or of
the thought process behind it. Tom's arguments were always
the result of in-depth thought, and were never prejudiced or
intellectually lazy. As a consequence, his views were always fit
for consumption, and I felt at liberty to consider the argument
before me, and not the reasons why it may have been made.

This seal of quality broke during this conversation. I knew
of course that Tom was a convinced Christian, but had never
given that matter much thought. I hold any religious, ideological or secular faith stance to be of equal potential value, and to
this day remain shocked when confronted with a view that
does not. And here was Tom, who openly seemed to suggest
that discrimination against others on the grounds of religious
affiliations was a perfectly viable ethical basis on which to
build your life. And the worst of this, as I said before, was that
it was *Tom* who made this statement, and not just anybody.

My intellectual home had taken a hit. My confidant, Tom,
had just pronounced himself unfit to judge ethical issues.
Would our friendship survive this test unscathed?

Those were the thoughts that flashed through my mind in
the few instants during which I was struggling to regain my

composure. I remember distinctly that Tom's viewpoint unsettled me so deeply that I briefly considered leaving the table – not in an act of huffed histrionics, but simply because I did not trust myself to speak.

In the end, however, my better judgement won out. Our friendship had developed over a decade at that point; would I really jeopardise it so easily? Deep down I knew Tom did not judge others on the grounds of peripheral attributes. There was more to this, and I needed to get to the bottom of it, needed to find out how my friend could have made such a statement.

I managed to pull myself together and found the strength to make a lame attempt at a light-hearted response. 'So no chance of you getting married to Aaron anytime soon, then?' was what I was able to come up with after a few seconds of wavering. Tom took the ball and said something like 'I would have to ask Jeanine first, I guess'.

Repairing the damage
So far so good. We had saved our friendship for the moment. But was I judging Tom? Yes I was. I found it unconscionable that anybody, most of all my friend and intellectual soulmate, should judge somebody unfit as a spouse because of her religion. If I am disarmingly honest, I need to admit that I almost judged Tom as a religious bigot and, by extension, was briefly doubting his ability to make ethical evaluations of *any* kind.

Almost, but not quite. Briefly, but not finally. Instead, I tried to understand Tom's reasoning and attempted to see the issue through his eyes. Doing so took up most of what was left of our evening and a lot more conversations during the weeks and months that followed. It was one of the most difficult and painful pieces of soul-searching I had ever done, but eventually I had some answers. Here they are:

- Tom thinks that in marriage it is best to avoid conflict that may arise from parental disagreements rooted in contrasting worldviews, religions or ideologies. The reason that

Tom feels strongly about this is that to him marriage equals kids. And when you are faced with the responsibility of bringing up children, he thinks it is best to create a home environment that is as free of strife and conflict as it can be. He reasons that if parents disagree about fundamental aspects of how to bring up the kids, they will create an atmosphere of discord ultimately detrimental to the development of their children.

- I understand this argument and have some sympathy with it. As an experiment, ask yourself what you believe in strongly. This may be anything – a religion, the absence of religion, a worldview such as socialism or capitalism, or a value system of some other description. For the sake of an example, let us pin this down. Say there is a couple who wish to have children. He is a devoted Christian and she is a Muslim. Christians regard the central figure of their religion as a deity. Muslims regard the central figure of the Christian religion as a human prophet. It is clear that if my hypothetical couple got married there could be fundamental, indeed insurmountable, issues of contrasting religious belief. It is true that these can be avoided easily by not getting married.

- So Tom was entirely justified when he formulated the interfaith marriage prohibition. It was just a pragmatic view. Or was it?

- Well, it would have been had he restricted the doctrine to himself and Jeanine. Tom and Jeanine are entirely at liberty to decide for themselves that they do not wish to get married to non-Christians. But this did not happen here. Tom decided on George's behalf that, in marrying a non-Christian, his twin violated an ethical principle that held for all Christians.

- But again, did he? On closer inspection, this also turned out to be my misconception. There was something I should have remembered: that Tom and George are twins. Tom once said to me that they were so close that they were practically the same person. So Tom did not feel that he was encroaching on somebody else's right to make decisions for himself. To Tom it felt *almost* as if he was applying the marriage maxim to himself when he expressed concerns about his twin.

- Of course, that was something that, as a single child, I was entirely unable to appreciate emotionally. I do not have any siblings, let alone a twin brother, and am therefore ill-equipped to understand the quality of the bond that runs between Tom and George.

- Does Tom extend the marriage maxim to Christians who are strangers to him? Does he judge Christians who marry non-Christians in general? I must admit I do not know. If he did so, I would strongly disagree with a stance that, when measured against my own value system, would show up as unethical.

But now I am judging one of Tom's ethical maxims and no longer Tom the person.

The two maxims
Let us see how my experience fares against the two maxims I formulated above.

Maxim 1 I shall strive to understand the reasons that motivated an action or that led to a statement of opinion.
I think I can say that I acted in accordance with this maxim in this instance. Paradoxically, I found it hard to do so at first precisely *because* I knew Tom as well as I did. My initial disappointment at finding him making a statement at odds with my own value system was very much the reason I judged him so quickly at first. But, at the same time, I was strongly motivated to preserve our friendship, and that gave me the strength to enquire more deeply into the reasons behind the statement.

As I was delving deeper, for one thing I understood his values better. But I also found out things I was unable to appreciate at first, things that placed his statement into a context that I did not initially have access to.

In doing so I found that my value system remained intact. As I became able to appreciate the *reasons* for his statement, it started to sound less outrageous than it had appeared the first time I heard it. Of course, in the most extended application of the statement, the ethical values it conveyed continued to clash with mine. But in that context I had developed an ability to judge Tom's statement and not Tom *himself*.

Maxim 2 *I will remember that no single character trait defines all that we are.*
This maxim I appreciated almost from the start. After a decade of close friendship, I knew that Tom would not hold views that discriminated on the grounds of ethnicity. After painful soul-searching, I confirmed to myself that Tom's statement only represented one aspect of his value system.

What is the point?
The point of telling you at length about my experience is that it speaks very strongly against judging.

I was able to execute the first maxim because I knew Tom very well indeed and was very close to him at the time. I was able to do this because I knew him very well.

But with most people we do *not* know them very well. We would not therefore normally have the incentive to find out more about a person's motives (it is not important enough) and neither would we have access to such information if we tried (we are strangers).

Hence, it is *probable* that our assessment would be wrong if we judged the person. Purely from a point of common sense, therefore, we would do better if we did *not* judge – it took a decade of close friendship to get this one right; how much hope is there if we do not know the person we are judging at all? Unless we are in possession of *all* the relevant information, it makes no sense to judge the person. But it *does* make sense, and I would claim that it is even essential to our own well-being, to evaluate, think about and judge the *action*.

The need to judge

Judging from insecurity

OK then. I think we have explored the reasons for judging, and its dynamics, to a fair extent. If we judge the action and not the actor, we maintain more emotional control, remain more balanced and generally more poised. And this should make for a less burdened, more liberated, happier state.

Fine. But I have not yet addressed those cases in which we judge out of a sense of insecurity. I mentioned at the start of this chapter that a tendency to judge others may reflect a lack of confidence in ourselves, or may indicate some level of frustration, of dissatisfaction with our lives.

I would like to conclude this chapter with the analysis of a case of judging born out of insecurity and a discussion of what we can learn from it.

A friend in need . . .

Before Ursina and I met, she was working abroad in a number of African countries in the employment of a global medical aid organisation. The institution ran camps in often remote regions of the countries and, as a consequence, aid workers often had limited contact with the outside world or with family members and friends at home.

We are back in the early days of my relationship with Ursina, when we were busy exploring each other's worlds. Ursina told me that as a consequence of the relatively isolated existence in Africa, interactions between workers were often more intense. Friendships could grow closer more quickly than they might have done in an unconfined environment, antipathies could rise to heightened levels, relationships formed more quickly and also dissolved more easily.

On one of her missions, Ursina became friends with Richard, a fellow aid worker. When we chatted about her time in Africa, Ursina described Richard as a fount of strength to her within a world that could often be emotionally testing – an isolated world far away from the comfort of home, often full of human suffering, degrading poverty, malnourishment, disease and even war. Ursina and Richard developed a close friendship, and she drew comfort from the close mutual understanding they shared.

Richard was in a long-term relationship with a woman in the US, his country of birth. When he had left for Africa, his partner had remained at home, but they intended to get married on his return from his missions.

But Richard had a weakness. Ursina said that Richard was unable to remain faithful to his girlfriend at home and at one time appeared to have multiple relationships simultaneously with fellow aid workers. After a while, Richard left for the US to marry his long-term girlfriend, but on his return continued being unfaithful to her.

Double judge

This sets the scene for what I would like to discuss. Richard's conduct, of course, is his business. His reasons are his own, and I do not know what they were. I may object to his behaviour from the vantage point of my own personal ethical standards, and on those grounds I may judge his *actions*, but I have no business judging Richard the *person*.

That is what I know now. But I did not know it then. Quite the opposite, really. In a heroic act of judging, I managed to judge both Richard and Ursina at the same time. I judged Richard the *person* for breaking his pre- and post-marital vows, and Ursina the *person* for continuing to regard 'such a man' as her soulmate.

And the point of this . . .?

You may imagine that this was a time of frequent and heated discussions between Ursina and me, and a time during which I was so often in the proverbial dog-house that I thought about moving furniture in.

But the point of my last story is simply this: the reason I judged Ursina and Richard is not just that I disagreed with Richard's conduct and would have preferred Ursina to be equally critical of it. The reason was more fundamental and had little to do with *them* and more to do with *me*. My act of judging was born of a feeling of insecurity. My relationship with Ursina was still young. I was still at the stage where I was testing how far it was safe to lower my defences and to expose vulnerability.

My experience shows that judging may highlight a lack of balance in the life of the person who does the judging, rather than a lack of balance in the life of the person being judged.

And, importantly, I believe that it is possible to reverse this dynamic! If I train myself *not* to judge, the chances are that I will start leading a more balanced life. Why? Because I remove some or most of the ambient anger I mentioned earlier. We get less worked up at what we see as the unacceptable behaviour of others, and as we do so we focus more on our own lives than those of other people. In this case, our egocentric focus is positive! In this case, the unintended benefit is that we will find it easier to think of ourselves as agents and to take charge of our lives.

I maintain that a tendency to judge may highlight dissatisfaction, frustration, disappointment, anger or other sentiments reflecting lack of balance. I also maintain that training yourself *not* to judge helps build a more satisfied, fulfilled, confident and balanced individual.

In conclusion, let me highlight the three key qualities of non-judging that will aid our training:

- *Understanding the reasons does not mean condoning the action.*

  A deeper understanding of the reasons behind a particular behaviour does not challenge our value system. And as our own ethical standards are not at risk, deeper understanding is safe.

- *Do not judge the person – judge the action.*

  The more we understand a person's reasons, the more naturally we focus on the person's *actions* rather than the person himself. As we separate the two, we are increasingly able to focus on the action itself, and less in danger of making sweeping value judgements about the person.

- *Do not judge the person – but **do** judge the action.*

  As we go through life, we need to develop a system of personal values that keep us on the straight and narrow. Judging the *actions* of others against such a value system may reinforce it (if the action is found to fall short of a standard) or enhance it (if the action is found to exceed it). Indeed, judging the actions may give us more confidence in ourselves as we develop a clear sense of where we stand.

A can of worms – ethics

Please note how obviously I failed to say what the phrase 'where we stand' at the end of the previous paragraph actually means. I also left you in the dark about how we might develop a sense of where we stand. How do I know what values I should have? How do I know whether those I *do* have are any good? How can I know whether my framework is strong enough to function as a benchmark? But surely it would have to be if I wished to judge the actions of others? And would I not need to do just that if I wanted to banish ambient anger from my life? In the end, therefore, does all this non-judging business unravel, just when I thought I had got to firm ground at the end of this chapter?

Well . . . I think it is time that we acknowledge something. There is a difficult issue here and at some point we need to address it. The issue is tricky, and we have encountered it once before.

It is the subject of ethics. In Rule 1 we saw it in the context of deciding whether an uncomfortable character trait can stand as part of our personality or whether we need to change it. This time we realise that we cannot avoid developing a system of personal values that guides us in life.

The subject of ethics seems to pop up unbidden when we least expect it. It seems always to be there, lurking beneath the surface. Indeed, I think this may be one of the deeper insights we can draw from our discussion thus far. The ability to like ourselves, know who we are, respect ourselves and develop confidence in ourselves ultimately rests on an ability to define ethical personal benchmarks.

We have come far enough to *acknowledge* this. But perhaps not far enough yet to *deal with it*. So for now I prefer to leave this particular can of worms unopened and concentrate on other aspects that we need to get right. I am going to let the worms out in the penultimate chapter.

Let us return to matters at hand. Judging others is not a good thing, we heard. But what about the other side of the spectrum? What if we do not feel inclined to *judge* but to seek help? What if we need to ask others for advice? This, it turns out, is another crucial life skill to learn. And – you guessed it – it is not as simple as it may sound.

RULE 6

Seek advice

How to listen to others

You do not take advice like a pill

As we continue to assemble our toolkit for a happy life, we are beginning to realise that the roots of happiness seem to be firmly planted in ourselves. EXPERIENCE MINING helps to improve self-knowledge. We get better at making decisions when we apply methods that render the unconscious conscious. We stand a fair chance of unlocking the power to act if we stop blaming circumstance. We find a heightened sense of balance when we stop judging others.

Fine. But what do we do when we are unsure of ourselves? Surely we are not alone on the planet? Surely we have friends and relatives and can turn to them for advice? Surely they would be able to guide us, would know what to do, would help us through rough patches?

Yes, of course. We all look to our friends for advice and to our confidants for guidance. We do this naturally if something is amiss, if we are uncertain about what to do or if we simply wish to share. And we do this, often unconsciously, when we hang out, go for a drink after work, have dinner or go on holiday together.

But let us not kid ourselves. They are our friends, some are our confidants, soulmates even, our mum and dad, our siblings or other relatives who know us intimately. But no matter how close we are to our friends, they are still different people and will judge a situation from their own vantage points, give advice that may be coloured, biased or reflect their own personal preferences. A parent, sibling or other relative may be protective, a confidant may be supportive but insufficiently assertive, a friend may lack empathy.

I believe that taking advice is a skill that has to be learned before we can add it to our arsenal of tools in the pursuit of happiness. What piece of advice feels *right*? Which should we follow? Which must we reject? And, since the seeking of advice is usually part of some form of decision-making process, can we use the decision tools to aid us? Can we use the DICE and ABACUS TESTS?

The four components of advice

Let us take that last one first. Yes, the situations feel similar and the decision-making tests may work to some extent. But if they do, they would come in at a later stage of the process; they cannot come first.

Remember the DICE TEST? This was a simple tool that only worked in relatively trivial situations. Shall we go to Cornwall or the Lake District on holiday? Shall I go out with that bloke on a second date? The chances are that for decisions like that we would not really seek advice. We may chat to friends and acquaintances in the pub, get a few recommendations and views, but that is it. We can use the DICE TEST to complement other people's views if the situation gets too confusing and no consistent view emerges.

So what about the ABACUS TEST? This was a more intricate tool that allowed an analysis of the underlying dynamics of a situation. The ABACUS TEST may indeed aid us in weighing up the advice, but it seems to me that we need to do a different kind of analysis first, and then adapt the test slightly if we wish to use it.

What we need to do first is understand the dynamics involved when we take advice. It seems to me that there are four fundamental components to advice taking. We need to develop an in-depth understanding of each before we go any further.

Component one: How well do I know myself?

Yes, I am afraid we are back at the beginning. I need to have a developed understanding of myself before I know what advice to take. I am aware that this sounds wrong – don't you need advice precisely because you do *not* know yourself well?

Well, maybe, but if I do not know myself well, I will be less able to separate good from bad advice. This may be unfortunate but it cannot be helped. It highlights yet again that self-knowledge is key in the pursuit of – well, anything really. The less developed my self-knowledge, the more I am at the mercy of my advisors, and the more I have to hope that my confidants know me well, or indeed that they know me better than I know myself.

But if I *do* know myself well, I will be able to sift through the advice given and weigh up whether and to what extent suggestions are appropriate for me, and whether they fit my personality and abilities. Advice will still be crucial, but I will be more expert at using it. I will depend less on my advisors, and it will be less important that they know me well.

Component two: How well do my advisors know me?

It is important that my advisors know me well. This is perhaps obvious, but still sufficiently important to note explicitly. The better my advisors know me, the more appropriate the advice I receive will be. If they only know me superficially, they may not know what is right for me; if they know me well, they might. *Might*, however, is the operative word – whether my advisors will give me appropriate advice will also depend on the degree to which they are able to empathise with me.

Component three: How well do I know my advisors?

For this reason, it would be preferable if I had an in-depth knowledge of those who give me advice. What is their personality? What is their background? What are their aspirations in life? If I am able to develop a fair understanding of who my advisors are, I will be able to assess why they are advising me in a particular way, and to what extent the advice may be coloured by their own personalities or life situations.

Component four: How well do I know how well my advisors know me?

This is a bit of a mouthful and may sound overly convoluted, but in my view it is a solid requirement when listening to advice. Put more simply, this requirement is similar to asking how much I trust my advisors to give me the appropriate advice.

I need to understand consciously whether my advisors are sufficiently empathetic and well-meaning to give advice that is not dominated by their own viewpoints but by their knowledge of mine.

Here is an example of what I mean. If I gave Ursina a box of dark chocolates, which I like but she hates, she would not have much use for the present. But if I gave her liquorice, which I detest but she loves, she would smile at me and be happy.

If you have somebody who gives you the liquorice equivalent of advice, you can relax. You are in good hands. You have found the highest calibre of advisor.

Interplay

Category 1 – maximise knowledge about myself

Of course, in real life the four components are usually tightly interwoven and inseparable. Still, let me briefly play around

with the concepts – I think we may develop a better understanding of how the four components interact.

I think components one and two may be the most obvious
pair to examine first. As a thought experiment, assume it is
possible to know somebody perfectly, 100 per cent. If my self-
knowledge was perfect, I would not need somebody else to
give me advice. It would be irrelevant how well others know
me, and I could be indifferent to the depth of their knowledge
of me.

But if my self-knowledge was low, say zero, I would need
my advisor to know me as well as possible. *Some*body needs to
know me. It is preferable if I am that person. But if I have a
'liquorice' advisor, that would be good too. And if it is both,
that would be best.

In reality, my advisor and I will both have imperfect
knowledge of me. The goal in taking advice, therefore, is to
maximise the sum. Put simply, I need to strive to know myself
as well as possible, and I need to ask advice of those who
know me best. This would make for the most powerful combination. It is a *necessary* combination if I seek advice on potentially life-changing issues. Of course, if I have such a friend, I
would be foolish not to ask her opinion on less pressing
matters as well . . .

Category 2 – maximise knowledge about my advisors

This dynamic combines components one and three. If I do not
have a friend who knows me well enough to give unbiased
advice, second best are those who are still close to me but who
are likely to give advice from their point of view. Put simply, if
the time-honoured basic question of advice seekers everywhere is 'What should I do?', they are the ones who would
answer, 'If I was in your situation, it would be right for me if I
did this . . .', rather than the more empathetic, 'Knowing you, I
think it is best for you if you do this . . .'

Advisors of this calibre are still very important, and we are
lucky to have them. However, with them I am more *on my own*

and need to be more on guard. It is relatively more important that I know myself *and* my advisors well, and I need to be consciously aware that the advice I receive has a strong subjective colouring.

Advice accepted

Not a big ask

As ever, let us now read through a few examples from my life and those of my friends and acquaintances. I will start off with some stories where advice was given and accepted, followed by others a bit later on where advice was rejected. We will discuss the dynamics of each and see what we can learn in the final section of this chapter.

The first story in this category is about Ursina and me thrashing out the terms of our life together. After more than a year of being together, we discovered that going from date to date and weekend to weekend before spending time together again had started to feel increasingly unnatural. So we made the decision – we would be moving in together. Ursina would sell her place, move in with me and we would look for a new place to buy together.

Good plan. There was just one niggle. As I mentioned earlier, I am a very private person at home and rarely have friends or family staying at my place. Ursina has a more normal attitude to hospitality and enjoys having friends over for a few days at a time. Still, while having friends over was just a 'nice to have', she made it quite clear that she would see it as a deal-breaker if her sister and her dad could not come down to London and stay with us.

Well, I could not really argue with this. And yet, the idea of having people staying over at regular intervals was alien to me and required some soul-searching. But whom could I ask? Ursina's position was clear. I would have to sit Tom and Aaron down for a chat. But I decided to do something else first. I would take a straw poll of opinions from people I liked as mates but who were not particularly close to me otherwise.

I must have asked about 10 people what they thought about it and what they would do. One said: 'Whatever dude. Sort it out.' Some acknowledged that this can be tricky but did not see a big problem with it. Nobody really appreciated my, admittedly extreme, need for privacy, and one person said something that still sticks in my mind to this day.

He said: 'That is not such a big ask, really.' Well. Not a particularly insightful comment but when he said it something clicked. I thought to myself actually, he's right. It is not a big ask. Her relatives will be over a few times a year, it will make Ursina happy, which in turn will make me happy, and that will be the end of it.

What had happened? Why did my reservations evaporate when I heard his simple statement? I think because it was just that: simple. His statement stripped the issue of deeper layers of perceived complexity, layers which I then realised were not really there at all. His sober, matter-of-fact statement carried the following message: 'Don't be such a fusspot. This is not a big thing so get on with it.'

And this message echoed what everybody else was telling me. By getting a straw poll of opinions from people who were not close to me, I managed to look at the issue from a detached, uncomplicated perspective. I still talked to Tom and Aaron about it but had basically already made up my mind. It was not a big thing so I would not treat it as a big thing.

Was this the right decision? After a year of living at mine, we finally found and bought a place together. It was big enough to have a small spare room, which we use as a study and which doubles as a guestroom for those who want it. When Ursina's family come down, I have found that it is a delight having them and that my private sphere is not threatened. I even had Aaron stay over, something that we had never done before, and it was good fun having him there.

So yes, the advice delivered in my straw poll proved exactly right. The experience has also demonstrated a surprising insight – sometimes it can be beneficial to seek the views of those to whom we are not that close. Views gathered in this way can add a disinterested perspective we may not be getting from confidants and soulmates. I still sought an in-depth discussion with my best friends, but learned to use the straw poll as an additional tool for gathering advice in situations in which it is appropriate.

Love, actuary!

Most of us will ask ourselves at some point in our lives what to do when our formal education is over, when we have passed GCSEs, graduated from college or university, completed voluntary training.

When Aaron was about to graduate from university, he was asking himself exactly that. What to do with a degree in Physics? Stay in research? Join a company? But if the latter, which company, which field, doing what?

The institution that offers counselling services for such existential questions is the Careers Advisory Service on campus. Most universities have one, and so Aaron went off to book a session. The advisor took a look at his course, recognised it to be Physics and pulled out a list with jobs deemed suitable for graduates of numbers-based subjects. The list was structured alphabetically and the second profession listed was actuary, right after accountant. Aaron asked the chap in the office about the nature of the profession and was informed that it was 'mathematics of insurance'. Actuaries, Aaron heard, can climb to the top of the managerial hierarchy in insurance companies if they are good enough. The training is mostly mathematical so should suit him down to the ground.

Well, Aaron did not really know about insurance, and it was not sounding very glamorous. But mathematics? Yes, that he could do, and a professional qualification was good to have.

So Aaron filled in a few application forms and eventually joined the insurance company where we met.

OK, maybe I was a bit too flippant in my description of Aaron's thought process and the quality of the careers advice. But Aaron confirmed to me that in essence my account is not much off the mark. Before his trip to the careers office he had never heard of actuaries, and his decision to follow the advice of the careers office was not based on much additional research into the nature of the profession.

Was that the right decision? Well, after qualifying as an actuary, Aaron worked in a number of jobs within insurance, consultancy and banking. I would be the first to say that he is having a successful career and has done exceptionally well. But when you ask him whether he is happy, he would probably tell you that he has never much enjoyed his life as an actuary, or even as a professional in the wider context of the City. Of course, there have been periods and projects that were challenging and intellectually rewarding, but I have never had the impression that Aaron regarded his professional life as fulfilling.

He would agree. Aaron recently quit his job to take time out and explore what he really wants to do, find out what would give his life purpose. It would be blatantly simplistic to trace all this back to the instance in the careers office when the advisor handed him the computer-generated list of professions. But Aaron's lack of work satisfaction is not entirely divorced from that experience.

I believe this is an example where the advice seeker did not know himself sufficiently to evaluate the advice he was given. Neither did the advisor know his client well enough to give more than the most perfunctory advice. Finally, the advice seeker did not treat his counsellor sceptically enough to see this. In the end, I believe Aaron would be the first to admit that he ended up in the wrong profession. The initial reason for this was insufficient knowledge of himself, of his advisor and of the relationship between his advisor and himself.

Class 4!

In England, national service was abolished in 1960 in favour of the establishment of professional forces, and the last conscripted soldiers were demobilised in 1963. In Germany, conscription existed between 1956 and 2011, when it was officially put into abeyance. Actually, for our purposes, what concerns us is not so much that national service is now no longer compulsory but that it very much was when I was a teenager. At the time, there was one event that every 18-year-old male adolescent would anticipate with mixed feelings. This was the medical examination carried out to assess whether a conscript would be fit to join the military. Feelings were mixed as most would regard national service as an unwelcome duty, a chore that had to be completed before getting on with your life. As such, there was always the fortuitous possibility that you might be pronounced class 5, meaning unfit to serve, for a trivial medical condition such as an allergy to nuts.

When the day came for me, I took myself down to the local draft bureau and entered the system. I was ordered[88] into the examination room, where I was addressed by an overweight man in a white coat. I was measured, weighed and asked to do a number of squats. I started my first exercise with my arms by my side but the army doctors were quick to offer helpful counsel on the correct form. 'Put your arms up or you fall backwards into the shit', I heard. Thus encouraged, I completed 10 squats correctly, and then presented myself for my heart rate to be measured.

The doctor listened attentively for a moment to the sounds in his stethoscope, and then turned to the clerk who was recording the results. 'Heart arhythmia. Class 4.'

I was devastated. I remember finding the whole process disconcerting and uncomfortable. The obvious pleasure on the

---

[88] Although potential conscripts were still civilians at the time of the medical assessment, the forces enjoyed making the point that military communications were able to dispense with expressions such as 'please' or 'would you mind'.

part of the examiners to show the civvies what was what in the army, the deliberate absence of polite conversation and the obvious disillusionment of the doctors with their own lives all combined to create a depersonalising, even hostile, atmosphere. The final medical verdict was worrying, to say the least. And class 4 meant that my draft would be deferred until I graduated from university, so I had not even gained the benefit of exemption for medical reasons.

I remember going home deeply unsettled and concerned. What did heart arhythmia mean? It did not sound trivial – did I have a heart disease? And if so, how would this affect my life? I arrived home – as usual for a German college graduate, I was still sponging off my parents – and told my mum about my concerns.

My mum proved to be the best counsellor I have ever had. She announced categorically that I did not have a heart condition and that the army doctors were impolite, useless scoundrels. She explained to me that I was of a nervous disposition and had always been oversensitive to what was going on around me. This tendency had first become obvious at a very early age when I developed a severe stutter. This condition had turned out to be purely psychological and had disappeared in the first year at school as my self-confidence grew. Mum asked me whether I had felt nervous during the examination and I told her that I had, and also why. When mum heard about the bedside manner of the doctors, she concluded that her earlier assessment of their professional qualifications had been entirely accurate and she advised me as follows:

'You don't have heart arhythmia. That's bollocks.[89] You have a nervous disposition and the doctors made you uncomfortable. That's it. Look on the bright side – you'll be able to go to university immediately and do what you like best. A few years in, you can take an independent medical exam if you

---

[89] Mum could be formidable.

want. For now, I wouldn't do anything. Don't worry. You are healthy, but you worry too much.' Then she gave me a big hug and the matter was forgotten.

Was I right to follow her advice to the letter? Are you kidding? Have I ever been that right again? I did exactly what she said. I started university and, as my self-confidence grew, I gradually became calmer and less worried. A few years in, I had a proper medical examination with a 72-hour heart monitor and the result came back fine.

This is a classic example of a situation where your advisor knows you better than you do yourself. My mum had no medical training but she did have a high level of penetrating self-knowledge. She knew my symptoms from her own disposition, and also knew that I took after her in this respect more than I did after my dad. I was out of my depth in the instance I shared with you, and too young and immature to know myself well.

But there was one thing I *did* know. I knew that I could trust my mum unreservedly to know me best. This knowledge may not sound like much, but it is crucial. If you do not know yourself well, you need an advisor who does. But you also need to understand, on a conscious level, that your advisor knows you better than you do yourself, and that counsel given is in *your* best interest, and not that of the advisor. If you do not know that, you will not be able to decide whether it is safe to follow the advice given or reject it.

Conflicting counsel
Recently I attended a school reunion party in Germany. As is the nature of these events, they reconnect you with lots of people you have not seen in a long time, in my case for more than a decade. At the event I ran into a chap with whom I had been good friends at school. We naturally reconnected almost immediately and after a few drinks he told me that a few years earlier he had decided to jack it in and start again. When we spoke he had just completed his qualification as a

physiotherapist and was waiting for his first employment at a local hotel to start.

But there was a catch. He had rather depleted the family's financial resources to pay for the tuition leading to his new professional qualification. He simply could not afford to do nothing for a month. So he had been looking for temporary employment and went off to an interview with a company that handled data management as an outsourcing agent for businesses. He rocked up to the interview and was immediately horrified. The company's premises were in a run-down area of town, the systems he would be using were old and of dubious origin, his work place was squalid and his boss rude. He left with an uneasy feeling, torn between the need to earn some money and his reluctance to work in the conditions he had found.

He told me that the situation started to affect his sleep patterns, and when he heard that he had been offered the job he asked his wife and his dad for advice. Unfortunately, the advice he got was not unanimous. His wife said it was just temporary for a month, that they needed the money and that he should knuckle down and get on with it until he started his new career. His dad said that if he felt uncomfortable on a personal level with it he should not do it. Money may be tight, but nothing was worth doing that he knew deep down was wrong for him. My friend decided not to take the job and was immediately able to sleep easy again.

On the face of it, this story is simple enough. However, I think it exemplifies some of the dynamics we were talking about earlier. Let me focus on three of the four components involved in the dynamics of advice taking.

How well do I know myself? My friend's knowledge of himself was relatively deep, at least as far as it related to the job offer. He knew he needed the money but, as his sleep patterns testified, he also knew he did not like the professional environment he was supposed to join.

How well do I know my advisor? In this case there were two advisors, and my friend knew them both well. He had been with his wife for 15 years, and as far as I could tell from our conversation, they had a good and trusting relationship. She had supported his decision to retrain and had stood by him through three difficult years. He also knew his dad well, with whom he had established a relationship of trust over the years throughout his life.

How much do I trust my advisor to know me? My friend was consciously aware that his wife, after three lean years, was approaching the end of her tether. Her advice was given primarily from the point of view of what was right for the family and only secondarily reflected his personal needs. She was giving him 'I want you to do this' advice, and my friend knew this!

His dad, by contrast, did not have the same intimate and practical involvement with his son. He did not live with him and had only observed the family's financial difficulties from a distance. Perhaps counter-intuitively this left him free to focus on his son the *person* and disregard his son the *breadwinner*. His advice was of the 'Knowing you, I think you should do this . . .' kind. He was able to empathise, whereas my friend's wife, in that instance, was not.

He took his dad's advice and we know that it was the right thing to do – his sleep patterns normalised immediately.

I believe the story demonstrates two things. Often we know instinctively what the right decision is since we know subconsciously what course of action we need to take. If my friend had used the DICE TEST to decide whose advice to follow, he would have felt dismay had the dice dictated that he heed his wife's counsel, and relief had they mandated his dad's.

If, in addition to this, we know *why* our advisors advise us in a certain way, we become invincible! In this case we will only heed the advice that is right for us and ignore that which is wrong.

Advice rejected

Sounds suicidal, mate!

A few years ago I had dinner with a mate of mine. I was in the process of moving to another firm and we were discussing the merits of various options and my preferred choice.

This guy was not a close friend, but we were easy in each other's company, shared the same taste in music and had good laughs together. We had worked together for a brief spell in the past, and occasionally went out for a drink or to have dinner. Neither of us had been to the other person's home.

My mate disliked my preferred choice of firm and advised me against it. He saw the small size of the broker house and its specialised business model as a 'suicidal' risk and advised me to wait for other opportunities at larger investment banks.

However, I knew him well enough to understand that it was his personal preference to work at larger houses. I knew that his personality was better suited to the culture you find in the banks known as bulge bracket. And, most importantly, I knew that he assumed I was like him, and that he failed to appreciate that I was not. I prefer to work in smaller houses, in environments which are entrepreneurial, where the culture feels hungry, where people have something to prove.

I did not take his advice and I joined the firm I liked. I enjoyed many happy and fulfilled years with that employer and know that I made the right choice at the time. I was able to reject his advice because I knew both myself *and* him well enough to detect the personal colour of his suggestion.

Get a dodgy geezer in!

A few years ago, Ursina and I decided that the little terrace at the back of our house needed some tender loving care. Well, more than some, actually. The terrace was a mess, with the floor stripped down to the supports, the walls discoloured and

discarded bits and pieces piled in every corner. This had to be
done, there was no question about it.

We spent some time thinking about how to do this renova-
tion work. Should we get a company in that specialised in the
design of small gardens? Should we design it ourselves and
ask a building company to complete the project?

This was not a big decision but I still asked one of my
acquaintances how he would do it. I knew he had just built a
terrace in his own garden so maybe his advice would be
valuable.

When I asked, he looked at me and said, 'Get a dodgy
geezer in, dude!'

Ah. So not that valuable then, his advice. It turned out that
he had paid his builders in cash and they had split the unpaid
VAT between them. I knew with certainty that this option was
not something we would consider. For one thing, there is the
question of liability. If the work was done inexpertly and as a
consequence damage to our or a neighbouring property
occurred, we would not have any legal protection. And also
we were uncomfortable with having the work completed by
dodgy geezers for, dare I say it, ethical reasons.[90]

So this was never an option. Truth be told, I never asked my
friend that seriously because I was half expecting him to give
me that kind of answer. There was no soul-searching involved
in this case, but the dynamics of the advice taking were still the
same. I knew myself and my advisor well. I knew what type of
person my mate was and that he always got away with things
like that. I knew that I was not like him, and I also knew that he
was not really giving me advice. He told me what he had done,
and therefore what he would do if he was in my shoes.

Bottom line: if you know yourself well, you will not follow
advice that does not work for you.

---

[90] Well, there it is again. A question of ethics popping up, as if out of nowhere.
Penultimate chapter . . .

A fast ride

A few years ago Ursina and I went off on holiday to a beach somewhere for 10 days. We had a great time. I loved it there – all the water sports you could name, plus tennis, golf, food (a lot of food, as I discovered after a cursory glance at the bathroom scales later) – and tubing.

Tubing is something we all know from beach holidays. Basically, it involves sitting in an oversized inflated ring and being pulled across the water by a boat. Typically, the experience is designed for two people and the idea is that you and a friend get into one ring each and the dynamics of the pull make them come together and bounce off each other.

Ursina loves this activity and, as we were whizzing across the water, shrieking and laughing, I had a thought at the back of my mind. The thought was this: 'This is excellent fun. I wonder what this would be like if the boat went any faster?' Back on the beach, I shared this thought with Ursina and asked her whether I should ask Etienne (the chap from the water sports business on the beach who had been driving the boat) to go faster. Ursina's advice was not to try that – in her experience the rings become more unstable the faster you go.

And you know what happened next, because this anecdote is under the heading 'Advice *not* taken'. Off I went to find Brad, another guest in the hotel with whom I had started to get along really well. Brad was one of those guys who was into extreme sports (waterskiing, wakeboarding, mogul-skiing, downhill mountain biking etc.). He also was easily twice my weight (all muscle mass, I am envious to report).

So Brad and I went down to the beach, put our names down for tubing and squeezed ourselves into the contraptions. Well, Brad did. He filled out his tube nice and snug, and his weight sealed it to the surface of the water. I sort of slouched in mine as though in a comfy chair. Then we asked Etienne to go really fast. Etienne was not surprised to hear this from us and he took off.

The boat's 100 hp outboarder roared. The water churned. The tubes tilted way beyond 45 degrees. The boat pulled away majestically, flicking the tubes into the horizontal and flinging them outside the wake.

I sensed immediately that something was different. It was not just that you had to hold on with real strength now; there was something else, and it was more subtle. The sound the tube made on the water was somehow lighter, like a flickering whisper, rather than the continuous prattle I remembered from my ride with Ursina. And the boat was still accelerating. Turning right. My tube was hurtling towards the wake. It felt light. There was Brad, closing in. My tube hit the wake. Brad smashed into my tube with full force. My tube jolted sideways. It left the wake and immediately became airborne. And something else became airborne too. I was flung like a stone from a slingshot into the air at 40 mph, hitting the water hard not long after.

When I got back to the surface, I saw Etienne's semi-concerned look and heard Brad's uncontrollable laughter. I shouted 'That's what I am talking about!' – an assessment that was as motivated by a desire to communicate to Etienne that I was fine (he had a professional duty of care) as by a need to show Brad that I was well tough (he was a lot better at extreme sports than I was), but also, most worryingly perhaps, by genuine delight.

Back on shore I discovered that I was not nearly as tough as I wanted to be. It turned out that I had hit the water hard head first and as a consequence my neck muscles had gone into spasm. By evening, my range of movement was limited and my neck was hurting.

This was not a serious injury and it cleared up in a day or so. But the moral of the story is clear. Ursina's advice not to go crazy on the speed was meant well and had turned out to be good advice. I ignored it because I thought that moderate speeds were boring and that I would be able to handle extreme tubing. Ursina had known me better than I did in that instance.

And no, I did not go tubing again for the rest of the holiday . . .

This would be great for you

After a few years of working for my first employer (an insurance company based in the countryside), I changed jobs and joined the branch of a German commercial bank in London. I was overjoyed at making the transition; for one thing, it meant I could move back to the big city. The other breakthrough was that I could leave life as an actuarial graduate behind and turn my mind to something I enjoyed more and, I hoped, would be better at.

At first, life at the bank was interesting and engaging. But after half a year or so I had started to notice that its culture was risk-averse and that the procedure for obtaining internal approval for loans was lengthy, bureaucratic and generally an uphill struggle. I had become interested in a certain class of non-standard transactions, and these proved even more difficult to promote than mainstream loan agreements known as plain vanilla. As a result, six months in I had already started to feel restless and moderately frustrated.

I started reading the job ads in the *Financial Times*. Not for any specific purpose. Just to see what opportunities were out there, in theory. One day I saw an advertisement which I just could not ignore. A firm of consultants was looking for somebody to join an interdisciplinary team of professionals to structure deals of exactly the nature I was interested in. I applied and after an initial chat was invited for the real interview.

In the interview it quickly became clear to me that I was out of my depth. I had heard of most things the interviewers wished to discuss but my knowledge was qualitative at best, and certainly not profound enough to work on a structuring team. However, unperturbed by this I proceeded to ask questions that were designed to demonstrate an intelligent, albeit not *informed*, approach to the subjects at hand. Since I had nothing to lose, I also freely criticised some standard approaches to certain problems, sharing my conviction that they did not make all that much sense.

Of course, you can see where this is going. It turned out that the standard approaches *did* make sense but that I just did not appreciate some of the subtleties. But it also turned out that my criticism had been reasonable, and my interviewers interpreted my irreverence as the quality of somebody who would be able to think outside the box. A week later I received a letter congratulating me and offering me the job.

Ah. Now I had a problem. Yes, as an opportunity this was exactly what I was hoping for. But I was certain that if I accepted the offer I would be setting myself up to fail. This had nothing to do with lack of self-confidence. Quite the opposite; self-confidence and a feeling of having nothing to lose, of playing a game, were the reasons I was in this predicament in the first place. But it was clear in my mind that I had delivered something in the interview that I would not be able to deliver on the job. It is one thing to look smart in a brief, largely theoretical discussion with somebody. It is quite another thing to deliver a marketable product as part of a structuring team working to deadlines. So I made up my mind. In the final chat to discuss terms and conditions I would invent some pretext allowing me to turn down the offer gracefully.

When I arrived for the chat on terms, everybody was all smiles. Excellent, I had done very well against more experienced competition and they were very pleased that I was coming on board. Would I sit here and would I like a coffee or some water? They would pay me twice what I was earning at the bank. The job would involve a lot of international travel, and the deal team I was joining was highly regarded internally. Of course, there was the option of a car and the potential for a hefty bonus.

Oh dear. This was not going to be easy. Twice my current salary? Plus bonus? And a car? And on top of that, everybody seemed to be courting me. It felt great. It was very seductive. I almost caved in, but there was the niggling sensation at the back of my mind that smiles would quickly turn into frowns when people discovered that I was not able to deliver. And then what? What would be next? How do you move on once you have established a track record of mediocre performance? So I braced myself inwardly and told them.

Why, you may ask, am I telling you this story in the context of taking advice? Because of what came next. They were not going to take my rejection lying down. They advised me to accept the offer. They went through my list of concerns and refuted every single one of them. I would not have sole responsibility, there would be some training, everybody would always be open and available if I had questions and I would be great in this role. When I remained steadfast in my resolution to turn down the offer, they finally accepted my decision but said they suspected there was something I was not telling them.

Smart guys. There was indeed. I knew that I had dazzled them in the interview by portraying myself as a far more accomplished professional than I really was. What my inter-viewers interpreted as irreverence and lateral thought in real-ity was merely a limited understanding of the standard tech-niques used in financial engineering.

I knew this, but they did not. I also knew that they did not know. And that is why I did not take their advice and accept the offer. I knew myself better than my advisors in this instance, and I also knew who my advisors thought I was. This knowl-edge enabled me to act against their counselling, even though the trimmings of the job were seductive, the evaluation of my abilities flattering and the opportunity a promise of escape from the frustration I was feeling at the bank.

Was it right to ignore their advice and turn down the offer?

Well. We can only make decisions and live with them; we cannot go back, make an alternative decision and observe the outcome. All I can say is that it felt right to turn down the offer and that I have had a fulfilling and meaningful career since then, progressing from commercial banking to stockbroking some 18 months after this episode. Had I performed a DICE TEST at the time, I very definitely would have felt relief had they simply accepted my decision to turn them down with no attempts to persuade me to change my mind.

Therefore, I would say that yes, turning down the offer despite advice to the contrary, and against the seduction of material gain and personal flattery, was the right decision.

Quit the rat race

Ursina was 21 when she left university with a degree in accountancy, 24 when she was a freshly baked ACA,[91] and 29 when she was ready to jack it all in. After a decade-long career in finance, she found that she was actually not enjoying what she was doing, that she was missing a deeper purpose in her job, that she was not living an authentic life. Ursina was at a stage in her life where she needed to feel that she was positively contributing to society, that the work she was doing had a measurable impact.

But what to do? Ursina told me that she had an epiphany while watching television. She was watching a documentary about Sean Devereux, an English aid worker for UNICEF who was active in a number of African countries before being killed in Somalia in 1993. Devereux's example inspired her to apply to the Red Cross, an organisation with which she was to work for three years on several missions to Africa, the Caucuses and wartime Bosnia.

But before she joined, there was advice. Some of it was neutral, some of it cautionary, but none of it encouraging. Her advisors were parents, friends and family. The closest to a supportive comment was the observation that she should go ahead if it was right for her. Everyone pointed out that there would be a serious hiatus in her business career as a

---

[91] Associate Chartered Accountant in the Institute of Chartered Accountancy in England and Wales.

consequence, that it would be difficult to re-enter and that aid work would put her in physical danger.

All of it was true. It is no secret that aid workers operate in politically unstable environments and that philanthropy is not in itself conducive to advancing a business career. And yet Ursina chose to reject advice urging her to rethink her decision and she joined the Red Cross anyway.

Why? Because she knew herself and because she knew her advisors. It is a parent's job to protect their children. Parental advice not to pursue aid work therefore was well meant but also one-sided. Most of her friends had pursued careers in business, and they focussed on the potential risk to continued development that a career break might bring. But her friends mostly liked their careers and saw them as fulfilling and meaningful. Their advice was therefore also given more from the point of view of themselves and less from a position of empathy.

Ursina, meanwhile, knew that she needed fulfilment just as much as her friends did. And she had discovered how to find it. When she made the decision to join the Red Cross, that decision was made as an examined stance. It was not made *against* explicit advice to the contrary, but it was made after weighing the concerns of her advisors and deciding that the benefits would outweigh the potential risks.

Was it the right decision to listen to herself more than to her advisors? I would say yes. A decade after leaving the Red Cross, Ursina discovered that the risks her advisors had warned her about at the time were real. Her time as an aid worker made it harder to develop a traditional career in finance. But Ursina says that was a price worth paying for what she received in exchange. A more balanced life. A knowledge of what is meaningful. And the satisfaction of making the right decision for herself.

Ursina was able to make this decision because she knew herself well, because she knew what she needed and how to get it. I believe decisions of this nature are the most satisfying in life, and although we must seek advice and weigh it up responsibly, eventually we answer only to ourselves.

Eventually, how well we know ourselves will dictate which advice to heed and which to reject.

A medical emergency

About six months ago my right arm started hurting. It just did, without warning. I went to bed one evening and it was not hurting; I woke up in the morning and it was. It was hurting inside the elbow joint, and within a few days it got so bad that it started disturbing my sleep.

Ever since I was little I have been a bit of a wild child. In my teens and during my 20s, I was into skateboarding, then roller-blading and currently it is skiing, waterskiing, wakeboarding and downhill mountain biking. The reason I am telling you this is because you need to know that aches and pains, muscle sprains and hurting joints are part of my life, to the point that I have stopped paying attention to them. My way of dealing with an injury of this nature is to ignore it. And although my body no longer heals as quickly as it used to, I am embarrassed to say that my attitude has yet to mature in a way commensurate with my age.

So you will not be surprised to hear that I ignored the pain in my arm, although I was not able to attribute it to a particular sporting accident or other specific cause. Still, I was waiting for it to get better, and when it did I paid no further attention to it.

Until one day it struck me that the pain had never fully disappeared and that the condition had not improved further. That is when I started to worry – an unexplained pain in the joint that just sprang up and that had lingered for months? What could be wrong? Some disease of the joints? Perhaps something worse – maybe other joints were going to be affected too?

Now this reaction may strike you as odd but, as much as I am perhaps a wild child when it comes to sports, I am also a

cry baby when things go wrong in ways that I have not encountered before. I told Ursina and she gave me the predictable
answer: 'You have had this for three months? Well have it
checked out, baby.'

But I did not follow her pragmatic advice. I know that
Ursina has an entirely different attitude from me to medical
problems. Something's wrong, you go and see the doctor, they
sort it out. End of story. But I was afraid of the insight that a
visit to the doctor might bring, and also was still secretly
hoping that the pain might vanish, thus exonerating my treas-
ured approach of doing nothing. In some really silly way, I still
thought that I was above aches and pains, and I thought that I
would be somehow acknowledging to myself that I was getting
older if I promoted the pain to an official condition by going to
the doctor's.

And so I lived with the pain for another three months,
pride and fear keeping me away from the GP practice.

Until finally even I had had enough and so gave in. I saw
the GP and she told me I had a condition known as lateral
epicondylitis, more commonly known as tennis elbow. She
prescribed some anti-inflammatory pills and suggested I see a
physiotherapist. The combination of six of the pills and five
sessions at the physio made the problem disappear, and the
cause was diagnosed as probably relating to the bad position I
had started to assume when sitting at my desk at home writing
this book.

Let me recap, then. I had a pain in my elbow because I was
sitting badly at my desk. After being diagnosed, the problem
disappeared after a few sessions at the physio. I had lived with
an irrational fear of a serious medical condition for months,
and for absolutely no reason. Had I listened to Ursina, the
problem would have disappeared much earlier. Although I
knew myself well, and also knew Ursina well, I did not trust
her to give me the advice that was fit for the occasion. After all,
who was the person doing extreme sports in the family? An
innocuous story perhaps, but it shows clearly that we need to

trust the other person to give us relevant advice before we are inclined to take it.

Confusion reigns

What does all this mean?
Well fine, you may think, this has been mildly interesting, and some of this I can relate to, but what is the *point* of all these stories on advice taking? Sometimes the advice works out, sometimes it does not; sometimes we know ourselves well, sometimes we do not . . . There is no clear pattern here, and I wonder what to take away from this . . .

This would be a valid point, and I think we need a few concluding thoughts. I would like to examine the stories and see if I can find some dynamic that drives success, or failure, in taking advice.

Analysis – the table
To do this I made a list of the stories and recorded a number of qualities for each. Have a look at the table.

	(1)	(2)	(3)	(4)	(Result)
	How well do I know myself?	How well does my advisor know me?	How well do I know my advisor?	How well do I know how well my advisor knows me?	Was it right to accept / reject the advice?
Story	Self-knowledge	Advisor quality	Advisor knowledge	Advisor trust	Success?
I. Advice accepted					
1. Not a big ask	Well	Not well	Not well	Well	YES
2. Love, actuary!	Not well	Not well	Not well	So-so	**NO**
3. Class 4!	Not well	Very well	So-so	Very well	YES
4. Conflicting counsel (dad)	Well	Well	Well	Very well	YES
II. Advice rejected					
1. Sounds suicidal, mate!	Well	Not well	So-so	Well	YES
2. Get a dodgy geezer in!	Well	Not well	Well	Well	YES
3. A fast ride	Well	Very well	Very well	Not well	**NO**
4. Conflicting counsel (wife)	Well	Not well	Well	Well	YES
5. This would be great for you	Very well	Not well	Not well	Well	YES
6. Quit the rat race	Well	Not well	So-so	Well	YES
7. A medical emergency	Well	Well	Well	Not well	**NO**

Fig. 6.1 The table summarises the outcomes of the stories. Stories are grouped into those where advice was taken (I. Advice accepted) or rejected (II. Advice rejected). The four components of advice taking are numbered (1) to (4) and the last column (Result) shows whether a choice to accept or reject advice turned out to be appropriate or not.

In the table are the stories I presented in this chapter. I split the one about my friend from school ('Conflicting counsel') into two, as it really contains two separate pieces of advice: the advice given by my friend's dad and that given by his wife.

Running horizontally to the right, you find the four components of advice that I discussed at the start of this chapter. The Result column records whether it turned out appropriate to accept or reject the advice given in a particular situation.

In the table I am basically subjecting each story to four analytical questions and recording 44 answers in total. This gives me a simple fact sheet that records the essence of each story.

Let me give you a few examples of how to read the table.

In the first story, 'Not a big ask', I knew myself well (column 1) but did not know my advisors well (column 3). My advisors did not know me very well either (column 2) and I knew this with confidence (column 4). Still, I got a positive result.

In 'Class 4!' I did not know myself at all (1) but my mum did (2). I would not presume that I knew her very well (what child really knows their parents . . .) but I knew with certainty that I could trust her counsel. The result was positive.

In 'A fast ride' I knew myself and Ursina well, and Ursina knew me very well too. Yes, wonderful, all the actors know each other extremely well here. What can go wrong? Funnily enough, I did not *appreciate* that Ursina knew me well in that instance. And . . . the result was negative!

I could go through each story in this way, but I will spare you the tedium of having to read through these obvious interpretations. Still, if I summarise my stories in this way, I believe some underlying dynamics start bubbling to the surface.

Analysis – bubbles

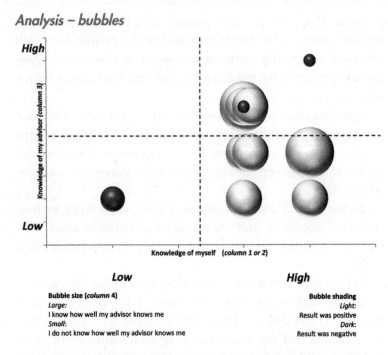

Fig. 6.2 The chart shows the same information as fig. 6.1. The graphical presentation brings out the dynamics more clearly than the table: (1) positive outcomes (light shades) tend to occur when I and/or my advisor know myself well (horizontal axis), but seem indifferent to how well I know my advisor (vertical axis). (2) Positive outcomes (light shades) also tend to occur when I have a high degree of trust that I am receiving quality advice (large bubble size denotes high trust). (3) But negative outcomes (dark shades) correlate only with trust (bubble size). This suggests that trust in the quality of advice (whether advice is appropriate or not, whether the advisor has the best interests of those she advises at heart) is the most important feature when taking advice.

The chart does not add anything that is not already in the table; it is just the presentation that is different. Let me first describe the set-up, just so that we can be sure we are all on the same page:

- The horizontal axis shows the degree of knowledge of myself, provided either *by* myself (self-knowledge) or by my advisor. This axis records answers to the first two components of advice (columns 1 and 2 in the table).

- The vertical axis records answers to the third component of advice (column 3 in the table). The position of the bubble along that axis will tell me how well I know my advisor.

- Bubble size denotes the fourth component of advice (column 4 in the table). Size tells me to what extent I know how well my advisor knows me. In other words, it tells me how much I trust my advisor to give me appropriate (or inappropriate) advice. If the bubble is large, the amount of trust is high; if the bubble is small, that trust is low.

- Bubble shading shows whether responding to advice turned out to be right or wrong. Light shades denote success (it was right to accept or reject advice), dark shades denote failure (it was wrong to accept or reject advice).

- Finally, some bubbles are superimposed, but this is only a graphical trick to show that more than one bubble occupies the same space – it does not mean that one is marginally more to the right or to the left of another.[92]

Now we are ready for some observations:

First, we note a cluster of light-shaded bubbles on the right-hand side of the chart. The bubbles are all in the high section of the horizontal axis, but more spread out along the vertical axis.

- This means that all positive (light-shaded) outcomes occurred when somebody knew the person seeking advice well. That somebody was either the advice seeker herself (self-knowledge) or her advisor.

- Digging deeper, I can go back to the data recorded in the table. There seems to be a high correlation between success and *self-knowledge*, but a much lower correlation between

---

[92] You may, in fact, wonder how I assigned the positions of the bubbles. The table only lists qualitative information; it does not show anything I can count or calculate. In order to get the bubbles into the chart, I assigned numerical values to each response (from 2 for 'very well' to –1 for 'not well'). I also assigned a 1 for success and a –1 for failure. The result is still illustrative – I do not pretend that you can calculate degrees of empathy mathematically – but the numerical values allow me to show the result graphically and to study the dynamics.

success and advisor quality (how well my advisor knows me). This suggests that self-knowledge is key. Advisor quality is also important, but less so. As I said before, it is important that *some*body knows me well. It is best if I am that person.

- Looking at the vertical axis next, my results would suggest that there is less correlation between success (light shades) and how well I know my advisor. In fact, there are five stories in which I did not know my advisor particularly well and yet made a right decision to accept/reject advice. There are still three, however, in which success occurred in situations where I *did* know my advisor well. This is therefore slightly inconclusive; the correlation is not strong. The evidence suggests that how well I know my advisor is not as important as self-knowledge.

So far, I am drawn to the conclusion that how well I know myself is a *primary* quality, and how well my advisor knows me is a *secondary* quality. Advisor quality (how well my advisor knows me) can enhance self-knowledge but it is self-knowledge that remains key. And both taken together are more important than how well I know my advisor. An ability to take the right advice seems to depend more on how well I know myself or my advisor knows me than on how well I know my advisor.

But we have not yet looked at bubble sizes. All light-shaded bubbles are large and the dark bubbles are small.

- This means that if I trust my advisor to give me appropriate/inappropriate advice, I tend to make the right decision. But if I do not trust my advisor to do so, I tend to make the wrong decision.

- Let us recap some examples to make this clear. In 'A fast ride' I did not trust Ursina to know me well, although she actually did. The result was negative. In 'Class 4!' I trusted my mum to know me well, although I did not do so myself.

The result was positive. In 'Conflicting counsel (wife)' my friend trusted his wife not to know him well (in that instance), and rejecting her advice was positive.

- This correlation seems strongest. *All* light-shaded bubbles are large! In other words, whenever trust was high, the person being advised made the right decision. And *all* dark bubbles are small! Whenever trust was low, the person being advised made the wrong decision.

There is something else, and it is rather interesting. The success bubbles (light-shaded) are all floating in the right-hand side of the chart. Success in advice taking seems to go together with trust and self-knowledge. But the failure bubbles (dark) are not clustered in a particular area of the chart. They are spread out across the space, a diagonal from left to right.

- This suggests that failure to take the right advice does not seem to depend on how well I know myself, or how well my advisor knows me, or even how well I know my advisor. If I do not know myself well *and* I do not know my advisor well, failure seems assured (the bubble in the south-west quadrant is dark). That much is intuitive.

- But even if I know myself very well, and also my advisor, I can fail to respond to advice in the right way (two bubbles in the north-east quadrant are dark).

- *Absence of trust* is the only common denominator for the failure bubbles. All dark bubbles are small!

This dynamic urges me to suggest something rather unexpected. An ability to take advice (to heed the right counsel and reject the wrong) relies crucially on the *trust* we have that our advisor counsels us well. Or, in other words, I can know myself as well as I like, and also my advisor, but that knowledge will be for nothing if trust is absent.

Critique and conclusion

We have come to the end of our discussion of how to take advice. Before making a few concluding remarks, allow me to make an observation on method.

It is obvious that my discussion would not withstand the cold glare of scientific scrutiny. The sample size of the stories chosen falls woefully below the number we would need to conduct a statistically significant investigation. The classification of the qualities into their categories, graded low to high, is to some extent subjective and different categorisations are conceivable.

These objections are valid, but I do not believe they invalidate the result of our discussion. My aim is not to develop a new sociological theory. What we are concerned with is the concept of happiness and how to achieve it.

If we consistently follow bad suggestions (or reject good ones), we will not be able to lead a satisfied life. If we know how to separate good advice from bad, we have added a skill to the arsenal of devices that help us to pursue a balanced, fulfilled life. We have discovered the general dynamics of advice taking in our set of stories, and the formal analysis has helped to clarify how they tend to interact. As such, we are able to dissect a complex problem with some level of analytical rigour. That rigour is certainly not enough to establish a scientific model, but I believe it *is* sufficient to provide some practical tools which may be useful to anyone.

To summarise:

- When taking advice, self-knowledge is key. Only if I know who I am can I establish what advice is appropriate for me and what advice is not.

- Advisor quality is also important. If my advisor knows me well, her knowledge may complement what I know about myself. This is even more important if I do not know myself well.

- Taken together, self-knowledge and advisor quality are a powerful combination that tend to generate successful outcomes when taking advice.

- How well I know my advisor remains important but has turned out to be secondary to self-knowledge.

- Self-knowledge may be key but, at least in the context of advice taking, it is a key that may not work if something else is missing. That something else is the well-founded belief, or trust, that my advisor has my best interests at heart. If that trust is absent, I may not listen to good advice even if I know myself very well. Trust is a condition for positive outcomes.

From this I would like to distil a few real-world action points:

(1) Develop as much self-knowledge as possible. No prizes for guessing I would say this.
(2) Recognise those among your friends who know you well enough to be competent advisors, and who therefore are able to complement your level of self-knowledge.
(3) Recognise those you can trust to have your best interests at heart. This may be among family or friends. If there *is* somebody, take active note and listen to them.
(4) If there is no advisor you think you can trust in this way, get one.

Get one? Does that sound a bit odd? Well, perhaps. But think about it. We are not alone in the world. Human beings are social animals and, as we have discussed in this chapter, nobody is a law unto themselves. The fact that self-knowledge is paramount in the pursuit of happiness does not mean that we have to, or even can, get there on our own, and certainly not that we have to *be* on our own.

We saw that trust is at least as important as self-knowledge when taking advice expertly. We are lucky if we have a family member or friend whom we can trust intimately. But we may want to have 24/7 access to a trusted advisor, to somebody who always has our best interests at heart, whom we respect and love, who loves us for who we are and who will not stray from our side.

No, I was not talking about a teddy bear or a dog.[93] I was talking about a friend who goes with us through life. These sorts of people can be difficult to find. But it is my contention that if we find a partner who is right for us, we have taken another important step towards finding happiness.

I deal with the complexities of this issue in the next chapter.

---

[93] Although, hey, whatever works . . .

RULE 7

Find a friend

How to choose your partner

To be single or not to be single

The very first thing we need to examine when we think about finding the right partner is whether the right partner may be no partner. I am convinced that life can be meaningful and fulfilled with the right partner, but I am not convinced that life without a partner is necessarily *less* meaningful. I know that I feel loved and understood by Ursina, and my life has gained warmth and a sense of belonging that gives me strength. But I have found the right relationship late in life, and for decades I was perfectly fulfilled as a single. What is more, during these decades I did not miss *having* a relationship, and certainly I never felt that I needed to develop a relationship as a goal in itself.

I therefore know with certainty, and from my own experience, that being single can be as fulfilling as being partnered. When I was single, I did not want to be in a relationship, and yet now the mere thought of not being with Ursina makes me unhappy.

So what happened? I can still recall some of the reasons why I did *not* want a relationship when I was younger. I would have hated to come back home at 2 am and not be able to put on Aerosmith really loud (well, moderately loud – I may have been single but I still had neighbours). I would have hated having somebody else's stuff sloshing around the flat. I loved decorating my place exactly how I wanted. I loved the freedom and the sanctity of my own space, and by space I am not referring only to the physical place where I lived but to my whole existence in the urban flux of London. I could go out whenever I wanted, pursue whichever interests I wanted, whenever I wanted, be part of whichever social group I wanted to be in.

And now? Surprisingly, I can still do most of this. I do not have to defend my personal space, since Ursina does not attack it. Ursina says a good relationship is like 1+1+1, where the first two 1s are the individuals in the relationship and the third is the couple. You do your own stuff as individuals, and you do joint stuff as a couple. This definition, I think, is succinct and evocative.

In my relationship I have found warmth and security. Ursina loves me for who I am, and vice versa. But there is more. We are friends, we laugh together, we love to hang out together. We respect each other, and when one of us is sad or has a problem, the other one tries to be strong. And since I have not lost my individuality (the first 1 in Ursina's sum) I have gained the third 1: enjoyment as a couple.

I confess that I feel my life enriched beyond measure through my relationship. Yet, I never missed anything when I was single, and I do not miss being single now. The point is that I did what I knew was right during the time when it *was* right. Both states, single and partnered, were examined – I knew consciously what I wanted and why.

Of course, I am going to say what you have been waiting for. Single or not single is a question we can only answer if we know ourselves. I believe that we need at least moderate, and preferably high, self-knowledge to get this answer right (check out the decision heat map again, discussed in Rule 2). In my case, the phase during which I wished to be single lasted a few decades. For others, it may only last a few years. For others still, it may last all through life. There is no absolute answer to this question. But there is a right answer for each of us individually.

In this chapter I am not concerned about how to find this answer – this is the domain of Rule 2, and part of the ongoing challenge to know ourselves. In this chapter I am only interested in how to go about it if, or when, the answer is 'I want to find the right partner'. Before jumping in, just to confirm what you may have suspected – I use the term partner independent of sexual orientation or marital status.

Phase I: Shopping around

What method?

First, I should like to chat a little bit about the settings in which we might run into potential partners. Before I do this, we need to remember what I wish to achieve here. We are not concerned with techniques for approaching people for a short-term relationship or a one-night stand. This is not a pulling guide or an advice section on great chat-up lines. But when (or if) we get to the point that we feel we are ready for a committed relationship, we still need to find a way to meet people who have potential.

To some extent this whole section on shopping around will be irrelevant to those who are still, or are permanently, in single mode. It will also be irrelevant to those who were lucky enough to find their life partner naturally, without conscious planning or deliberate input. Readers in the first group may want to jump to the next chapter, and those in the second may find that it makes sense to skip to the next section in this chapter.

But to those of us who struggle with how or where to approach people, the present discussion may prove helpful, or at least amusing. In the next few paragraphs I will introduce settings in which I have met, or failed to meet, ex-girlfriends. Let us see what we can learn from it.

This did not work . . .

Got the time?

While I was at university, my best friend and I decided to go off to Mallorca for a wild holiday filled with sunshine, beach and partying. One evening we were walking around aimlessly, trying to decide which club to go to, when something unusual happened. I was leaning against a lamp post chatting to my mate: 'NRG or Timepiece? NRG is huge but there were these dancers in cages at Timepiece – they were cool.' While I was saying that, my eyes were automatically scanning the area for 'eye candy' – I was 22, genetically programmed to do this and had as much control over this action as I do over breathing when I am asleep. I spotted a stunning-looking woman on the other side of the street – this was not unusual in the place we were staying. This woman then started crossing the street, clearly heading towards me. Now that *was* unusual. When she got to where I was standing, she looked me in the eyes and asked, 'Excuse me, what is the time?'

You can see that the experience must have impressed me deeply, since I still remember it clearly today after more than 20 years. And what do you think was my response? Was it (a) 'Time to part*aaaaaaayyyyyy*!' or (b) 'It is 10.25 pm'? And where do you think I was looking? Was it (a) into her eyes or (b) at my watch?

Yes, you guessed it. It was (b). Both times. No pulling tips from me.

What a slapper!

A few years later I was in the army and eight of us decided to go on holiday together – this time it was Ibiza. It was great fun and we stayed in two self-catering apartments next to each other – you can imagine what that was like. After a few days we had made friends with a few girls we had met clubbing or on the beach – I cannot remember.

One of us was an annoyingly good-looking bloke who would not have looked out of place in an underwear advertisement. This had two effects: first, it facilitated meeting girls for us as a group. But unfortunately second, it tended to accentuate, by contrast, that my looks were more on the bookish side of things.[94]

Perhaps not surprisingly, I decided I needed to compensate for what I regarded as an inappropriately academic look and to invent the persona of someone who was full of chat-up lines and confident in his effect on women.

One evening we were in a bar and I decided to act out my newly crafted character. So I set to work on one poor girl who just happened to be in the wrong place at the wrong time. After half an hour of witty aphorisms and generally seductive charm she must have decided she could bear it no longer.

Slap! The sound of her hand making full contact with my left cheek rang out, stopping for a moment the chatter around us. My mates looked at me. She looked at me. I looked at no one in particular. *A moment, frozen in time* – you will only think this is a cliché if something like that has never happened to you.

She turned out to be at least as shocked as I was. After the moment had thawed out, she apologised profusely to me and I to her. The matter was forgotten but, you guessed it, this is not the point of the story.

Not my market
The point of the two stories is simply to demonstrate this. When I was about to get pulled, I tended not to notice. When I tried to pull, I tended to get slapped. Sure, in the two stories I was not trying to establish meaningful relationships, but the basic character traits that the stories reveal survived to an older age, to a time when I *was* interested in meeting women for a long-term relationship.

---

[94] In fact, somebody once said to me that I looked very much like Franz Liszt. Turned out she was massively into classical music and that might have skewed her judgement . . . Still, you get the idea. Franz Liszt, not Brad Pitt.

Indeed, I have remained broadly consistent in my life in terms of pulling talent. As I got more confident in myself, I was able to chat more naturally to people, and I met some of my former girlfriends in everyday settings – in the supermarket, at university, at a friend's house. But never in a noisy pub or bar. I have consistently been unable to function in settings characterised by blanketing ambient noise and, until the introduction of the smoking ban, by thick layers of carcinogenic fumes.

And since I had repeatedly encountered this inability in many episodes in my life, I was consciously aware of it when I came to the point of wanting a long-term relationship. The point of my story about pulling, therefore, is again to know who you are. Know your personality, know what social settings make you comfortable, which ones make you feel awkward, and act in accordance with this knowledge. In my case it was not to seek social contact in bars or clubs. In your case it may be the opposite. Who knows?

Who knows? Well I suppose you do. When establishing a relationship, it is important to find your potential partner in a setting that puts you at ease. Hence, the first lesson is to know what that setting is or, if you do not, to find out through active deliberation (EXPERIENCE MINING would not be the worst method . . .).

. . . but this did!

Peoplesupermarket.com

After two decades of blissful existence as a single, punctuated by one longer-term and several shorter-term relationships, I had come to the point where I was asking myself whether there was something missing in my life. Would it not be nice to go out for dinner to romantic restaurants with a girl, go on dates, have long conversations, share things? But there were not many women in my life – after my two-year relationship with Mary had come to an end, I'd had enough and had focussed on life as a single guy. Also my job consumed more waking hours than I would have liked and, as a consequence, I did not really meet a lot of women.

So there was a problem. I was ready to go back 'on the market' but did not really know how to find potential buyers for the merchandise. As we discussed, the chances of meeting somebody in a bar or a club were basically zero. But what to do? Most of my friends were of an age where their own acquaintances had partnered up, so the traditional English route of matchmaking was pretty much closed to me. Also I would have loved to meet people from different walks of life, not just from my own extended social sphere.

The solution came when I was travelling on the tube one evening. I was idly scanning the advertisements in the carriage and saw one suggesting internet dating as a means of meeting new people. A little bit of research revealed that all it took was to pay the site a fee and put up a profile of yourself. I was immediately taken by the idea and signed up, a little bit sceptical about whether I would receive a single hit, but generally in curious anticipation of what my new venture might turn up.

As it turned out, it changed my life.

The first date
The next few stories are just a few I selected from a large number of dates I had as a member of the site. I chose them because they tell a story, and I think we can use them later to illustrate another important ingredient in the hunt for your partner – that of waiting until you find the right one and not settling on second best because you are getting anxious and perhaps frustrated after so many dates, or relationships, that did not deliver.

After spending a while checking out how the social dynamics on the site worked, I received an email from somebody. 'Hey, you look nice. How tall are you – I am 1.80 m in heels.'

Saucy. I liked that. I pinged back, 'I am 1.84 m in cowboy boots.' This was not a lie, depending on the boots, and after some more good email banter and a nice chat on the phone, I asked Eleanore to meet up for coffee. She agreed, and we had a nice evening. Coffee at a Starbucks, noodles at Wagamama's, a nice stroll through Soho back to the tube station and air-kisses to say goodbye. The conversation had been a bit slow and laboured at times, but all in all this had been a lovely evening. She was enthusiastic about meeting up again, but had to go away for a few weeks to see her parents. She would contact me when she got back. After a month, I pinged her an email asking how she was but never received a reply. She must have found the conversation a bit laboured too.

Proper dates

After a while I got into the swing of it and dates were coming in regularly.

The first date that had potential to go somewhere was with Naomi. We got on like the proverbial house on fire on our first date. Still, I felt a bit out of my depth when we left a club at 2 am, on a school night. I was about to thank her for a great night out, expecting naturally that we would now go home, but instead of saying nighty night or something she said 'Let's go in here – they have great music'. I was like, 'You have *got* to be joking – it's 2 in the morning! I need to go home.' After a few more dates like that, I decided that I enjoyed her company enormously but could not go the distance with her. I would get up at 5.30 am normally and needed more than three hours of sleep to function.

My next date was with Jamila. We got on well, we fancied each other, one date led to the next and we woke up to have breakfast together. Nice. After a few breakfast dates she suggested that we get married – not immediately, but eventually. How did I feel about that?

Oops. Unexpected. I would have thought relationships should develop before getting to the stage where partners are discussing marriage. It turned out that she was perfectly happy to let it develop, as long as she knew that at the end of this process would be the certainty of marriage. To cut a moderately long story short, I could not deal with this scholastic view of marriage and decided to run a mile.

A dictatorial food choice

The second date that promised to lead to something more meaningful was with Mei-Xing. However, as our relationship progressed, there were several incidents that made me doubt whether we had a compatible outlook on life. The first doubt came when we were walking down Bond Street one weekend. When I stopped to look at a display in a shop, she stopped and looked at it too. When I resumed walking, so did she. I thought that was strange. Was there nowhere *she* wanted to go? No shops *she* wanted to visit? It struck me as odd, but I did not think about it at the time and just filed the experience away. However, things like that kept happening and one evening at dinner something finally dawned on me. What dawned on me did so in light of the following experience.

We were sitting down for dinner in a restaurant in the West End. The waiter arrived and handed us two menus. Mei-Xing excused herself to go and freshen up in the bathroom. I half rose out of my chair to acknowledge that she was leaving the table. She looked at me quizzically and disappeared. In her absence, I looked at the menu and when she returned I had decided on what I was going to have. Then we had the following conversation:

Why did you get up when I got up?
I was just being polite.
Is this something men do in England?
I don't think so . . . It is quite old-fashioned, I suppose. But I like it. It's a nice gesture. Respectful.
Ah OK. Men would not do that in China . . . Have you chosen?
I have indeed. Have a look at what you would like. Shall we have wine?
I thought you had chosen?

I did, yes. But you haven't yet . . .?

No, I take what you have. In China, men choose for women.

Do they really? Well, in Europe they don't. Or if they do, they shouldn't. Certainly I won't choose what you have for dinner.

But that's how we do it in China.

And that would be perfectly fine if we **were** in China. But we're not. We're in London. And in 21st-century London only chauvinists choose for women. I certainly won't choose for you.

And so I did not. Mei-Xing went along with it since she must have found it unconscionable to talk back to a man, even if it was for the purpose of upholding her cultural rules of decorum.

A few days after our dinner we ended our fledgling relationship. No prizes for guessing that I was the driving force behind the split. Even so, I was very sad to bring it to an end – she was fun-filled, sweet, intelligent and had a disarming innocence about her which I found very attractive.

What had dawned on me was this. For me, a meaningful relationship has to be a bond of equals. My experience with Mei-Xing made it very clear to me that I need a strong and independent partner who walks through life with me side by side. Who leans on me *only* when she needs support, as I only lean on her when I do. The fact that I get up in a restaurant when a woman leaves the table is nothing more than a quaint mannerism that I find delightfully old-fashioned but essentially is meant as an expression of respect, not of chauvinism.[95]

---

[95] I picked this up from a movie, actually. I was watching *Kate and Leopold*, starring Meg Ryan and Hugh Jackman. Hugh's character Leopold is a time-displaced French lieutenant from the 19th century, who is taken in by Meg Ryan's character Kate and whose old-world manners tend to clash with those of early 21st-century New York. In one scene Leopold stands when Kate leaves the table. I thought that action was delivered with so much panache, and pride in himself, that I decided to make it my own. The first time I used it in public I made a complete idiot of myself. Reality is not like the movies. Regardless, I love the gesture and have fun using it, although I am a modern man to the core.

I do this just as I hold doors open for people, help Ursina with her coat and would open the car door for her, if I did not always forget. But Mei-Xing interpreted my slightly dusty gesture as servile and my independent food choice as offensive. I knew who I was, and I knew we had no future together, much as I enjoyed her company.

Do I like what?

Another date that had the potential to turn into something longer term was with Shakina. Shakina was a lawyer, fiercely intelligent, loved a good argument and had a malicious sense of humour. That she was able to defy what you would think of as social norms became clear on our very first date. We were in a bar, sitting down with our drinks, starting to chat about ourselves, taking the first steps to explore what the other person was like. She asked me why I was looking to meet somebody through an internet site, and I asked her the same. Then she said, 'Can I ask you something personal?' I said of course. She continued, 'This may sound like a bit of a strange question, but . . . do you like anal?'

I could not believe anybody would ask me that in a social setting. Here we were in a chic bar, swirling our cocktails, reclining in our seats, while Soho was beginning to come alive around us. Also how do you respond to such a question? What exactly is a good answer? Is yes a good answer? Or maybe 'Only after coffee'? I must admit I was not as shocked by the question as I was enormously amused. I decided to stick with the truth and said something like, 'I never felt the urge to try so have no experience to offer – was that a good answer?' Turned out it was. A previous boyfriend of hers had been obsessed with that sexual practice and she just wanted to make sure that I was not. I liked her no-nonsense approach, in particular because I remember seeing something of a coy smile on her face when she asked the question.

We got on well and had quite a number of dates before we called it off. She liked competitive debating just a bit too much for my taste. I like it too as a mental sport, but more than debating I like a proper intellectual discussion where at the end you go away knowing a little bit more about something than you did before. With Shakina I felt it was difficult to have a normal conversation. Pretty much everything would be debated in controversial style, and I remember finding this mode of interaction quite exhausting.

The mentalist

I only had a few dates with Susan. Although our relationship was extremely brief, it bore the hallmark of psychological anguish. Our first date was great. We had an enjoyable dinner near Tower Bridge in a restaurant close to the *Thames*. The conversation was easy, we laughed a lot and time flew by. On our way to the tube station, she was a little bit less sprightly than she had been in the restaurant, but we continued chatting and said we would meet again. On the second date I found her in less high spirits, the conversation was more laboured, her eyes less twinkly and the date not as much fun. Still, we decided to give it another go and put a date in the diary for two weeks hence, since I was away travelling on business for a week.

We met up on the day and, instead of greeting me with a smile, she said: 'You never sent an email asking how I was.' *Well, why would I?* I was asking myself silently. *It's not as if we are married – we've just had a few dates together* . . . 'I need support, you know, and the feeling that you care for me,' she continued. This conversation went on for a while, we then had a drink together in a bar and I made an early exit pretending I had a work commitment first thing next morning.

But what I was actually doing was consciously taking stock of what I had been sensing all along. A woman who is sprightly one minute and noticeably less sprightly the next. Relaxed on one date, morose on another. Who is complaining about lack of emotional support from a guy on the fourth date. I am no medical expert but, if the evidence had been any more pronounced, I would have thought that this was what manic-depressive looks like. I was getting a bad feeling about the situation and decided to distance myself – after all, we had only had a few dates together, and we were miles from the stage where either of us could reasonably have expected emotional commitment from the other person.

For about a month I heard nothing more from Susan, then an email arrived at work. It was from her. She said she had been admitted to hospital and would I come visit her. I was immediately cautious and wondering what sort of condition she might need treatment for.

I checked the hospital and the specific ward on the internet. It turned out to be the ward for patients who suffer from an acute mental illness.

I sent her an email in response saying that work was terribly busy at the moment and that I had started seeing somebody else. Both of these were true but neither of them would have prevented me from paying her a visit, had I absolutely wanted to. I did, however, think that any such gesture would have been misunderstood, and I certainly did not feel that it would have been ethical for me to create a false hope in her mind. She sent me a nice email in return, wishing me luck and asking me, jokingly, to send a good man her way if I knew one. I never heard from her again but hope she found what she was looking for.

Finding a partner is like house hunting

Let us pause here. I could go on with stories from my dating phase for a long time, and I hope you had fun reading through them. But there is a reason why I told you about my dating experiences. The reason is to illustrate how we can know who is right for us. We have already encountered the method I want to propose. It is EXPERIENCE MINING!

Here is what I suggest. When you are on a date, have fun and be natural, but also note consciously *why* you are having fun, or why you are *not*. Be honest with yourself – you are not an equal opportunities employer: you do not have to pay heed to non-discrimination on the grounds of height, race, looks, intelligence, whatever. If something makes you feel uncomfortable, or comfortable, take note of it. Let me present my thoughts on what this might feel like:

- The conversation with Eleanore was a bit difficult to sustain. Why was that? Often she did not get my jokes and took what I was saying seriously. Does this tell me something about myself or what I need? I have more fun with somebody who gets my sense of humour. Somebody who is not too serious.

- Naomi was exhausting. She was great fun, but I have not got the energy to go clubbing into the wee hours of the morning. I would probably want somebody with more depth too.

- Jamila was too full-on. I mean, who talks about marriage on the third date? I have no interest in exploring why she needs that psychological assurance. Why not? Because I need a relationship to develop naturally. Because I may not be able to deal with somebody who is psychologically fragile.

- Mei-Xing was lovely but *come on*. A relationship with somebody who does not believe they are my equal, who constantly expects me to act first, or on her behalf, would be disastrous. I am looking for a partner in life, not somebody to take responsibility for. No way.

- Shakina was great. Our conversations sparked, crackled and popped. But they were *always* like fizzy drinks and never like, for example, a cup of herbal tea. I like competitive debating, and she is a great challenge intellectually, but I need some non-conversations too once in a while, or merely a discussion to explore a topic, with no winners and losers. I need balance. And also why is she always intellectually competitive? Perhaps she is not as self-confident as she seems. Again, I need somebody to stand next to me in life. Not somebody who feels compelled to prove to me on a daily basis that she is able to do so.

- Sorry, Susan, I cannot deal with mental disorders. You need somebody who is close to you, truly loves you and gives you strength. That is not me.

You have probably noticed that there is a common theme here. I need a partner who is my equal, and I would not be happy with somebody who tried to lean on me. The relationship I want is a bond of equals, where the partners support each other when necessary but do not need to support each other all, or even most, of the time.

And there it is. Another self-insight, distilled from the more than 30 dates I had during my time on the dating site. And I got there through EXPERIENCE MINING.[96]

Finding the right partner, I therefore suggest, is similar to the process through which we start to know who we are. I suggest having as many dates as it takes, and having them consciously. In the process, we learn something about ourselves. Knowing who you are is the most important element in finding the right partner – only if you know who you are can you know which partner you need. Only if you know yourself can you be a strong partner in a relationship.

---

[96] You know what else you can do? After a bit of dating, do the DICE TEST. I assure you it works. An example: Amoli and I got on very well and there was definitely some romance going on. Sadly, on our third date she was a lot less 'romantic' and when I asked her if everything was OK she said that her ex-boyfriend had contacted her and asked her out for dinner. She said she really liked me and was not sure what to do. I explained the DICE TEST to her and suggested she use that to find the answer. She said that she would, and I never heard from her again. The DICE TEST works.

This leads me to another element that I believe is important in a successful search for a partner. Do *not* settle for second best! Do not get frustrated and stay with somebody because you start telling yourself that after so many attempts, so many dates, you finally need to settle or it will never happen. You owe it to yourself to find the person who is best suited to you. If you dislike this statement because you think it sounds egotistic, turn it around. You have a responsibility not to stay with somebody whom you would make unhappy because you are imperfectly matched.

And this is where the search for a partner is similar to house hunting. I put it to you that we subconsciously know what sort of home makes us comfortable. This flat is on the ground floor and lacks privacy. This one is a basement flat and does not have much light. This one does not have a balcony where I can grow herbs. This one is too far from clubland. This house is too far away from the local school. And so on and so forth. We know. The trick in house hunting is holding out until you find what you know is right.

OK then. I guess by now you may be asking yourself whether I actually have at least one piece of positive evidence that EXPERIENCE MINING and avoidance of premature settling actually *works*.

Let us see. I had just received an email from a person on the site. She said she had noted my profile and was inviting me to chat. I checked her out and decided I liked what I saw. In her profile she was talking about reasons why she would go out with somebody on a date. I did my usual banter-initiating email and pinged her this: 'Read your profile. Fair enough. But give me one good reason why I should go on a date with *you*. ☺' Her response was: 'No way. You first, matey!'

Uuuuuh. Gutsy . . . Challenging . . . I *like* her . . . We had a telephone conversation and, about two weeks later, I went on my first date with Ursina.

Phase II: Test drive

Strong enough to be vulnerable

Basically, what I have taken away from my time as a member of the dating site is twofold. In finding a partner, you must not settle for second best, and it is important to date *consciously*. These two guidelines can be applied to any date, and I believe they should also be remembered in the early phases of a relationship.

I believe relationships pass through phases. The phase I call the test drive is the time in which we are exploring the other person's world and are slowly initiating the other person into ours. It is the phase after the chat about being exclusive,[97] but before consciously going steady. Going steady is a third phase, and is typically sealed by a public ceremony (marriage, civil partnership) or personal vows.

The test-driving phase has no set duration. Mary and I split up after two years, so by definition our test-driving phase took 24 months. The test drive for Ursina and me was shorter, and definitely over once we decided to live together.

The test drive is a key time in a relationship. It is in this phase that we are still free to go our own ways if it does not work out. It is in this phase that we need to trust our intuition. It is in this phase that we slowly dismantle our protective walls and let the other person in, bit by bit.

In order to do this well, we need to apply the same principles I discussed before. We must not settle for second best, and we need to test drive *consciously*.

Still, being consciously aware of things is one thing. How to act on this knowledge is quite another. Let me give you a few examples of the sort of things we might notice during the test drive:

---

[97] I assume most people will at some point have a chat about not going on dates with others any more. At the very least I certainly recommend such a chat.

(1) He has a tendency to drink too much when we are out on a date. I do not like it when he is becoming less attentive as he gets more tipsy. Also he is often a bit rude to people when he gets like that.

(2) He tends to look openly at other women when we are out. I hate the way his gaze wanders in mid conversation. One minute we are chatting, the next I've lost him. He does not even have the good grace to hide it.

(3) When she stays over at mine, she constantly tells me what to do. I do not drink enough water, I do not eat the right things, the arrangement of stuff in the kitchen is not optimal, my furniture looks crap.

(4) She constantly phones me up to get stuff for her. Arrange pedicures, change her hairdresser's appointment, bring her that bread she likes so much on my way to her apartment.

(5) When we have an argument, he seems to get a little carried away. His voice is raised, he shouts, his eyes sometimes flash at me angrily. He seems to have a short fuse – he might put a cup down on a table forcibly, fling a book he is holding into the sofa, slam his hand on the back of the chair.

(6) She has had quite a number of ex-boyfriends. Some of them have treated her quite badly, it seems. Some of her exes seem to have 'overlapped'. She says she was not actively cheating, that one relationship had already run its course when she met the next person, but still . . .

(7) He always suggests dates *he* likes, but does not seem to be very interested in what *I* want.

(8) She always makes comments as if she would like to change me, like 'What do you think of that haircut for you?' or 'Oh, these shoes would look really good on you. Much better than the ones you are wearing' and 'You are always wearing jeans. Don't you think you should try some more grown-up trousers?'

(9) She is constantly going on about how this person mistreated her, that person was rude to her, how she is being constantly slighted by everybody.

(10) He tends to cancel dates with me at the last minute because he's had a better offer, usually to go somewhere with his mates.

Which of the behaviours in the list is important enough to justify concern? Which ones are innocuous and may disappear after you get to know each other better? Which ones do you need to address and discuss? Which ones do you simply need to observe? And which ones are just symptoms illustrating that you are leaving your comfort zone and finding it difficult to let somebody else in?

The tricky thing about the test drive is that nothing is settled yet. On the one hand, you need to protect yourself. You need to protect your world and must not invite somebody in who may treat you badly. Behaviours (5) and (6) in the list might qualify.

But equally, you need to give the other person the chance to get in. If you do not run at least some risk of getting hurt, you can never develop trust in another person. The trick is to do this in stages, in small steps. But even so, we need to develop the psychological tenacity to deal with potential emotional distress; we cannot be 100 per cent sure in the early stages of a relationship whether trust is deserved or misplaced. We need to be strong enough to be vulnerable. Examples (2) and (6) may be cases in point.

None of the instances we pick up during the test-driving phase may be strong enough in themselves to justify an action (either end the relationship or move on to the steady state), but all of them taken together will create a quality, a dominant feel. This can either be strongly positive (potential to move on to steady state), strongly negative (potential to break up and go your separate ways) or undetermined (unsure whether to stay or go).

It is in that third, indeterminate state that a relationship is often said to need work. Often when I discuss this subject with friends, I hear the view expressed that you need to work at a relationship, that somehow a good relationship does not come about entirely naturally, that conscious input needs to be made to find common ground, to create practical solutions for practical relationship problems.

I would say this is, at first sight, a reasonable observation. It is without doubt the case that we need to communicate with each other in the test-driving phase, and throughout a relationship. We need to do this with the aim of exploring each other's needs, understanding each other's personalities and finding common ground in practical problems of everyday life. This is the hallmark of a healthy and functioning relationship.

But how much work can reasonably be expected? How much is too much? How little is too little? At which point are we simply trying to keep incompatible personalities together because we are afraid to face an emotionally jarring split? Even worse, when is a relationship one-sided, with one person accepting all the compromise and the other person accepting none?

These are crucial questions to answer in the test-driving phase, and as usual the answers are not easy to come by. Equally as usual, the answers lie in us, and in the extent to which we know ourselves. But this time the problem is even more tricky. This time there are two people involved. In addition to knowing ourselves, we also need to know what quality the relationship needs to have for us as individuals.

I am going to illustrate what I mean in the next section.

Venn does a relationship need work?

My basic premise is that partners in a relationship need a certain level of overlap. They need to be attracted to each other's personalities, but that is not enough. They also need to share some views, some ambitions, some tastes, some fundamental convictions.

Some. Not all. In fact, some personality traits work best in relationships if they complement each other, like pragmatism and creativity (she negotiates the mortgage with the bank, he does the interior decorating), or practical and intellectual intelligence (he fixes things around the house, she helps the children with their homework). But if you never laugh at the same things, if you never want to watch the same TV shows, if you never wish to go to the same holiday destinations, live in the same place or enjoy the company of similar people, you will not have much fun together in the long run.

I believe this statement is intuitive, and perhaps incontestable. If Sue is a mercenary, fighting in theatres of war all over the world for personal gain, and Jerry, who loves children, is a paediatric nurse working in an NHS hospital in Slough, Sue and Jerry are unlikely to have much of a future together. They may still fall in love if they were to meet, but it is unlikely that they would form a meaningful mutual bond.

If I chose to represent Sue and Jerry's relationship by the overlapping circles we find in Venn diagrams, I would draw two isolated circles in two different parts of my notepaper. But how would this – admittedly simplistic – tool represent more successful relationships?

Let us pick out two at random and take a look.

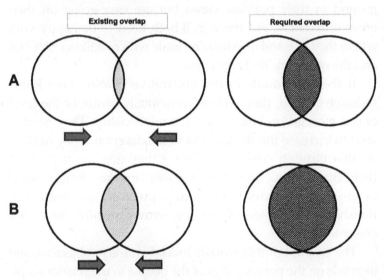

Fig. 7.1 The Venn diagrams illustrate the extent of work required in a relationship. Two relationships, A and B, start out with different amounts of natural overlap. In both cases the partners feel that they need a higher degree of common ground to form a sustainable bond. The arrows indicate that the relationships need active inputs ('work') to achieve the overlap required. The amount of overlap needed is subjective; relationship A requires less, relationship B more. Relationship B has a natural overlap equal to the required overlap in A, and yet relationship B requires work, just as relationship A does.

On the left-hand side I show the common ground two people in a relationship have *naturally*. This is the starting point, and it will differ between individual couples. In the diagram the partners in relationship B have more natural overlap than those in relationship A. To be less abstract, let us say the partners in A have different tastes in music and like to watch different TV shows, differ in their views on politics and one would like to live in the city, the other in the country. Their counterparts in B like the same music and have similar political views but like different telly and also differ about where they want to live.

On the right-hand side I show what level of overlap the partners *need* in order to form a meaningful bond and live sustainably as a couple. This is also subjective and will differ between couples. Say the people in A need to find common ground in their political views but are easy-going on their other differences, but those in B both need to be happy with where they live and also have an issue with one liking *Star Trek* and the other *Say Yes to the Dress*.

If the individuals in my illustrative relationships know themselves well, they will be consciously aware of the level of common ground they need in a relationship. They need to start to increase the shared area in the diagram. They need to do this through conscious effort – they need to talk about their differences, find compromises, maybe change some deep-seated attitudes. They need to put work into their relationship, as indicated by the two arrows pushing the circles closer together.

The amount of this work is indeed entirely subjective, and depends on the personalities of the people in the relationships. We could, for example, imagine couple B saying things like, 'Why do things have to be so complicated with you? Look at our friends from A – *she* is completely happy to commute into town, and they are still great together. Why do we always have a row over this?'

Well, the answer is that the level of common ground that people need in a relationship differs from couple to couple. We need to know how much overlap we have naturally, and how much we need to have. If we know this, we get a good sense of how *much* work we need to put in.

This does not yet tell us whether putting in this amount of work will be worth it, but conscious knowledge of these dynamics is definitely an advantage. Knowing this, we are less likely to make the mistake and rate our progress by the standards set by other couples we know.

So far so good. But before we move on, let me look at one more example:

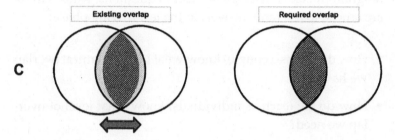

Fig. 7.2 If natural overlap is larger than required overlap, a relationship can survive strain and is naturally resilient.

These guys are lucky. They need as much common ground as couple A to be happy in a relationship. But look how naturally well suited they are! Their *natural* overlap is already larger than what they would require for a meaningful relationship. Arguably, their relationship is the strongest of the three. Even if they move slightly further apart as individuals during their lifetime, their relationship will not be at risk. Only if they drift apart materially would they need to put work in to push their circles back together.

Epiphany recognition

Of course, my diagrams are simplistic. Relationships between people are complex, the dynamics are not constant and in addition they are embedded in a wider social context. All true. But the diagrams still capture an important, essential even, quality of relationships.

This quality is natural suitability. If a relationship is to work long term, I believe it is absolutely essential that the partners have a high level of *natural* overlap. If they do, the relationship will be naturally strong, and hence able to withstand pressure and stress more easily. How does the relationship fare if one partner's parents die? If one partner falls ill, or loses his job? I suggest that relationship C would withstand pressure of this kind more easily than A or B.

Looking at relationships with the simple model of Venn diagrams focussed me on a number of questions, which I think are crucial to ask (and answer) in the test-driving phase:

- How do we (as a couple) know what level of natural overlap we have?

- How do we (each as individuals) know what level of overlap we need?

- How large is the gap? How much work would we need to put in? If it is too much, we may never get to our comfort zone. If it is manageable, it may be worth it.

- Will it last? If we put the work in and then stop, do the circles snap back to their natural positions? Or do they stay in the required state of overlap?

These are all important questions. But the last question, I think, is crucial. Does a relationship require *constant* work to keep it at a level where the partners find the common ground which they need to be happy? Or is the work that they need to put in something like an acquisition cost, a one-time talking through of issues between the partners, which, once successfully completed, lays the foundation for a strong and sustainable relationship? Only if we know the answer to this question will we know how to respond to the time-honoured suggestion that relationships need work. Only then will we know whether ours is a relationship that will withstand stress tests, and hence is worth the effort, or will falter under pressure, and hence is not.

The goal, therefore, is to develop a relationship similar to that shown in the third diagram. If we find a partner with whom we have that naturally, excellent! We are there. If we can get there by working out some issues and finding some compromises, great! It is definitely worth the effort. But if we cannot get there, or if we drift apart if we do not constantly find new compromises, we should accept that we do not work as an item. There is no more efficient recipe for unhappiness than to stay in a relationship which is not right merely because we feel a false sense of duty.

'OK, OK!' I hear you say, somewhat impatiently by now. 'We get it! Natural overlap, sustainable relationship. All very good. But how do you get there? What are the tools?'

I believe that the answer to all my questions is nothing more earthshattering than drive consciously. We have encountered this principle already when we were still shopping around, and I think it is fundamental. However, in the test drive phase I would like to give this tool a different name, because I think it has a slightly different quality. I call my tool for the test drive EPIPHANY RECOGNITION.

EPIPHANY RECOGNITION works like this. We take note of experiences and record how we feel about them. We need to be honest with ourselves and not censor our emotive responses. There is no such thing as an immature response, an inappropriate reaction or an embarrassing emotion. All responses are private, and we take note of them *in* private.

I suggest we take brief note of our responses and then move on. None of them is likely to be significant in itself, but over time they will bind together into an ambient or dominant feel.

This feel can be positive or negative, but it will be there, mostly in our subconscious.

But there will be events that bring this quality out! There will be experiences that make the elusive feel tangible, that turn it into something that we consciously understand. These events are important. They can be anything: a look, something a person does or says, something a friend says, a shared joy, a shared concern.

When these events happen, we need to sit up and take note. These are the events which we need to analyse. These are the emotions we need to understand. It is not important what these events are, but it is important that we recognise them *for* what they are and that we do not let them go. These events are glimpses into the quality of our relationship. They are the epiphanies I refer to in the name of my tool.

An aborted test drive – the ride

My first test drive is a practical example that demonstrates how a series of unconnected experiences, each in itself unremarkable, coalesced into a dominant negative feel over time. EPIPHANY RECOGNITION helped me to become consciously aware of this and made me realise that the relationship was not right for me at the time.

The test drive I refer to is my relationship with Mary. I am going to present a series of experiences, which I narrate first and then annotate. In the annotations I record the thoughts and emotions I remember having at the time. The annotations represent the dynamic I referred to earlier: we take brief note of our emotional response and move on.

As you read on, some further questions may occur to you. Why did we stay together for two years? Why did we not work more at the relationship? Did we not think it was worth saving, and if not, why not? These are important questions which go right to the heart of the matter of how we can know whether a partner is right for us. I think the answers will become clear as I present the evidence.

But first evidence. Then interpretation.

Birthday girl
Mary and I had been going out for a few months and her birthday was coming up. It was the first 'diary event' between us and I thought I would do something nice to mark the occasion. I was thinking of inviting her out for a romantic dinner, or perhaps taking her to the theatre or a classical concert.[98] I had not made up my mind yet, but needed to make sure that she was available on the day of her birthday. So I told her I was planning something special for her first birthday with me as a boyfriend and that I required her presence on the evening of the day.

I did not expect her to decline, and yet that was what she did. She said that for years it had been a tradition for her friends to organise something for her birthday and that she always looked forward to the surprise. But she said she would love me to be there with her.

Hmm. Being told unequivocally that she preferred her friends' do to mine hurt a bit. But then it was early days, we were exploring each other's lives, and if this was something her friends had been doing for years, I might as well initiate myself into her life on this occasion. Even so, I did not like her preference.

More activity, please
After going out for a year or so we were beginning to be aware that we had different ideas of what constituted a pleasant weekend. Mine would involve waking up in a leisurely way, reading until after lunchtime then either getting out of the

[98] I would have preferred jumping around for two hours in a cloud of headache-inducing noise produced by the likes of Megadeth or Metallica, but this was about her, not about me.

house for some activity (rollerblading in Hyde Park, waterski-ing in the water sports club close by, rock climbing on the climbing wall) or reading some more or playing a videogame. Then in the evening either going out for dinner or to the cinema, or staying in with a movie or a book, or meeting up with friends. Mary's ideal was to get up quite early and go and visit different friends around London during the day, followed by a dinner party at a friend's house in the evening. As you can see, I am a curious mix between homebody and extrovert, and Mary was happiest when she felt part of her large social sphere.

Unfortunately, we were quite seriously mismatched in that regard. The trouble is that an active social life tends to domi-nate easily over a quiet contemplative life. In our case, the active things I enjoyed were out of Mary's comfort zone, so she was not able to share them with me. This mismatch led to a large number of weekends where I accompanied her to vari-ous social gatherings, at first enthusiastically as I found it interesting to meet her friends, but increasingly grudgingly as the novelty value wore off.

And Mary cannot have been happy with the mismatch either. One weekend when I was still lounging around the flat at 2 pm reading, with no sign that I intended to stop this activ-ity any time soon, she sat me down for a heart to heart. Our conversation was longer than what follows, but the part that is relevant went a bit like this:

> Mark, I am not happy with my weekends.
> What's wrong with them?
> I don't know . . . it's like . . . we don't do enough . . . When I get
>   to Sunday evening, I feel that I haven't . . . that I didn't . . .
>   cover enough ground.[99]

---

[99] Of course, the dialogue is not verbatim. But I remember Mary using this exact phrase. She pronounced it with that light emphasis that reflects the satisfaction we feel when we grope around for an expression, which at first we cannot quite find – and then are satisfied when we do.

> Well, I have a similar but opposite feeling. I feel that I cannot
>   read with as much . . . abandon as I used to.
> But why not? Look at me. I read all the time.
> Really? Like when?
> All the time. On the tube, when I am on a train going some-
>   where . . . just all the time.

On the tube? On the train? Mary had an attitude to reading that was
fundamentally different from mine. When I read, I like to immerse
myself in the book. Feel the language evolve. Live in the plot if it is
fiction. Grapple with challenging concepts if it is non-fiction. Mary
treats reading as a means to fill the brief interludes between consecu-
tive social activities. There is no common ground on this matter, and
she will never understand the way I read, as I will never understand
the way she does.

Not the bookshop!

The brevity of the experience that follows contrasts with the
profound impact that it had on me at the time. Mary and I were
on our way to a dinner party given by Donna, her best friend.
But Mary had to stop off briefly on the way to get a present and
decided to look for something in a bookshop. I let her go in and
waited outside.

That is it. That is the experience. You may wonder how that
even qualifies as an event. If you do, it is only because I have
not told you enough about myself yet.

When I enter a bookshop, I tend to *be* in the bookshop. I
browse in this section and in that, walk through the aisles, wait
to be inspired by something new, feel attracted by a colourful
display, mesmerised by the graphic novels, drawn in by the
books on philosophy or science, stand fascinated in front of a
crime author I had never heard of before, discover a new
edition of a classic novel. I can spend hours doing this, and
very frequently have done – I remember long evenings in the
Borders bookshop on Charing Cross Road, lounging in the
armchairs or sitting on the floor reading, drinking coffee from
the in-store coffee shop. And when I finally left my temporary

home, I would do so laden down with books, to be carried home and cherished in weekends to come.[100]

I tell you this because you need to know how much I love reading, and how much I love bookshops. The point is I would *never* not enter a bookshop. I would *never* wait outside. And I would *never* not buy anything inside.

The reason I did not want to follow Mary in was this: I knew there would be many things in the shop that I would have liked to read and did not want to face up to the disappointment that I would no longer have the time, or the peace of mind, to read them.

I realised this consciously when I was waiting for Mary to leave the shop. It was the first time it occurred to me that something fundamental was not working between us. It sounds like a small matter, but if one partner in a relationship is removed from their natural comfort zone constantly, it is time to notice. And notice I did. This was an epiphany, and I recognised it as one.

This is for my nephew

After the bookshop interlude, we were on our way to Donna's evening do. When we arrived, most of the other guests had already settled in and were chatting over nibbles and cocktails. They were all thirtysomethings, but they all acted as if they were much older than that. Actually, it is more likely the case that I just felt mentally much younger than a typical 30-to-40-year-old. For example, if they were talking about skiing, they would not be speaking about hand drags or flatspins but about the quality of the food in the restaurants. Skiing tuition would not be mogul training[101] but the ski school for the kids. You get

---

[100] I used to do this a lot. The flipside of this activity was that the pile of unread books tended to tower over the pile of those I *had* read. This used to stress me out as I felt the need to get through what Umberto Eco called the 'anti-library', the library of books purchased but not read.

[101] Just to be clear, I am not any good at free skiing. My point is that I like to muck about in the fun park when I go skiing, even though I cannot do a single trick.

the idea. And of course I realised that *I* was the odd one out, not they.

This fact was also clearly illustrated by the following interaction I had with Donna. Donna and I were chatting when I spotted an Offspring album on the kitchen table. I was surprised to see this but also naively relieved. Perhaps we could chat about music for a while? So I said 'Hey, Donna! You listen to the Offspring? Respect!' But her response was a sobering 'Well no, it's a present for my 12-year-old nephew.'

Ah. OK then. At least my mental age is clear now . . . I did not have much in common with Mary's friends. It was not as if they were old before their time – it was more that I was young for my age (still am . . .). Again, I noticed the mismatch consciously and stored it away for inspection at a later time.

Down below

Of course, this was not the last time I was to feel uncomfortable around Mary's friends. Next up in my parade of events is the weekend sailing. Before I get into this, a word of apology to those among you who are sailors. I had never been on a sailing boat before that weekend, so my knowledge of anything nautical is woefully inadequate. I will no doubt be guilty of using the incorrect terminology, so I apologise in advance.

One of Mary's friends owned a small sailing boat and had invited us (well, Mary, really, but I was tagging along by unspoken consent) down for a weekend of sailing. I believe his boat is appropriately referred to as a cruising yacht and was some 20–25 feet in length. The plan was to go from Bosham, where the boat was berthed,[102] to Southampton and back the following day.

As I said, I had never been sailing before and was looking forward to the experience. By now you will not be surprised to hear that I was hoping for strong winds. I had seen pictures on telly where yachts ran hard at the wind, leaning dramatically

---

[102] I may have said 'parked', initially . . .

against the water, and that was something I was eager to experience for myself.

Turned out we were 'lucky' with the weather. About two hours into our trip the wind started to pick up. Then dark clouds appeared and the wind picked up some more. The boat's forward motion had changed from a sedate glide to a heavy lurch. We were speeding along nicely at an angle that allowed me to dangle my hand into the water with ease from where I was sitting. Then the wind got more forceful still and Mary's friend, in his capacity as skipper,[103] told me that it may be safer not to sit on the side of the boat any more. Then he ordered me not to. And then the wind started to crack into the sails and the little boat was *driven* across the surface with real force.

The skipper was concentrating but not concerned. I was in my element. This is what I had been hoping for! Then Mary's friend suggested I go down below and make tea for everybody.

So I did. Unfortunately, the task turned out more difficult than I would have thought. By now we were being propelled along by a gale force 5 or 6 and the space below deck was commensurately challenging to occupy. There were no windows so it was impossible to know where you were relative to sea-level outside. As a consequence, I was rattling around like a ball in a pinball machine. Up, down, sideways, forward. Down again. Now sideways. Then a period of calm. OK good. Now is the chance. Where is that milk? Where are the cups? Teabags. I need teabags. Lurch! Ah crap. Spilled the water. Then from above deck a shout: 'Are you all right?' 'No!' I shouted back. 'Where is the fucking milk? And where do you keep the teabags?' After a few more minutes of undignified thrashing around I found a way to wedge myself in and complete the job. I emerged from below deck with five steaming cups of tea, proud of my accomplishment and relieved that I was able to rejoin the action. I was greeted by five facial

---

[103] I think I called him 'driver' . . ..

expressions, four grinning with expectation and one (Mary's) with some concern.

It was only much later that I understood the significance of this incident. Apparently, it is customary to send the sailing rookie down below for a while on a pretext and derive amusement from the condition of seasickness this brings about.

What Mary's friends did not know is that I do not get seasick. Frequent air travel is part of my job and in some 300 flights in all weather conditions I have not once had second thoughts about the movements, even severe ones, of the aeroplane. On rollercoasters I never feel anything but squealing delight. I am sure it is *possible* for me to get seasick, but all I can say is that making tea below deck in gale force 5 on a sailing boat was not enough to bring it on.

But of course, the point is not whether I get travel sick or not, or whether Mary's friends were playing a mild prank on me. The point is that Mary could not have known that my physical constitution was robust enough to withstand that particular test. The point is that she did nothing to warn me, or to dissuade her friends from carrying out the prank. In short, she did not protect me.

This may not sound like a big deal, but I understand that seasickness can be severely unpleasant. We were all planning to have dinner together that night and, even so, Mary went along with a prank that, for all she knew, may well have spoiled my enjoyment of the day out. I can say with certainty, on the other hand, that Ursina would never allow harm to come to me, if it was in her power to prevent it. Nor would I have stood by if I had been aware of an intended prank on Mary. On that day, Mary chose to side with her friends against me. This is true, even though she did so with a feeling of discomfort.

Uzi nine millimetre

A few months later, Donna was getting married to George, and Mary and I were at the wedding. I found myself sitting next to people whom I had never met, but I was enjoying the conversation. I noticed that Mary was deep in conversation with somebody who she later identified as Charles. Charles was the 32-year-old son of Lord Wolseley. The Wolseleys, I heard, were an aristocratic family which traced its origins back through the centuries. They owned a splendid estate in Scotland and Charles had invited Mary up to 'the house' for a weekend of country pursuits. I was told that he would later seek me out to extend the invitation to me as well.

And so he did. I was lining up to get some hot food from the buffet when I was addressed. Please remember that at that stage nobody had officially introduced me to Charles, so as far as I was concerned, I did not know who he was. We had the following conversation.

Hullo.
Hi there.
You are Mark, are you not?
Yes?
Mary pointed you out to me.
Uh-huh. And you are . . .?
I am Charles.
Hi Charles. How's it going?
I am very well, thank you. Very well indeed. I was wondering whether I could invite Mary and you up to the house.
Sure. Thank you for the invitation . . . Where is your place?
My family owns an estate in Scotland. You would be staying for the weekend.
Cool. Yes, that sounds fun.
Mary said you are not a country man, Mark?
No, I am not . . . Why do you say that? Have you got some country pursuits in mind?
Yes. Well, we were thinking you could join us on the shoot.
A shoot? That's when you walk through the countryside and kill birds, isn't it?
Yes. So I was wondering – can you handle a gun, my boy?
Well. As a matter of fact, I can. I was trained in a range of weapons in the military, and I came second in the German army marksmanship competition in two disciplines. One was the Uzi SMG and the other the Walther P1.

Charles looked at me uncertainly.

> To the uninitiated, SMG stands for sub-machine gun. The Uzi is
> an automatic weapon capable of firing 10 rounds per second.
> The Walther P1 is a semi-automatic pistol with a design that
> is based on the P38 used by the Wehrmacht in WW2.[104] And
> if you were wondering whether second place means
> anything, there were 500 contenders in the competition.[105]
> Ah. Yes. I think that will do.
> Well, I am wondering, Charles. Will it? I was trained to kill people,
> not grouse. I am not sure my skills are easily transferable.

Now he looked at me as if I was slightly unbalanced.

> In fact, thinking about it, I am sure my skills are not applicable
> to grouse. With regret therefore, I need to decline your kind
> offer.

Now he looked profoundly shocked. I do not believe he was
used to commoners turning down his invitations.

Again, I felt severely out of place in the company of Mary's friends
and acquaintances. My response to Charles may amuse you, and I
am certainly smiling now recalling this incident more than a decade
later, but I was not smiling at the time. My response was deliberately
adversarial, and clearly defensive. The point is that again somebody
in Mary's social circle had made me feel uncomfortable and I was
taking conscious note of this fact at the time.

What do you think about fox hunting?
A short time later, Mary was invited by her friend Joanna to
go down to Devon for the weekend to stay with Joanna and

---

[104] The army drills this stuff into you. I was trying to forget this information,
but I am not sure I ever can.

[105] This was a little bit embellished, I have to admit. . . . It is true I ranked 2/500
in the competition, but the contestants were all drawn from army HQ, where
I was stationed as a conscript, and as such presumably not as true in their aim
as some in the fighting units may have been.

her parents at their house in the countryside. As usual, by polite consent, my presence was also requested and so I went along.

Joanna was nice but a bit guarded, her mum was delightful, open and charming and her dad was – well. Joanna's dad was a retired physician who, judging by the number of publications to his name, all displayed on the bookshelf in the living room, must have been an eminent doctor and researcher during his active working life. By the time we stayed with the family, he was retired and had developed a habit of dominating conversations. At dinner I discovered that he had also developed a habit of drinking heartily, as evidenced by the fact that there was a stationary bottle of wine next to his place setting, whereas the other guests were served from roaming bottles.

The dinner conversation was pleasant enough, until Dad addressed me from the head of the table. It was a long table, with eight people seated around it, not including him. I was sitting quite a distance away from him and was surprised to be singled out in a somewhat imperious manner.

This is what he said: 'What do you think about fox hunting, Mark? I understand you live in London. We are all very big hunters down here.'

Huh. Unusual. What to say? I was a guest in his[106] house, eating food his wife had kindly prepared and until now we had shared an evening of gentle, pleasant conversation. Best to prevaricate. 'Well, as you said, I am a townie and don't understand the ways of the countryside. I don't really know.'

But he would not be defeated that easily. 'No, no. Please tell us what you think. We would all very much like to know.' I felt cornered. I looked at Mary for support. Mary looked at me apprehensively but did not offer any help. I knew Dad was her hero. She admired him for a kindness and intelligence

---

[106] I assume it was his. But of course it could have been his wife's. The way he was acting said 'his' though.

he no doubt possessed but had just chosen not to display that particular evening. So I tried to put an end to this line of debate before it got out of hand, and without being too impolite. The only response I could think of was to address the issue directly, so I said: 'I apologise, Sir. Please accept my answer that I don't understand the ways of the countryside. I can assure you that if you ask me again, I will no longer be this diplomatic.' I am not sure he got the message, but the other guests were rapidly starting up conversations, and the tension dissipated.

Once again, I felt that I was singled out by one of Mary's acquaintances. This time I was addressed confrontationally but the social setting I found myself in made it impossible for me to respond as I would have liked. Yet this again is not the point. The point is that Mary let it happen and did not try to defuse the situation. Surely it must have been in her power to do so, as she had told me she knew the old gentleman like 'a second dad'. This situation was similar to the yachting incident. I noticed consciously that Mary did not jump to my rescue, and that she had not done so on her friend's sailing boat either.

V Day

Another few months later, Mary and I had a Valentine's date. We were now quite far into our relationship and I had started to feel sceptical about whether we had a future together.[107] Perhaps for that very reason, I had been looking forward to our dinner date for a long time, and I was cherishing the prospect of an evening of *just the two of us*. We arrived at the restaurant, a nice French place just off the King's Road, and I had taken her a flower to make the night a little bit more special. I remember giving her the flower outside the restaurant, deliberately before we sat down to eat.

---

[107] I can hear you say 'Glory be! He finally got it!' This would be justifiable sarcasm, and of course it is the heart of the issue we need to discuss after this last story.

We entered the restaurant and were greeted by the waiter. Mary had asked for a vase, so I was shown to the table first. We arrived at our destination and the waiter showed me the table with a satisfied 'Voila, Monsieur!' The following three things then happened in quick succession:

(1) I noticed that the table was set for six and started saying 'This must be a mistake . . .'
(2) Mary shouted 'Surpriiiiiiise!'
(3) Four of Mary's friends arrived.

And there they were again. Mary's friends. A ubiquitous presence. Even a Valentine's date was not strongly fortified enough to keep them out. I remember that I felt betrayed – it was not actually the fact that Mary had, without my knowing, invited somebody to our date. That in itself might have been OK. But she had invited only her friends and, as I found out later, had not even tried to invite mine.

An aborted test drive – interpretation

Questions asked
A few months after V day we mutually agreed to end our relationship.

The point of my eight stories is to present some evidence that we can use in our quest to find answers to the questions raised earlier. How can we know whether a relationship is right? How much natural overlap do we have? Does our relationship need work? More importantly, does it deserve work, or are we fundamentally mismatched? Are we trying to fit a round peg into a square hole?

These are the big questions in the test drive. Let us consider the evidence and see what we can learn.

First, an initial comment. The experiences I selected were all negative (certainly from my perspective, but presumably from Mary's as well). When you read them all in one go, it must seem as though this was the relationship from hell. That impression would be wrong. It was a good relationship, but between two people who were fundamentally ill-suited to each other. Initially, the positive aspects were more important, but slowly the negative ones started to dominate. But it took two years for this dynamic to run its course.

How is it possible for a badly matched relationship to continue for so long? Why did neither of us acknowledge the evidence earlier? The answer to this question, I think, reveals the first dynamic of a relationship which is in test drive. Each experience in itself is not severe enough to lead to an emotional break. Each individual event can be explained away: I just ran into a strange chap at that wedding, I did not want to go into the bookshop anyway, the prank on the boat was not really important . . . That sort of thing. You recognise the signs – we have all been there. And between the negative events are long periods during which the relationship is nice, enjoyable, fantastic even. Hence, if there is not something fundamentally wrong (cheating with somebody else, physical or verbal/ psychological violence, rows every time you see each other), relationships have a tendency to be resilient. It is human nature.

But each time something happens, we unconsciously take note of it and tag it with a memory – sad, hurt, infuriating, charming, noble and so on. Over time, these unconscious interpretations of events (either positive or negative) bind together and leave a feel, a certain overall quality. This quality becomes tangible when triggered by a certain event. We have no idea when this will happen, or what it will be, but it *will* happen.

Epiphany recognition
So let us see what my relationship with Mary looks like with hindsight, and where these epiphanies fall in the timeline. Have a look at the diagram.

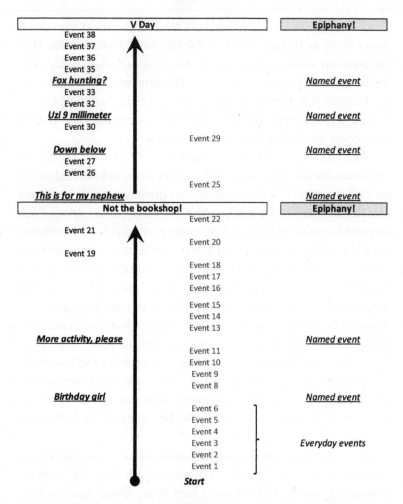

Fig. 7.3 A relationship starts out with a preponderance of events seen as positive. In a relationship between ill-suited partners, these tend to become less frequent. Conversely, events seen as negative increase in frequency until they dominate. The timeline is punctuated by epiphanies, experiences that illustrate the essence of a relationship as right or wrong. It is paramount to recognise these epiphanies consciously, and accept their message, if the partners wish to make accurate interpretations regarding the dynamics of their relationship.

Some observations, if I may:

• At first, positive events dominated. Gradually, negative experiences began to occur more and more frequently until they became the norm.

- Not all events are important or stand out in any way. Most are just everyday things – a look or an evening spent together.

- In the run-up to the first epiphany, there were two named events, two events that I remembered later and that therefore stood out from the rest. At the time they occurred, I did not consciously analyse them, but they had some significance and I stored them away in my subconscious.

- And then I had my first epiphany! The bookshop incident had a profound effect on me and demonstrated clearly that something was wrong. I realised that I was no longer able to engage in an activity that I needed for my own well-being. Indeed, the incident showed me, possibly for the first time in my life, how much I had taken for granted that I would always be able to sit down with a book, and how much I missed it now that it was gone.

  I remember that I consciously thought about the reason for my loss and realised that Mary and I were fundamentally different people. Mary existed as part of a social nexus. For her to be happy, she needed to feel part of a wider group.

- But the epiphany was not severe enough to break off the relationship. It was followed by some positive events, and I thought maybe the relationship merely needed work. However, negative events soon tended to appear more frequently, among them several which disquieted me at some level.

- And then I had the second epiphany. When Mary's friends 'invaded' the restaurant on V Day, something became clear to me. I realised, with the clarity of conscious insight, that Mary was a social being through and through. Not only did she enjoy the company of her friends, she also defined herself to a large extent by the benchmark of the position she occupied within the society of her friends and acquaintances.

This insight helped me connect the dots. I realised that events I called 'Birthday Girl', 'Down Below' and 'Fox hunting' were all of a similar nature. Mary did not 'have my back' in any of these; she was siding with her friends and did not try to shield me from her friends' behaviour.

I also realised that a partner suitable for Mary would need to want to build an extended sphere of social contacts and immerse himself in Mary's circle. Her partner could only ever hope to hold a moderately elevated status: he would be first among her friends. But for me the position of first friend was not enough. I needed more of Mary and less of her friends.

- The second epiphany therefore made it clear to me that our personalities were incompatible to the point that we could not find sufficient common ground.

And that, I think, answers most of our questions. At the end of our test drive, I knew that Mary and I had very little natural overlap. Our Venn diagram was of the first kind. After the bookshop epiphany, I knew that I needed a large area of overlap to be happy in a relationship. It followed that our relationship would need a lot of work to get to that level. But the nature of the mismatch turned out to be profound – of our two personalities, one was essentially *social* and the other essentially *private*. It is difficult to find common ground in a relationship lived between these two qualities. A dominating social sphere swamps the private one; a dominating private sphere imprisons the social one. Hence, no amount of work could create a stable foundation in this case, and the circles would always have snapped back into their natural positions.

Many of you may think that it took me a long time to get to that insight. True enough. But the point is that I got there, and also *how* I got there. The most important tool I used was EPIPHANY RECOGNITION. This, I believe, is the most important insight in this discussion, the most important lesson. When epiphanies occur, we need to take note. We must not let these events elude us, and we must not try to explain them away.

This tool, if used constructively, allows us to gain insights into the nature of relationships that will mandate the right actions. Even work does not benefit a relationship between two personalities who are essentially incompatible. If we find ourselves in such a relationship and we are still in the test-driving phase, the responsible choice is to call it a day. If we allow the wrong relationship to continue because of a false sense of duty, or guilt, or because we wish to avoid the emotional turmoil of break-up, we will with certainty create an unhappy life for ourselves.

Of course, turn that statement around and you have: work benefits a relationship between two essentially well-suited personalities. Does my method work in these cases as well? Is EPIPHANY RECOGNITION able to detect well-matched relationships, even though they may have problems?

Well, I cannot prove scientifically that the method works in *all* those cases, but I am confident that it will work in many. And I *know* that it has worked in at least one test drive.

A successful test drive – the ride

The experiences and events that illustrate a positive relationship are all taken from my test drive with Ursina. There are essentially two reasons for this. First, our relationship has stood the test of time, and the positive epiphanies I have experienced are therefore proven to have worked. And second, Ursina and I did not get to where we are now without work.[108]

I can therefore present you with a case where work *was*

---

[108] There may be a third reason . . . If Ursina got to this part and it was *not* full of positive stories about her, I'd be in trouble.

required as an initial cost, and where following its input the circles in the Venn diagram settled into a position of abundant overlap.

Again, first the stories, then the interpretation.

Dinner is served

My first story is from the early days of our relationship, from the time that we were getting to know each other and were just generally seeing how we got on. We had sorted the exclusivity chat some time ago and were officially test driving.

This is a story about having dinner together in a restaurant. Actually, it is not just *one* story, but a blended memory from many dinners, and as such a generic story about having dinner together.

A typical dinner would go like this. We would meet up at some restaurant in town and first we would have a drink and chat. Then we would go to the table and chat. The waiter would arrive after a polite 15 minutes or so and I would discover that I had barely got beyond the part on the menu where it mentions the name of the restaurant. We would then make a conscious effort to concentrate on the menu, place our orders and chat. Chatting would change to talking, perhaps to debating or discussing, and back to chatting. There was always laughter and sometimes there were silly things. And then one of us would order a latte and the other tea, and I would be incredulous at how quickly the time had passed, and that we had come to the end of dinner seemingly without having eaten anything.

You are, of course, getting what I am saying. Time flew by. Our conversations were interesting, intelligent (mostly hers), funny and easy. But there was another quality to our dinners, and it was deeper down. Although I knew on a rational level that we did not know each other that well, we never felt like strangers. I always had a feeling that it was right to be there with her, that people who were close to me would approve, that I was in good hands.

Illustrated strips

After a while, we thought it would be a nice idea to go to Paris for the weekend. We booked a room in a small hotel in the Jewish quarter and arrived on Friday night on the Eurostar. It was a nice weekend in April, still a bit cold perhaps, but the city was filled with the promise of summer and life was good. We spent our time strolling through town, window-shopping in the Rue du Faubourg Saint-Honoré, or in the furniture shops in the sixth arrondissement. Finally, we got to the Champs-Elysées, and I knew what I wanted to do there. So I asked her whether she would mind if I popped into the megastore for some browsing. She said she did not and would meet me in there in an hour, while she investigated the shoe shops.

What I had not told Ursina specifically was that I wanted to go into the bookshop to browse the comic books. From the age of 12 I had been an ardent fan of French and Belgian comic books. Unlike in the UK, where comics are invariably associated with the *Beano*,[109] in France and Belgium *bandes dessinées*, or illustrated strips, are considered a form of literature in their own right and are held in high artistic regard.[110] I liked the well-known characters *Astérix* and *Tintin*, but also titles like the detective story *Ric Hochet*, the series *Bruno Brazil* about a team of secret agents or the atmospheric Western series *Blueberry* by Jean Giraud, who also won critical acclaim for his avant-garde drawings published under the pseudonym of Moebius.

I will stop here but, trust me, I could go on. I realise that an interest in art and design, and by extension in *bandes dessinées*, can mark you out as a major bore if shared too openly. And I did not necessarily want to share it with Ursina, unless she showed an interest,[111] but I *did* want to browse the large

---

[109] Or the *Viz*, which is actually cool.
[110] If you find this hard to believe, check it out on amazon.fr. Under 'livres', you'll find *bandes dessinées* as a subgenre next to *littérature*, showing more than 10,000 different comic books.
[111] She did not.

selection of titles on offer. So I did. And, as you will have no trouble believing, I lost myself a little bit. So many titles I had never heard of! Some early stories I had never seen. Biographies of authors. Signed editions. Director's cuts which showed drafts and the genesis of classic titles. Fantastic – I was like a kid in a candy store.

Oh crap. Was that the time? It was half an hour after we said we would meet up. Where was Ursina? I hoped I could find her and that she would not be angry. But hang on . . . there she was, sitting quietly on a chair, looking idly at some comic books, waiting for me to finish.

I could not believe it. Most people would have announced their presence, either quietly making a point or openly urging me to get on with it. But Ursina just sat there and appeared to be in no hurry at all. That was the first time I noticed a quality that was to become characteristic of our relationship. We do not urge each other to live in accordance with the other person's preferences. If I am browsing in a book shop and Ursina is not interested, we meet up somewhere else in an hour. If Ursina is looking at bags and I am bored, the same. We complement each other well, and the Paris browsing session was an early signal that we were well suited.

We are not going to push past this, are we?

You must not think, however, that our relationship started off on cloud nine and never came down to earth. We had our share of issues to work through, and one of these I want to share with you now.

As I mentioned already, in the test-driving phase of a relationship we explore each other's lives, decide to what extent we can trust the other person with our more intimate thoughts, test how many layers we can remove from our protective walls. This process takes time; we are cautious as we do not want to get hurt. It is a bit like trying to sit down in a very hot bath – you lower yourself slowly, recoil briefly from the heat, then lower yourself again, stop, get used to the temperature for a while, then lower yourself a bit further.

And this is what we were doing. As we were climbing into the bath, so to speak, we encountered a tricky issue. I already mentioned it before, in the context of judging. Remember Ursina's friend Richard from her days as an aid worker in Africa? He was the chap who found it difficult to remain faithful to his wife and had frequent extramarital affairs, sometimes more than one at the same time. Ursina and Richard had developed an intimate friendship and Ursina told me that Richard was her rock in an alien, and sometimes hostile, environment.

I remember that I found this difficult to accept. We have already discussed that I was judging Richard and Ursina at this point, and that the reason I judged them was basically vulnerability and insecurity. At the time, we had not yet developed an in-depth understanding of the other person's motivations. I was evaluating Ursina's actions from the point of view of how a similar action could affect *me*, and not with the primary intention of understanding *her*. The way I saw it was that Ursina had been able to build a meaningful friendship with somebody who I did not believe had demonstrated himself to be worthy of trust. And, by extension of this sentiment, I was not sure whether Ursina valued the personal qualities I believed I possessed. In short, I was unsure whether ethical standards were something that Ursina valued or not. And if she did not, could that not bring problems further down the line if we stayed together?

From Ursina's point of view, of course, the issue looked different. She *knew* the deeper reasons she liked Richard and why she was able to overlook, or at least not focus on, an aspect of his character that she also saw as a weakness. In our many intense, heated and emotionally draining discussions, she tried to make me see that Richard, indeed people in general, were complex and have many personality traits, weaknesses and strengths. Ursina tried to make me understand that the ethical weakness Richard undoubtedly demonstrated did not dominate his character, that at least in *their* friendship he projected the kindness, strength and empathy that Ursina loved in him.

Well, Ursina tried to make me see this. But our relationship was young and I would have needed to pretty much *blow up* my protective wall, rather than lower it by a few inches, had I wanted to accept her explanation. In short, I was afraid. During this traumatic time in our relationship, I did not feel strong enough to make that leap of faith. I was not strong enough to be vulnerable.

All this was brought to a head in a telephone conversation on a Saturday morning. The evening before, we had eaten dinner at a nice place on the *Thames* and, sure enough, after a while we got on to The Subject. Most of dinner was spent again in a draining discussion of the issue and we decided that we each needed to go to our separate flats to gain some distance.

The next morning I called her and we discussed it again. We got to a point where we were hitting a brick wall (probably my protective wall, which was still there, proud and erect). I remember Ursina saying, with some real sadness in her voice: 'We are not going to push past this, are we?' And I did not know whether we would. So I said nothing, and we agreed to hang up.

And that was the moment that I had one of these epiphanies I keep talking about. In that moment, I felt a sadness so fundamental, so profound that I was unable to ignore it or make light of it. I had a feeling that we might just have ended something that had been developing into the meaningful friendship and trusting relationship we had both been hoping to find. And once we ended it, it would *never* come back. And we would have ended it lightly, for no real reason.

That was it. In that moment, I knew that I *had* pushed past it. If I thought that we would have ended our relationship *lightly* for this reason then the reason lacked substance. And if there was no substance then I did not need to be afraid, and I had no reason to be insecure.

So I grabbed a chocolate bunny from the fridge (it was a week after Easter), jumped into the car and drove 30 miles across London to her flat. I rang the doorbell and a small voice weakly asked 'Yes?' I said 'Delivery!' and the voice squealed with delight. I ran up the stairs and she said 'That was exactly the right thing to do, sweetheart!'

It turned out she was not referring to the delivery of the chocolate bunny. Both of us felt an intense sense of relief, a sense of deep joy that we could continue building our relationship, that we would not have to split up and that we had a future together.

Of course, this did not end all our issues. There were more to work though, but we had made our leap of faith. The point of this story is that we put a lot of work into our relationship in its infant stages. Work that took the form of discussions about issues that we both thought were fundamental. These discussions were held in a spirit of openness, and we always tried to be well-meaning when listening to the other's point of view. This, however, does not mean that it was easy to get through some of the issues. Some, like the one I told you about above, were emotionally draining, traumatic and took courage to work through. And yet we have continued doing this ever since, and have developed the confidence that we will be able to resolve any issues if they arise. This confidence is one of the components that forms the bedrock of our relationship.

Dinner is served again

A few months after our epiphany, we decided we needed to go on a holiday. We went somewhere hot, with a beach, a nice hotel and a lovely spa. There was scope for some activities, but mostly we were relishing the prospect of a quiet and relaxing two weeks off. It was the time of Ursina's birthday and I was planning to do something special as a gift.

I thought I would arrange the romantic dinner to end all romantic dinners. I had a vision of a lone table on a beach, just the two of us, and probably some champagne and a nice bottle of wine. In my vision I also needed romantic music and therefore knew I had to investigate what she would like – I sensed that my preferred choice of hard rock ballads would probably not hit the spot. So I steered conversations in the direction of music and was able to find out that 'Moon River' was her all-time favourite song. Of course, I had no idea what her favourite arrangement was so I downloaded 20 different versions of the track to my i-Pod and also got Rod Stewart's American Songbook collection for good measure.

I then started an email conversation with the hotel management asking them whether dinner on the beach for two was something they would be able to organise. I was delighted when they said yes, and booked this as a special treat.

When we arrived at the hotel, the manager took me aside briefly and asked whether I would be happy if they reserved an area around one of the swimming pools for Ursina's birthday dinner. I said that would be fine, and thought nothing more about it.

When the day came, I asked Ursina to dress up to mark the occasion of her birthday. After getting ready, we left our room and, on some pretext, I steered her towards the pool area.

As we approached the pool, we saw that management had lined the garden path with large candles standing on the ground. Then we got to a stony staircase that led down to the pool. It too was lined with lanterns. At that point Ursina realised that something was up. She squealed 'You have *done* something!' and before I could deny it, we had walked round the corner, passed through the archway into the pool area . . .

. . . and were speechless. The hotel had not reserved an area around the pool for our table. They had reserved the *entire* pool area for our table.

Please do not think that this was a small area. We are talking about possibly 50,000 square feet, and in the middle of it there was *one* table. The table was on the beach, bordered on one side by Mayan-looking architecture framing the pool and to the other side by the sea. The pool area was adorned with massive torches, which formed part of the architecture and had been lit for the occasion. The sea was gently rolling against the beach. There was a gentle breeze and we had dinner into the sunset.[112] In the background, 'Blue Moon' was playing.

'Blue Moon'? Not 'Moon River'? Yes, well spotted. I had messed it up and downloaded 20 different versions of the wrong song. Well, what can I say? I would not have got it wrong had Ursina wanted 'Back in Black' by AC/DC.

The point of this somewhat longish story is simply this. I love organising surprises for Ursina, and this was the most romantic surprise I have ever been able to pull off. Not from any huge input of my own – I just set the ball rolling with the management of the hotel and they delivered something truly outstanding and genuinely special. But why do I love doing this? It is for Ursina's reaction. The look in her eyes when I do something like this, or give her a present, or buy her chocolates, is absolutely priceless. One of Ursina's friends said once that it was easy to have a good relationship. You just get up every day and make your partner happy. Well said. But you also need a partner who allows themselves to be made happy. Ursina and I try to make each other happy, and it is working. This is easy when you click in this way. But it is not if you don't, as the Birthday girl story about Mary and me demonstrated.

Angst and serenity

Ursina had informed me some time before that one of the bank holiday weekends in May would be reserved for my birthday treat and that I was not allowed to plan anything for that weekend.

I could not wait. What would she have prepared? Dinner and a treat? Cinema perhaps, or a surprise party with friends? But it was to remain a secret and Ursina would not talk.

A few days before the weekend, I was told to brace myself as we would have to get up early on Saturday and drive somewhere. I was told to bring sporty clothes since it would involve cycling. I was beginning to get an idea what this might be all

---

[112] I've tried five different versions of this story. I am sorry but it always sounds corny written down. You just had to be there.

about and I was proven right on the day. We were driving down to Surrey for a half-day induction into downhill mountain biking!

I was over the moon. Fantastic! This would be great. Those of you who know what this is do not need further explanation, of course. But for those of you who do not, let me say that downhill biking is to mountain biking what downhill racing is to cross-country skiing. There are graded runs, and black runs include drops, rock gardens, artificial obstacles and other stuff. I had always wanted to do this and was hugely looking forward to the opportunity of getting a proper introduction to this sport. As it turned out, we were both having a fantastic time.

After downhill biking, I was told that we would continue onwards to a hotel not far away, where we would spend the rest of Saturday and all day Sunday. When we arrived, it turned out that Ursina had booked dinner and a spa treatment for the following day. I was in heaven. Sunday night came and it was time to drive home.

Or so I thought. But I was informed that we would be spending another night in the hotel and then driving on to another location, yet to be disclosed, for another treat. This time Ursina gave in to my incessant begging and revealed that we would be going to Thorpe Park for a wild day on the rollercoasters. My best friend was also coming down for the day, and Ursina had booked preference tickets that allowed you to get onto the rides by queuing in the fast lane.

What a birthday weekend. We had so much fun. But the fact that we had fun is not the reason why I am telling you this story, as you might have guessed. The real point is what the weekend reveals about Ursina. She put together the perfect weekend for me. Action sports, relaxation and innocent fun. She knew what I would enjoy and went to huge trouble to get it all organised. If you find somebody who thinks only of you when giving presents, you pretty much know you have found the right person

I do not want to go home ...

The final story I want to share with you is quickly told. It is another epiphany, and as short as it is meaningful.

Ursina and I had spent two weeks together on holiday and had just walked through the arrival gate at Heathrow airport. The holiday had been wonderful; beach, sun and halloumi.[113]

So there we were with our suitcases, about to go to our respective homes. Only one thing left to do, really, and that was to say goodbye and agree when we would get together next. And that is when it hit me. I did not want to go home. Or rather, I did not want to go home *on my own*. I wanted to go home together.

That is it. End of story, so to speak. Ursina had been feeling the same for a while longer, but had never pressed me about it. We basically decided there and then that we would live together and a few days later started discussing the practicalities. This story answers the question, 'How do you know when the test-driving phase is over?' You know when you feel that you are happier together than apart. Our test drive was over that afternoon at Heathrow airport.

A successful test drive – interpretation

Catching a fish

So here we are again, at the end of a test drive. Only this test drive led to a stable relationship, while the other one we discussed did not. I am consciously aware, pretty much on a daily basis, that my relationship with Ursina is right, while, certainly towards the end, I was consciously aware that my relationship with Mary was wrong.

What makes my relationship with Ursina different? And how did I know that it was different? How did I know that this relationship was worth working on?

Before I discuss these questions, a reminder of why they are important. The goal of this chapter is to explore how to find a

---

[113] Guess where we went ...

fulfilling relationship. The anecdotes I shared with you are all taken from my relationships, but of course the object of the exercise is not to talk about *me*. The stories are simply examples, and I chose them because I know them well. I wanted to demonstrate how a dominating feel develops in a relationship, how we can become consciously aware of it and then act accordingly.

So what was the overriding feel in the test drive with Ursina?

It is simply what people refer to as chemistry. When Ursina and I did[114] something together, I always felt that I belonged there with her, that it was right for me to be there and nowhere else, that I was in good hands, that people close to me would have approved. On the rare occasions that I had dinner with Mary (on her own), I never quite felt that we shared the same values, wanted the same things in life, clicked the same way. Mary loved the countryside and felt at home there. Ursina is urban, and although she does not dislike the country, she never expresses a particular urge to go there. Mary wanted to have kids and was drawn to the sheltered existence of village family life. Ursina never actively made a choice against kids, but never saw a family as her goal in life either.

Yet, even this is not the essence of the matter, and it does not explain why Ursina and I clicked and Mary and I did not. The essence lies in the way Ursina smiles when I do something nice for her and in the way Mary did not. The essence is that Ursina would stand her ground for me, where Mary chose to side with friends. The essence is that Ursina loves me for who I am, and Mary loved me for who she hoped I would become.

And importantly, I *knew* this. The respective qualities of the two test drives were known to me while I was 'driving', mostly on a subconscious level, but sometimes consciously. I could always see a potential future with Ursina, but hardly ever with Mary.

---

[114] In accounts involving Ursina, the past tense refers to events in the test-driving phase.

This is the reason why epiphanies highlighted that I was out of sync with Mary and in step with Ursina. However, do not get me wrong – this does not mean that things have always been easy with Ursina and were always difficult with Mary. Quite the opposite. You may recall that 'Ursina epiphany #1'[115] marked the end of a draining and quite traumatic process of soul-searching, while 'Mary epiphany #1'[116] came after a number of innocuous events. However, the epiphany itself highlighted that my relationship with Ursina was essentially right, whereas the one with Mary was not.

And this, really, is it. This is how we know. This is how *I* knew. A relationship in which I was afraid to enter a bookshop lest I should find things I would like to read cannot be right. A relationship in which the thought of ending it makes me fundamentally sad may be right, but one in which the prospect of not having to end it fills me with relief is almost certainly right. A relationship in which I cannot breathe because I am constantly expected to be somebody I am not cannot be right. But one in which the thought of going home alone makes me sad, and the prospect of going to a shared home makes me happy, is right.

It comes down to these simple recognitions. In the end, we know. We know subconsciously if a relationship is right or not. But our rational mind may get in the way, and we may not allow ourselves to act in accordance with what we know on a deeper level. The things we tell ourselves to explain away a negative feeling take many forms: a relationship requires work; things take time; he has a lot of qualities; my parents really like her; he has a good job, is really sexy, has cool friends . . . But deep down I maintain that usually we just know. The trick is to let the subconscious do the work and capture the moment when it rises to the surface and delivers an insight.

In this, EPIPHANY RECOGNITION is like catching a fish. We must not let it slip away, but once caught, we still need to

---

[115] See 'We are not going to push past this, are we?'
[116] See 'Not the bookshop!'

prepare it. We need to recognise the insight for what it is, but then need to evaluate it consciously and understand its significance intellectually. If we learn this skill, and allow ourselves to act on it, we have taken a huge step towards finding the right partner in life. And if we find the right partner in life, we have taken a huge step towards finding happiness and balance.

A huge step *towards* it. But we are not there yet. To find happiness we still need to sort some other things out. Things which may seem less important or less fundamental. Like where to live. What job to do. How to act towards others. How to do what we would like to do, and not always do what others would like us to do.

But do not kid yourself. These things *are* important. They may not seem as fundamental as self-knowledge, self-confidence or finding our life partner, but if they are out of sync you know that something important is missing. I will discuss how to try to get these things right in the next chapter.

RULE 8

Shape your world

How to build your comfort zone

An introduction to sculpting

Each of us needs to shape our own world. We want to design our world in accordance with our preferences and desires; we want to give it a shape that allows our strengths to shine and our weaknesses to fade; we want to keep it free from pressures and unencumbered by responsibilities that we cannot handle.

In such a world we would be free. We would be able to spread our wings, explore our full potential, do what brings us fulfilment. We would never have to take on tasks we are ill-suited to accomplish, engage in activities we find onerous or allow others to put us into a bad mood.

But how to achieve such a utopia? Surely this is impossible? Surely life would get in the way when trying to construct such a world? And what are the building blocks of something like that anyway?

These are the questions I would like to discuss in this chapter. First off, let us be clear again that, of course, utopias do not exist and nobody can build a *perfect* personal world. But this does not mean that we cannot try to build the best world possible. Certainly, I do not accept the view that a halfway house is the best that we can ever expect to achieve. If we know ourselves and act in accordance with what we find, we will be able to shape a world that is largely free from pressures we cannot handle, and largely filled with pursuits that fulfil us.

As ever, the task starts with us. *I* shape my world. The world does not shape *me*. I am aware that this statement invites objection if presented in this deliberately simplified form. But remember what we discussed in the chapters 'How to control your life' and 'How to control fate'. What is important is mind-set. A mindset that blames circumstances relinquishes control. A mindset that empowers you to act for yourself establishes control.

This principle also applies when we build our personal worlds. Only *I* can shape my world in accordance with my wishes. Nobody else can. Indeed, if somebody else could, that might be bad. If you allow others to be the architects of your world, you may end up with a life that pleases others more than it does you, and hence fails to bring you contentment.

So let me restate what I wish to discuss in the current chapter. We need to find a way to create a world in which each of us can be ourselves, in which we do not have to pander to the expectations of others. But equally, we need to do this in a way that it does not detract from the happiness of others. We need to find a balance between our happiness and that of others and create our world responsibly.

The construction of such a world will require a variety of tools. At times we need to be uncompromising and make sure that the desires and goals of others do not become dominant. At other times we need to realise that we interact with others and so our happiness is entangled with that of friends, family or even acquaintances.

Some building blocks of our world may sound trivial, such as where to live or how to behave towards people we meet in our daily lives. Other ingredients seem more funda-mental, such as what career to choose or how to define goals in life. All of them together, however, shape our world. And since they do, each of them individually requires conscious attention.

Be unreasonable

The first tool I would like to discuss is like a shield. When we use it, we attempt to shape an emotional reaction into an uncompromising statement. However, if this response remains purely instinctive, we have not yet learned to use this tool. Then, we would merely be stroppy or defiant. But if we learn to tap into the strength of the emotion and channel it into a conscious response, we have a tool that can protect our world from attack. In using the emotive response consciously, we aim to bend circumstances to our will, rather than bending our will to circumstance:

> The reasonable man adapts himself to the world: the unreasonable one persists in trying to adapt the world to himself. Therefore, all progress depends on the unreasonable man.[117]

Well then. Maxim 124 in George Bernard Shaw's list of aphorisms for the modern revolutionary certainly seems to capture this same essence. Of course, it can be interpreted in a number of ways, and can lend moral support to a wide range of actions. And yet, I have always found this to be one of Shaw's most evocative pronouncements. I have to confess that I love it, in the interpretation that I choose to give it.

My interpretation is simply this: a person is not accountable to the expectations of others.

In this interpretation, Shaw's *bon mot* provides a useful mindset to draw upon when shaping a world. In the first section of this chapter, I would like to talk about the nature of this attitude. Put simply, this is the mindset where we exert personal strength; this is the no pushover faculty in our arsenal of world-shaping tools.

---

[117] Shaw, George Bernard. 'Maxims for Revolutionists'. *Man and Superman*. The University Press 1903. Reprinted by permission of The Society of Authors, on behalf of the Bernard Shaw Estate.

And now for some anecdotes. Just as a reminder, before we get stuck in, that the stories from my life are simply the raw material which I analyse to make some more general points.

Back to ASD

My first job was with an insurance company headquartered in Surrey. I was one of the annual intake of actuarial graduates and my first assignment was a two-year stint in the Actuarial Services Department, or ASD for short. To those of you who are puzzling over the expression actuary, I revealed in Rule 6 that this is another way of saying insurance mathematician. Actuarial science is a branch of applied mathematics that concerns itself with the quantification and modelling of financial dynamics in funds made up of life assurance policies or insurance products such as motor or household policies. For example, if you are a 30-year-old male and you wish to purchase a life assurance policy that pays out the sum of £100,000 on your 60th birthday, an actuary could work out the premium you would have to pay every month for the next 30 years, assuming payment in arrears, a suitable return on the insurance company's investment assets and mortality in line with an appropriately chosen statistical table.

This gets even more technical if you investigate, for example, what the solvency of the life office is at any given point in time if you bunch a million of these policies together in a fund, all with policyholders of different ages at inception, different premium payment patterns and different contractual payout amounts.

So you can see this is highly fascinating stuff. The reason I am telling you this is simply to illustrate the nature of the tasks that came up in ASD. They were highly technical, and many of those drawn to this type of work were, let us say, more at ease when they communicated with computer programs than when they did with people.

There was, for example, our head programmer on Modelling,

who would spend days drawing up technical specifications, the purpose of which was to define in great detail naming conventions for computer files. Or there was the chap who headed up the mainframe programming team and who in his spare time loved to do something called track-spotting. This is different from the more widely known trainspotting, and involves covering every mile of railway track in the UK by personal train journeys. He once took a journey on the Eurostar to Paris solely for the purpose of having covered the UK portion of the rail track. He told me that once he arrived at Gare du Nord, he immediately boarded the next train back to London. But he said he had an excellent weekend, since the journey also allowed him to verify the speed of the train by counting the mileposts next to the track and keeping time on his stopwatch.

After two years in ASD, I was ready to leave and delighted that I was being moved to the pensions department. Not much of a move, you may think, but compared with ASD the pensions department sounded like a breath of fresh air. A chance to talk to normal people and to engage with the outside world, even to have a light-hearted chat by the coffee machine, perhaps. And I was overjoyed to find this was indeed what it was like.

But after a year of bliss in pensions,[118] my boss revealed to me that he had to transfer one of us back to ASD.

Shock. My young professional world crumbled. I could not possibly go back to that nether hell of nerd-dom. It had been bad enough in ASD when I was there, but in the meantime all my friends had transferred out, so I would be surrounded by techies all day long. The prospect seriously depressed me but I had no idea how to avert disaster. There were three of us in pensions, and one of us would have to go.

My boss talked to all of us and we gave the following evaluations of the situation:

---

[118] Yes, I know what that sounds like. Don't ask . . .

Sean: I'll resign if you stick me into ASD. I mean that.

Mark: If you put me back into ASD, I'll kill myself.

Aaron: Well, it would not be my preference, I must say. If you did not mind awfully, I should very much like to stay in pensions, but of course I understand the necessities of the job . . .

Guess who got picked to go to ASD? Tip: it was not me, and Sean remained my team leader.

Back to ASD – interpretation

Clearly, it would be absurd to contend that in the instance narrated above I consciously channelled my emotions into a statement designed to signal intransigence to my boss. The emotion I felt was pure frustration. My response reflected this emotion. It was pure and unadulterated, certainly immature, possibly childish. I would not have killed myself. My boss knew that.

However, and of course unbeknown to me at the time, the vigour of my response contrasted with the reasonable and mature stance that Aaron adopted in his interview. When I heard that Aaron had drawn the short straw, I asked Sean what he had said in his interview and noticed that his response had been similarly uncompromising. It dawned on me that my boss must have chosen Aaron because he expected him to be the most motivated of us three. I guess my boss made a profes- sional decision after weighing up the evidence presented to him. I realised that, had I been more reasonable, more mature, more *professional*, my stint in pensions may well have been cut short, and my career in the company would very likely have suffered as a consequence.

The lesson I learned from this experience is that defiance may, at least in certain circumstances, be an effective defence against adverse developments. However, I also realised that defiance has to be controlled consciously before it can blossom into a tool that can be used to master circumstance.

A few years later, there was one instance where I was able to channel similar frustration into a consciously controlled response.

Can't make me!

It was the first day of my employment with the firm of stockbrokers in London. I was very excited – in my mind, I was leaving the world of small commercial banking and I was about to spend my first work day in the City proper. Now I would be able to develop a career as an equity analyst, something I had secretly been wanting to do pretty much ever since I escaped ASD. I arrived and the person from HR showed me to my desk on the dealing floor. HGV greeted me cordially, and I sat down to sift through the various goodies on my desk, arranged for the induction of the newcomer. A mobile, a leaflet on how to use something called a dealerboard, induction manuals, something about Datastream and Reuters and – two textbooks. Asked what they were, HGV revealed to me cheerfully that I needed to read these and sit the exam administered by the FSA[119] to become an approved person in accordance with the Financial Services & Markets Act.

This was unexpected, but I should probably have known that I could not just start talking to financial institutions recommending the sale or purchase of stocks without some formal qualification. I asked my new boss when the exam was going to be held. He had just got up from his desk and, moving away, he shouted back, 'In two weeks! But don't worry, it's a doddle!'

Yeah right. Doddle. OK, it was multiple choice, but there were some 100 questions to answer in two exams on the day. And these books had a combined 700 pages or so. Blimey. Two full weekends and a lot of late nights lay ahead of me.

---

[119] Financial Services Authority, at the time the regulator of financial institutions in the UK.

And there would be absolutely no room to fail this – for one thing, failing would extend the time during which I would not be authorised to talk to clients; but more importantly than that, I would never live down failure on something considered as basic as the FSA registration exam (even though customarily rookies were given six weeks to study for it).

So I knuckled down, waded through two tomes of impossibly dry information on regulation, custodianship, clearing systems, money laundering and similar things. My previous schooling (business school, actuarial exams) helped with some of it, but it was still an incredibly tedious process.

The day of the exam came, I braved the onslaught of questions designed to check that I had learned all this information by rote, and got back to work just happy that it was over. A week later I received a slip of paper saying that I had passed and, to my utmost relief, I would now be able to concentrate on my job. This was the last exam I would ever take!

Or so I thought. When I triumphantly brandished my pass in front of HGV, he said, 'Told you it was gonna be a doddle. But still, this will be a good introduction for the CFA exams.'

I was not sure I had heard right. The what? To get to the bottom of this, I asked, 'The what?' – I was slightly shell-shocked at the prospect of sitting yet more exams and my eloquence had suffered a bit.

'CFA exams. Every new joiner sits them. Nothing unusual.' Enlightened, I sat down on my chair and did some investigations into this new requirement of the job. The CFA, I learned, is the Chartered Financial Analysts Institute and awards the professional qualification of CFA to those who complete a three-year programme and are able to pass three exams, one for each level. Looking through the syllabus for the exams, I discovered that it covered little I had not studied before at business school or in the Institute of Actuaries. The subjects did not have the mathematical bent everything had in the Institute, but they were comprehensive and eminently 'failable'. I decided not to study for this qualification and informed HGV of this decision.

After a short and controversial chat with HGV, I found myself at the desk of the Head of Research. We had the following conversation:

HGV told me you would rather not sit the CFA exams, Mark?

Actually, I will not sit them.

You are **refusing** to sit them?

Absolutely. There is no way I'm going to study for this.

But all the new joiners do. It is a requirement we have at the firm.

Well, I was never told during the interview stages that this was a requirement. God knows, with seven interviews there were plenty of opportunities to slip that one in. I want to be absolutely clear about this. Had I known about this requirement I would not have joined.

But why not? What is so hard about these exams?

It's not that they are hard necessarily. It's that nothing in the syllabus is new to me. I have studied all of this before, and it would just be a waste of time for me to study it again. In fact, it would mean that I can devote less attention to the rollout of the European product – I would have to dart off home all the time to learn facts from a textbook.

But hang on, Mark. If you studied all this before, these should be easy to pass. You should be able to take all three exams in one go and be done with it.

Well, first off, nothing is easy to pass. Exams can be failed, and I would still have to study for them. Second, what is the point of studying for something I already know? Why do you want people to qualify – so that they know their stuff, or so that they have uniform letters behind their name?

It's just to level the playing field, Mark, and make sure that everybody has the same level of qualification.

OK, I am up for that. Let all those who have a Bachelor degree top it up to a Masters, then obtain a separate postgraduate qualification, and then get a technical certification as an actuary. When everybody in the firm has got that, we can talk again. Until then, I will not take these exams.

And that, it turned out, was that. HGV supported me, probably because he was also a failed actuary[120] and had not taken the CFAs, and they decided to 'delay' the decision about whether or not I would have to sit them until after the European product was up and running. Three years later, the firm officially waived the requirement for me to sit the CFAs.

Can't make me – interpretation

This experience was, in some respects, quite similar to the one I had in the pensions department of the Surrey-based insurance company. Both times I felt intense frustration in response to a demand that had been made of me. Both times I felt that my professional, and by extension my private, world was threatened. And both times I felt driven to avert this threat. However, this time I consciously tried to channel my frustration into a steely resolve, into a mindset that would not accept the possibility of sitting the CFA exams as an option.

When I sat down for my chat with the Head of Research, the emotions were real. I was furious that the firm had not informed me of the study requirement. I was frustrated that I was asked to sit yet more exams, after two decades of passing exams almost continuously[121] and after finally sitting what I thought would be my last exam.

But this time I used my emotions consciously. This time I *allowed* them to deliver the passion that supported an otherwise rational argument. This time I used my emotions just enough to convey a lack of willingness to compromise. To be fair, I also counted on HGV supporting me since his qualifications looked similar to mine.

---

[120] No disrespect to HGV, of course. Those who discontinue the actuarial exams after the purely mathematical part of the syllabus used to receive a document called a certificate of actuarial techniques. I suppose it is possible to refer to yourself as 'partly qualified' if you got that far. The expression I use here is firmly tongue-in-cheek.

[121] School, university, business school, actuarial exams, FSA registration exam. There was also a driving test and a PADI scuba certificate.

This, I believe, may be an example of Shaw's unreasonable man, albeit on a very minor scale. Had I been reasonable, I would have had to accept the firm's statement that a CFA qualification was a condition of employment. But a controlled measure of defiance, added to a calculated gamble that my boss would be on my side, produced a result that facilitated my progress at the firm and gave me strength to face the professional challenges I knew were lying ahead.

To summarise, if we can learn to harness the power of our emotions in a way that means they lend resolve, conviction or spirit to a rational argument, and if we are not afraid to be responsibly uncompromising, as opposed to merely stubborn, we will have mastered an important skill which will help to protect our world from threats:

> . . . any one can get angry – that is easy . . . but to do this to the right person, to the right extent, at the right time, with the right motive, and in the right way, that is not for every one, nor is it easy . . .[122]

Zero tolerance

The second tool I would like to talk about is similar to being unreasonable. This tool is also defensive, but is more like an umbrella than a shield. When used appropriately, this tool allows us to make sure that our world does not get swamped with things we do not like.

We would use this tool for minor decisions, such as whether I really would like another pint, or to watch this movie or go to that party. Trivial though these choices may sound, if we constantly do things we do not really want to, the result will almost certainly be a sense of dissatisfaction. The sentiment may not run deep, but if we allow these small encroachments

---

[122] Aristotle. *The Nicomachean Ethics*. Translated by WD Ross, The Internet Classics Archive, http://classics.mit.edu/Aristotle/nicomachaen.html, II.9.

to continue unchecked, there is a chance that we may feel discontentment without consciously knowing why.

Indeed, this type of discontentment is most likely elusive. It is like ambient noise: we cannot quite put our finger on it, but it *is* there. For example, I do not do the sports I used to enjoy any more. My weekend was spent ferrying the kids around to the rugby and the ballet lesson. I have not spent time with my mates in a while. I never watch the sort of movies I really like.

Any of that sound familiar? Let us see whether we can wrest back some basic enjoyment from life.

Broken windows

In 1982 two American social scientists published an article in the reputable literary and cultural magazine *The Atlantic Monthly*.[123] The authors explored the dynamics that escalate crime from trivial beginnings, and argued that collectively shared indifference to petty crime may serve to create an atmosphere that fosters more serious unlawful acts:

> A piece of property is abandoned, weeds grow up, a window is smashed. Adults stop scolding rowdy children; the children, emboldened, become more rowdy . . . Teenagers gather in front of the corner store. The merchant asks them to move; they refuse. Fights occur. Litter accumulates. People start drinking in front of the grocery store; in time, an inebriate slumps to the sidewalk and is allowed to sleep it off. Pedestrians are approached by panhandlers.[124]

In a later more extensively researched publication,[125] the authors suggest that this theorised escalation of crime can be stopped by repairing damage when it is in its early stages: keep the

---

[123] Wilson, James Q and Kelling, George L. 'Broken Windows: The police and neighborhood safety'. *Atlantic Monthly*, vol. 249 (1982), pp. 29–38.
[124] Wilson 1982, p. 33.
[125] Kelling, George and Coles, Catherine. *Fixing Broken Windows: Restoring Order and Reducing Crime in our Communities*. Touchstone 1996.

abandoned building in shape, repair broken windows quickly, tend to the communal areas surrounding the building.

For our purposes, it is of course irrelevant whether the Broken Windows theory has validity as a sociological model. I mentioned the concept of zero tolerance because of its possible value as an analogy. Is it fruitful to employ a version of zero tolerance in our own lives? If so, what would it look like? Under which circumstances might it be an appropriate guide to our behaviour, and under which ones would it be counterproductive?

In this section, I shall argue that it *is* possible to adapt the theory of zero tolerance to carefully defined occurrences in our lives. However, as you may already suspect, we need to treat this maxim with caution – it is inappropriate in many life situations and will only be a useful tool if we learn to use it responsibly.

Do not act to please others – where zero tolerance works

Let me start by identifying the types of occurrence that I believe can be seen as analogous to Broken Windows. I define occurrence as a demand on our time, or an expectation from others of how we should behave. The occurrences I see as valid analogies are simple events that happen in everyday life:

(1) I am on my own at home. I am trying to finish a novel that I started a week ago. I am half way through, but it is boring. I'd rather put it on the shelf and do something else. But something compels me to read on. Maybe it will get better? Surely I cannot simply stop in the middle?
(2) I am in the pub with my mates. It is 10 pm and I would rather go home. My mates would rather stay for another while. 'Just one more drink, Mark. Then we'll go.'
(3) Ursina and I are in the theatre watching a play with two friends. Our friends are quite intellectual. They are enjoying the play enormously. We are bored and think it is a waste of time. But surely we can't just leave?
(4) I am at a bar with Aaron and a large group of his friends. One person suggests we all go to a restaurant in the

vicinity. I do not like it there. I came over mainly to chat with Aaron. Do I need to bite the bullet and go to that restaurant, even though I do not like it?

All these events are similar. None of them matter hugely in themselves, but in each of them something holds me back from doing what I would rather do. My preference to engage in a different activity is not overwhelming; I would not *hate* doing what the group dynamics suggest, but I would be incrementally happier if I went against the flow and did something else.

So let me examine next what would happen if I applied the maxim of zero tolerance in each case:

(1) This is the only occurrence in which the action does not depend on the desire of others and in which my decision would not affect anybody but me. The answer in this case is therefore easy. Zero tolerance would dictate that I stop reading a book I do not enjoy, put it on the shelf or take it to the charity shop and do something more productive instead. Those of you who do not enjoy reading as an activity may be bemused by my example – but if you enjoy reading, you will, at least at some point, have been in a similar situation.

Can't bring yourself to stop reading the boring book? No. Put the book away. Zero tolerance.

(2) Now this is marginally more difficult. In this example, I am not on my own. I am in the pub with my friends and we are enjoying a nice evening. We are having fun, we are laughing, chatting, we have drinks, crisps and pork scratchings. But I'd rather leave now, since it is getting late and I have an early meeting the next day. Zero tolerance dictates that I march out immediately and go home. And this is exactly what I should do. Not that drastically, perhaps, but I should say to my friends why I need to leave and then leave. After all, they are my friends. I know they understand – there is no problem here.

Force yourself to stay longer than you want? No. Say goodbye and leave. Zero tolerance.

(3) This is marginally more difficult still. Here, Ursina and I have arranged to come out with another couple. We are not the closest friends in the world, but we like each other and enjoy each other's company. We meet up maybe every three months or so and have dinner at the other couple's place, or go out to a restaurant or to see a play.

Ursina was unhappy, but our friends were really enjoying it. I could see Ursina was ready to leave, but something was keeping me. I was not sure whether our friends would find it rude to abandon them in the middle of our evening together.

Zero tolerance requires that we get up and leave the theatre with no second thoughts. And that is, eventually, what we did. After listening to a particularly absurd outburst from one of the characters, I had had enough. I became consciously aware that I was not enjoying myself. But we were there voluntarily, nobody forced us, and it was our evening. Our friends would understand, and they still had each other to chat to – it was not as if we were abandoning somebody to an evening of solitude. So we made our excuses, left and had dinner in a nearby French restaurant to finish the evening in good spirits.

Suffer through a performance because of a false sense of politeness or pride? No. Leave respectfully, but leave. Zero tolerance.

(4) A situation similarly difficult to (3), but for different reasons. Aaron is my best friend, and we know each other very well. I met up with him that day in the hope of having a conversation with him, and to meet some of his friends. It turned out that I did not find the people there very engaging, and Aaron's attention was largely taken up by the group he was with that evening. No big thing, but when people suggested we go to a restaurant which I dislike, I decided I'd rather go home and watch television. It was also drizzling moderately, so not the

nicest of evenings in London. The potential issue here was that, by leaving, there was a risk that Aaron might have taken offence – were his friends so bad that I had to escape immediately? But Aaron would understand, so I pointed out the facts that the weather was awful, the restaurant sucked and I was tired. Aaron did not mind, as I knew he wouldn't.

Suffer boredom because of a false sense of loyalty? No. Leave kindly, but leave. Zero tolerance.

I hope I have been able to illustrate what I mean by zero tolerance, and in which circumstances I believe it to work well. It may not yet be totally obvious to you why I chose the sociological essay with the Broken Windows theory as an analogy, but think about what would have happened had I not acted in accordance with zero tolerance in the above cases: spending precious leisure time after work by forcing my way through a book I do not enjoy. Sitting in a pub, impatiently waiting for my friends to get on with it so that I can leave and go home. Torturing myself in an uncomfortable theatre seat, longing to be somewhere else. Getting depressed in an awful restaurant watching the drizzle outside, and knowing I could be at home watching telly – I would not be reading, 'cause my book is boring.

The analogy is not perfect – Broken Windows suggests an escalation in which a minor infraction eventually leads to a petty crime. But the effects of the four incidents, if they occurred in quick succession, would compound. If you do not take a stand with a boring book, you may end up drunk against your will because you have not learned to say no. And if you constantly allow things you dislike to encroach on your time, eventually your time will be filled with things you dislike. If that happens, you may become aware that your enjoyment in life is only *so-so*: things are not really bad, but you are not really happy either, and you do not *consciously* enjoy yourself.

And this is where the analogy of Broken Windows comes in. Do not let the window stay broken for too long. Repair it quickly. Do not do too many things you dislike. Stop doing the first thing quickly, and do something you enjoy instead.

But, as I said at the start of this discussion, zero tolerance is a difficult principle to get right. The trick is to know in which circumstances it can be used safely so that it has large benefits and negligible drawbacks. The situations in which the principle will work well are *trivial* – they are small everyday occurrences – and *contained* – any potential repercussions will fade and not entail unintended consequences.

Entangled states of happiness – where zero tolerance does not work

Clearly, there seems to be a fine balance here. I think we can all agree on the method of zero tolerance if it means not acting to please others. But at what stage will the principle turn into intransigence, and at what point do we start hurting others and putting our own well-being *above* that of others?

This problem arises if our personal happiness is affected by the personal happiness of others. For example, the relationship between parents and their child or within a couple. The chances are that parents would be unhappy or concerned if their child was unhappy. I know that if Ursina is pensive, unhappy or depressed, her emotional state affects mine. This, I believe, is healthy and a natural state between life partners, parents and offspring, close friends and siblings. For the purposes of this discussion, I shall refer to these dynamics as entangled states of happiness.

Let us consider three more examples and discuss whether zero tolerance would work in each case:

(1) Polly's husband Brian has received an invitation to the wedding of Bill, his brother. Polly is Brian's wife, so of course she is also invited, but more than this Brian's family *expects* her to attend. Polly has nothing against Bill, but is not big on family events and would strongly prefer not to go. Can she say to Brian that she does not want to attend? Will he mind? Will his family mind?

(2) Your parents are celebrating their 50th anniversary. You know that your sister, of whom you have a low opinion and with whose family you do not get on at all, will be there. Your parents retired to France 10 years ago, so on top of a potential fallout with your sister, you will incur an expense of transporting your family abroad for a weekend, and will need to put up with the complaints of your teenage kids. Can you tell your parents that you cannot, or will not, attend?

(3) Your girlfriend has received an invitation to a social event at a hotel in the countryside. It is a momentous occasion to celebrate the centenary of her best friend's family business. Acquaintances of your girlfriend's are arriving from far afield to attend the event. Not only would she love you to be there, but you can clearly sense that she expects you to attend as her other half. You are freshly in love, your relationship is still young and a bit fragile and so you do not wish to upset her. But equally, you hate the idea of functioning as a social accessory. Can you turn her down with good grace?

These events are different from the first batch in two important aspects. While the first examples were all simple events, those in the second batch carry more significance. A wedding, an anniversary, a commemoration are events where the hosts contemplate their past and future as members of their social and familial sphere; they are not merely parties, just as many of the invitees are not merely guests.

The second difference is that each event is embedded in a skein of interdependent relationships. Personal emotional states are entangled in a far more profound manner than they were in the first batch of events. And since this is so, personal choices are likely to have consequences; their impact will not just fade, as in the first examples, but reverberate and perhaps intensify.

Events of this nature are not suited to the unmodified application of zero tolerance. Let us analyse each event and then ask to what extent we could have used the method:

(1) The situation is a good example of an entangled state of happiness. Polly's happiness depends to some extent on that of her husband, Brian. Brian's happiness is influenced by that of his brother Bill and his family. But equally, Brian's happiness is affected by Polly's.

To pick this apart, Polly would need to understand the relative strengths of all of these relationships. First, how important is it to Brian that his parents and brother are happy? How important is it to his parents and brother that Polly attends? Do his parents want Polly to attend because of social convention? Would they feel *embarrassed* if Polly was not there? Or do they *like* Polly and want to see her?

If Polly feels able to discuss these issues with Brian, that is great. If she thinks the matter is too sensitive, she needs to make an executive decision by herself. This decision should be based on whatever she expects will have the greatest benefit to her.

For example, let us say she cannot bear appearing at the wedding simply as Brian's accessory. If this would affect her sense of self-worth, it is likely that any incremental happiness she created for Brian by forcing herself to go would not offset the reduction in her happiness (her self-worth). If this was the case, Polly should not attend. By choosing this course of action, Polly would also set boundaries for similar situations that may arise in the future; by not attending she would teach others how to treat her.

Conversely, if Polly thinks she cannot refuse because her happiness would suffer as a consequence of Brian's disappointment, she needs to ask herself (a) whether her happiness is unduly dependent on Bill's and (b) whether she should choose Brian's happiness over hers in this case. If she is able to analyse the situation in this way and the answer is (a), deeper issues may be present which will need to be addressed over time. If it is (b), she will consciously have made a decision against the application of zero tolerance and her choice will be an examined one.

(2) This example seems less entangled, since the relationship between your parents and you is dominant. We need to perform a similar analysis, and the answer will again depend on the greatest net benefit you are expecting your decision to generate. Perhaps in this case you decide to grit your teeth and make your parents happy. But only you can know – the circumstances that drive the decision are personal.

(3) In this example, the emotional entanglement seems more indirect. On the first level, there is the relationship between your girlfriend and you. On the first indirect level, there is the relationship between your girlfriend and her friend, and on the second indirect level that between your girlfriend's friend and her family. You may find that because the relationship between you and your girlfriend is still young, it is appropriate to set boundaries and turn her down on this occasion.

There is no mechanistic model that can be employed to analyse entangled emotional states. Each state has its own dynamics and needs to be considered on its own merits. However, the goal of the analysis is to ascertain which outcome results in the greatest *net* benefit to ourselves. Sometimes it will be necessary to teach others how to treat us. And sometimes it will be best to be conciliatory and do something we may dislike, but which we know will make somebody close to us happy, and in turn have a positive impact on our emotional state.

When we think through the dynamics of an entangled state, we may also discover that our actions tend to be unduly driven by consideration for the happiness of others. Worse still, we may discover that the happiness of others entirely determines our own. If that is what we learn, we have uncovered a more deeply rooted issue, the solution to which is beyond the scope of this chapter and resides in a deeper analysis of self-knowledge, as discussed at the start of this book.

Tolerance versus zero tolerance

In conclusion, therefore, I maintain that zero tolerance works.

Used responsibly, it can prevent the build-up of dissatisfaction by avoiding experiences we dislike. This may not sound like much but if we constantly engage in activities that do not make us happy, we create a world for ourselves in which our life enjoyment is only lukewarm.

But we need to be careful about when and how we use the method. The tool will only work well if nothing much is riding on our decision and if we can control its potential to produce unintentional consequences.

Compromise well

Am I not full of contradictions? In the previous two sections, I was expounding the virtues of actions that were the opposite of compromise. First, the advice was to be unreasonable, and then to use zero tolerance. Now we are back to compromise. Which one is it?

Well . . . all of them, really. Being unreasonable essentially meant not to be a pushover. We have seen that zero tolerance works in carefully defined situations. Our goal is to assemble tools which, used in their proper contexts, enable us to construct a personal comfort zone. Every tool has its proper use, and there is a proper time to use it. Some experiences in our lives demand the presence of Shaw's unreasonable man, and some demand the use of compromise.

But compromising, as with everything else, is a skill that needs to be learned. In this section I want to discuss the nature of compromise. Which type of compromise is good and which type is bad? In which situations is it desirable to compromise?

The nature of compromise
To start, let us look at the definition of a compromise. My dictionary[126] tells me that the word came into English from Latin via medieval French and literally means something like

---

[126] Collins Dictionary of the English Language. Editors Urdang et al., Collins 1984.

together (*com-*) making a promise (*promittere*). The modern definitions given are 'settlement of a dispute by concessions on both or all sides' and 'an exposure of one's good name, reputation, etc. to injury'.

These two definitions are striking. Together they reveal something fundamental about the nature of compromise. The first definition tells us what a compromise is technically – an outcome in which all parties involved in the negotiation make concessions. But it does not tell us anything about the quality of the compromise – how severe was the concession a given party had to make? And, given the nature of these concessions, is the outcome workable? Is the compromise good or bad?

There is clearly a danger that the compromise will not be workable, that the solution could damage the integrity of one or several parties. This risk, apparently, is sufficiently prominent in our minds that it expressly lives on in one meaning of the verb to compromise, while the opposite possible interpretation has no semantic value. When we say that somebody's integrity is compromised, we only ever mean damaged; we never mean enhanced.

So a few minutes after looking up what the phrase means in a dictionary, we have penetrated the core of the issue. A compromise seems to be something worth striving for, but there is a risk that compromises achieved in real life may be suboptimal, that at least one party may emerge from the negotiations with the upper hand at the expense of the other(s).

We are not concerned here with the nature of compromise in the various disciplines where the concept plays a role, such as politics, philosophy, science or logic. Our interest is quite practical. How can the ability to compromise enhance the quality of our lives and hence improve the enjoyment we draw from it?

To answer this, I will simplify the concept and discuss it in the context of two players only. These will often be members of a partnership (marriage, civil partnership, boyfriend–girlfriend, unmarried life commitment), friends or family, but can also be work colleagues or be drawn from other social dynamics.

I regard a compromise as an agreement in which both parties lose something individually but gain something collectively. Each partner makes a concession, and this concession detracts from the happiness each partner would feel in isolation. But by making the concession individually, the partners create a solution that enhances their collective happiness. As such, I think compromises can most prominently be found in situations where entangled emotional states prevail – the more entangled, the more material, in theory, is the collective gain.

Actually, my discussion in the previous section suggested that zero tolerance is unlikely to work in emotional states that are highly entangled, and my analysis of compromise hence seems to be consistent with what I said before.

So I would say that a compromise is good if individual concessions generate a collective benefit. A compromise is bad if individual concessions do not generate such a benefit.

Let me give you two examples to make this less theoretical.

The bad . . .

One of the most bemusing cases of bad compromise I have ever come across is the abbreviation for 'co-ordinated universal time'. This is a scientific time standard based on an average of measurements taken by more than 200 atomic clocks located in national laboratories all over the world. The standard is used to define time zones, which today are expressed in terms of a number of positive or negative offsets from the time standard.

OK, whatever. So what is the abbreviation? It is UTC, which stands for . . . actually, what *does* it stand for? When the standard was developed in the 60s, the English-speaking delegates proposed CUT as the abbreviation (for co-ordinated universal time), while the French-speaking delegates opted for TUC (for *temps universel coordonné*). No agreement could be reached so the sides compromised on UTC, which does not mean anything in either language but with a bit of goodwill is accepted to refer to a syntactically awkward 'universal time, co-ordinated' in English and a grammatically incorrect '*universel temps coordonné*' in French.

So well done. Of course, most of us are entirely indifferent as to which of the six possible abbreviations were used and whether they make intuitive sense or not. But my example was supposed to serve as an illustration of a bad compromise, and I think we can immediately detect its characteristics. Each party accepted an abbreviation that did not stand for an idiomatic expression in either party's language. That was each party's concession. The collective benefits were twofold. First, the solution broke a stalemate over an issue most would consider trivial, and it allowed the standard to be launched. Second, each party gained the satisfaction that the other party's language would not be exclusively associated with the new standard.

I would argue that in this case the collective benefit fails to offset either party's loss. We ended up with an abbreviation that makes no sense to anybody and both English- and French-speaking commentators refer to the standard in their natural languages, rather than use the artificial construct. Both parties, it seems, lost more than they gained in this compromise.

... and the good

To illustrate what I mean by a good compromise I shall turn again to personal experiences. In fact, this is one that I have mentioned before, in the context of taking advice ('Not a big ask'). To recap briefly, the issue was to find a compromise between Ursina's desire to invite her family down to our place whenever they wanted and my need to control the frequency of these visits to protect my need for privacy. The solution was that Ursina promised me that she would watch my back in this and manage any expectations of her family in this regard. As a result, I no longer felt the need to protect my space and now feel that I actually enjoy it when her relatives come to stay.

This mode of operation has stood the test of time and is proven to have worked for years. So this is an example of a good compromise. But let me analyse the dynamics of why it is so in a bit more detail.

First, let us identify the concessions each of us made. My concession was to give up some of my need for privacy. Ursina's concession was to give up some of her need for social inclusion. But there are several deeper layers here.

First, Ursina and I represent an *entangled emotional state*, if I may call it that. This means that by diluting my need for privacy, I could see that I removed an obstacle to Ursina's happiness. Ursina's incremental happiness in turn served to enhance mine. This dynamic is also present for Ursina, and hence our individual concessions were offset by the increase in happiness we knew the concession would generate for the other person.

Second, Ursina and I explored each other's needs and preferences in a series of discussions. These discussions were not always easy, and we did not get to the bottom of our respective personal issues before we abandoned our protective walls and became disarmingly honest with each other. At that stage of our engagement, we revealed the issues for what they really were. We achieved a mutual understanding of the true motives of the other person and it was this understanding that allowed us to craft a solution to the problem.

In the final analysis, therefore, our individual concessions are more than offset by the resulting collective gain. Our relationship has become stronger and less vulnerable to potential external threats. Put simply, I am happier as an individual because Ursina is happier, Ursina is happier as an individual because I am happier, and we are happier as a couple because we are holding our world free of concerns that might threaten it.

When to compromise

Broadly speaking, I would say that entangled emotional states are the realm of compromises, and isolated emotional states the realm of zero tolerance. For the most part, I believe that common sense will dictate which events belong to which realm. You are suffering as you watch a movie because it is boring? Even if you are there with a large number of friends, zero tolerance would potentially be appropriate. It is hard to think of a compromise that would solve this, unless you simply stay and sweat it out. Family visits in your house? You do not need me to see that zero tolerance will not lead to workable outcomes.

But what about things which straddle the line? What about that wedding which you really do not want to go to? I believe a good guide is a maxim of 'When in doubt, talk!' We saw in our previous discussion that Ursina and I reached a solution only after understanding the other person's viewpoint in depth.[127] If you are in a relationship, out with your friends, at work or engaged in some other form of social interaction, I strongly advocate seeking the point of view of the other party first. Other than in particularly clear-cut situations, where zero tolerance or being unreasonable may decide an issue in your favour, a well-crafted compromise represents a more durable solution.

The skill is to identify which situations call for which approach. If we decide that compromise is called for, these are the tools for crafting good compromises:

- *Know who you are.* Here it is again. But clearly, unless I understand my needs and why I have them, I cannot enter into a discussion in which the goal is to explore how to craft a good compromise. I cannot do so because I do not know how much concession is too much and why.

---

[127] Perhaps not surprisingly, thorough investigation of parties' interests in a negotiation has been found to generate outcomes seen as more beneficial by participants in a negotiation process. See for example: Thompson, Leigh and Hastie, R. 'Social Perception in Negotiation'. *Organizational Behaviour & Human Decision Processes*, vol. 47 (1990), pp. 98–123.

- *Know who the others are.* This is almost as important in this context as self-knowledge. Without it, I do not know how much concession is too little and why.

- *Talk to others.* We need to enter into a dialogue with the other party. Without it, we cannot understand the other party's needs or communicate our own.

Sounds daunting? Well, it probably is. But it is not new. We have been here before. Knowing who you are remains the key to everything, and EXPERIENCE MINING is a powerful tool to develop it. Knowledge of the other party in a compromise is very similar to the advisor knowledge we discussed in the context of advice taking. The fact that these skills come up again and again lends powerful testimony to their fundamental importance in building a life that is filled with happiness.

Be nice

Mental and dental health

My toothbrush smiles at me. It is electric and has a wireless connection to a display unit that keeps track of brushing time. For each 30-second interval of brushing, a circular segment on the display turns solid. Once you have collected four segments, two dots and a bendy line appear in the middle of the – now complete – circle. I get a smiley in return for being a good boy and brushing for two minutes!

Fig. 8.1 The display on my electric toothbrush, showing time of brushing and a smiley face as reward!

When I bought the brush I thought the display was just an elaborate gimmick. Still, the gadget was on sale for the price of a normal electric toothbrush so I thought I might as well get it. I set it up at home and to my surprise found that I actually like getting the smiley. I guess regular use for two minutes at a time must be good for my dental health too. But of course that is not why I am sharing the story of my tooth-brushing habits with you. What I have found is that my toothbrush actually puts me in a good mood.

Yes, I know what this sounds like. But I *am* serious. Of course, the stimulus we are talking about here is mild. It is hardly that I leave the house singing and dancing in the morning, and my toothbrush cannot turn a grumpy mood into a sunny disposition for the day. But on a normal morning, when I am forced to get out of bed too early and my mind is focussed on coffee rather than the *FT*, the little smiley makes me smile for a brief moment. It is only a fleeting moment and quickly forgotten, but it *is* there.[128]

Now think what would happen if I could keep this up throughout the day. If I could get more smiles or friendly words out of people on my way to work, at lunch time, on my way home. Would there be a compound effect? Would I not get nice, friendly reactions all day long? And would that not make me feel good?

The answer to each of these questions is yes. And yes, I know this for a fact. I have tried it and it is working. Let me trace a normal, uneventful day for you and comment on my interactions.

---

[128] In fact, the psychological impact of a smiley face is very real. Next time you see an advertisement for watches in a magazine, take note of the time the watch shows. In fact, if you have access to the internet, why don't you type 'watches' into the search engine and do a picture search? Do it now. Do the watches show 10 past 10? Most of them do? Indeed – this is because in this configuration of hands the watch looks like a smiley face. Ad people keep creating this effect in the overwhelming majority of watch ads launched. They wouldn't do that if the effect was not real enough to help sell the product.

A ☺ day

I leave the house and walk to the tube station. At the foot of the stairs is the guy who hands out *City AM*.[129] I never take a copy but I always say good morning and give him a friendly nod. I have no idea whether that makes him feel any better on a cold, wet London morning. But I know that it makes *me* feel better. I think it is much nicer than simply shuffling past the guy with my head down, barely acknowledging his presence. I feel, for a brief moment, *empowered* – I am able to exchange a friendly gesture with a stranger. I do not stagger into work like a zombie. I keep my head up and I interact with the world.

Next up is the coffee shop at Liverpool Street Station. I get a latte there almost every morning, so they know me by now. I always try to be cheerful to the barista serving the customers, and when it is not too busy there is usually time for a brief chat. 'Howzitgoing? Weather sucks again.' Sure, this is not deep, but usually stimulates a friendly or smiley response. After doing this for years, I can now have longer chats with the guys there. I know what country they are from, where they want to go on holiday, how long their shifts are. I ask how their holidays went, if I remember, how their family is, what that party was like they told me about. Very often we have nice, brief chats in the morning, we smile, I get my coffee and off I go.

I get in, do my stuff for the morning meeting and usually after that go down to get breakfast. Again, I normally go to the same place so they know me well too. The chap who is there most mornings is a football fanatic. I know nothing about football but we still manage to chat about it. He is enthusiastic about it and we banter our way through my order. Again, this makes me happy. I think he is having fun as well.

At lunch time I get a salad from a place I know well. The people there are delightful – all young staff, chatty and with interesting stories. One dude is putting himself through music college while doing that job. I checked out his stuff on

---

[129] A free daily distributed in the City of London.

SoundCloud; his music is good so we chat about it when I see him. People sometimes offer me free coffee, we have a good laugh and I usually leave the salad bar smiling.

In the evening when I go home, most of my non-serious interactions during the day have been positive and put me in a good mood. Not into an ecstatic mood, just a moderately smiley mood. Each interaction adds a faint layer of happiness, and if nothing happens at work or in other areas of my life to offset this, I usually go home with a bit of a smile on my face.

No goody two-shoes

I am aware that there is a risk of sounding excessively naive or 'happy-clappy'. But I am actually serious about this. I maintain that we put ourselves in a good mood by acting in a friendly or respectful way towards others. Of course, this will not work every day. If we are in a grumpy mood we often cannot act cheerfully towards others, and even if we could, any positive feedback would not lighten the mood. Often we are apprehensive about something the day holds in store for us: an exam, a deadline, a visit to the GP. But I would strongly advocate trying to act in this way on days where we are in an indifferent mood.

Next time it does not cost you anything to be friendly, choose to be! Treat it as an experiment – act in a smiley manner towards people a few days in a row and observe the result. I am sure that you will at least not feel the worse for it, and you will probably feel better.

A few ☺ experiences

I adopted this method years ago and now find that it has become second nature to me. I always try to be friendly or smiley in everyday-type interactions. And my experience is that in the overwhelming majority of cases you are rewarded with equally friendly feedback. Let me just share a few of my experiences with you.

M&S checkout – Liverpool Street Station
I am at the M&S food store on my way home. I am picking up
flowers and chocolates for Ursina. There is no particular reason
for this but, as I said before, I like the way her eyes light up and
she jumps around when I do something nice for her – I selfishly decided I would like to see that again tonight. So there I
am, in the queue lining up at the checkouts, acutely aware that
I look like a cheesy advertisement for a dating site.

When it is my turn to pay, I approach the cashier and say, 'I
got roses. I got chocolate. What more can you want?' She looks
at me and laughs. I smile back. She asks, 'Special occasion?'
and I say, 'No, it's just that my girlfriend likes flowers. And I
eat her choccies.' We both chuckle, I touch my card to the
reader, say goodbye and am on my way. But I am still smiling,
and perhaps so is she. There is no downside here.

Taxi into town – Zurich
I have just arrived at Zurich airport and get into a taxi to take me
into town. I tell the driver the address of the hotel and ask him
how things are and how his business is doing. He says business is
tough in the recession and he is beginning to feel it now. But he is
not complaining. 'You need to go where the customers are. If you
park your cab in the customers' line of sight you get a little more
business.' I observe that this is an excellent attitude. 'You are not
sitting there blaming the recession, you are doing something about
it.' He agrees, saying you have to. 'I am OK. You can always do
things to make stuff better.' We are continuing our chat and I am
finding his attitude refreshing. I arrive at the hotel in good spirits.

Bookshop – Frankfurt airport
My flight out of Frankfurt is delayed so I have a little time on
my hands. Of course, I go to the bookshop – maybe I can find
some untranslated writers I would not find in the UK. I am
browsing and naturally find something that looks interesting.
I carry a book and a magazine to the checkout and smile at the
lady sitting there. 'Hi! How are you?'

She looks at me with a slightly incredulous look. There is a small but notable pause. Then she says, 'You know, you are the *first* person today to ask me that.' 'Really?' My surprise is genuine. 'That is weird. I mean – that sort of stuff is important, no? Of course I need to know how you are – how can we transact business otherwise!' She starts laughing, and so do I. I say, 'See – we are smiling and are a little bit happier. Not much. But a little bit.' She agrees. And we *were*.

Newsagent – Hampstead

Ursina and I are enjoying a walk on Hampstead Heath at the weekend. We are walking back into the village to get a coffee somewhere when I spot a newsagent to get a bottle of water. I go in, pick up my water and carry it to the counter. 'How's it going, mate?' I say to the chap sitting there. This is what I get in response: 'I am extremely happy.' I am surprised by that. 'You are? That is great – any specific reason?' 'No, I am always happy!' Now he's got my full attention. 'What's your secret?' He says, 'The reason people are *not* happy is because they want things before the time is right. And they want the wrong things. They don't follow their destiny. I don't want things that I can't have and I know there's a right time for everything in life. Because I know that, I'm calm and I have no stress.' Blimey. I did not expect to hear something like that when I popped in for a bottle of water. I am impressed. The encounter makes me even more confident in my view that it is possible to find happiness. There are many ways to get there, and the guy at the newsagent has clearly found his. It is uplifting to hear his view.

Monolitten Café – Oslo airport

I am flying back to London and have some time to kill at the airport. I decide to go to an airport restaurant – this one looks inviting and the menu says they are serving traditional Norwegian food. Perfect. I sit down and the waitress brings the menu. I say, 'Thank you very much' and make eye contact. I always do this – I do not find it polite to stare at the table and mumble something unintelligible while somebody goes to the trouble of bringing you something. Lapskaus is the same word in German and brings back memories of something unsavoury. But there is reindeer! And moose! Excellent – a new experience. I ask the waitress which one she prefers. She likes moose, so moose it is. I am having soup as a starter and tell the waitress that it was excellent when she comes to clear the bowl away.

By now, there is definitely a good vibe going on when she comes over – we are both smiling and I always acknowledge her effort. I am genuinely curious to find out the taste of moose and am pleasantly surprised. I tell the waitress I enjoyed my meal greatly and ask for the bill. I leave her a solid but not exaggerated tip, and when I get up to leave, she gives me a kiss on the cheek and thanks me for being so nice. I am stunned but break out into a huge smile immediately. 'Surely not more so than anybody else?' I ask. 'Oh no. Customers here are normally quite grumpy – not very nice.'

Well, it *is* an airport restaurant so people are probably pressed for time. This sets the benchmark quite low, so perhaps it is less astounding that being polite and friendly stands out in this environment. But still, getting a peck on the cheek is a novelty! I am hugely flattered and cannot stop smiling until it is announced that my flight is delayed by another 30 minutes.

Conclusion: Be nice!

All my smiley stories make the same point. If you are friendly to people, the chances are that they will be friendly back. This is not a new idea, and most people will be aware of it *in theory*. But I am not sure how many of us use it as a maxim by which to live – in two of the experiences I shared with you, people expressed surprise when I acted in a friendly way, and hence there is some evidence that many of us do not.

The conclusion, therefore, is simple. Whenever you can, be friendly, engage with people and smile. You will find that people respond in kind, and that will bring you joy. The benefit of each positive experience will be marginal, but over time benefits add up and may even compound.

Build your comfort zone – your job

This section will get me into trouble with management consultants. When I was at business school, my tutors programmed me to believe that staying in your comfort zone was wrong. In fact, leaving your comfort zone was considered the hallmark of the young, up-and-coming professional. Application of this maxim meant you were going places, while failure to apply it would inevitably lead to a dull existence, in which neither professional nor personal evolution was possible.

And this made total sense to me at the time. Until I got half way through my second year and discovered that it was time to interview with companies. At that stage I discovered that I had no clue what career I actually wanted. I did not really know what my strengths were, and I was not sure which part of my course I enjoyed most. I realised that before I could *leave* a comfort zone, I first had to *build* one.

Indeed, as I know now, building a comfort zone is difficult and requires a lot of skill. I would even claim that leaving a comfort zone is insane – if you are skilful enough to build one then that is where you should stay. In the next sections of this chapter, I shall examine two key components of a personal comfort zone that I regard as important: your job and your home. I am not claiming that this is an exhaustive list. There clearly are other important components, like family and health, but we dealt with a key component of family in the chapter 'How to find your partner', so I will not repeat the messages here. And as for health, well, this is clearly important, but a discussion of fitness is firmly outside the scope of this book.

Why is career important?

First, let me explain why I believe that our career, or at least our job, is a part of life that we need to get right. If you think about it, most of us will spend roughly eight hours at work, eight hours at play and eight hours asleep. This is a crude analysis of a typical day, but it will do for starters. So even in this most simplified view of our life, we are likely to spend one third of it at work.

But if we are more realistic, an altogether more sobering view is emerging. I think the reality for most of us is that we spend closer to 10 or even 12 hours at work daily. Surely most of the cabbies in London work 10-hour days? Ursina's sister's husband works three jobs, and her sister has official 12-hour shifts as a midwife. I recently chatted to somebody who used to be a truck driver – his day was also easily 12 hours. On a typical day, I am in the office for 11 to 12 hours, and when I am travelling or at peak times in the year, days are a lot longer. Ursina leaves the house at eight and gets back at eight. I was just at a school reunion and many of my ex-classmates are doctors who work 12-hour days in hospitals. My point is that it is not at all difficult to find people who work 10- to 12-hour days.

The second eight-hour phase, the one I labelled play, is hardly all play either. Some of this phase is consumed with commuting time to and from work, with doing domestic chores like going shopping, preparing meals for the kids, cleaning the house. There is also a 'twilight-hour' in the mornings, when we are waking up, having a bit of breakfast and getting mentally ready for work. Let us say then four hours are chores and four are play. Now our day looks more like 12-4-4-4 hours for work-chores-play-sleep. Or worse, 12-4-2-6, if I assume that we need six hours of sleep to function.

Realistically therefore, we probably spend half of the calendar day at work! With that much time spent at work, and only between two and four hours at play,[130] I believe it is obvious that we need to get the part of our lives right that is dedicated to work. If I find that I do not like what I do, or that my job gives

---

[130] I use the expression 'play' to denote waking hours that are not spent on work or chores. 'Play' can therefore refer equally to activities like sitting in the pub with mates or playing videogames, as it can to spending time with our partner or our kids.

rise to pressures I cannot handle, a large chunk of my life will be difficult to cope with. What is more, as that part of my life tends to pay the bills, I will find it difficult to extricate myself from it or change it if I need to. Hence, the chances are that any frustration will spill over from my work life into my private life, and since there are only around two to four hours of that left in a typical day, I cannot afford to have those compromised.

So before we know it, our whole life is out of balance. We are generally unhappy, perhaps without even knowing why. This is why I believe our jobs, our careers, are important parts of our lives and it will pay off to spend some thought on getting them right. Let me illustrate what I mean, and how we might get it right, by looking at two examples.

Beyond business school

Let us start with me. As I said, I was getting to the stage at business school where graduation was in sight. I needed to start interviewing with companies in an attempt to persuade them that I had acquired skills that would prove useful in helping develop their business. It was then that I discovered I did not have a clue what career was right for me, nor whom to approach for interview. So I had interviews with a wide range of companies and in a variety of functions: manufacturing, publishing, FMCG[131] and consulting. I interviewed for jobs in marketing, accounting, consulting and general management. In none of my interviews did I know why I was interested in the job, and hence none of my interviewers were interested in me.

This could not go on. I needed to understand what I really wanted and why. So I sat down and tried to think it through. First, I needed to understand what I enjoyed most about my course, since that would presumably show me what my strengths are. In order to get to the bottom of that, I tried to recall the assignments which I found most engaging, where I had the most fun doing them and why. It turned out that these

---

[131] Fast-moving consumer goods.

were assignments that required the application of analytical methods to get to a conclusion, like business law, accounting, finance, and the like. Second, I tried to isolate the parts I found tedious or onerous, as these would illustrate my weaknesses. I found the answer to be consistent with my previous insight. I found tasks that involved group thinking fatiguing, and I disliked areas that required practical skills, such as marketing, sales or organisational aspects.

So there I had one part of the answer: I liked analytical tasks, but not practical ones. I also liked getting creative in inventing new analytical methods, and usually found that what I read in textbooks was only the start of a story. Finally, I did not hugely identify with any particular product or corporate ethos. So there was the second part of the answer: I needed an industry which was a little bit abstract, which did not sell tangible things.

Third, I tried to identify industries which would fit the bill. My criteria ruled out most manufacturing industries, and even management consultancy, but financial services sounded about right. I started interviewing with companies in that sector, and decided to accept an offer to join an insurance company and take professional exams to become an actuary.

Granted, I had to adjust that choice of profession twice before I landed in stockbroking, the industry in which I am still working today as a research analyst. But essentially I had made the right choice. Financial services is the right industry for me, and I am still working in a professional sphere that plays to my strengths, and hence minimises psychological pressures of the kind I would find difficult to handle.

Midwife
Ursina's sister is a qualified midwife and started her new professional life at a local hospital close to where she lives.

But she was not always in a good place professionally. After leaving school with limited qualifications, she worked as a secretary at a local business. However, although work colleagues and bosses were great, the pay was extremely low and barely sufficient to make ends meet. What was worse, her job did not give her a sense of achievement, she did not regard what she was doing as meaningful and hence she found that her life lacked substance.

But she had always had a connection to children and, when her own son left the parental home to pursue his aspirations, she took the plunge, left her job and enrolled in a four-year course to qualify as a midwife. These four years were hard. She had to go back to the classroom, obtain a formal qualification and find the strength in herself to meet ongoing challenges, often doubting whether she would be able to pass the academic requirements of the qualification.

But she did, and she is now a midwife, with a proper professional qualification. She is much the happier for it. Her job gives her the sense of meaning she was missing when she worked in an industry she had no interest in, and beyond that gives her more confidence in life generally.

The point of these stories?
The points I want to make are these:

- It pays off to think about what you wish to do in life professionally and why. If you are happy in your job or career, you have sorted out a large part of your life.

- One way to understand what you are best suited for professionally is to research your strengths and weaknesses. You can do this analytically by using a modified ABACUS TEST, by writing down all the things that bring you joy and all the things that you find onerous. Or you can trust your intuition.

- It is irrelevant whether you are studying for an academic degree or are about to leave school. The method of asking yourself what you have liked and disliked is a powerful one, and will work just as well with school or extracurricular activities as it will with a formal academic degree.

- Once you have started in a particular career, assess your professional happiness at intervals. Are you still happy? Is it still fun? If not, what are the parts of the job that you dislike? What bits do you like? The answers to these questions pointed me towards equity analysis as my professional comfort zone, and Ursina's sister towards midwifery.

Stay inside your comfort zone

Of course, Ursina's sister and I are not the only people who have found their comfort zone professionally. One of my earliest childhood friends just sent me an email saying that he was made head of controlling at a local business in Germany where he lives. The hair stylist whose customer I have been for years completed a course a few years ago enabling her to teach classes in advanced styling in the organisation in which she works.

But I also know of people who are not in their professional comfort zone and are clearly unhappier for it. Ursina's sister's husband told me he would rather be unemployed than continue working in the firm of graphic designers where he is employed. Aaron never completely enjoyed his life in the City and I do not think he has ever been truly fulfilled professionally.

If we feel satisfaction at work, the chances are that we will be more confident and well adjusted outside work as well.

I can best speak for myself in this matter: As a 'Cityboy', I work in an industry which highlights my strengths and not my weaknesses. This means that I do not have to be somebody who I am not when at work. I can be natural and concentrate my energy on the professional demands of my position. As I have found a natural fit, I do not tend to be confronted with pressures that I find impossible to handle. For that reason, I find fulfilment in my professional life – for the most part.

And this is what I mean when I speak of a professional comfort zone. A word of advice to those who have not (yet) built it: do ask yourself what you like and dislike, and maybe write the answers down. But do not believe that life outside work is the only real life, that somehow an unfulfilled work life is something we should accept or tolerate.

And a word of advice to those who have been successful in building it: do not leave it. Stay inside your comfort zone. Feel free to stretch, test and expand it, but do not leave it.

Build your comfort zone – your home

OK, so let us leave the sphere of work now. We have come to the end of the working day. We leave work. Where do we go next?

To the pub? OK, fine. So after drinks, then where do we go? That is right. Home. We go *home*. Minus an average of four hours spent on chores, we are likely to spend the next eight to 10 hours at home, some of them at play (watching telly, having dinner, reading, bathing the kids) and about six hours asleep.

Clearly, therefore, our home will play an important role in our lives too. So we ought to spend some time thinking about getting that right, I think.

Before I get to this I need to make something clear though.

First, this is not about money or the value of your house. Even if money was no object, we would not all choose to live in a mansion in the country.[132] Some of us would choose to live in a cosy semi close to friends and family, some would live in a flat in the suburbs, some of course *would* like to reside in a stately home, but yet others would opt for a modern penthouse in the metropolis. It is important to find out what is right for you and then try to get there.

Second, this is also not about an ideal state. Some might push back on my point and say that you can never live in your dream home. I would be inclined to agree.[133] But even so, we should certainly try to get as close as possible. We may not get

---

[132] If your first instinct is to disagree, watch a few episodes of *Country House Rescue* . . .

[133] If you agree too, though, watch a few episodes of *Grand Designs* . . .

all the way there, but we will get closer than if we accept defeat before we have even started.

A home truth

Let me tell you a few short stories to begin with. What I would like to explore is how we know where we want to live.

I remember an experience when I was 17 years old. I was coming back from holidays abroad to my home town in Germany. Several friends and I had been touring Europe using a general rail ticket that entitled the bearer to travel on most trains within a number of specified European countries. On our inter-rail tour we travelled south through Austria, the Balkan countries and Greece, and then came up through Italy to arrive at the Côte d'Azur. We spent a few enchanted days in Monte Carlo and then travelled home.

Our holiday had been full of fantastic experiences. That was the first time I had been abroad for a full month without parental supervision. The places we visited were varied and each impressed me in its own way. Athens crackled with mad energy, Vienna paced aristocratically and Rome was both ancient and modern. Pompeii unhinged our composure and Monaco dazzled with glamour and style.

And then we were back home. Back in the industrialised region of Germany, a large conurbation that lacked the charm of the exotic because we knew it so well. It had no landmarks of renown because it was largely industrialised. Do not get me wrong – I was happy to be back home, happy to see my parents and I liked where I lived because it was, well, home. But I remember thinking, we have just been all over Europe, we went to famous and exciting places and there are people who actually *live* in those places. Would it not be exhilarating to live in Rome, or Paris or Monaco? Why can't I live somewhere more . . . *exciting*?

That was my first glimpse into the big, wide world outside Germany. And my first inkling that I might want to live somewhere I would consider more recognisable, more iconic.

Home is where the heart is

My second glimpse came on an inter-rail tour the following year. This time we were touring the UK and our first stop was London. To this day I cannot say why, but I instantly fell in love with the place. There was nothing specific that impressed me, and I was not bowled over, as I had been in Monte Carlo.

It was a certain atmosphere, the way red buses crossed Westminster Bridge, the way people would competently walk through the thickest of traffic, the way world-famous land-marks seemed just to *be* there, without taking themselves too seriously. I felt as if London was welcoming me as a friend, as if we just *got on*. It was not an infatuation; we just liked hanging out together. I knew that London was my home. I just did not live there yet.

Home runs

It was more than a decade before I moved into my first flat in London. And I certainly did not return from holiday with a burning desire implanted in my mind to move to the city. But when business school led me back to the UK, and I started my professional career in Surrey, I remembered my 'old friend'. The first weekend that I was free I decided to visit the place again. I discovered that we still got on as well as we used to. And, as you know, after a few years spent in pursuit of an actuarial qualification, I decided to change careers and looked for employment in the banking sector in London.

Which simply means that I knew where I wanted to live because I knew who I was in this respect. And the reason that I knew this aspect of myself was simply that I had listened to myself, that at an early age I had become consciously aware of my attraction to London. And, when the time came, I consciously combined a professional change I had to make anyway with a move towards my preferred location. It was still not easy to actually get there – a sideways move from the actuarial route into banking proved difficult, and at one point I became so frustrated that I considered going back to Germany. But perseverance won out in the end and I landed a job in the London branch office of a small German commercial bank.

Tom was basically the exact opposite. He worked in London but lived in Surrey. The commute never bothered him much until he and his wife had kids. After the birth of his second daughter, Tom started looking around professionally and landed a few offers. He joined a firm of consultants that had offices five minutes away from his house, and in doing so he turned down a couple of high-profile jobs that would have required him to work in London.

For Tom the choice was also easy. He would have hated the idea of living in London; he loved the countryside and suffered emotional trauma when he was forced to be on the train to Surrey while bath-time was going on at home!

Mary, as you know, also hated the city and when we were together lived in a cottage in Oxfordshire. I do not know where she is now, but at the time she used to commute between London and her home. A friend of Ursina's lives in a small village in Ireland and loves it. He told me once he would pull pints in the local pub after work if that was a requirement to continue living in the village.

Everybody in these stories consciously decided where to live. Some put up with some measure of inconvenience in order to live in their preferred location. This is no surprise, really – I know with certainty that I would have been deeply unhappy in the countryside, and so would Mary or Tom in the city. So the point I am making is relatively simple: know what your preference is by listening to yourself. Then seek to set up home where it suits you best. I maintain that living in an environment you love is good for the soul, will give you pleasure and will contribute to the level of composure you create in your life. Know who you are and where you need to live. Find your comfort zone.

A few house points

Of course, it is also important to know what type of dwelling you prefer. Flat, house, maisonette? Basement flat, pied-à-terre, penthouse? Cottage, terraced, Georgian, Victorian? On the water, near the park, close to the action, far from the crowd?

However, I do not think we need an in-depth discussion of the options and how to decide what is right. Essentially, the point is the same as above – know yourself and try to get as close to your ideal as possible, constraints allowing. Just one point in this context – if you are not pressed to find a home and have some leisure, I would strongly advocate actually *taking* whatever time you have. Provided you know yourself well enough, you will know what is right when you see it. Do not commit too early; it pays off to bide your time. To sum up:

- A comfort zone is a space where you can be yourself. A space where you do not have to conform to the expectations of others, where things are natural and where you are free from pressure. We all need to build such a space.

- We will all have different ideas about what the most important aspects of the comfort zone are. However, given that most of us will spend most of our lives at work and at home, it follows that we need to get these two components of our lives right. Or as right as possible given practical constraints we may face.

- We all have choices that are open to us. Some of these choices may not be immediately apparent, some may be difficult to make or involve some measure of courage, but we *do* have choices. We can *choose* our career and we can *choose* where to live.

- The game of like and dislike works! Ask yourself what you enjoyed most at school, college or university. What you uncover denotes the natural strengths and talents you have. Ask yourself what you hated most. What you find shows your weaknesses and the sort of stuff you are not suited for.

- Now you know your strengths and weaknesses, your likes and dislikes, identify a career where many of your strengths are required to be successful, and where few of your weaknesses will detract from progress. Do not be a bartender if you hate long nights or cannot keep five things in your head at the same time in a noisy environment. Do not be an engineer if your idea of mathematics is checking the bill in a restaurant.

- Identify where you need to live. Yes, *need*. Not *would like*. If you suffer from hay fever and are afraid of dogs and horses, do not live in a village in the countryside. If you suffer from claustrophobia and are afraid of taxis and buses, do not live in the big city.

- And then *do it*. Get that career, or one close to it. Live in that place, or in one not far away from it. As a result you will feel balanced and more natural about yourself. You can be yourself when you are at work, and as a consequence will (mostly) enjoy being there, or at least will not mind it. You will feel that you are yourself when you are at home, and as a consequence will like spending time there.

- I am convinced that your comfort zone will make you happy. Having a fulfilled work life is good for self-confidence. Heightened self-confidence will spill over into other areas of your life and make you generally more fulfilled, more balanced. Living in a place you love or like is good for the soul.

And finally, something I said before. It is important so I will say it again. Your comfort zone is one of the most precious things you can get in life. Once you build the zone, do not leave it! Feel free to stretch, test and expand it, but do not leave it.

Nothing to prove

The chances are that, as you are building your comfort zone, you will discover something interesting and perhaps surprising. You will increasingly feel that you have less, or even nothing, to prove to the world. And perhaps you will even discover that you have less or nothing to prove to yourself!

This statement needs to be digested with care, since it can easily be misunderstood. I am not talking about a state in which you lose ambition, drive and motivation. I am not talking about a situation where you abandon existing goals or cease to set yourself new ones.

Quite the contrary, I think it is vital for our well-being to have goals and find the energy to pursue them. But I believe it is important to have these goals for the right reasons. And the right reasons are those that are consciously examined and have substance.

What do I mean by this? Let us consider a simple example. Say you own your own home and now wish to extend it, for example by adding a conservatory or, more ambitiously, by digging out a basement. Why do you want to do this?

(1) Do you want to impress or keep up with the neighbours?
(2) Do you want to show somebody that you have the financial means to do it?
(3) Do you derive personal satisfaction from the fact that you have the means to do it?
(4) Are you fulfilling an old dream of yours?
(5) Do you need more space for the kids and is this the most feasible way of getting it?

I would say that reasons (1) to (3) have less substance than reasons (4) and (5). The first two reasons 'keep up with the Joneses' and therefore derive the motivation for an action from the standards of others. You may not care much yourself for a conservatory but everybody in your street has one, and the nasty Joneses from next door certainly have one and you are gonna show them. Reason (3) is borderline. Here you may not define your actions by the standards of others, but you still need to prove something to yourself. The reason for acting does not lie so much in what the action is meant to achieve, but more in the knowledge that it is in your power to achieve it. But in the last two actions, the motivation to act springs from the desire to achieve a goal, either for yourself (4) or for others and for yourself (5).

If you act because you wish to achieve a goal, rather than to demonstrate that you are *able* to achieve that goal, you have attained a level of self-awareness that rests in itself. In this state, you have nothing to prove, you focus on the substance rather than the form and you have set yourself free.

Just think how liberating it would be to exist in a space where we truly could afford to define ourselves by *our* standards and not by those of others. A space where we could act independently of what we believe others think of us.

Not sure yet what I mean, or why that would be liberating? Let me give you a few examples.

Skiing with daddy

I am 16 years old and I am on holiday skiing with my dad. We are in Val Gardena in Italy. For me, this is the second time skiing, after I was introduced to the sport during a school trip a year earlier. I am a teenager and it is *hugely* important to me what my peers think of me. I would just *love* to be a competent skier and dance down the slope with no obvious care, rip through the moguls laughing and be the focus of admiration.

I am a teenager. That is how my mind works. That is what I *do*. So I am setting about to do just that, and I choose the black run down to the village of La Villa to be my stage. So here goes. I am gaining speed. Two swings – easy. I am dancing. This is great – I am the man. Surely everybody is looking? The front ends of my skis cross. I panic and try frantically to avoid the inevitable. I tumble head first into the slope. The skis are off. I am sliding down the slope on my jacket. It is a rather steep slope and I come to rest some 50 metres further down.

There is a faint crackling sound next to my ear. My dad slowly comes to a rest next to me, skis perfectly lined up, his arms full of my errant sports equipment. 'Mark, are you OK? Did you hurt yourself?' 'Nah, I'm fine.'

This was not true. My leg and my pride were hurting badly. But what he said next I remember to this day. 'Mark, look. I know you think that everybody is looking at you and you need to be cool. You know, the truth is nobody is looking. Those who are still learning have so much to do themselves the last thing they want is to look at others. Those who are experts do not care about what other skiers are doing. The truth is, nobody gives one.'

I know today that his assessment was spot on, but I still remember what I thought of it at the time. I thought he was wrong. I thought that people were definitely looking and were admiring expert skiers. And I wanted to be the object of their admiration, maybe even more so after my tumble than before.

The point of this story is that there is a time in life when it is OK, or certainly excusable, to define yourself by the standards of others. When you are young, peer-group respect does matter, and there is often no harm in that. But my dad's point of view marked the position of a mature, well-balanced adult. He was able to see my action for what it was. However, his advice not to care what others think fell on immature, and therefore deaf, ears. The point is that you need to have attained maturity before you can understand that others do not constitute a viable benchmark for your actions.

Britta

I am still 16 years old and we are back home. I am going to school but my interest in the classwork is beginning to be complemented by interest in other things. It is the time of parties pretty much every weekend, of going out to clubs and of girlfriends.

A girlfriend, I am beginning to discover, is something the cool kids on campus have. They are the sorts of dudes who display admirable irreverence to the contents of the school curriculum, who hang out with slightly older kids and hence have a lot of street cred. The guys I am hanging out with are not really that sort – but I know a lot of people on campus and there are house parties every week. We are enjoying trading stories of who has got a girlfriend, who split up and who started going out with whom.

I am in two minds about all of this. I rather enjoy going out skateboarding with my friends. But then, it would be cool to have a girlfriend. Now some of my closer friends have started to go out with somebody. The social dynamics are changing but I am still not sure I would actually *like* going out with a girl. Also I am totally awkward with girls. There are a lot of them in the group I hang out with, but I do not think any of them think of me as boyfriend material.

I am at a house party and things are getting out of hand as usual. I am a reasonably good gymnast and one guy at the party challenges me to do a handstand in the host's bedroom. I am in no mind to let anybody think I would not be able to do that, least of all Britta, who is there with her friends watching. I can do a handstand anywhere, so let me show them!

I straighten out to a handstand nice and clean, but rather close to a bookshelf. Surely this will impress Britta! Unfortunately, one of my mates chooses that moment to come in and shout 'Oy Mark! You are a wanker!' – I start laughing and lose my balance, unable to avoid the host's bookshelf. I tumble down with the shelf and end up in a heap of books on the floor, giggling uncontrollably. And – miracle – Britta is laughing too and clearly enjoying the show.

Half an hour later I find myself on the balcony with Britta. We are chatting a bit, and I know what I have to do. The moment is here! I am closing in. There is the kiss. Boy, this is awkward. People actually *enjoy* this? Whatever. This is gonna seal it, and I will have a girlfriend after this.

And I did! What a success that party was. Now I was going out with somebody and that was rather cool. But the point of this story is that I had to force myself to a certain degree to take the opportunity. I had to prove to myself that I was able to get a girlfriend, and I had to prove the same to my peers. My action was almost entirely driven by what I perceived to be the expectations of my peer group and not by what I wanted myself.

Do what you bloody well like!

It is decades later. I am sitting on the sofa at home in Surrey watching television. Billy Connolly is on a chat show in Australia. He has just turned 50 and the chat show host asks him about his new piercing. Apparently, Billy has just had his belly button pierced and is sporting a shiny stud of some description. Billy gets up and lifts his T-shirt to show the audience. He sits down to a general cacophony of appreciative howling and whistling. The chat show host asks him the predictable question: 'Billy, you just turned 50. Do you think getting piercings is what a 50-year-old should do?'[134]

Billy responded: 'Why not?' And what he said next impressed me deeply and I remember it to this day. You need to imagine a Scottish accent accompanying the next statement.

'You do what you like, mate. You do what you bloody well like!'

That is it. It was nothing more profound than that. But it made an impression on me that I will never forget. In that moment something clicked. I realised that he was right. Absolutely. Who would stop you doing what you want? Why would you not get a tattoo, or a piercing, or shave your head, or take time out of work to travel, or do a million other things you would like? Only you decide. Only you *can* decide. Do not

---

[134] This is not a direct quote. I remember seeing this show but I was not able to find any trace of it. All quotes are substantially true, but I am quoting from memory.

let others make that decision for you. Do not live your life by the standards, indeed the *perceived* standards, of others.

Of course, we need to evaluate this maxim with care as responsible adults. I believe it reflects the immature attitude of the teenager if we derive the motivations of our actions from a desire to attain peer-group respect. But it would be equally immature to swing the pendulum to the other extreme and contend that our individual desires are the only valid benchmark for our actions. It goes (one hopes) without saying that we cannot do anything illegal, but it does not go without saying that we should not do anything unethical.[135] We may not wish to engage in activities that make somebody close to us unhappy or bring about pressure we cannot handle. If my partner hates tattoos and I do not feel that strongly about getting one, I will not get one. I would also think twice before tattooing my face, even if I felt a desire to do so, since I can see that such an adornment may not project professionalism in a business meeting. But in cases where nothing much is riding on a decision, the maxim of 'doing what you bloody well like' is a sound one, and if followed will set you free of the expectations of others.

It may also give you the strength to use the method of zero tolerance when needed, or to conjure up Shaw's unreasonable man. My next story illustrates this.

Teetotalling
It is a few years later still. I have just started working for the English brokerage house. I passed my FCA exam, and the decision about whether I need to sit CFA exams has been deferred in light of my intransigence. I therefore have time to concentrate my efforts on the job, and I am also initiating myself slowly into the culture of a City institution.

One such cultural aspect is an urge to go out after work to a pub or bar and consume vast amounts of alcohol. This may not be exclusive to stockbrokers or investment banks but the

---

[135] Haven't seen that one in a while, but here it is again. Popped up all by itself, as before. See penultimate chapter.

culture is certainly present at the firm; not more so, I believe, than anywhere else, but it is certainly there.

It is Friday night and the first night in months that I do not have to work late. The lads are going to the pub and of course I am joining in. Now, there is something about me that I have not told you yet – I do not actually like drinking alcohol. This is not an ideological preference: I am not a teetotaller and I enjoy a glass of wine over dinner or a gin and tonic from time to time. But I rather detest beer and in general I do not like to drink alcohol very often.

So picture the scene. Here I am in the pub with my new work colleagues, my bosses and a bunch of traders. I am pretty much the new kid on the block and I would like my peers to think that I am one of the lads and that I blend well into the social setting and the culture of the firm. I have not yet established a reputation as a broker inside the firm – I have written one large piece of analysis that my boss liked but that is about it. I would like to follow this up with another one and am anxious that my boss should see me as future partner material.

TJ is 'getting them in'. TJ is a senior trader. He brings in millions for the firm and he is highly respected. He is part of the firm's DNA because outside work he lives a lifestyle that finds approval internally. As traders sometimes do, he comes over as highly abrasive and totally no-nonsense. I am with a group of analysts, within earshot of the partners, when TJ comes round and points at each of us in turn, taking orders.

I am not in the mood to drink alcohol. It is my first free weekend in months, I am meeting up with Aaron later and I have no intention getting there in a state of semi-inebriation. Let me describe the group dynamics that unfolded.

TJ is counting down the orders.

Pint of Pride, mate.
Stella here!
Pint of cider, thank you, mate.
Lemonade please.

TJ is already pointing at the guy standing next to me. Now he freezes and looks back at me. 'I don't do non-alcoholic orders. What do you want?' His voice sounds like his vocal cords have been put through a cheese grater.

What I say next, I say clearly, but with no exaggerated emotion. 'Well you can fuck off then. Nobody tells me what to drink. I'll get it myself.'

There is total shock and disbelief among the analysts. I am the rookie! I am talking to TJ! This is unheard of.

TJ pauses and looks at me. Then he smiles broadly. 'Pint of lemonade!' He points at the next guy, takes two more orders and proceeds to the counter.

I never had a problem with TJ during my stay at the firm. I would not exactly say that he respected me because of the incident – this would be a slightly romantic version of reality. But he respected my choice and the fact that I upheld it. And some of the analysts looked at me with a mixture of bemusement and respect.

So here it is. A prime example of not caring what others think of you. Of course, I was feeling the pressure when TJ revealed his alcohol-only policy, in particular because partners in the firm were there and I would have liked nothing more than to blend in. But at the same time, TJ's comment triggered the naturally defiant streak in my personality. Nobody tells me what to do in my spare time, or how to behave and certainly not what to drink! In that instant I did not care what my peers thought of me, even those whose respect I was ultimately striving to secure. And, as it turns out, my uncompromising attitude won me the respect of some, including TJ, at least to some extent. What the incident taught me was that it is better to be true to yourself and 'do what you bloody well like' than to allow your actions to be dictated by the standards of others. In the process, you might even rise in the esteem of those whose respect you no longer seek.

Doing cups

It is a few years later. It is summer, the sun is shining, it is the weekend and people are out in droves in Hyde Park. For a

while now I have been coming here to 'do cups'. This activity
is basically freestyle slalom on rollerblades. Over the previous
few months I have fallen in with a crowd of rollerbladers who
seemed to be there every weekend. There is usually a long line
of cups, and the game is either to rip through them as fast as
possible or to weave in and out in an intricately choreographed
dance.

I am lining up at the cups and try a figure that I have not
mastered before. It sort of works but there is no flow to my
performance, and it shows that I am still thinking consciously
about how to execute the moves. Next up is Ma-Yong. She does
the same figure, but you would not think so for watching her.
She dances down the line, she feels the rhythm, her blades are a
blur. Then she stops dead. Ma-Yong stands frozen in the middle
of the slalom, her body rigid, suspended. It lasts for two seconds.
Then she resumes the flow as if there had never been a break.

Wow! Fantastic! I wish I could do that.

One of the guys I have started hanging out with steps up.
He says, 'She did that better than you.' 'Of course she did!
She's in a different league.' 'That don't bother you?' 'Why
should it, mate?' I was genuinely surprised. 'This is not a
competition . . . I have nothing to prove.'

And then it hit me. I did have nothing to prove! It was true! That was
the first time in my life that I became consciously aware of this fact.
And when I did, I also became aware of the freedom that goes with it.
Yes, I would have loved to be as good at cups as Ma-Yong, and while
I was at it I was trying my hardest to improve. But I noticed I had zero
to prove to others, and I genuinely did not care whether others
perceived me as a good rollerblader or not. I was there for myself and
because I was having fun.

What did I want to show?

My stories show a progression from teenager to adult. When
we are teenagers our personality is not yet fully formed, we are
struggling to find our identity and as part of this struggle it is

normal, healthy even, that we would strive to attain the respect of our peers.

However, we can think about winning respect in two ways. We can strive to attain the respect of others by earning it. In that case, any respect we gain would show that others appreciate a personal achievement. This achievement may be a good track record in academic subjects, or PE when at school, professional success when at work, proper upbringing of kids when at home.

Or we can strive to earn the approval of others by acting in ways that we perceive would please them. Approval earned in this way is not proper respect; it does not show that others appreciate something we did, but merely that they recognise it as conformist behaviour.

And as such, the latter does not help us form our personality, develop self-confidence or find a personal identity. It has its place, or can at least be condoned, in the brief time during which we are teenagers, but it has no place in the behaviour of an adult. As mature individuals we need to strive for a confidence that rests in ourselves and is not fuelled by a desire to gain the admiration of others. Once we develop the courage to trust our own instincts, and the confidence to know that our personal goals are valid, we find that any perceived need to live by the standards of others falls away. Then we will no longer care what others think of us. Then we will care what we think of ourselves.

The stories I shared with you are all innocuous, and each one is hardly significant in itself. But if you read through them you can detect a certain progression. The need to impress others with sporting skills was present in Mark the teenager, but absent in Mark the adult. Teenager Mark impressed Britta with antics born of lack of self-confidence, but adult Mark stood out briefly for being true to himself when he turned down the offer of an alcoholic drink.

If we live our lives by the standards of others, we are still caught up in a struggle to find our identity. But as we are finding out who we are, what we need and how to get what we need, we find it less and less important what other people think of us. We have increasingly less to prove, we are set free of other people's expectations of how we should behave and we learn how to do what we bloody well like.

Goals and dreams – land on the moon

But having nothing to prove does not mean having nothing to achieve. As I said in the introduction to the previous section, I consider it vital that we identify the right goals for ourselves and then go after them. But what are the right goals? This is another skill we have to learn, another tool for our toolbox.

I can express the essence of my goal-setting tool by formulating two maxims. I advocate using these maxims whenever we set ourselves goals. Here they are:

Maxim 1 *I will always set myself unrealistic goals.*
There is no typo there. I did mean unrealistic. Do not be realistic and reasonable. Be *un*realistic and aspirational. Goals have to be ambitious to the extent that they are *just not* impossible to achieve. Reach for the stars and you might land on the moon. Reach for the moon and you may never leave earth.[136]

Maxim 2 *I will learn to deal with disappointment.*
If I follow my first maxim, there is a very real chance that I will not achieve my goal. If this happens, I will be disappointed, and it is important that I learn to deal with any psychological fallout. I

---

[136] I modelled this phrase on an adage that you sometimes hear people use. It is something like, 'Reach for the stars. You may only get to the moon, but that is better than staying on Earth', but there are many different versions that all carry the same meaning. I am unable to find an originator to whom I could attribute this phrase, but I am aware of a similar metaphor, although used with a different meaning, by American motivational speaker and speech coach Les Brown: 'Shoot for the moon. Even if you miss it you will land among the stars.'

need to be strong enough to fail, just as we saw before that, in finding a partner, I needed to be strong enough to be vulnerable.

When I was discussing this with a friend recently,[137] he asked me a very good question: 'Mark, doesn't the second maxim negate the first one? If I am not going to be too upset if I do not achieve an ambitious goal, are my goals really ambitious in the first place?'

This is an excellent point, and I would like to comment on it immediately at the start of the section to avoid confusion. My maxim does not say learn *not to be* disappointed but learn to deal with disappointment *if* it comes.

This distinction is important, but I realise it is also subtle. I believe the former interpretation to be a grave error – if I teach myself to be *indifferent* to the outcome of the goals I am setting myself, I will have no genuine motivation to achieve anything, and my goals will no longer be goals. But it would be equally wrong to avoid ambitious goals for fear of being disappointed. That is why we need the second maxim. I must never *avoid* potential disappointment but develop the means to deal with it if or when it arises.

As ever, though, we need to be careful about how we interpret these ideas, and in this these two maxims are no different from any of my other methods, tools and suggestions.

I shall look at the two maxims in turn and start with goal-setting.

Goals and dreams

So what does it mean to be unrealistic? The first point to make is that we have to distinguish between specific goals (short term) and non-specific aspirations (dreams). They are both important, and each has its place in the art of goal-setting, but we need to keep them separate in the discussion. Let me first illustrate the difference by giving you two statements, each of which describes essentially the same goal:

---

[137] Tom's twin brother George, whom you met earlier.

(1) 'One day I would like to have a degree in Physics.'
    The speaker may well feel strongly about his desire to achieve
    the goal, but has not yet taken tangible steps towards it. The
    speaker has not enrolled yet at a university and may well still
    be at school. The goal is unspecified and as such is a long-
    term aspiration in the mind of the speaker. This is a dream.

(2) 'In three years' time I will graduate with a BSc in Physics.'
    This speaker talks about a tangible, specific goal. She is an
    undergraduate at a university and enrolled in a taught course
    in Physics. The course takes three years to complete and, at
    the end of it, she aims to hold an academic degree in the
    subject of her choice. This goal is specific. It is short term in
    that it is possible to achieve the goal within a clearly deter-
    mined time frame (even if that time frame may be three years).

Maxim 1: I will always set myself unrealistic goals

I advocate that we formulate goals that are specific and clearly
defined.

However, there is a trick here that we must not miss. I claim
that short-term goals need to be two things at once, unrealistic
and inspirational.

But hang on, I hear you say, surely this is a contradiction in
terms? How can unrealistic goals inspire? Let me illustrate what
I mean with an example. Consider the following two goals:

- In three years' time I need to graduate with a first-class
  degree and rank first in my year.

- In three years' time I need to graduate with a first-class
  degree and win the Nobel Prize for Physics with my final
  dissertation.

Clearly, both of these goals are ambitious. They are both unrealistic – nobody can reasonably expect to attain a first-class
degree at the start of their course, before even opening the first
textbook. But the second goal is, at least nowadays in the

modern world of academia, not merely unrealistic. This goal goes a step further and is *impossible* to achieve. An undergraduate degree does not go into the depth that would be required to publish in learned journals. Even if it did, the chance to come up with something worthy of perhaps *the* most acclaimed prize science has to offer is basically zero.

Only the first goal will therefore inspire. It is unrealistic, in the sense that it is extremely ambitious. But it is something that could *potentially* be done. As such, it will focus the energies and harness the willpower of those who define it for themselves. And, in doing so, it is likely that it will inspire a better outcome than a goal which aims lower.

The second goal is unlikely to inspire. It is also unrealistic, but no longer merely ambitious. This goal is so far removed from reality that those who formulate it set themselves up to fail, and therefore will abandon it early on. The danger with such a goal is that its owner is not likely to replace it with something that is ambitious but potentially achievable. Such a goal is likely to frustrate its owner to the point that they lose, rather than gain, motivation.

In the terms of my metaphor, the first goal is reaching for the stars. The second is reaching for the edge of the universe.

Maxim 2: I will learn to deal with disappointment

Fine, if we reach for the edge of the universe, we will be frustrated, lose our motivation and give up. But is there not a similar danger with extremely ambitious goals? What if we do not measure up to our deliberately inflated targets? What if we fail? How do we cope with that? And would it not therefore be better to follow conventional wisdom and set our sights lower? To be realistic? To be reasonable?

These are good questions. But the answer is not to lower our sights or avoid disappointment. The answer is to *deal with* disappointment if, or when, we need to.

This, I believe, is a fundamental principle in life that pops up all over the place if you look for it. When we invest money, to name only one example, we may opt for a safe class of security, like a savings account or a life assurance product. The risks associated with these products are low and so we can only expect to generate a moderate return on our investment. Riskier investments, like equities or futures and options, generate a higher potential return, commensurate with the higher risk assumed by the investor. My analogy works like this: in expectation of a higher return, an investor must be prepared to accept the risk of losing some, or all, of the capital. In expectation of a better outcome, a person must be prepared to deal with disappointment in the case of failure.

Another analogy is finding the right partner. Here also some might consciously resist opening up to another person for fear of being hurt. We discussed this issue in the previous chapter and I believe the analogy is obvious. To find the right partner, we need to be strong enough to be vulnerable. To achieve stretching goals, we need to be strong enough to fail.

But there is a problem with this, and it is lurking below the surface. If the analogy from investing holds, would we not need to find our personal preference, our utility, in goal-setting, just as we do when we are investing? Say I am happy to receive a modest return from my investment because, *to me*, the risk of losing outweighs the chance of winning (even if the probabilities are identical in either case). Surely I should opt for the safe investment in that case? Similarly, if I am happy to receive a merit as my degree class because, *to me*, the risk of disappointment outweighs the elation of over-achievement, would I not *have* to opt for the safer goal? Surely if I *deliberately* act against a consciously examined preference, I would not be able to sleep well as an investor, and would not be able to focus as a student. So in the end, would I not have found my *comfort zone*? Would self-knowledge and the ability to understand my personal preferences not guide me to the goal that I need to set for myself? And is the attainment of self-knowledge not the key principle that I promote in this book?

The answer to these searching questions, I think, is a pragmatic one. Yes, *perfect* self-knowledge would indeed allow us to pinpoint exactly our position between the polar regions of disappointment and achievement. Then we would know exactly how much disappointment we can handle and how much potential achievement that would buy. But it is impossible to attain *perfect* self-knowledge. We can know ourselves extremely well, but we will not know *exactly* where we stand in terms of disappointment versus achievement. Which means we have two choices. We can play it safe and aim low. *Or* we can take a risk and aim high.

I advocate aiming high and learning how to deal with disappointment. I believe this is the option of choice because it may generate two benefits. The first is obvious – if we are successful, we achieve more and build self-confidence, which in turn inspires other areas in our lives. The second is less obvious perhaps – if we fail, we are forced to deal with disappointment. If we are successful in doing this, our life competence grows. This again builds self-confidence and enables us to embrace challenges that allow us to grow.

I believe this interpretation is consistent with what I said before. If we set ambitious targets, we stretch our comfort zone, but we do not destroy it. If we are facing disappointment, we remain in control by searching for the reasons in our own actions.

So this is what I mean. I used the word unrealistic in a deliberately provocative way. I believe we can maximise personal benefits if we set our goals deliberately high – so high, in fact, that others may say they are unrealistic. But not so high that they are unattainable.

Stars which seem out of reach are worthy targets. Stars which are out of sight are impossible targets.

Dreams are aspirational long-term goals

So far, so good. We have tackled specific, short-term targets. But what about aspirational, long-term goals. I said before that they also have a place in our arsenal of targets, so where do they fit into this?

Well, they complement the specific, short-term goals we set ourselves. We need to have both: ambitions *and* dreams. Or, perhaps even more to the point, ambitions and a dream (one at a time). Having a dream gives us an overall direction and will make it harder to get lost in the multitude of stimuli that we encounter every day.

To illustrate this, let us consider two hypothetical life paths.

Lisa wants to become an acclaimed scientist one day. She chose a good breadth of subjects at school, but focussed on numbers-based ones. She set herself the goal of getting straight As in every subject. She enrolled in a suitable course at university. On graduation, she lined up her PhD topic, aimed for a job at a university and eventually achieved tenure. At each step of the way, she set herself unrealistic short-term goals that inspired her.

Iggy is indifferent to what he may achieve in the long term. He just goes with his interests. He liked Maths and Physics, so he focussed on numbers-based subjects at school. A year later he met a charismatic actor who headed up an amateur dramatic work-shop after school. He started to focus on that and neglected his schoolwork. A few months later he went out trial biking with Ionni, whom he met at the workshop. It turned out that he was quite good at it and, boy, what a thrill that was! So he left the workshop and went out trial biking every day after school. Also he really started to enjoy reading, something that the theatre workshop inspired, and changed his subjects to focus on the humanities.

Lisa's life has a dream, and because it does it is a *journey*. Iggy's life lacks a dream, and because it does it is an *odyssey*. Again, we need to be careful to put my examples into proper perspective. There is nothing wrong with having a wide range of interests and being enthusiastic about everything. Quite the contrary, such personality traits are admirable and ought to be embraced and developed, certainly not stifled! But there is a mature way to do this – Iggy would have benefited from a dream. A dream, by definition, is a long-term goal that is not clearly defined. It can be something like 'I want to be a famous actor'. Then you can still go biking and study a broad range of subjects. But you may more seriously focus on the acting classes rather than burn out your interests in short stages, and in the process achieve nothing, hamper your personal development and perhaps look back on a life of missed opportunities.

On the other hand, if you *do* have a dream, you may find that it keeps you more solidly aligned as you go through various life stages. You may eventually even *achieve* your dream, but it is actually irrelevant whether you do or not. What *is* relevant is that the dream lines up the short-term goals into a series of targets and therefore makes it harder to lose your way in life.

The dream might also change and be replaced by a different dream. Our lives may change direction entirely, move off in a direction we never imagined and do this more than once! I am not advocating following a rigid, unimaginative or unwavering path in life. Far from it! What I *am* saying is that each stage in our lives ought to be traversed with good understanding and steady aim. Changing direction is fine, and potentially productive. Shooting around like a ball in a pinball machine is not.

To return to my metaphor of the heavens, an aspirational long-term target, or dream, is like a fixed star. It is so far away that we cannot reach it, but it helps us navigate our ship.[138] And of course, we can change our ultimate destination; but if we do, we stand a better chance of reaching the new one if we have another fixed star in our sights.[139]

---

[138] Astronomers of antiquity referred to stars that did not appear to change their position in the night sky over time as 'fixed'. The change in apparent position generated by the movement of the Earth (parallax) is highly pronounced for bodies relatively close by, like the Moon or the Sun, but negligible for vastly distant objects, such as the North Star. Current estimates put the distance to the North Star at 323 light years. By comparison, the Sun's distance from Earth is 0.000016 light years. Put differently, the North Star is 20 million times farther away from Earth than the Sun.

[139] The Roman Egyptian astronomer Ptolemy (c. 90–186 AD) published a star catalogue as part of his treatise *Almagest*. He counted 1,022 fixed stars visible from Alexandria. I'd say that's enough dreams to last any of us a lifetime.

Odysseus and the fixed star

Let me conclude with a simple illustration of the dynamics we discussed. Have a look at the following diagram.

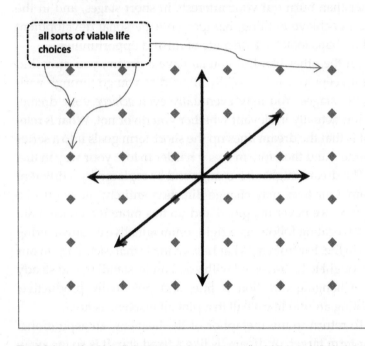

Fig. 8.2 A case in which all short-term goals appear equally viable to an individual. As none stands out, there are a bewildering number of possible ways to navigate through life. The individual has trouble deciding on one preferred goal and, as a consequence, risks drifting through life with no clear path to follow.

The dots represent possible short-term goals in life. Choosing numbers-based subjects at school. Choosing humanities. Concentrating on sports. On soccer. Or maybe rugby. No – gymnastics. Amateur dramatics. Woodworking classes. Starting a job after GCSEs. At the local supermarket. Maybe at the dentist's office? Getting a professional qualification. As a carpenter. As a physiotherapist. And so on. There are thousands of choices, thousands of goals.

But all the dots are exactly the same distance from each

other! All life choices are viable, but all seem *equally* viable! None stands out. What should our life path be? How to navigate through this?

In fact, there is no single path that stands out. I have illustrated six on the diagram, out of an infinite number of equally viable paths. And since they are all equally viable, in this scenario there is not a single direction that suggests itself as the preferred one through the jungle of opportunities life has to offer. We have just as much justification to move west or east as we do to move north, south or indeed any combination of directions. The result is that we run the risk of zigzagging through life, where each goal is as good as the next, and in the end we get nowhere. This is similar to what happened to Odysseus when it took him 10 years to travel home to Ithaca after the Trojan War.

But look what happens when we have a dream:

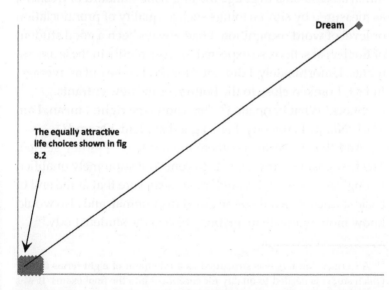

Fig. 8.3 The same chart as shown in fig. 8.2, this time with a long-term goal added. The long-term goal defines a steady path through the multitude of choices considered equally attractive to the individual without a long-term goal, now shown bunched up in the lower left-hand corner.

Now the previous potential choices are bunched up in the bottom left-hand corner of the chart, their scale dwarfed by the emergence of the dream, the long-term goal. Yes, it seems so far away that we cannot hope to reach it (certainly not in one go) but, like a fixed star, it helps us navigate through the bewildering range of short-term life choices.

Odysseus could have benefited greatly from focussing on a fixed star. Before concluding this section, let me give you one example of how this may work in practice.

Apollo 11

I remember my first month at university. It was an odd feeling – I was full of trepidation and uncertain whether I would measure up against the challenging standards that undoubtedly prevailed at this lofty institution.

The department of English philology ran a number of initial assessments to gauge the linguistic standard of freshers, as measured by simple things such as quality of pronunciation or level of word recognition. I had always been a good student of English at school, so expected to score highly in these assessments. Unfortunately, I did not. Nor did I come out as average. In fact, I ranked close to the bottom of the new entrants.

Shock! What happened? That cannot be right. I mean, I am *Mark*! Not just anybody. I am a good student. Or am I?

And this, basically, is where my academic journey started. The first goal I set myself was to come out supremely qualified in English grammar. I would make *damn* sure that at the end of basic studies[140] I would be an *expert* in grammar, and also would know more words than anybody else in the student body.[141]

---

[140] A German Masters was structured as a minimum of eight terms during which students needed to qualify for enrolment into the final exams. It was not possible to enrol earlier, and the first four terms constituted a block of basic studies, with the later four focussing on research.

[141] Yes, I had something to prove. Well spotted! But this motivation has its place when we are setting out to achieve new goals. It is misplaced only if it inspires actions we would not choose if the need to prove something was absent.

That was my first short-term goal, and it was unrealistic. But it inspired me, and from there, other short-term goals developed. By the end of the first term, it was my declared goal to qualify within the shortest possible time, graduate with the highest academic honours and secure an academic scholarship. None of these was remotely realistic, which is why I chose them at the time.

Today, there is no doubt in my mind that the achievements I *was* able to secure at university were possible because of the inspiration I drew from these goals.

These were the specific, short-term goals. But there was something else too. Half way through the first year, after starting to feel comfortable in my new environment, I became fascinated with the stature of some of my professors. There was Professor Eastarmy, a delightfully erudite Shakespeare scholar and linguist. Professor Real, a charismatic man of boundless energy and peerless standing in 17th-century History of Ideas. Professor Germountain, who, as eminent *ordinarius* of Historical Sociology, dominated the department of History.

And then there was Professor Hebwood, who had achieved eminence in the field of something or other by his acclaimed series of monographs on such and such. Well, there wasn't *yet*. But there would be. *That* was my dream. As you can see by how I phrased it, this was not a very specific dream. I had no idea which field I wanted to specialise in, or even what was actually involved in gaining tenure. But I decided I wished to become a tenured professor at a university. I never told anybody about this – it was my secret. Psychologically it provided me with a deeper purpose at university. Basically, it just felt good to have a dream.

Five years later I had had enough of the world of academia. However, by that time I had replaced my dream with another, which was to work in the City of London, and I supported this with a different short-term goal: to graduate from business school as the best in my year.

Moonwalk

I only gave you one example, although I am aware of many more. But I believe my story will serve to make the points I wish to illustrate, which can easily be generalised:

- We all need to set ourselves goals in life. There is no downside to being as ambitious as we can and to setting our sights as high as possible.

- I can see only one constraint involved in the setting of short-term goals. They need to remain inspirational and thus spur us on to achieve what we otherwise would not achieve.

- As we set ourselves ambitious goals that inspire us, we also have to take into account the possibility of failure and need to develop techniques to deal with disappointment.

- A dream makes it easier to navigate the multitude of possible short-term goals we may set ourselves. It keeps us on the straight and narrow for as long as we maintain it. Dreams can change, but we should always have one that we are following.

Shaping our world

Well then. At the end of this chapter, what have we learned? In previous chapters we discussed key *methods* for building our world; in this chapter we were concentrating more on particular *tools*.

All very well, you may say: the discussion of each individual tool may have made some sense, but it is quite difficult to see how these maxims fit together. Some are similar; some positively contradict each other. What are we to do with this chapter? How do we bring this together so that we can use it in the real world?

I think I can answer this by dwelling a little while longer on the metaphor of tools. Have a look at the toolkit you have at home. I am doing it now. There is a hammer, a pair of pliers, a screwdriver. My power drill. Sandpaper. A brush. All laid out nicely in front of me. Now let us build a shelf.

Each of my tools has a specific purpose. Some of these purposes are similar and others seem at odds with one another. I use the power drill to insert holes into metal clamps that hold the boards together. I use a hammer to drive a nail into a piece of wood. I use pliers to remove a nail from a piece of wood. I use sandpaper to smooth rough edges, and a brush to apply paint. Some of the tools I use in isolation and some, like a hammer and a chisel,[142] in conjunction. But I am not going to use a hammer to apply paint. And I am not going to use a saw and a brush to complement each other.

It is the same with the toolkit we assembled to build our world. I will use each tool as necessary, and for its proper purpose. But, just as a carpenter needs to learn and then master the skills to build a shelf, so we need to learn how to use and then master the tools to build a world.

So let me recap the essence of each tool and see whether we built a reasonable kit.

The toolkit

Land on the moon. This is a goal-setting tool. It works by being as unrealistic as possible while remaining as realistic as necessary. Which is to say that I need to be as ambitious as I dare without losing touch with what is humanly possible. If I manage to do that, my ambitious goal will inspire me; if I do not, it will frustrate. This goal works well when complemented by a dream, a long-term goal that aligns the short-term goals, and in so doing makes sure that I do not lose myself. This tool provides motivation. It is like an engine or a rocket to take me to my destination.

---

[142] You can see I am no carpenter. Work with me here . . .

Compromise. This is a tool that cultivates my world and helps it grow. In order to master this tool, we must have advanced knowledge of ourselves, and of the person(s) with whom we are seeking to enter into a compromise. To use it we need to enter into a dialogue with the other person(s). For this dialogue to be successful, we need, at least to some extent, to drop our guard and lay open the true motivations that are behind the outcome we personally favour. This is the most difficult aspect of handling this tool. But if we master it, we will arrive at good compromises that enhance the parties' collective happiness. Good compromises enhance our world and make it grow. This tool is like a watering can.

Zero tolerance. If we use this tool wisely, we are making sure that our world is not slowly taken over by activities we dislike. It is a tool difficult to master since it requires a measure of self-confidence and a true understanding of the circumstances in which its use is appropriate. And yet, it is at its most effective if we are able to develop it into a habit and make it second nature. This tool cannot be used in conjunction with compromise. It is its opposite, but in a passively defensive way. This tool is like a raincoat, or like an umbrella.

Be unreasonable. This tool is the big brother of zero tolerance. It is an actively defensive tool, like a shield. When we use it we protect our world from infractions or attack. It is very difficult to master as it requires active control over our emotions. It is used to best effect in situations where genuinely felt emotions, like anger or defiance, are consciously channelled into an uncompromising attitude. This, therefore, is literally the opposite of compromise. But the two tools *complement* each other. This tool provides a protective wall behind which we can cultivate our world and let it grow.

Be nice. This technique makes you feel good about yourself by being nice to others. The goal is to make *yourself* happy, not others, but in doing so others feel better about themselves too. And this makes it a win–win technique. It is easy to use and it does not take much effort – all that is required is that you are friendly to people, rather than indifferent. Each instance in isolation is small, but if you make sure you are friendly on a regular basis, the positive effects will compound.

Comfort zone – our job. The comfort zone is something we should aim to build with our tools. Our job is an important component of the zone. Because we spend almost half our day at work, it is important to get this component right. If we hate what we do, we diminish our chances of finding fulfilment and hence happiness. This does not mean that we all have to be medical researchers or renowned artists. All it means is that we find a job or a career that is *right* for us. We can identify this part of the zone by playing the game of like and dislike. We can build it by going for a job that has most of what we like and least of what we dislike.

Comfort zone – our home. The other key component of the zone is our home. This is not just how we live (renting or owning, sharing or non-sharing, flat or house), but also, and I would say more importantly, *where* we live. An ability to build this part of the zone rests on how well we know ourselves. Am I the countryside type, the city type or the suburb type? Am I happy in the country of my birth or do I want to live abroad? We can find out by EXPERIENCE MINING. We can build this area of the zone by going for it. There is no other way to build your comfort zone than by acting on what you know. And once you have built the zone, do not leave it. Stretch it, test it and expand it, but do not leave it.

Nothing to prove. If we use all these tools, apply all these techniques and follow all the methods we have discussed in the book so far, and in this chapter specifically, eventually we will notice something. We will notice that we have nothing to prove. Certainly not to others, but much more importantly, not to ourselves. Once we achieve this, we are pretty much there. We still have goals, but we have them for the right reason. We are still competitive, but responsibly so. We do the things we do because we know they are the right things to do, not because we feel compelled to impress others with the results or ourselves with the act. We do things because we wish to attain a result *for ourselves*. Once we achieve that, we have given our world the foundation it needs to flourish. Once we achieve that, we are in harmony with ourselves. Big words? Not really. Talk to the owner of the newsagent's in Hampstead. He's there.[143]

---

[143] See experience #4 in 'Some ☺ experiences' above.

RULE 9

Know what's right

How to tell right from wrong

Why let the worms out?

Why are we talking about this again?
Oh dear. It is the chapter about ethics. I warned you that I would
be opening this can of worms, and I am about to do just that.

But before we start, let us remind ourselves *why* we are talking about this, and also think about *how* we are going to do it.

During the course of our investigation, we have come up
against the subject of ethics several times. We never *planned* to
talk about it, but it sort of popped up unbidden, all on its own.
It was centre stage when we talked about judging, or rather non-
judging, others. How can we not judge if others fall demonstra-
bly short of ethical standards to which we adhere? It came up in
the context of taking advice. Knowing which advice to take and
which to ignore is influenced by an awareness of our personal
ethical standards – I would hardly follow advice if I thought that
I would be acting unethically as a consequence. It came up in the
context of EXPERIENCE MINING. When I discover something about
myself I do not like, do I need to change it or do I need to accept
it, embrace it even, as part of my personality? Just as much as I
embrace my positive traits? How do I know when a character
trait is bad enough to warrant a change? How far can it still be
good enough for me to welcome it as the yin to a yang?

And these are just some of the big ones. Ethical questions are pretty much part of everyday life. They may not arise every single week but they *will* come up from time to time. Can I send my child to a high-quality faith-based school although I reject the teachings of that faith? Can I get married in a religious ceremony although I do not believe in the tenets of the religion? My current boyfriends overlap with each other – is that cheating? Is it OK to hunt animals for pleasure? Is it OK not to give to charity? Is it OK not to recycle, to water the garden if there is a hosepipe ban on, to use tax-avoidance schemes?

Some of these issues are more important than others, and some of them do not appear to be very important at all. So, I hear you ask, what is the problem with not having a view on these? It does not seem much of a crime just to remain indifferent? My response to this question rests on the study of two hypothetical cases:

(1) Sue, whom I made up, likes to engage in fox hunting. She loves the thrill of the chase, the idea that she is part of what she sees as the fabric of the countryside and the social standing that goes with the activity. And yet, she feels that perhaps there is something not quite right about deriving pleasure from bringing down an animal for sport. Her doubts begin to nag at her, they interfere with her enjoyment when she is out on a hunt and she is starting to have feelings of guilt. When challenged by others about the ethics of this hobby, she is unable to defend herself with confidence and she is starting to feel less assured about this part of her life.

Her friends are of little help. Not troubled by doubts themselves, they suggest that ethics are entirely subjective and therefore form a meaningless benchmark. Besides, foxes are pests and hunters are delivering a service to country dwellers by reducing their numbers.

But Sue's general confidence in life has taken a knock. Not a huge one – she is certainly not thinking about the issue all the time – but severely enough that she can no longer justify an activity she used to love with quiet unbridled enjoyment.

Would it not be great if Sue could find a way to think the issue through and come up with an answer that restored her confidence? If she did, she would feel more at ease with herself, would regain balance and would be able to like herself again.

(2) Hugh, whom I have also made up, discovers in the course of regular sessions of EXPERIENCE MINING that he has a tendency to manipulate others for personal gain. He is not engaging in anything illegal, and it is not necessarily monetary gain, but he tends to play others with the goal of deriving a personal advantage from it. He might plant gossip about others in the workplace, hoping to discredit those whom he sees as a threat, and to elevate others he sees as potential patrons. He would make up stories to get out of unwanted social obligations, align himself with those he sees as powerful and avoid those he regards as damaging to his professional or social standing.

Hugh is discovering all this about himself and it is beginning to bother him. Is this a character trait that he needs to change? Or is it something that he can allow to stand, something that he regards as negative in his personality and yet embraces as part of his character? Would it not be great if he could find a way to think the issue through?

Both cases have something in common. Sue and Hugh are both troubled by an issue that throws off their life balance. To restore it, both need to find a benchmark against which to measure the issue. But this benchmark is an ethical standard and as such it is, to some extent, subjective! So what to do? If they do nothing, they allow a problem to remain unresolved. And in staying indifferent, neither of them develop the life competence they potentially could, neither of them develop an examined stance and as a consequence neither of them are able to like themselves as much as they otherwise might.

So there you have my answer. Indifference to ethics is not in itself an issue. But unless we develop an examined view on ethical issues if they arise, or find an ethical benchmark when we need one, we will not be as centred as we otherwise could be, and therefore we will not be all that we can be.

Interestingly, it is actually irrelevant *what* answer we find to these ethical issues. The important thing is *that* we find an answer. If we do, the insight we have will restore our life balance and build self-respect. It will enable us to approve of the way we live our lives, even to be proud of our actions. In short, a clear understanding of our position on ethical issues will enable us to like ourselves. And, as I stated before, if we like ourselves, happiness is within reach.

How are we going to talk about this?

So far, so good. Now you know why I think it is important to find examined positions on ethical problems if they impose themselves on our lives. But how exactly are we going to do this? Is ethics not a hopelessly esoteric subject, and entirely subjective to boot?

Actually, I think I have some good news on this. We do not need to develop a system that can separate good from bad in absolute terms. We can leave this task to the philosophers and go about our business in a much more pragmatic way.

As I said before, it does not matter *what* answers we find, what matters is *that* we find them. Therefore, my goal here is simply to come up with a method that we can use *in practice* to think through the issues.

The method that I propose, and that I want to discuss with you in this chapter, is ultimately *practical* in its outlook. But because of the complexity of the subject matter, I will need to discuss some other people's thoughts on ethics first and appreciate the benefits and limitations of their models. That will give us a framework in which we can develop our own model. Then we will put ours to the test and see whether it is any good, and whether it is a useful tool.

The key difficulty in this discussion is that ethics will always retain an element of subjectivity. It will be our task to develop a method that allows us to think about a particular issue in a disinterested way, and then test it against a number of possible benchmarks.

After reading this chapter, we will be able to say things like: 'This conduct is ethical when measured against this general benchmark, but it is unethical when measured against another, more exacting, standard.'

And we will be able to produce verdicts like: 'My action passes several benchmarks. Yes, there are more demanding benchmarks against which my action fails to show up as ethical, but *I* am happy with its moral fibre. *To me*, my action is ethical enough.'

The judgements we will learn to make will be the result of analysis and thought, and not of indifference. As such, they will represent *examined* views on ethical issues. Hence, they will be strong enough to serve as a foundation on which we can rest with confidence.

This, I believe, is all we can hope to achieve when defining where we stand in the ethical flux. I call my method ETHICAL HYPOTHESIS TESTING and will describe it later on.

Ethics – what is it?

Two encounters and three definitions

We have already caught a glimpse of the key issue with ethics: subjectivity. One society will differ from another in what it sees as ethical behaviour, but even views within societies are not fixed. They differ between individuals, change over time and the whole thing appears to be quite a mess.

So much so, in fact, that some have given up on any efforts to penetrate the issue and blankly refuse to discuss it.

For example, this chap I met at a dinner party once – he was fascinating to talk to, he had interesting and well-thought-out views on a wide range of subjects, his comments made you think and he was a delightful conversationalist. Until the subject of ethics came up. When it did, his body language changed, he became defensive, even slightly belligerent, and his frustration was almost tangible when he said: 'I always think I should find ethics more interesting than I actually do. It is entirely subjective, it changes over time and it is different in different societies. I think it's a waste of time to talk about it.'

Ah well. We would not be discussing ethics that evening after all.

My very *first* encounter with the subject of ethics was no more enlightening. I was at college, attending the first lesson of my course in philosophy. The teacher came in and announced that in the first lesson he would just like to brainstorm some of the concepts of philosophy with us. We would ask questions and he would answer. One of us asked, 'What is ethics?'

Before this, the teacher had been gradually leaning back in his chair, relaxed, ready for discussion. At this he slowly turned his head to look out of the window and said, 'Yeah. What *is* ethics?', all the while nodding his head up and down as if pondering some grave responsibility. Then he puffed out his cheeks and audibly exhaled, letting the air escape in a long, long sigh. Finally, he suggested we postpone a discussion of ethics until later in the semester.

OK. Looked as though we were not going to be discussing ethics in class at all.

Still. Why did somebody with a university degree in philosophy find the subject of ethics so daunting that he did not even *attempt* a definition? Why did an intelligent dinner guest with an inquisitive mind tremble with frustration when the subject of ethics came up? What *is* it about ethics that strikes such fear into the minds of people? What, indeed, *is* ethics?

Well, let us have a look. Turning to my trusted dictionary, this is what I find:

1. The philosophical study of the moral value of human conduct and of the rules and principles that ought to govern it; moral philosophy. 2. A social, religious, or civil code of behaviour

considered correct, esp. that of a particular group, profession, or individual. 3. The moral fitness of a decision, course of action, etc.[144]

Hmm. Definition number 2 is the most helpful, but how do I define correct? And the other definitions are useless if I do not know what moral means. But luckily I can look that up too:

> 1. Concerned with or relating to human behaviour, esp. the distinction between good and bad or right and wrong behaviour . . . 3. Based on a sense of right and wrong according to conscience . . . 7. A concise truth, maxim. 8. Principles of behaviour in accordance with standards of right and wrong.

OK, a bit better, but still murky. So this has to do with a knowledge of what is right and wrong. This is not exactly a new insight. That is what we all think that ethics or morals are concerned with, but there is still no definition of how to determine what is right and what is wrong. Maybe I am asking too much of my dictionary? But wait – definition 3 sounds promising. It defines the benchmark for right and wrong as conscience. So looking up the definition of conscience should bring some enlightenment:

> 1. a. The sense of right and wrong that governs a person's thoughts and actions.

Fine. I give up. We are talking about something that is based on a sense of right and wrong according to a sense of right and wrong. No surprise that the issue deflated my teacher and frustrated my conversation partner.

The issue with ethics
My treatment of this subject so far is a *little* bit too tongue-in-cheek to be taken entirely seriously. Of course, we cannot

---

[144] Collins English Dictionary, as annotation 126.

expect a conclusive and insightful discussion of a complex subject from a dictionary.

But light-hearted as it was, our first attempt at defining ethics has highlighted precisely the issues that make the subject so difficult:

- Ethics is about deciding what is right and what is wrong. To do this, we need a benchmark.

- This benchmark may be human conscience. But that in itself is also defined in terms of right and wrong and therefore does not provide a yardstick that is objectively useable.

- Indeed, an individual's conscience is a personal thing, and ethical behaviour itself is defined as something that is considered so by a particular group, profession or individual. Hence, subjectivity seems to be an intrinsic quality of ethics.

- And yet, it is also said to be a concise truth or maxim. At least the former suggests a concept that exists independently of subjective interpretation, and the latter implies that the ethical code in question is at least *felt* (by a person or a group of people) to be sufficiently robust to serve as a maxim.

And now my head hurts again. But I think the issue with ethics has become clear just by looking up the concept in a dictionary. We all think, at least at some level, that it is desirable to know how to act in accordance with right and wrong. We all have some idea of what the *majority* of people would regard as right and wrong. And we have an idea of what we *personally* would regard as right and wrong.

But what if we are confronted with issues where this intuitive compass fails, where it may seem insufficient or get confused by strong self-interest? How can we decide whether it is OK to take part in a fox hunt? How can we know whether having an abortion is right or wrong? Is it OK to have an affair

with a married person if you are single – after all, you are not
the one cheating, are you? Can I bank this money that has
arrived in my account because of a clerical error? Is it OK to do
some of these plumbing jobs 'on the sly' – after all, I need to
make ends meet in this recession and surely this is excusable?
Can I cheat on my expense account? Should I join a legal tax-
avoidance scheme?

All these are real-world, practical issues. And yet, we do
not have to evaluate all of these as part of a theoretical exercise
in philosophy. We only have to find answers to those that may
emerge as actual problems in our lives. And it does not matter
which answer we find. It only matters that we *do* find one.

Still, even with these caveats, the task remains fiendishly
difficult. What methods should we use? How can we define
where we stand? How can we know?

It is to this question that I am turning next. Before I describe
my method of ETHICAL HYPOTHESIS TESTING, I would like to
discuss two important systems of ethics in popular thought
and in philosophy: the Golden Rule and Immanuel Kant's
Categorical Imperative.

The Golden Rule

Origins

Before chatting about the origins of the maxim that has become
known as the Golden Rule, let me first state it. There are several
versions, but most of these fall into one of two general ways of
expressing it:

- Treat others as you wish to be treated (the positive version of
  the maxim).

- Do not treat others as you do not wish to be treated (the
  negative version).

I believe most of us will be familiar with these maxims, even though we may not know them as the label Golden Rule. To me they make intuitive sense, and I can see why they have become a crucial part of popular morality: I would like to be treated courteously by others, so I will treat others courteously. I do not want people to punch me in the face, so I will not punch people in the face.

In fact, the nature of these two maxims as pragmatic guidelines for everyday behaviour is probably the reason they remain near-universal concepts in ethics and are not confined to a particular time or region.[145] The label Golden Rule appears not to have been in use until after the 16th century, but as a *concept* we encounter it far and wide.[146]

It is present in the Mahabharata, one of the two major Sanskrit epics, in stories rooted in the 8th and 9th centuries BC. Going north and jumping forward a few centuries in time, we find it is a key concept in the dialogues between teacher and students attributed to Confucius (551–479 BC):

> Tsze-kung asked . . . 'Is there one word that may serve as a rule of practice for all one's life?'
>
> The Master said, 'Is not Reciprocity such a word? What you do not want done to yourself, do not do to others.'[147]

---

[145] The classic monograph on this subject unfortunately remains untranslated; see Dihle, Albrecht. *Die Goldene Regel. Eine Einführung in die Geschichte der antiken und frühchristlichen Vulgärethik*. Vandenhoeck & Ruprecht 1962, p. 8 n 1.

[146] For a good overview see the Wikipedia article at https://en.wikipedia.org/wiki/Golden_Rule.

[147] Confucius. *Analects*. The Internet Classics Archive. http://classics.mit.edu/Confucius/analects.1.1.html. The quoted passage is section 3 part 15; see also, for example, sec 1 pt 5 ('Tsze-kung said "What I do not wish men to do to me, I also wish not to do to men"') or sec 1 pt 6 ('Chung-kung asked about perfect virtue. The Master said, "It is . . . not to do to others as you would not wish done to yourself . . ."') The Golden Rule abounds in the Analects in its negative formulation.

In the Middle East of antiquity, the concept seems enshrined in Maat, the ancient Egyptian concept of truth, in stories dating back to the 20th century BC. Fifteen centuries later, it is still present in the region, this time expressed as an ethical imperative: 'Do not seek revenge or bear a grudge against one of your people, but love your neighbour as yourself.'[148] And after the 4th century BC, the principle starts appearing pretty much everywhere; it is present in Greek oratory (Demosthenes) and literature (Xenophon, Ovid), just as much as in historiography (Cassius Dio, Diogenes Laertius).[149]

But I do not think a modern reader would intuitively associate the concept with these texts of antiquity. I believe a *modern* reader would have encountered the principle most naturally in a religious context. However, as we have seen, the ethical concept of the Golden Rule is much older than certainly the Abrahamic religions, and I think there is reason to believe that these theologies felt an urge to assimilate a moral code that they found deeply embedded in popular morality.

Certainly, it seems that the historical Jesus did not teach the concept. On the contrary, he appears to have positively *criticised* the Golden Rule and spoken out against the idea of the moral reciprocity enshrined in it.[150] In Luke 6:31–6, no sooner has Jesus declared the moral imperative to do 'to others as you would have them do to you' than he sets out criticising it as morally flawed:

> If you love those who love you, what credit is that to you? Even 'sinners' love those who love them ... But love your enemies, do good to them ... Then your reward will be great, and you will be sons of the Most High, because He is kind to the ungrateful and wicked. Be merciful, just as your Father is merciful.

---

[148] Leviticus 19:18.

[149] Meier, John P. *A Marginal Jew. Rethinking the Historical Jesus, Volume IV: Law and Love.* Yale University Press 2008, p. 554.

[150] See Meier 2008, pp. 556–7. Also Betz, Hans Dieter. 'The Sermon on the Mount'. *Hermenia – A Critical and Historical Commentary on the Bible.* Fortress Press 1995, pp. 306–10.

This passage from the Sermon on the Mount seems to owe more to the philosophies of the Stoics than it does to Leviticus. In Seneca's essay *De Beneficiis*, we find both the maxim of extending kindness to those who show themselves as ungrateful and also the doctrine of divine imitation: 'If . . . you wish to imitate the gods, then bestow benefits upon the ungrateful as well as the grateful; for the sun rises upon the wicked as well as the good, the seas are open even to pirates.'[151]

It is therefore plausible that the Golden Rule entered the Gospels via assimilation. The historical Jesus is unlikely to have taught it, opting for a principle which was more altruistic in essence and openly criticising the Rule's promotion of reciprocity. But the pragmatic wisdom of the Golden Rule resonated more naturally with ordinary people, and the authors of the Gospels must have felt it impossible to ignore.

This conclusion seems even more compelling as, by the time of Jesus's ministry, the principle must already have been assimilated into rabbinic Judaism. We find evidence supporting this hypothesis in the funny story of the Gentile and Rabbi Hillel. According to the anecdote, as told in the Babylonian Talmud,[152] one day a Gentile came to the shop of Rabbi Shammai, who was as famous for his teachings as he was for his rigid temper. The Gentile challenged Shammai to explain the whole of the Torah to him in the time that he could remain standing on one foot – if Shammai was successful, he would convert to Judaism. Shammai may have felt that the Gentile was making fun of him, as he drove him away with his measuring rod. Failing to receive the instruction he sought, the Gentile next proceeded to the house of the equally renowned rabbinic scholar Hillel, known for his wisdom and mild temper. Hillel must have thought that he could easily meet this

---

[151] Seneca. *De Beneficiis*. Book IV, XXVI. Project Gutenberg http://www.gutenberg.org/files/3794/3794-h/3794-h.htm#link2H_4_0006. See Meier 2008, p. 545.
[152] *Babylonian Talmud*. Tract Sabbath. http://www.jewishvirtuallibrary.org/tractate-shabbat-chapter-2. Also see Meier 2008, p. 555.

challenge, and responded succinctly, 'What is hateful to thee, do not unto thy fellow; this is the whole law. All the rest is commentary to this law; go and learn it.'[153]

What is interesting in this comment is that Hillel did not collapse the whole of the Torah into a principle identical to the Golden Rule. What he said is that the Gentile would need to learn the principles of the Torah to become a Jew. But he presented these principles as though they were a commentary on the Golden Rule, an ethical theme that the Gentile would already recognise. In doing so he presented him with something familiar and hence succeeded in attracting him into the religion rather than driving him away, as his learned colleague had done, literally. The Talmudic anecdote thus allows us a glimpse into the extraordinary power of the Golden Rule. It represented a principle of popular ethics to which ordinary people could intuitively relate, and as such both Jewish and Christian teachers of the 1st century assimilated it into their respective, often far more complex, theologies.[154]

It is hence not surprising that we also encounter the principle in the Islamic world. Although it is not stated as clearly as in the Gospels, we find the essence of the Golden Rule in the Koran, for example in the maxim of forgiveness:

> And let them pardon, and let them overlook. Do you not love for Allah to pardon you? Allah is All-Forgiving, Most Merciful.[155]

Even stronger than in the Koran itself, we find the Golden Rule stated literally in the Kitab al-Kafi, a collection of *hadith*, sayings and anecdotes attributed to the prophet Muhammad:

---

[153] *Babylonian Talmud*. The quote is from a paragraph in the commentary on Mishna VI. p. 50.

[154] See Meier 2008, pp. 555–7.

[155] Qur'an, Surah 24, 'An-Nur – The Light', v. 22. The Holy Qur'an. Translated by Talal Itani. http://www.clearquran.com/024.html.

A Bedouin came over to the Prophet and . . . grabbed one of the reins of his riding animal, and he said . . . 'Teach me a deed by which I can enter the Paradise'. So he said: 'Whatever you love the people to come to you with, so go to them with it, and whatever you dislike the people coming to you with, so do not go to them with it.'[156]

It is remarkable that again the Golden Rule is presented as a principle of essential morality. We have encountered the form of question and answer three times now: between student and master (Confucius), gentile and rabbi (Talmud) and believer and prophet (Hadith). Each time, the request is general and seemingly unanswerable in succinct form. And each time the wisdom teacher gives a simple answer by using the Golden Rule as an essential principle which he can be sure the person asking will intuitively understand.

It therefore appears that the Abrahamic religions preserved the Golden Rule as a core moral principle and allowed it to travel within their more complex theologies. The fact that the three major non-Oriental religions all hosted the Golden Rule in this way speaks to the extraordinary power of this intuitive concept of popular ethics and helps us understand how it could have survived the millennia as a pragmatic guide to everyday life.

Three test cases

A pragmatic guide it may be, but is it useful for our purposes? Let us see how the Golden Rule fares if we apply it to some of the problems in our list. I am going to pick out three real-life dilemmas that have happened to people I know and use them as test cases, not just for the Golden Rule, but also later, when we go on to discuss Kant's Categorical Imperative and my ETHICAL HYPOTHESIS TEST.

---

[156] Al-Kafi, vol. 2. Translated by Muhammad Bin Yaqoub Al-Kulayni. HubeAli asws. http://www.hubeali.com/alkafivol2/, The Book of Belief and Disbelief, Part 5, ch. 66 H 10, p. 27.

Case 1: Girlfriend overlap

Remember the story about me getting slapped on that holiday in Ibiza? The good-looking bloke I told you about was called Chad and, not surprisingly perhaps, he used to be a bit of a lad. We got on really well as friends and one day (when we were safely back in Germany) he took me aside and said, 'Mark, can I ask you something?' I said he could. 'Look – I met this really cool chick and we have sort of started dating.' That was not unusual where Chad was concerned, so I just looked at him expectantly. 'The thing is though, I am still going out with Irena.' Ah. Problem. 'But it's really basically over with Irena, she's not into it any more, and Mona's really cool.' 'Soooo?' Of course, by now I knew what he was going to ask. I just did not want to make it too easy for him. Not that I had any particular axe to grind. I was just having fun.

'So what would you do? Just get on with it and hope the situation with Irena will sort itself out? I don't want Mona to think I am not into her or whatever . . .'

What I said in response is actually irrelevant for our purpose. What is relevant is that Chad started drifting into his new relationship without ending the one with Irena. Although he seemed powerless to stop himself, he was still not entirely happy with what he was doing. It took about half a year before he managed to sort himself out, but during that time he became noticeably less easy-going and we could all see that something was wrong.

Case 2: Tax avoidance

It is an ordinary day in the office. I am preparing my models for the start of the corporate reporting season, chatting with investors about what to expect, publishing a few preview notes.

The phone rings. I pick up and a voice says, 'Am I speaking to Mark Hebwood?' Reassured by my answer, the voice continues. 'Well, Mark, what would you say if I told you that we have developed a product that lets you recoup all the income tax you've paid over the last five years?' 'I don't know. *Are* you saying that?' 'Yes, that is certainly what I *am* saying, Sir.' 'In that case, I would tell you that you are a criminal and that I'm hanging up.' I hang up.

Anybody who works in the City, indeed anybody who is in permanent employment, gets these sorts of phone calls every so often. By now, you know me a bit and may therefore not be surprised to hear my response – as we know, I can be stroppy.

But I can also be wrong. And of course, in this case, I was. The person on the phone was not a criminal. Tax avoidance is legal. Tax *evasion* is illegal. This case study is not about me, it is about the work colleague who got called next by the same people. He started talking to them but remained unconvinced. For several months he was agonising over whether to sign up to the tax-avoidance scheme. He was clearly tempted by the prospect of saving a considerable amount of money but could not make up his mind whether he should agree to do something moderately dodgy. But how to decide?

Case 3: Fox hunting
This case study takes us many years back to a restaurant in London, and to one of my very first dates with Mary. At that time we did not yet know very much about each other, but we were getting on well and dinner was romantic. There was candlelight, there was wine and we were holding hands across the table.

I could tell something was on Mary's mind. She was building up to telling me something. 'Mark, you know, there is something you should know . . . and I don't know how you will take it . . .' Uh oh. This ain't good . . . 'Next weekend, I'm going to do something I really love . . .' 'Uh-huh?' 'But I don't know what you will think of it. Next weekend, I'll be taking part in a fox hunt.'

The conversation may have been a long time ago, but I still distinctly know my reaction to this revelation. I snatched my hands away as if somebody had poured acid on them, breaking our tender hold in a most unromantic manner. Or rather, that was my immediate impulse – I was able to control myself and leave my hands where they were for just long enough not to look entirely impolite. I withdrew my hands slowly about two seconds later and tried not to look too shocked.

And this moment started several months of soul-searching for me. Could I be with somebody who engaged in a pastime I saw as clearly unethical? Actually, why did I think fox hunting was unethical? I had never scrutinised my position hugely, nor did I have to defend it among my circle of friends and acquaintances. What I needed to do first was to understand thoroughly what I thought about fox hunting and develop an examined verdict on the practice. I knew that I needed to do this before I could allow myself to take my budding relationship with Mary any further. But how to think about it?

Let us put the Golden Rule through the ringer and see whether it helps us decide what to do in the three cases.

Test driving the Golden Rule
Girlfriend overlap

Let us start with what is perhaps the easiest problem. Let us apply the Golden Rule. The first thing Chad needs to do is turn the problem around and then decide whether he would be OK with the treatment he would receive.

The analogous situation is that he is not seeing anybody else but has a feeling Irena is. Chad needs to ask himself whether he would mind.

If the answer to this question is yes, the Golden Rule would indicate that a girlfriend overlap constitutes unethical behaviour. If Chad would not like Irena seeing other blokes while she was still officially going out with him, it follows that he should not engage in analogous behaviour. If he took this insight to heart and acted in accordance with it, he would have to initiate The Chat, they would have to break off their relationship and then he would be free to pursue other interests.

Easy enough, really. But there's a snag, and here it is: what if Chad's answer to the question was no? What if he was indifferent? The relationship is over anyway, she can do what she wants and so can he?

If this was the outcome of the test, the Golden Rule would have failed. I do not believe the correct interpretation would be to conclude that girlfriend overlap is ethical, but certainly it is not prohibited by the benchmark of my ethical tool. And yet, somehow we feel that letting a relationship peter out in this way is disrespectful to the other person, it feels sloppy and it is unlikely to make us feel especially proud of ourselves.

This ambivalence is a deep-seated issue with the Golden Rule, and I will return to it in just a moment.

Tax avoidance

Let us move on to something a little bit trickier. With this problem, it is not even immediately clear how my colleague might apply the Rule. If it was a wrench, he would not quite get purchase on the bolt. He would fumble around and, when he finally got a grip, the bolt would prove difficult to turn, the wrench would slip and he would have to start all over again.

OK, so let us see. Tax is a payment of funds by residents of a country to a government. The government uses the proceeds to provide public goods and in this way achieves wealth redistribution. Maybe the Rule works like this then: I would not like to pay more than my fair share of tax as a consequence of other people paying less than theirs, so I will pay my fair share and no less. Or perhaps: would I mind if others paid less than their fair share of tax and as a consequence I had to pay more? I think most people would answer yes to this. The Rule would therefore say that tax-avoidance schemes are unethical and my colleague should not sign up to them.

But here is the thing. It is not difficult to imagine my colleague saying no to my last question. He might think that everybody is free to regulate their tax affairs as 'astutely' as they can, and if somebody chooses not to make use of tax-avoidance schemes, that is their decision. My colleague might say in response to my question, 'Well, I *would* mind but only because somebody else had found a way to avoid taxes that was more effective than mine.' Paradoxically, if my colleague felt inclined to respond in such a way, he might actually feel *encouraged* to join tax-avoidance schemes by applying the Rule, rather than see such action as unethical.

Dilute to taste

There is this ambivalence again, the same issue that diluted the rigour of results derived in the first example. George Bernard Shaw saw this weakness in the principle when he quipped, 'Do not do unto others as you would that they should do unto you. Their tastes may not be the same'.[157]

Indeed. The problem with the Golden Rule is that it elevates subjective interpretation of ethical behaviour to an objective benchmark. If overlapping boyfriends is not an issue for *me*, it follows that I can let my girlfriends overlap with no regard for what my girlfriend might think of such a practice. If I think it is everybody's prerogative to aim for the minimisation of their personal tax bill, the Rule will not prevent me from joining a tax-avoidance scheme.

So unfortunately, the Golden Rule appears to falter at the first hurdle. Chad and my colleague are still none the wiser – the Rule was not able to provide a conclusive answer!

It is unlikely to get any better if the issues get more involved still, but let us at least check.

Fox hunting

How do I apply the principle now? This is even worse than before – this time, I do not even know how to hold the wrench.

Treat others as you wish to be treated. Well, there is only the fox, but clearly it seems bizarre to ask questions like 'Would

---

[157] Shaw 1903, as annotation 118, maxim 1. Reprinted by permission of The Society of Authors, on behalf of the Bernard Shaw Estate.

I like to be hunted like the fox?' This question would miss two points at once:

(1) We cannot conclusively state that the fox possesses self-awareness equal in quality to that of a human being. Hence, it does not help our purpose to see the hunt from the fox's perspective.
(2) It is the ethical conduct of the *hunter* that is under scrutiny, not the presumed psychological strain of the *hunted*. Even if it *did* make sense to assume the standpoint of the fox, that would not teach us anything about the ethical quality of our conduct in this context.

Hence, I do not believe it is possible to use the Golden Rule as a tool in this case.

Critiquing the Golden Rule

So where do we stand with the Golden Rule? Despite my criticism above, I still like it. It may fail when we apply it to complex ethical issues, but that does not seem to be the Rule's fault. There is a reason why it has survived the millennia as a benchmark of ethical behaviour. This reason is that it is *simple*. It works best when understood as a pragmatic guideline that governs human interactions on a daily basis:

• Would I like my girlfriend to cheat on me? No? Ah. I cannot cheat on my girlfriend.

• Would I like it if somebody stole my property? No? Ah. I cannot steal other people's stuff.

• Would I like to be murdered by somebody? No? Ah. I cannot murder people.

All these are examples of how we would apply the negative version of the Golden Rule. The negative version *prevents unethical behaviour*, and this is where I think the principle is strongest. The positive version *promotes ethical behaviour*, and in this it is less effective. It often fails altogether when applied to complex issues or ethical dilemmas. But for all its weaknesses, I believe we should remember it as a first port of call when trying to decide on ethical issues in our lives. It may solve the issue or give us insights into its complexity.

But if it does *not* solve it, who do we call? It seems we need to resort to heavier tools. We need tools that are resistant to the subjectivity that seems to inhabit ethical problems and which softened up the Golden Rule.

It is to the most famous of such tools that I am turning next.

Kant's Categorical Imperative

Background

Immanuel Kant is considered by many to be the greatest of modern philosophers. Even those who would not place him in such an elevated position hardly deny that his writings profoundly shaped modern thought on ethics and metaphysics.[158]

Kant was born in 1724 in Königsberg, East Prussia (today Kaliningrad, Russia), and died at the age of 80, still living in Königsberg. In fact, he lived a very ordered and outwardly uneventful life. When he died he had famously never travelled a distance more than 80 km from home. His day was rigidly structured: he rose at 5 am, interrupting his work day only for his afternoon walk, starting at precisely 4.30 pm and ending after precisely eight turns up and down his street. So unwavering was he in this ritual that it is said that his neighbours were able to set their watches by his walks.[159]

---

[158] For example, Russell, Bertrand. *History of Western Philosophy*. Routledge 1946, p. 639.

[159] For a well-written introduction into Kant's life and philosophy, see Wharburton, Nigel. *A Little History of Philosophy*. Yale University Press 2011, pp. 110–120.

Possessed of an acutely intelligent mind, he devoted himself to academic studies from an early age and published numerous philosophical treatises while still employed as tutor to families in the catchment area of his hometown. At the age of 45, he was appointed professor of Logic and Metaphysics at the University of Königsberg, from which position he was to publish the works that secured him a place in the philosophical pantheon.

He developed his system of ethics in three major works: *Groundwork of the Metaphysics of Morals* (1785), *Critique of Practical Reason* (1788) and *Metaphysics of Morals* (1797).[160] Most of his fundamental thought on ethics is laid down in *Groundwork*, and hence I shall briefly summarise some key ideas taken from that work before we test Kant's thoughts on ethics in the cold light of the 21st-century day.

Groundwork
Preamble
Kant's *Groundwork* has received unparalleled acclaim as a key contribution to philosophy, and many consider it the most important work ever written in the history of ethics.[161]

First off, I should like to apologise to those who are intimately familiar with the work – my summary will only be able to skim the surface and will hardly do justice to the complexity

---

[160] I have always felt that metaphysics is just a big word for anything that talks about the structure of the world. The Greek word *meta* means beyond or upon. So I could, without losing too much subtlety of meaning, translate metaphysics simply as 'on physics'. Hence, Kant's title 'Groundwork ...' simply means 'How ethics basically works', and the title of his later book published in 1797 means 'How ethics works'.

[161] See Koorsgaard, Christine M. 'Introduction'. In Kant, Immanuel. *Groundwork of the Metaphysics of Morals*. Translated and edited by Mary Gregor, Cambridge University Press 1997, pp. vii–viii. See also Kraft, Bernd and Schönecker, Dieter. 'Einleitung'. In Kant, Immanuel. *Grundlegung zur Metaphysik der Sitten*. Felix Meiner Verlag 1999, p. XIII. All quotes from the text are from the freely available edition on Project Gutenberg, www.gutenberg.org 2004.

of Kant's thoughts. Still, we need to remember why we are looking at this at all: we are not trying to run a philosophy seminar[162] – we are hoping to come up with a system that will allow us to answer ethical questions more confidently, and as a consequence become more grounded, more balanced and more proud of ourselves.

Moral imperatives

Kant distinguished two general forms of moral precepts: hypothetical and categorical imperatives.

Hypothetical imperatives are precepts that are qualified. They are moral principles that mandate you to do something if you wish to achieve a certain goal, or if you wish to avoid punishment. 'Do not steal if you do not wish to go to prison' would be an example of a hypothetical imperative. Another: 'Be polite to others if you wish others to be polite to you.'

I think we all recognise the general form of the last example. It is the Golden Rule! In fact, I believe that by studying Kant we have just had an insight: the Golden Rule is a general hypothetical imperative! 'Treat others as you wish to be treated' means 'Treat others in a particular way if you wish to be treated by others in this particular way'.

As such, Kant would argue that the Golden Rule is inferior in moral quality to categorical imperatives. A categorical imperative does not need to be justified by reference to a particular benefit or penalty. A categorical imperative stands as absolute and is immutable. The categorical version of our first example is 'Do not steal!' End of story. No further elaboration necessary. The categorical version of our second example is 'Be polite to others!' That is it. Does not matter how others treat you.

---

[162] Although you may be beginning to wonder . . .

The Categorical Imperative

So the question might now be, what are the categorical imperatives that ought to govern my conduct? Is there a list?[163]

Kant, you will not be surprised to learn, did not seek to
publish an exhaustive list of categorical imperatives that
would give people a set of ethical maxims to live by. He was
interested in developing a general system of ethics and so he
formulated a basic, fundamental categorical imperative that
was intended as a blueprint for all others. This imperative has
achieved fame as 'the Categorical Imperative' and may, at least
by name, be one of the most universally recognised ethical
norms.

In fact, Kant names three versions of it, but he preferred the
first one because of its technical formality:[164]

> There is therefore but one categorical imperative, namely this:
> Act only on that maxim whereby thou canst at the same time
> will that it should become a universal law.[165]

A few lines further down, Kant offers an alternative reading of
this principle, which I find a lot more accessible:

> [. . .] the imperative of duty may be expressed thus: Act as if the
> maxim of thy action were to become by thy will a **universal law
> of nature**.[166]

A moral law of nature

Now, this is a bit convoluted and academically stilted, but in
essence it sounds promising. This maxim seems to address the
problem of subjectivity that we found so daunting when

---

[163] In the Torah, the decalogue is such a list. I have counted four categorical
imperatives of wider ethical applicability. Religions, of course, tend to have a
strong component of moral guidance. See Exodus 20:1–17.

[164] See Sullivan, Roger J. *An Introduction to Kant's Ethics*. Cambridge University
Press 1994, pp. 28–9.

[165] Kant 2004, section 2.

[166] Kant 2004.

dealing with the concept of ethics generally, and that revealed itself as the key limitation of the Golden Rule.

The Golden Rule said treat others as you wish to be treated. Kant said your treatment of others must be such that you would want to see it elevated to a general moral norm. In essence, therefore, Kant's benchmark for moral conduct is not subjective preference (Golden Rule) but universal applicability. Shaw's warning that the taste of others may not be the same as yours would not apply to the Imperative. Taste, Kant would point out, does not come into it – if all of human creation could not potentially live by the moral norm embodied by your action, your action is not good enough, pardon the pun.

The universalisation test

OK, that is all well and good, but clearly there is still a piece missing. How do I know whether my action is good enough to form the blueprint for a universal moral law? Subjectivity has not been banned entirely – *I* am still the one who decides whether I would wish to campaign for the morality of a given act to be accepted as a universal law.

The answer to this important question is already contained in the way in which Kant expressed the Imperative. Basically, for an act to be pronounced moral, there must not be a contradiction between an individual acting in this way and everybody else acting in the same way. If such a contradiction arose, Kant would see this as proof that the action of the individual was not morally permissible. Kant himself said that he believed ordinary people tend to challenge actions where the morality is found to be dubious in this intuitive way, by asking, *what if everybody acted in this way*? He goes on to illustrate the universalisation test in four examples.[167] I do not think it is necessary to go through these here, but I shall apply his test to a simple principle in order to illustrate how it works.

---

[167] Suicide, false promises, hedonism, lack of social conscience; see Kant 1998, 422–3.

Consider the following maxim: 'I shall steal to enhance my personal wealth.' Kant's test demands that the person who proposes to live by this principle must be able to will it to be a universal moral law without creating a contradiction. The expression 'will', in Kant's interpretation, is far stronger than 'want', and more akin to 'bring into existence' or 'enact'.

In this case, I would have to enact my precept as a universal law. I would have to campaign actively for a universal adoption of the maxim 'stealing to enhance wealth'. If I was successful in this, everybody would then need to live by this principle, and everybody would always steal for personal gain. However, in such a world, personal property would cease to exist in a meaningful way. All my stuff would constantly be nicked by somebody else, and I would constantly do the same. As personal property would cease to have any practical meaning, the act of stealing itself would become meaningless. In other words, the individual maxim of 'stealing for personal gain' cannot coexist with the identical universal maxim. This contradiction denotes that the individual maxim has no moral substance and is therefore prohibited.

Usefulness

It is tempting to summarise Kant's philosophy of ethics in the following way: we ask ourselves what the world would look like if everybody acted in the same way as we did. If no contradiction arises as a consequence, we would pronounce the maxim morally sound; if one did arise, we would pronounce it morally prohibited.

But does Kant's system actually *work* in practice? Is it useful in solving the ethical problems that we encounter in real life? And importantly, does it work *better* than the Golden Rule? We note, perhaps with some measure of bemusement, that the Golden Rule would have been perfectly adequate to tell us that stealing is not ethical. To bring this to a light-hearted point, let us contrast what the Rule and the Imperative have to say on the subject of stealing:

- *Rule: I do not want people to nick my stuff, so I won't nick theirs.*

- *Imperative: Everybody is always nicking everybody's stuff, so there's no point in nicking anything.*

The net result is the same. Both tests have identified stealing as unethical. The key difference between the two is this: the Golden Rule elevates subjective preference to an objective benchmark; the Imperative aims to identify a universal benchmark and apply it to the individual.

But even though it is stated in a grossly simplified way above, there is something about Kant's universalisation test that makes me uneasy. In the end, is it not self-interest that we discover again when applying the test? If everybody stole, stealing would not work, so I will not steal. If everybody lied, lying would not work, so I will not lie.

Indeed, does Kant's test not transform a categorical imperative into its weaker hypothetical version? 'I will not steal because stealing would cease to make sense if everybody did so.' Not: 'I will not steal because I understand that stealing is unethical.'

If Kant's Categorical Imperative does indeed have these weaknesses, we need to ask ourselves whether the Imperative is truly more useful than the Golden Rule.

Well. Let us see.

Test driving the Imperative
Girlfriend overlap

To test whether the practice of girlfriend overlap is ethical, I shall require it to be a universal law mandating everybody to act in accordance with it. In such a world, nobody would ever tell a partner in a fading relationship that they have moved on to somebody else. It might be argued that it does not conflict with a personal maxim to act in this way and that it is therefore possible for the individual to will this as a law of moral nature.

Intuitively, this does not feel right, though. At least the Golden Rule, in one interpretation, would have identified this sort of behaviour as unethical. I guess most of us still feel that a practice of girl/boyfriend overlap is not quite right. The question remains, why do we feel this (if we do) and how do we know? The practice appears to have passed the universalisation test of the Categorical Imperative, but not necessarily the self-test of the Golden Rule.

Tax avoidance

This one seems more clear-cut. To make it easier to translate this problem into the terms of the test, I shall re-express the issue as, 'Is it OK not to pay tax at all?' To test this, I need to will non-payment of tax as a universal law and explore its implications. So what sort of world would we live in if nobody paid any taxes?

The answer is a world in which there would be no public goods. Infrastructure would only exist in locations where it is commercially viable to have it. Train links between remote villages would disappear, leaving the poor or disabled in a state of immobility and, one presumes, social isolation. Health and education could only be funded by the grace of individual philanthropists. Development of the arts would again be subject to patronage of the wealthy.

While it is conceivable that some may be perfectly happy to live in such a world, Kant would argue that even they would not be able to will such a world to exist. Kant would argue that the entrepreneur may find herself in need of infrastructure to transport her goods; that an individual might be in need of healthcare he would not be able to provide for himself; that a person may develop a taste for culture that could not be satisfied.[168] Anticipating such needs, a rational individual would not be able to will a world of no taxes into existence without contradicting his desire to benefit from the non-payment of tax.

So the Imperative, appropriately interpreted, would lead to the same answer as the Rule but, true to form, more

---

[168] Kant did not give these exact examples. I am interpreting his analysis of the fourth example, Kant 1998, 423.

categorically so. The Rule allowed a way out; the Imperative does not. According to Kant's Categorical Imperative, it would always be unethical to use tax-avoidance schemes.

Categorical self-interest

And yet, again there is this twinge of uncertainty. Is the Categorical Imperative actually categorical in this instance? Is it not self-interest that governs what I would will as a universal law and what I would not? Could I conceive of somebody who wills a world of no tax to exist if that person judges the cost–benefit to himself as outweighing the downsides? Kant may well have said no, but I am not convinced.

I believe we are sensing that the Imperative may not provide the ultimate answer either. We were not able to judge the moral fibre of our easier examples conclusively by either standard. In the end, neither the Rule nor the Imperative managed to provide compelling insights with finality.

Fox hunting

Let me see whether I can derive an examined stance on the moral quality of fox hunting from the Imperative.

First, I need to translate the activity into a personal maxim. We have already seen in the application of the Golden Rule that it is the ethical conduct of the hunter which is under scrutiny – the fate of the hunted may not be irrelevant, but it is secondary.

A maxim needs to have general applicability, so something like 'I shall always hunt for fun' does not quite cut it. What I need to find is the essence of why people like to engage in a fox hunt. From my discussions with proponents of the hunt, I believe most participants in a fox hunt value the activity as an adrenalin sport, see the social aspects of it as important but secondary, and justify the practice ethically by focussing on the fact that foxes can pose a threat to the livelihood of farmers in rural communities.

So I will focus first on the potential function of the hunt as pest control. I can see immediately that Kant would not agree with a fox hunter's claim that this justifies the activity on moral grounds. Kant would argue, in agreement with the sentiment of most hunters, that the driving motivation to participate in the hunt is personal enjoyment. Therefore, as the possible culling of the fox is secondary, the fox hunter does not act out of a *sense of moral duty* when engaging in the hunt. The hunter would have hunted anyway; it is not as if he feels compelled, out of a sense of responsibility for the community, to take part in an activity in which he would not otherwise have participated. This absence of duty, in and of itself, does not make the activity unethical, but it *does* mean that I cannot build pest control into the formulation of my maxim.

I shall therefore propose the following maxim: 'I shall chase and kill a predatory animal for personal pleasure.' I believe this captures the essence of a fox hunt, and I would not expect objections to this point from either proponents or opponents.

Now I have the maxim. Next, I need to universalise it. Can I will this maxim to be a moral law of nature? Well, if everybody were to hunt predators for fun, and I wished to do the same, no contradiction between individual and universal maxims seems to arise. There is also no paradox that would make such activities meaningless, so again the maxim appears to be passing the test.

But still, there remains something in the formulation of this maxim that makes me uneasy. Is it really OK to chase and bring down a living being for no other reason than the pursuit of personal pleasure? Why would a hunter feel this pleasure? Is it merely the adrenalin? There are other adrenalin-producing activities that could be substituted, such as downhill mountain biking, car racing, bungee jumping – the list is endless. So perhaps there is something specific in pitting your wits against that of the fox, in chasing the animal? There seems to be something atavistic or primeval about this activity. But there is also something that does not feel quite honourable. The hunter is not meeting the fox on a level playing field. He is on horseback, he has a gun, he is supported by an army of footmen and hunting dogs, and he is in the company of other hunters, who are also on horseback and who also have guns. He is chasing the animal without any real risk to himself. Is there something about the hunt that is at odds with the dignity of a human being?

I cannot answer these questions with the tool of the Categorical Imperative. Neither was I able to apply the Golden Rule to develop an examined understanding. But in thinking about the issue in the context of the Categorical Imperative, at least I was able to ask a series of questions that highlighted the problems I have with fox hunting. It seems I got a little bit further than before. But I am not there yet.

Critiquing the Imperative

The Imperative has certainly provided verdicts. Applied in a strictly mechanical way, it would pronounce girlfriend overlap and fox hunting as ethical and tax avoidance as unethical. But I feel this method has not quite cracked it yet.

To me, the main shortcoming of the Imperative is just that – that it feels *mechanical*. The universalisation test is necessary in deciding the moral fibre of an act, but it produces its verdict by reference to a technical indicator. If there is a conflict between an examined personal maxim and its proposed universal equivalent, the personal maxim is pronounced unethical. But we do not necessarily understand *consciously* why it has been so pronounced. Working through the application of the Imperative does not necessarily enlighten us.

The Imperative identifies stealing as unethical. It does so because stealing would not make sense if everybody did it. But it does not explain why stealing is unethical. It does not lead to an insight that, for example, the personal property of a person is part of an individual's private sphere. It does not discuss whether, and why, such a sphere may be inviolable. It does not examine the extent to which a person who violates the private sphere of another may diminish his own self-respect or dignity. The test is a perfunctory device. It may give us an answer, but often it does not tell us the *reason* for the answer.

Neither the Golden Rule nor the Categorical Imperative therefore seem entirely useful if we wish to develop an examined understanding of how to behave properly in certain situations. Both leave something open, we do not get closure, we are unable to banish the noise in our lives, we do not yet act with our head held high. But that is what we want. That is what we *need*. So what can we do?

I believe all we *can* do is attempt a case-by-case analysis of ethical questions that allows us to judge each issue on its merits. But to do that we need a method.

I guess it is time to do some DIY. Let us see whether we can develop a method ourselves.

Ethical Hypothesis Testing

The tool
The problem with the Golden Rule is that its pronouncements changed with the subjective verdicts of each individual. The problem with the Categorical Imperative is that it tried to banish subjectivity entirely and produced rigid verdicts in the process. In short, the Rule is too subjective and the Imperative not subjective enough.

What I would like to develop is a tool that works with the inherent subjectivity of ethics and keeps it at bay as long as possible, before allowing it in when evaluating the result.

What I require of my tool is twofold:

- It must allow us to think about ethical questions with a large degree of analytical rigour. It must not arrive at solutions in a mechanical way. It must foster genuine insights into the nature of an ethical issue.

- It must find verdicts on where we are *comfortable* to stand, not where we are *ordered* to stand in response to the outcome of a prescriptive model.

In this chapter, I discuss how we may build such a tool. I call this tool ETHICAL HYPOTHESIS TESTING.

Ethical invariance

The first task we face when starting to build our tool is how to deal with subjectivity. We need to make the tool as objective as we possibly can and treat any residual subjectivity as responsibly as possible. Let us approach slowly how we may be able to do this.

Let us think back to how Kant originally defined the Categorical Imperative. He said that only those individual maxims that could potentially be elevated to a universal law of nature could stand as ethical.[169]

A universal law of nature. This, I think, is interesting. Kant used this expression as a metaphor. But what if we stopped looking at the concept metaphorically? Why do we not look at the properties of *actual* laws of nature for a moment?

One of the most fundamental qualities of a physical law of nature is invariance. Invariance basically means that the properties of the law will not change in different locations, in different centuries or depending on how you look at them. According to Cox and Forshaw:

> It doesn't matter whether you are pointing north, south, east, or west, gravity still has the same strength and still keeps your feet on the ground. Your TV still works when you spin it around, and your car still starts whether you've left it in London, Los Angeles, or Tokyo. These are all examples of invariance in nature.[170]

Cox and Forshaw go on to say that 'if the laws of nature remain unchanged irrespective of the direction in which we are facing, then there exists a quantity that is conserved'.[171]

---

[169] Kant 1998, 421.
[170] Cox, Brian and Forshaw, Jeff. *Why does E=mc²?* Da Capo Press 2009, p. 59. Reprinted by permission of Da Capo Press, a member of The Perseus Books Group. Brian Cox and Jeff Forshaw © 2010.
[171] Cox and Forshaw 2009, p. 60.

So back to ethics. There are two concepts in our brief foray into the world of physics which I think may be fruitful in our attempt to control subjectivity in ethics. These are invariance and conservation. Would it not be useful if we could identify ethical qualities that are invariant and therefore conserved? For these conditions to be met, we require that these ethical qualities remain unchanged, irrespective of who you are, where you are, when you are or how you look at them. As a consequence, these ethical qualities would be conserved through time and space: they would be equally binding to people who lived in the 12th century, who live today and who will live in the 24th century. They would be equally relevant to people who live in England, Japan and Iran, and would be no less imperative if a person was stationary or moved from one location to another.

If we could identify some such ethical principles, we would have made an immeasurably important step forward. We would be on the same road that Kant travelled, but we would have a bagful of objective benchmarks by which we could measure the moral quality of specific actions.

Can we identify such principles? Well, we can try.

Ethical axioms – exioms

I believe that in order to find such principles, we need to observe what is already quite close to the surface. I believe we all have an intuitive understanding of fundamental ethical principles. A friend of mine pointed out to me recently that if we did not, nobody could make sense of how characters on soap operas interacted with one another.[172]

What I am proposing to do next is to find some ethical principles that are universally binding. I am looking for principles that we would regard as self-evident, in the same way as, for example, a mathematical axiom is taken to be self-evident. I

---

[172] Although another friend remarked that *Coronation Street* only shows that cheating on your girlfriend gets you into trouble, not that it is wrong.

like this analogy with axioms, and I think it is a useful one for our quest. The reason I like it may become clear if we look at what some mathematical axioms look like. Here are some, which I found in an old book:[173]

A point is that of which there is no part.

And a line is a length without breadth.

Things equal to the same thing are also equal to one another.

And the whole is greater than the part.

We see that an axiom is merely a statement the validity of which can be taken as self-evident. In other words, it is a 'statement of the bleeding obvious'. I do not believe any of the four statements I listed above are contentious or inspire strenuous effort to find counter examples – the statements stand up to common sense and can be taken as true with no further proof.

This is the sort of thing that I am hoping to find in ethics too. I am hoping that we will be able to agree on a set of simple ethical truths, statements that can stand as self-evident and that require no deeper justification. By analogy with an axiom, I shall call such statements ethical axioms, or 'exioms'.[174]

A list of exioms
The first three
Let us try to find some exioms. The way I will do this is more by stream of consciousness than by following a methodical

---

[173] Euclid. *Elements of Geometry*. Translated and edited by Richard Fitzpatrick, 2008, pp. 6 and 7. http://farside.ph.utexas.edu/Books/Euclid/Elements.pdf. The Greek mathematician Euclid (c. 300 BC) wrote this famous mathematical and geometrical treatise, which lists definitions, postulates, propositions and proofs of propositions. The work consists of 13 books, and in book 1 Euclid lists a series of axioms, postulates and 'common notions'. The first two axioms in my quote are from the section 'Definitions', the last two from the section 'Common Notions'.

[174] I hope you can forgive me this little intellectual vanity – I have always wanted to coin a new word.

analysis – I will bring it together at the end of the section. What you *will* notice, however, is that I am using principles embodied in the Golden Rule and the Categorical Imperative to get to my exioms.

We are looking for fundamental truths, so we could do worse than to start with a fundamental need all organisms share, that of *self-preservation*. This principle is universal and all life forms have developed mechanisms that ensure the preservation of their individual existence, and by extension their species.

Hence, an action that is designed to violate this principle can be pronounced unethical with no further burden of proof. The corresponding exiom is: 'It is unethical to kill.'

So there's the first one! And yes, I hope you are not disappointed. Like the mathematical axioms we briefly introduced, much of what we will discover will sound obvious, even trivial. It lies in the very nature of an exiom to be self-evident, so we cannot hope to discover novel principles that nobody has ever heard of. Whether the method we are building is any good will depend on how we use the exioms that we are discovering.

But let us explore the essence of our first exiom. Killing leads to the more generalised concept of harming. I think we can postulate that harming others is not a good thing and that we should refrain from doing so, certainly as a deliberate act. This principle is applicable in a wider sense, to include harming others in not only physical but also psychological ways. So my second exiom is this: 'It is unethical to harm others.' This would mean that I should not physically injure others deliberately, but also that I should not hurt others emotionally, for example through bullying or through breaking promises.

A third exiom, 'It is unethical to steal', sort of comes out in the wash, since it would violate the second one in its widest sense – when we steal, we also violate the private or personal space of another individual, and this action infringes the no harm principle.

Let us check whether our first three exioms are compatible with the Rule and the Imperative. I do not wish to be killed, harmed or have my stuff nicked, so I will not do it. The exioms have passed the Golden Rule. I would not wish to live in a world where everybody killed and harmed others and nicked other people's stuff, because in such a world it would not make sense for me to do the same. This conflict shows that actions such as this are ethically forbidden. More difficult to state, but the exiom has passed the Imperative too.

A qualification

It seems that we have found our first set of exioms. Now, let us check whether they are intuitively watertight. Do these exioms govern all possible cases? Or may there be some cases that fail against the exioms when stated in their rigid form, yet feel ethically justified nonetheless?

Going back to the principle of self-preservation, we immediately find one qualification that appears sensible. If somebody wishes to kill me, surely it would be ethical for me to defend myself? And if in the course of doing so the aggressor should come to harm, or even die, surely that would be ethically acceptable?

It seems we have found a valid qualification. We could restate all three exioms in this way:

*It is unethical to inflict harm on others / kill / steal **unless for the purpose of self-preservation**.*

For example, if I am about to starve to death and I have no other means of rescuing myself, it would be ethical for me to steal food (but not if I stole something the value of which exceeded the price of the food necessary to keep me alive, and not as a habitual life choice). If I was attacked, it would be ethical if I killed my attacker to defend myself, but only if the threat was sufficiently severe that any action other than killing would not result in removal of the threat. If I was able to neutralise the attack by any action less severe than the killing of my attacker, and I still ended his life, my action would qualify as doing harm and would therefore be prohibited by a higher-level exiom.

Passive forms

Next, let us see what happens if we consider passive versions of the active prohibitions we discussed above. 'It is unethical to inflict harm' is fine. But what about failing to prevent harm done to another person? I believe we would all agree that if it was in my power to prevent an attack on another person, I would be acting unethically if I chose to ignore the assault and withhold aid I could otherwise have offered. The same goes for killing or stealing. In one fell swoop, we have found another six exioms: 'It is unethical to allow harm to be done/killing to occur/stealing to occur' and their qualified versions 'It is unethical to allow harm to be done other than for self-preservation' and so on.

This last exiom deserves a comment. Consider the following case. An elderly, wheelchair-bound woman turns a corner in the street and comes face to face with a mugging in progress. The mugger is holding someone up at gunpoint, threatening to kill him unless money is handed over. In this situation, it would be perfectly ethical for the elderly woman to flee the scene of the crime and not attempt an active intervention lest the mugger turn on her next. However, if she is able to get herself out of harm's way, it would be unethical for her not to call the emergency phone line and report the crime in an attempt to help. Leaving the scene of the mugging would not violate the exiom, but failing to call the emergency services would.

This example would hold true in exactly the same way if we replaced the elderly woman with an able-bodied young male. Fleeing the scene of the crime may not be *courageous* in this modified scenario, but it would be *ethical*.[175] Remember,

---

[175] Provided the young man has not received training that would allow him to neutralise the threat to the passer-by, for example as a soldier or police officer. The key is whether it is within a person's power to help.

we are only concerned with trying to build a method that can measure the moral fibre of individual actions, not their valour as measured against some other standard.

The ethics sieve

Let us pause here. Clearly, we could continue in this way for a long time. But we must not lose sight of what we want to achieve: we would like to build an analytical method that allows us to think through ethical problems on a case-by-case basis. The reason we want this is because we need a benchmark we can use to judge the moral fibre of actions that bother us or of character traits which we discover in ourselves.

So let us see what we have accomplished thus far:

• We have discovered nine exioms. These are self-evident ethical truths which do not require further proof.

• We discovered them by finding a fundamental need shared by everybody (indeed, every living thing). We then explored the implications of self-preservation as such a need.

• We added self-defence as a fundamental qualification and explored the passive form of the exioms found. This yielded further exioms.

• Each set of exioms (three under each heading: no killing, no stealing, no harm) contains a hierarchy. For example, 'Do not allow harm to be done' has a wider remit than 'Do not (actively) do harm', and both are subject to a valid qualifier, 'other than for self-preservation'.

• The same is true for no killing and no stealing, although each can be seen as a subset of the wider remit no harm.

We could continue to fine-tune the exioms we have already found by subjecting them to further case studies. We could continue to look for more exioms and add more to our list

– clearly, the ones we have managed to find do not represent an exhaustive set.

I do not propose to do that here, but I do believe that, as we add further exioms to our list, we develop an increasingly more effective tool to judge the ethics of a situation, action or intended action.

So how would we use our tool in practice? We can construct an ethical decision tree, or ETHICS SIEVE. Let us do an example. Say the able-bodied but untrained young man we encountered earlier failed to prevent a mugging during which the victim was harmed physically. He ran off, but once out of harm's way called the emergency services to alert the police.

I can define the hierarchy of exioms that we can bring to bear in this case as follows. I am using increasingly exacting versions of the widest remit we found, no harm:

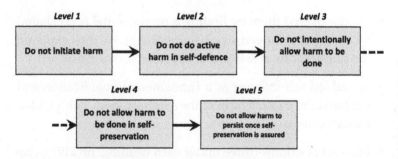

Fig. 9.1 A hierarchy of exioms with five levels. Higher levels are associated with more exacting versions of the basic exiom. An action that is ethical by the benchmark of a level-5 exiom, for example, conforms to a more stringent interpretation of ethics than an action that is only ethical when considered against level 4 (say) but is not ethical when measured against level 5.

Before I analyse this example, a quick word on the exioms:

- I deliberately designed the exioms in such a way that they form a hierarchy. However, the design I show in figure 9.1 is not the only one possible. We can construct filters that include a larger number of even more finely tuned layers. In fact, the method I am proposing is flexible, not set in stone. We need, to some extent, to start from scratch with each new case and develop the sieve that is most appropriate.

- Level 1 means: Do not deliberately set out to inflict harm on others. For example, do not walk into the street and punch somebody in the face.

- Level 2 means: When defending yourself against attack, do so proportionately to the level of the threat perceived. For example, if somebody approaches you with the intention of punching you in the face, run away, protect yourself or wrestle the attacker to the ground (in accordance with your level of training or skill), but do not shoot the person with a gun.

- Level 3 means: Do not withhold help if it is in your power to offer it. For example, if you see somebody in distress, do not deliberately ignore their plight and go about your business.

- Level 4 means: Do not withhold help by overprotecting yourself. For example, if you escape the scene of a crime for the purpose of protecting yourself, know when you are out of harm's way. It is OK to run away, but not OK to run away, get on the tube and take a 30-minute ride to another part of town. During the time it takes you to do that, you would be allowing harm to continue.

- Level 5 means: Do not withhold help once out of harm's way. For example, if you escape the scene of a crime, do not forget about the issue and go about your business once you deem yourself to be safe.

Filtering out the ethics – an example

Armed with these layered exioms, our test person is now ready to check whether he acted ethically. Troubled because he ran away, he gets out his ETHICS SIEVE. Here it is:

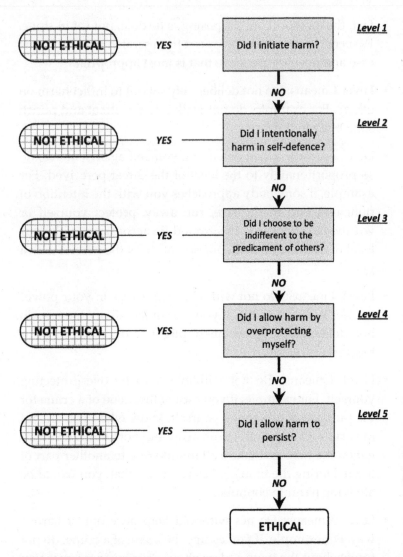

| | | | Level 1 |
| NOT ETHICAL | — YES — | Did I initiate harm? | |

| | | | Level 2 |
| NOT ETHICAL | — YES — | Did I intentionally harm in self-defence? | |

| | | | Level 3 |
| NOT ETHICAL | — YES — | Did I choose to be indifferent to the predicament of others? | |

| | | | Level 4 |
| NOT ETHICAL | — YES — | Did I allow harm by overprotecting myself? | |

| | | | Level 5 |
| NOT ETHICAL | — YES — | Did I allow harm to persist? | |

ETHICAL

Fig. 9.2 An **ETHICS SIEVE**. An action is progressively exposed to increasingly stringent ethical benchmarks. The example shows a sieve with five layers, but there is no reason why sieves with more layers cannot be constructed. If an action passes an exiom at one level, but not at the next level up, we can conclude that the action is ethical against level x, but unethical against level x+1. This type of analysis allows us to pinpoint an action's position within the ethical flux. It is up to the subjective interpretation of an individual to decide whether he wishes to accept this position or would feel urged to attain a higher one, effectively deciding to hold himself to a more exacting ethical standard.

Here is how he might analyse the situation.

He starts out with the most general question. He did not initiate harm. Hence, he passes level 1. In this case, therefore, he immediately passes level 2 as well, since it follows he cannot have inflicted harm in self-defence either.

But now he needs to move on to the next, more restrictive exiom. Did he allow harm to be done? This exiom has a wider remit as it captures a higher number of possible cases. Hence, this exiom is tougher to pass. Unfortunately, if he is honest with himself, he *did* allow harm to be done as he took off when he could have gone in and protected the victim. But there is the qualifier of self-preservation – he is asking himself next whether such an intervention would have been made at a potential cost to his health or his life. The answer is yes; he is not a trained fighter and does not possess the tenacious mindset required to neutralise a threat to another person safely and effectively.

Hence, he was not indifferent to the predicament of others. Neither did he overprotect himself – as soon as he cleared the scene of the crime, he stopped running and started to reflect on the situation. So he also passes levels 3 and 4.

How about the final test? Once out of harm's way, did he do something to help or not?

Yes, he did. He called the emergency services and therefore, if anything, got more effective assistance to the victim of the mugging than if he had intervened himself and ended up unconscious on the ground.

Filtering out the ethics – results

Phew! He passed the level-5 exiom, which in the sieve that we custom-made for this specific case happens to be the final level. Our test person can rest assured that he has acted ethically on this occasion. He may still be troubled that he chose to run away, but as we said before, our test is about ethics, not about any other behavioural standard.

And knowing that he acted ethically in this situation, he has brought closure to a problem that may otherwise have continued to disquiet him. Am I a good person? Did I do the right thing? Was I acting selfishly? Should I change something about myself? All these are questions he was able to answer and lay to rest. As a consequence, he will be more self-assured, more centred and incrementally happier. He knows a little bit more about who he is and will be able to like himself more.

But what if he had *not* called the police? In that case, he would have acted unethically since he did not call for help when the situation allowed him to do so. In that case, his action would have failed at level 5 of the sieve.

What if he had been a trained professional, for example a police officer off duty, a soldier on leave, a security professional such as a bodyguard or even a trained fighter, like a boxer or a martial arts teacher? In that case, his action would have failed at level 3 of the sieve since he could have been expected to possess the means to neutralise the threat to the victim but he chose not to. This would qualify as withholding help that it was in his power to give, and hence would violate the exiom 'Do not allow harm to be done in self-preservation'.

So what is the power of this analysis? I believe it lies in the following observation: without filtering his action through the layers of the sieve, a trained fighter could, in theory, claim that he had acted ethically. 'So what?' he could ask. 'I didn't actively hurt anybody so what's the problem?' But using the tool of the ETHICS SIEVE, he would be able to realise that his action did not stand up against a level-3 exiom, although it does against both a level-1 and a level-2 exiom. In not calling the emergency line, the young man would have to realise that his action passes exioms at levels 1 to 4, but not at level 5. Using these results, the fighter and the young man may have found out something about themselves they did not like and would have been free to hold themselves up to more exacting ethical standards in future. The decision to do this or not is still a conscious choice, but after analysing the situation with the ETHICS SIEVE, the decision they make is an examined one.

And this, I believe, is all we can hope to achieve when analysing ethical issues. We can subject an action to progressively harsher ethical tests and observe at which level of the sieve it has stopped. We deliberate whether the action is sufficiently ethical at that layer to be adopted as a principle for personal behaviour. An action complies with more exacting ethical standards the later it gets stuck in the sieve, or if it never does.

This is what I meant when I said that I wanted my method to be capable of holding subjectivity at bay for as long as possible. The ETHICS SIEVE is a tool that allows the user to analyse ethical situations with some rigour and some level of objectivity. Whether an individual deems the ethical quality of an action to be sufficient at a given level is again subjective and largely at the discretion of the person asking the question.

But subjective though that decision may remain, we will have achieved a *conscious knowledge* of which level of the ethical continuum we are at, and will have made an *examined choice* about whether or not we are comfortable with that position.

Ethical Hypothesis Testing

Now let us see how we can incorporate the ETHICS SIEVE into a formal procedure that allows us to examine the moral fibre of an action with some measure of objectivity. I call this procedure ETHICAL HYPOTHESIS TESTING (or EHT) and base it loosely on a method used in statistics,[176] so any similarities you may notice do not occur by chance. I will use the ethical dilemma of girlfriend overlap as an example:

(1) We start by stating the hypothesis. This is a simple statement such as 'Letting your girlfriends overlap is ethical'.
(2) Next, we need to analyse the action and find its essence. In this case, I am moving on to a relationship with somebody else without formally ending the one I am in. I am doing this without exploring the views of my partner in the

---

[176] Statistical Hypothesis Testing.

fading relationship, and without consulting my partner in
the blossoming one (assuming I am not telling either of
them). I am putting self-interest first, perhaps because I
wish to avoid confrontation, or because I am indifferent to
the psychological well-being of others, or even deliberately
to inflict emotional distress on my existing partner.

(3) Next, we formulate this essence as a maxim. In this we
need to be careful not to express the maxim too narrowly.
For example, 'I shall always let my girlfriends overlap'
does not capture the essence and therefore lacks general
applicability. Perhaps we could say in this case, 'I shall
give priority to the pursuit of my self-interest and shall only
secondarily concern myself with the well-being of others'.

(4) Often, the formulation of the maxim itself will provide a
strong hint as to whether the action is ethical or not.
Certainly in this case the reader may agree that the prioriti-
sation of self-interest over that of others feels unethical.

(5) But why? To find out, we need to measure the moral fibre
of the maxim against exioms. This is where the ETHICS SIEVE
comes in. We may already have identified the exioms in
previous deliberations, or we may have to find fresh exioms
for the purpose of the specific test. For this example, let us
see whether the sieve we developed above will serve.

a) We are starting with the most fundamental exiom. The
one we found earlier is 'Do no harm'. In a literal sense,
we can claim that we did not actively initiate harm and
so the exiom is not violated.

b) But what about the next one down? Well, I certainly did not
act in self-defence, and so I have passed my level 2 exiom.

c) Next up, level 3. The formulation we used in the sieve
does not work well in this case, so let us replace it with
our original exiom, 'Do not allow harm to be done'.

Did I do this? Well, again, *strictly* speaking I have not
allowed harm to be done either. But I created a situation
which has the potential for harm. If my existing partner
finds out, she might object, feel hurt or think she is being

betrayed. This might not *actually* be the case – but *potentially* it could be. And I did not worry about this *before* I acted, so I allowed a situation to arise in which psychological harm to my partner was a realistic possibility.

(6) Next, we interpret our findings. In this case, my action violates a level-3 exiom.

(7) Finally, we formulate the conclusion. In this case it is: 'Girlfriend overlap is unethical when measured against a level-3 exiom. We need to reject the ethical hypothesis at the third level.'

You may think this way of expressing the result is unnecessarily convoluted. But in fact it is essential to do it in this way. By saying it this way, we preserve the insight that ethical standards will often remain subjective. A verdict such as 'This action is unethical when measured against a level-3 exiom' implies that the action *may* be ethical when measured against a less exacting standard. In the end, it is up to the individual to decide whether a standard of less than x is good enough.

I believe that EHT ought to allow an individual to work out where they stand in the ethical flux. The analysis is conducted against invariable benchmarks and therefore remains objective as much as possible. The conclusion is formulated in a deliberately scientific way and is not subjective in itself. Only the examined decision to accept a particular position is derived by reference to personal standards and remains subjective.

But pragmatically speaking, how subjective would this decision actually be? Have a look again at the sieve and at the conclusion of the girlfriend overlap example.

Level 2 is all about self-defence. But surely I can never claim in a situation such as this that I acted out of a need to defend myself? I may not have the courage to face up to an uncomfortable conversation, but self-defence this is not. A threat to self-preservation needs to be fundamental (physical injury or death; severe psychological trauma), so uncomfortable conversations do not qualify. Hence, level 2 does not really apply and it turns out that I failed at the second hurdle really. An action that is only ethical against an exiom which states that I should not actively inflict harm on others does not seem to carry a lot of moral fibre. In short, I conclude from my analysis that girlfriend overlap is pretty damn unethical.

Therefore, there really is only one plausible conclusion: we cannot let our girl/boyfriends overlap and need to deal with the situation in some other way. I am afraid there is no way that we can ethically avoid 'The Chat'.

Test driving Ethical Hypothesis Testing
Girlfriend overlap

We know the result – no reason to dwell on this again. I just wish to point out an interesting fact: girlfriend overlap passed the Categorical Imperative (it was not pronounced unethical) but not the Golden Rule. However, the Rule left a back door open and therefore failed to give a categorical verdict. So far, EHT is the only method equipped to state categorically that the practice is unethical against all but the widest ethical standards.

Tax avoidance

Let us apply EHT to find out.

Hypothesis	Tax avoidance is ethical.
Essence	I am attempting to reduce my share of tax through the employment of a scheme the only purpose of which is to bring about such a reduction.
	Since I am attempting to pay less than my fair share, I prioritise self-interest over the interests of others. The effect of my action is to reduce the overall contribution to public funds and so does not induce any indirect public benefit.
	As such, the essence of my action is to place self-interest over the interests of others.

Maxim	I shall always attempt to reduce my fair share of responsibility at the expense of increasing the burden of others.
Ethics sieve	*Level 1. Did I initiate harm?*

Well, I suppose this is debatable.

My intention was to lower my own tax burden, not to increase that of others. I believe it is possible to argue that I might not actively have initiated harm. However, as the increase of other people's tax burden is a direct consequence of my action, I believe it is possible to argue that I violated a level-1 exiom. For the purpose of this analysis, I choose to go with the softer interpretation and say that I did not initiate harm.

Level 2. Did I intentionally harm in self-defence?

No.

Level 3. Did I choose to be indifferent to the predicament of others?

I believe it can be argued with confidence that I did.

Consider an analogy. You are a member of a ball club. You do not want to miss training sessions but cannot take the kids to the club as it does not have a crèche. Other members are in a similar situation, so eventually everybody decides to chip in and collect sufficient funds to establish a crèche service at the club. Say it costs £15,000 to run this service for a year and the club has 50 members. Each person's fair share (tax burden) in the establishment of the crèche service (the public good) is £300.

However, you find a way not to put money in. By avoiding contribution of your fair share, you have increased the burden for everybody else to £306 each. Now, that may only be a bit more than a fiver each, but I think most of us would see such conduct as unfair, indeed unethical.

So why might we think that similar behaviour is acceptable in the context of tax and the wider economy? Presumably because we see the impact as diluted, our action as anonymous and the public benefit as abstract.

I would argue that by joining a tax-avoidance scheme, a person does indeed ignore the additional burden this choice inflicts on others.

Conclusion	The practice of tax avoidance is unethical when measured against a level-3 exiom. We need to reject the ethical hypothesis at the third level. In a more rigid analysis of the dynamics, the practice might even be pronounced unethical when measured against a level-1 exiom.

Fox hunting

Let us see whether my method helps me define what I think of fox hunting, hence making it easier for me to go through the early stages of my relationship with Mary.

Hypothesis	Fox hunting is ethical.
Essence	I derive pleasure from chasing and bringing down a (predatory) animal.
Maxim	I shall chase and kill a predatory animal for personal pleasure.
Sieve	*Levels 1/2.* Before we answer this, we need to remember that the test applies to the ethical

integrity of the hunter, not that of the hunted.[177]
An animal is not a person, so a fox hunter does
not actively harm some*body*. Strictly speaking,
therefore, she has not violated a level-1 exiom
and was not acting in self-defence.

Level 3. But did she allow harm to be done? Well,
this is subtle and exceedingly difficult to answer.
I would argue yes. I would argue that she
allowed her ethical integrity to become compromised, as she is engaged in bringing down a
living being in the pursuit of pleasure. This
motivation dominates; she is not hunting to
survive, or combining pleasure with the supply
of food (as in a grouse shoot, for example) and
she is certainly not motivated by the urge to
provide a public service (in the alleged culling
of a pest).

As pleasure dominates, I would argue she may
diminish her own personal integrity, and by
extension that of the society hosting the activity.
Few would deny that the banning of practices
such as cockfighting or bear-baiting has elevated
the integrity of society at large.

Level 4. Last way out! Did she allow harm (against
herself) to be done for reasons of self-preservation?
Not unless the hunter in question is, for example,
a farmer whose livelihood depends on livestock
which the fox routinely endangers. But even then

---

[177] I use this opposition loosely. Ethical judgements can only exist as self-
reflecting thoughts and hence presuppose an advanced degree of consciousness. This is a wide field and I am relieved we do not have to go into this
subject as part of our quest for happiness. For the purpose of the argument I
am presenting here, I shall assume that animals are not sufficiently self-aware
to be moral agents.

there would be defensive ways to protect the livestock (fences, for example, or a professional culling of the vulpine population), not driven by the
pursuit of pleasure.

Conclusion   The practice of harming or killing a predatory
               animal for the purpose of personal pleasure
               alone, or for purposes dominated by personal
               pleasure, is unethical when measured against a
               level-3 exiom. We need to reject the hypothesis
               at the third level.

OK. It seems I am getting somewhere. I may not have an absolute answer, but I should not have expected one in the first
place. What I *do* have is a balanced verdict that pronounces the
activity as unethical when measured against certain exacting
standards and ethical when measured against other less restrictive benchmarks.

So where do I choose to stand on this? As far as my analysis
goes, there seem to be three possible positions. A fox hunter
could say:

(1) 'I can see that the activity may diminish my personal integ-
    rity, but the infraction is so subtle that I regard fox hunting
    as sufficiently ethical for me to engage in it.'
(2) 'I am troubled by the potential compromise of personal
    integrity and will desist from fox hunting until I have done
    some further soul-searching.'
(3) 'I realise that the preservation of personal integrity is
    more important than the pursuit of personal pleasure and
    will stop participating in fox hunts.'

All three stances are possible, and all three are equally valid.
Which one a hunter chooses is again *subjective* – there is no way
of eliminating subjectivity from ethics.

At the end of this process, I did of course not know where
Mary stood, but that was not the point of the exercise. I knew

where *I* stood, and I also knew why.[178] I had developed an examined stance, and I was confident that I could argue it. By extension, I had developed an understanding of where Mary might
stand and why. My ethical exercise enabled me to be more empathetic with Mary, and made it easier not to prejudge her on limited
knowledge. As a consequence, I was able to lay the issue to rest,
engage with Mary confidently and regain my emotional balance.

Critiquing Ethical Hypothesis Testing

So . . . in the end, does EHT work? Did it do something the other
two methods were not able to do? Did it find answers where
the other two did not? Is it a tool that we can use to define an
ethical view, and hence to achieve balance and happiness?

To critique EHT, it is helpful to see it in the context of the
methods we discussed. Here is my checklist:

	Ethical system		
	Golden Rule	**Categorical Imperative**	**Ethical Hypothesis Testing**
General characteristics			
Treatment of subjectivity	Used as benchmark	Tries to eradicate	Tries to qualify
Benchmark used	Self	Moral law	Axioms
Ease of use	High	Low	Low
Verdicts			
1. Girlfriend overlap	Ethical / unethical	Ethical	Unethical at level 3
2. Tax avoidance	Ethical / unethical	Unethical	Unethical at level 3
3. Fox hunting	N/A	Ethical	Unethical at level 3
Quality of verdict			
1. Girlfriend overlap	Ambiguous	Final	Differentiated
2. Tax avoidance	Ambiguous	Final	Differentiated
3. Fox hunting	N/A	Final	Differentiated
Pros & cons			
Key weakness	Subjective	Mechanical	Case-by-case analysis
Key strength	Simple	Reduces subjectivity	Can produce examined views

Fig. 9.3 Strengths and weaknesses of the three ethical systems in comparison. The systems
differ most fundamentally in how each strives to deal with the issue of subjectivity. The Golden
Rule is the easiest to apply and is intuitively accessible, but essentially subjective. The other
two methods cannot be applied as easily and require conscious thought and effort, but they
have the potential to yield less subjective results. EHT has the potential to generate examined
views, a feature not necessarily present in the other two systems.

---

[178] Note that I am not revealing where that is. As I said before, it is not important *what* the answers are, what is important is that there are some.

I believe the key weakness of EHT is that it is not easy to apply. It does not use an intuitive benchmark, like the Golden Rule, or feature a mechanical indicator that decides the ethical fibre of an action, like Kant's universalisation test. Instead, EHT needs to be freshly worked out each time it is applied. We may need to think about appropriate exioms to use as benchmarks if we encounter a moral dilemma we have not analysed before. We may need to reformulate exioms that we already found in order to customise them for the problem at hand. We may need to redefine, or newly define, the hierarchy of exioms in a particular moral issue. We need to find the essence and formulate the maxim. And we need to decide how a particular behaviour filters through the ethics sieve we constructed for the case at hand.

In short, EHT is a method that needs to be custom-made each time we use it. But I would argue that this is a blessing in disguise. The need to customise the method forces us to think about the issues in depth when we encounter them. And if we apply EHT often enough, we build the method into a more elaborate tool, a tool that becomes easier to use with practice.

This leads me to the key strength of the method, as I see it. After analysing a problem using EHT, we are likely to have produced an *examined* view. I do not believe either of the two other methods I presented in this chapter is able to do this. The Golden Rule only works in comparatively simple cases, and has a tendency to produce ambiguous verdicts depending on the subjective stance of the individual who applies it. The Imperative is rigorous, both in its demand on intellectual analysis and in the finality of its verdict, but the method does not necessarily provide further insights into the nature of the ethical issue at hand.

EHT aims to avoid these shortcomings. My method does not try to banish subjectivity (Imperative), but neither does it allow subjectivity to stand unmodified (Rule). It does not aim to generate verdicts with finality, but neither are its findings ambiguous. EHT accepts that subjectivity is printed into the ethical DNA and therefore tries to shape and structure it and keep the analysis as objective as possible for as long as possible. Its verdicts are commensurately gentle, but they do have teeth. Behavioural maxims are pronounced as unethical with finality, but only at a given level of ethical stringency. It is this feature which I believe makes EHT useful in defining a personal position within the ethical continuum. After applying EHT, two individuals may still forcibly disagree about the ethical quality of an act, but now they do so from a position of *insight* and not merely of subjective preference.

Having examined our relative positions, we are now able to argue them with confidence and conscious understanding. This in turn means that we have become a little bit surer of ourselves, that we feel moderately more anchored and that we have carved a modicum of extra meaning out of life. If we do this repeatedly, the effects build, even compound. Eventually, we will be able to decide which negative traits in our personality can stand and which ones need to be modified. We will become more centred, we will like ourselves more and we will be happier.

RULE 10

Know who you are

The Happiness Test

A finish to the start

We have travelled together for a while now and, dare I say, it has been quite an adventurous journey of discovery. We set out to discover that most elusive being of all, ourselves. We have cooked up a number of methods to get closer to it, including EXPERIENCE MINING, the DICE and ABACUS TESTS, EPIPHANY RECOGNITION and also the game of like and dislike. We have been thinking about whether we are to blame for everything that happens to us, and we have met a master of survival. We have practised how to let go of the tendency to judge others, but also how to take advice *from* others. Half way through the journey, we discussed how we might find a permanent travel companion, and were starting to put together a toolkit for the construction of our world. Late in the journey, we turned our attention to deeper matters and were thinking about how to tell right from wrong. All this was to achieve one goal – the goal of finding balance, liking ourselves and being happy.

Are the elements we discussed helpful in developing happiness? Before we can answer this question, we need to have some idea of how happy we actually *are*. I left this task to the final chapter of the book.

'Yeah, great,' I hear you say, 'but perhaps that would have been a useful *first* chapter, rather than coming up at the end of the book?'

Well, yes. It probably would have been. But I think we needed to appreciate what has gone before to understand where we are now. In a way, we have now reached the starting point, not the finish line. We need to know ourselves in order to understand how happy we are, and we need to know how happy we are in order to understand how happy we wish to *become*. This sounds as if we have come full circle, but I do not think that is quite the right metaphor. It is closer to climbing up to the first floor on a spiral staircase – we may have got back to the starting point, but our position is now *elevated* above the level from which we started. We have more insight into ourselves and into the way we need to shape our lives, and as a consequence we will be able to probe the quality of our happiness more competently. In essence, if we had not completed the journey that went before, we would not stand a chance in the HAPPINESS TEST.

So let us see then. How happy are we at the moment?

The Happiness Test

No multiple choice

First off, I have to disappoint those who thought that this would be a multiple-choice test of the nature you find in some of the glossy magazines. Neither is it a survey of yourself, like those carried out by the government for the UK population. In my test you will not find any direct questions asking you to rate your happiness levels actively. For example, participants in the government survey are asked to identify satisfaction levels on a scale ranging from zero (low) to 10 (high), responding to questions like, 'Overall, how satisfied are you with your life nowadays?'[179] This type of question invites the respondent to measure his satisfaction levels directly, by reference to a benchmark which is only loosely defined and known only to himself. And as there is no requirement that the respondent evaluates his benchmark in some way, I believe a direct question may invite positive bias – my guess is that few people would admit in a survey, even if they know it to be anonymous, that they are dissatisfied with their lives.

I do not think that this problem invalidates the findings of the government survey but, for the purposes of a *personal* investigation, I would like to introduce a benchmark to which we can perhaps relate more intuitively. So rather than asking for a direct evaluation of an element in our lives, I shall be asking how much *less* happy we would feel if it was taken away. Rather than asking, for example, whether I am happy in my current relationship, I shall be asking how much *less* happy I would feel if it was gone.

The life stuff – a sketch

My questions work broadly on the adage 'you don't know what you've got until it's gone'. But what is 'what'? Where is the list?

Well, each of us has to make our own list. When I tried this test on myself, I started out by jotting down a list of everything that is and is not important in my life. I did not think about any single item specifically, I just sat down and let a stream of consciousness take over. I did not censor anything or structure the list in any way. I just wrote down whatever came to mind. I would suggest you do that too.

Why don't you do it now? I already have my list. Here it is:

---

[179] Office for National Statistics. *Measuring National Well-being: Personal Well-being in the UK, 2014 to 2015.* 2016, p. 5.

> *Car*
> *Home (my house)*
> *Home (location where I live)*
> *TV sets*
> *Playstation*
> *Club membership*
> *Job (financial security)*
> *Job (meaningful activity)*
> *Sports activities*
> *Acquaintances*
> *Friends*
> *Ursina*
> *Family*

Fig. 10.1 I jotted down this list on a sticky note.

Analytical methodology – the happiness grid

Rating your happiness – part 1

So you have got your list? Doesn't look like much?

Well, it does not have to. You can expand it later if you wish. But this is a good start. Now I want you to think about every item on the list in the following way: *If it was gone, how much less (or more) happy would I feel?*

That is it. No more than that. Think about it honestly (only you see the results of this) and grade the answer on a scale of –5 (devastated) via zero (indifferent) to +5 (ecstatic).

Rating your happiness – part 2

After you have done that, however, there is a second part. This one is slightly harder. I said before that the list should not be structured – we are just writing down the items as they occur to us. But this, of course, does not mean that all the items we come up with are equally important. Some will mean more to us than others, and the second part of the exercise is addressing that.

So next you need to go back to every single item and ask yourself the question, *Why did I feel that way about this?*

Let us do an example. Consider the item 'car' on my list. First, I ask the question, *How much less happy would I feel if my car was gone?* Say my answer is only a little bit – I like my car but it is not that important to my overall happiness. In accordance with this sentiment, I am grading it –1.

Now I need to ask myself, *Why do I feel this way about it?* Well, let us see. I like the shape of the car, I like looking at it when I get back to it after doing something and I like the sound the engine makes and the acceleration. But I live in London and, from a practical standpoint, I could certainly manage without a car. So *not* having the car would not matter very much. I am not entirely indifferent, but its loss would be no major issue.

At the end of that short thought process, I know why the loss of my car would make me slightly less happy: I regard my car as a toy. It is not essential to my life, but I like having it. So I am writing down *toy* next to the rating of –1.

Rating your happiness – part 3
With this insight we have arrived at the third and last part of the grading exercise. This is the hardest, and it requires an advanced level of self-knowledge and maturity. We need to grade the quality of the reason we have found. Is the reason for my loss of happiness superficial in nature, or does it reflect a quality that I feel is essential to my life? To stay with my example, I need to ask myself whether the loss of a toy (and specifically this toy) is non-essential or elementary.

This is a separate evaluation and needs to stand in its own right. It is difficult to make because it requires a measure of objectivity. We need to find a way of standing next to ourselves to answer the question as a disinterested observer. So the question to ask would take a general form, for example: *Do toys represent a superficial happiness, or are they the essence of a person's life?* I need to grade my answer on a scale of 3, from –1 (non-essential) via zero (neutral) to +1 (essential).

Rating your happiness – an example

As an example, let me illustrate how three different people might rate the loss of their car. Let us ask Larry, Jo and Ann. None of these people exist; I made them up so that I could illustrate how to look at the different parts of the rating exercise.

Larry is a bit like me. He would wind up mildly less happy if he lost his car. He regards it as a toy, and he feels that toys are nice things to have but that they do not represent the essence of life. His answers to the rating questions are *not much* for part 1, *toy* for part 2 and *non-essential* for part 3. His ratings are accordingly {–1; toy; –1}.

Jo sees her car as a utility item. She lives in a rural area and needs it to get around – get to work, do the shopping, do the school run. The loss of her car would make her life noticeably more difficult. For her, losing her car would reduce her independence significantly and would therefore have essential repercussions. Her ratings are {–4; utility; +1}.

Ann does not need her car as she lives in a metropolitan centre with excellent public transport. But it is a classic and she loves it. She found it, negotiated a price, bought it, rebuilt the engine and lovingly restored it from the ground up. Her grandfather used to drive one just like it and the car therefore carries a lot of sentimental value for her. A loss would devastate her but she is a mature and well-adjusted individual. She realises that at the end of the day, the car is only an object and could be replaced if lost. She can find another one and restore that, and at any rate she knows that the memory of her grandfather lives more vividly in herself than it does in a tangible thing. She realises that the car, as much as it means to her, is non-essential in quality and rates its happiness value as {–4; sentimental value; –1}.

And that is the reason for the double ratings – three different people can feel identically on how much something means to them and yet feel this way for entirely different reasons. Jo and Ann would both be devastated by the loss of their car. But this is where the similarity ends. Jo would lose an essential utility item and she knows that her car is fundamental in her life for that reason. Ann would lose a replaceable object and knows that in the end her car is non-essential.

Or consider Ann and Larry. Both realise that their car is a non-essential item and yet they rate its contribution to their overall happiness differently – Larry does not feel it would be a big issue if it was gone, but Ann does.

Constructing the grid

If we evaluate every item on our list in this way, we end up with a large table. The table shows three things for every item in our list (for every element of our lives that we listed):

(1) The *severity* of the loss of happiness if it was gone. This is equal to how much the item contributes to our overall happiness. I call this *happiness intensity*.

(2) The *reason* why there is a loss of happiness. This is a subjective evaluation. It is the reason why I personally believe there would be a loss of happiness for me.

(3) The *quality* of this reason. This is a pseudo-objective evaluation. It is what I think the importance of the loss in happiness *should* be in somebody's life. Phrased differently, it is what I think the importance of the item's contribution to my overall happiness should be. I call this *happiness quality*.

OK. So I now suggest you grade your list in accordance with the three steps we discussed. If you want, you can expand it if you are getting more ideas as you grade the items on your list, or you can structure it by putting similar items together into categories. When you are finished, you will have a grid that allows some insights into both the *intensity* and the *quality* of your happiness.

To illustrate what the results may look like, let us take a look at my HAPPINESS GRID and then discuss some of the insights we derive. Here it is:

Mark's happiness grid

The grid

Component	Happiness intensity (−5 to 5)	Reason (Why?)	Happiness quality (−1, 0, 1)
Possessions			
Car	−2	Toy	−1
Home (my house)	−5	Safety	1
Electronics			
TVs	−2	Joy	0
Games consoles	−2	Joy	0
Hi-fi	−2	Toy	−1
Music streaming site	−2	Joy	0
Books	−5	Essence	1
Musical instruments			
Board games			
Jewellery	−2	Vanity	−1
Clothes	−3	Vanity	−1
Job (financial security)	−5	Freedom	1
Savings	−5	Freedom	1
Activities			
Courses			
DIY			
Education	−3	Essence	1
Sports			
Rock climbing	−3	Joy	0
Hobbies			
Gardening			
Travelling	−3	Joy	0
Job (meaningful activity)	−1	Essence	1
Charitable work			
Social nexus			
Club memberships			
Sports club	−2	Joy	0
Debating club			
Social sphere			
Social media			
Acquaintances	−2	Joy	0
Friends	−3	Joy	0
Best friends	−4	Essence	1
Partner, spouse	−5	Essence	1
Family	−5	Essence	1
Home (location where I live)	−4	Freedom	1

Fig. 10.2 A HAPPINESS GRID is a structured list of life components identified by the person analysing their happiness. The grid shows two major components, 'happiness intensity' and 'happiness quality'. A person evaluates their happiness intensity by grading how much the loss of a specific item would detract from overall happiness. A person evaluates their happiness quality by grading whether the component is superficial or fundamental in nature. The reason why the loss is felt is also recorded. The result is a three-dimensional grid, with a label and two numerical values assigned to each life component.

In fact, you do not have to create this grid yourself; I have prepared one earlier. You can download an interactive spreadsheet from my website that will allow you to list and grade the items you want, and also to create a chart showing things graphically.[180]

When I looked at my grid for the first time, I must say I was a bit underwhelmed. All I could see was a jumbled mess of dots and crosses. The table certainly did not generate immediate insights into the nature of my happiness, or even tell me how happy I was.

However, when I looked at the results one by one, things started falling into place. It is worth staying with your grid for a while and interpreting your responses first in isolation and then in context. If you immerse yourself in your grid, you will find that it is a powerful tool for analysing your current state of happiness.

Allow me to use myself as an example and let us look at my grid together. We will see how we might interpret its components and what we can learn from the evidence.

First observations

I grouped the elements loosely into three categories. Some items in the list do not apply to me and I merely included them to illustrate the sorts of things different people might include.

We have already discussed my reasoning behind the grading of the item 'car', so let us turn to the second item on the list. Here I wish to see how the loss of my home would affect me. This item refers to my home as a physical property – I use the word house loosely; a home can of course be anything you like – a house, a flat, rented or owned, even the freedom you enjoy if you are a traveller.

I know that the loss of my house would affect me intensely and so rate the loss of happiness −4, only one step away from devastated. Next, I ask myself why this would be such a

---

[180] The spreadsheet will generate a **HAPPINESS GRID**, a **HAPPINESS CHART** and a **HAPPINESS PROFILE**. You can download the file at http://www.markhebwood.com.

problem. It turns out that I regard my[181] house as a sanctuary. It is where I can let go of the world, it is where I can hole up with a book on the sofa, feel comfortable and enjoy the view from the window. In short, it is where I feel protected. So I note down safety as the reason for the severity with which I would feel the loss. Finally, I ask myself what quality that reason might have. The notion that I have somewhere to feel safe is essential to me. It represents an essence in my life and I rate happiness quality accordingly as +1, or essential.

As I discussed earlier, others may rate this item differently. Larry, whom we met earlier, may also be near-devastated by the loss of his home but for different reasons. He may keep an impeccable home to 'keep up with the Joneses', and derive his confidence from the kudos he receives from it in his social nexus. As a self-aware individual, he would note peer-group respect as the reason for his happiness and rate its quality as non-essential.

The next items on my list are electronics. Things like TV sets, my video games console, my hi-fi system, the music streaming site I use. The list is not exhaustive, and I could add to it if I wanted to, but the sample is representative.

I like watching TV. It is fun and can be educational, but in my case it is mostly escapism, I am afraid. If it was gone I'd do something else, but some of the fun would have disappeared from my life. Similar ratings apply to the other items in this group. I rated the quality of the reason why these things contribute to my happiness mostly as neutral. Clearly, the joy these items can provide is not essential but neither is it actually superficial. We need to be honest with ourselves and recognise that we all need fun and joy in our lives.

Books, you will not be surprised to see, play an important part in my life and if they were gone my happiness would be severely compromised, and for this reason I regard them as essential.

---

[181] The possessive pronoun 'my' is not supposed to denote legal possession but rather refers to the position that home has in my life. It is mine in an emotional sense, irrespective of whether I own it solely, jointly or not at all.

And so on. I am not going to discuss every single item, but I would like to point out the importance of financial security, education and friends in my world. You will not be surprised to see Ursina in pole position – other than my parents, she is the only influence in my life whose absence would leave my overall happiness in tatters.

One item that stands out is my job. If I think about it as a meaningful activity, rather than a means to provide financial stability, I have to concede that its absence would make me moderately happier! This may surprise you as I have stated repeatedly that I derive fulfilment from my job. However, this was not always so and my grid represents a snapshot in time when I was engaged in several strategies designed to bring job satisfaction back into my life.

OK then. So far I have my initial observations as I eyeball my responses. But if I want to learn something more from my grid, I need to look at the factors as a whole, rather than in isolation.

First insights
Solid dots first:

- Negative ratings clearly dominate, as indicated by the shaded area. In fact, there is only one dot in positive territory.

- Most ratings seem bunched in the −4 and −2 ratings. The distribution of ratings suggests that I am generally happy. If you take away any item on my list, I would be either near-devastated or sad. And this means in turn that most items in my life contribute solidly to my happiness.

- There are two other possible distributions of dots which we may encounter when constructing our grids. A grid which shows most of the ratings around 0 may suggest a general absence of joy in somebody's life – if you are vaguely indifferent to most things in your life, I would suggest that something is missing. And a grid which shows most of the intensity ratings as positive would be potentially alarming.

- If most ratings are in positive territory, this means that if you take any element of your life away, its absence would make you happier – it follows that all or most elements in your life make you unhappy.

Dots and reasons together:

- Items which contribute most to my happiness (−4 or −5 ratings) tend to be associated with two reasons in the main, *freedom* or *essence*. Both these reasons are fundamental. It seems that elements in my life that contribute most materially to my happiness are fundamental in nature.

- This finding suggests my happiness is of a robust quality. It seems that fundamental qualities tend to contribute more to my happiness than non-essential ones. In short, I am happy because I believe I have freedom in my life and have real friends, not because I have a noisy car and loads of superficial acquaintances.

- In other words, my HAPPINESS GRID appears to confirm that I have shaped my world into something that is close to my comfort zone.

Dot ands crosses together:

- Finally, let us look at the two quantitative ratings in conjunction. I believe this is where we may gain the deepest insights into the structure of our happiness. I am looking at them now. Are you looking at yours? My head hurts – I am just seeing a swirling cloud of crosses. You too? Time to change the format of the grid then. Let us put the results of our grid on a chart.

Mark's happiness chart

Here is the chart:

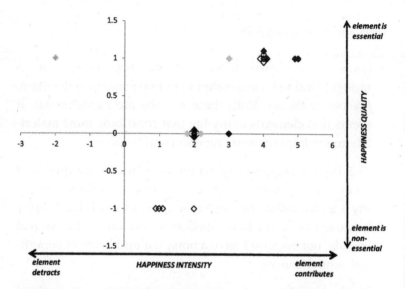

Fig. 10.3 A **HAPPINESS CHART** shows the numerical values of the **HAPPINESS GRID** as a three-dimensional cluster. Happiness intensity, the degree to which an element contributes to personal happiness, is shown on the horizontal axis (I reversed the negative values of the **HAPPINESS GRID** to positive numbers, as this is more intuitive in the context of a chart). Happiness quality, an evaluation of whether an element is essential or non-essential, is shown on the vertical axis. In this way, each element in our lives is represented as the sum of two distinct components. A third dimension can be specified by adding shading to elements in common groups. A **HAPPINESS CHART** gives more intuitive insights into the nature of a person's happiness than a **HAPPINESS GRID**.

Let me first describe what the chart shows:

- The chart presents the same information as the HAPPINESS GRID. Happiness intensity is shown on the horizontal axis and happiness quality on the vertical axis.[182]

---

[182] To avoid confusion, allow me to repeat a point made in the commentary below fig. 10.3. The ratings for happiness intensity are shown as positive rather than negative numbers. I think it is more intuitive to have positive numbers to show how much something contributes to personal happiness.

- This means that every item I single out in my list is presented as a combination of two components. The first component defines how much a given factor contributes to my general happiness. The second component evaluates the reason why it does so as essential or non-essential. Now I can see quite easily how the two components interact – my head hurts less.

- In addition, I have shade-coded major groupings on the chart. Factors shown in the grid under the headings possessions, activities and social nexus are represented as transparent, grey and black dots respectively. This dimension of the chart is not that important but nice to have.

Deeper insights

Let me now make a few observations on what I can learn about the structure of my happiness when I present the information in this form:

- First off, I see more easily what I had already observed when looking at the grid. Most dots are located in the right-hand area of the chart. Their contribution to happiness is *positive* and only one element detracts from overall happiness. This is an encouraging start. Most elements in my life appear to make me happy in some way.

- Looking at the chart vertically (just considering the vertical axis) we see that happiness qualities are distributed in three layers. One layer is situated in positive territory (above the horizontal axis), one is neutral (on the horizontal axis) and one is in negative territory. The elements I have singled out are distributed across the spectrum; some are essential, some indifferent, some non-essential.

- But I can also see that *more* elements are located in positive or neutral territory than below the line. Factors are above the line if they contribute to happiness in a fundamental way, and below if they do not. So my third glance suggests that most factors that make me happy do so for fundamental reasons and do not tend to be superficial in nature. This is also promising.

- Now I bring the two components together. I can see three clusters, and if I joined them up I would get a slash (/) sitting in the area of the chart to the right of the vertical axis. This, as we will discover, is a heartening outcome.

- Let me focus on the top right cluster first. These are factors that contribute most materially to my overall happiness (they are on the far right horizontally). And all of them do so for fundamental reasons (they are sitting high up on the vertical axis). It appears that a significant proportion of my happiness is based on qualities that I consider meaningful in my life. Just checking quickly what is in the cluster: four black, for social nexus – these are my best friends, Ursina and my parents. Plus the location where I live, defining social nexus in a wider sense. Three possessions, but these are my savings, my home and my books. I am happy with that.

- Next up, the middle cluster. Seven dots bunched at 2, contributing solidly but not materially to happiness. All of these are neutral in nature – I would consider these factors as neither fundamental nor superficial. Quick check: two social nexus (acquaintances and sports club, although the latter is also an activity), three possessions (TV, games console, music site) and two activities (sports again and travelling). This is all fine – factors that I would consider somewhat neutral in meaningful significance contribute proportionately to my overall happiness (that is, their contribution is neither marginal nor dominant).

- Last cluster to consider is the one below the line. Three items contribute marginally to my happiness, and I would grade them as commensurately superficial. Three transparent dots for possessions – this is my car, what little jewellery I have (a watch, basically) and my hi-fi (which I do not tend to use very much).

In summary, therefore, I think for the moment I can be satisfied with the structure of my happiness. Factors tend to contribute to my overall happiness proportionately to their importance in my life. Those that contribute most materially tend to be associated with qualities that I regard as meaningful. Conversely, things that I do not believe possess fundamental qualities contribute only moderately. Also virtually all factors that I have isolated in the analysis contribute to happiness, and only one detracts from it.

In short, most elements in my life make me happy, and for what I think are the right reasons.

'Perfect' happiness

I think it may be possible to generalise the results of my analysis to an extent. If I was to describe general HAPPINESS PROFILES in the context of my chart, I would be tempted to say that we should strive to develop a funnel – a slash which is narrow at the base and widens towards the top right corner of the chart. Ideally, no dots should be situated to the left of the vertical line. Such a HAPPINESS PROFILE would basically say this: *Everything in life makes me happy, and for the right reasons.*

If I lose the detail of the HAPPINESS CHART shown in figure 10.3 and just focus on its general shape, I could represent it like this:

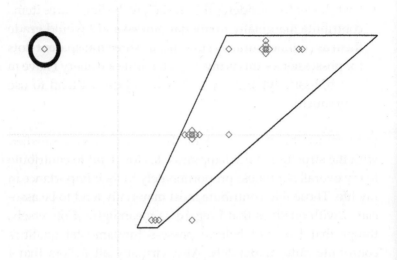

Fig. 10.4 A **HAPPINESS PROFILE**. This is the **HAPPINESS CHART** of fig. 10.3 in stylised form. This presentation focusses on the general shape of the chart, moving on from a detailed analysis of happiness to an evaluation of its overall quality. This example shows a strong profile where most factors contribute to happiness, and do so in proportion with their significance in the individual's life. There is one element that requires positive action as it detracts from the individual's overall happiness.

On the right-hand side is the funnel I was hoping to discover – that is encouraging. But there is one element that stands out, and I have circled it with a black doughnut in my stylised profile. There is an element in my life that detracts from my happiness, and unfortunately it does so for fundamental reasons! This item is *job satisfaction* and, since I took this snapshot of my HAPPINESS PROFILE, I have been taking steps to address the issue, with the goal to shift the dot horizontally to the right.

This last point also illustrates another quality of the analytical method I chose to adopt: the chart will allow us to gauge which factors fall *outside* the ideal HAPPINESS PROFILE, and also for what reason. Once we have identified these elements in our lives, we have taken a huge step forward. Now we know what it is that stands between us and 'perfect' happiness. And once we know, we are empowered to change these elements, preferably without affecting the quality of other factors that already contribute to happiness. The mindset that will help us change the offensive factor is none other than 'everything is my fault'. We should now be able to use MOCK SELF-INCRIMINATION as a tool to accomplish a specific purpose. This purpose is to maximise happiness in our lives.

Happiness profiles

The happiness doctor is in the house

I believe we might now be ready for a few general observations, a series of diagnoses and some practical advice. I am going to discuss some other HAPPINESS PROFILES that are theoretically possible, then diagnose the nature of the profiles and finally give some practical advice about how to mould their shapes into the ideal positive slash over time.

Profile 1: Negative backslash

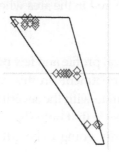

Description
(1) All dots are located to the left of the vertical line. This means that all factors examined by the respondent in her HAPPINESS GRID *detract* from her overall happiness – none contribute.
(2) The profile is a *backslash*. Points to the far left of the horizontal line (factors that detract from happiness most severely) are associated with points sitting high up on the vertical line (reasons for unhappiness are regarded as

fundamental). Equally, the respondent believes that factors detracting from happiness only moderately are less important or superficial.

(3) The backslash has a narrow base. This means that there are fewer factors that detract from happiness only a little bit and more that detract a lot.

Diagnosis

It is likely that the respondent is severely unhappy in her life. Everything in her life makes her unhappy, and mostly for fundamental reasons.

Example symptoms: Person may wish to have children, something she regards as fundamental in life, but is physically unable to do so. Person is seeking a job she sees as meaningful but is unable to define an appropriate arena of employment. Person seeks a life partner but is unable to find a way to go about meeting people. Person has few or no confidants with whom to discuss her predicament. Person cannot engage in the sporting activities she likes as they are not offered in the area where she lives.

Treatment

Arguably, this is a theoretical profile and few people may fall into this category. However, 'treatment' in this case presents challenges that are commensurate with the severity of the condition.

The first thing to realise is that only she can treat the condition; there is not necessarily going to be outside help, at least not at first.

Second, it will take time to turn her life around and achieve happiness.

Third, she will need to apply everything we discussed in the previous chapters to improve her situation. Most important will be to develop self-knowledge. Without it, she cannot hope to understand why the various stress points in her life exist. The HAPPINESS TEST itself should provide insights into which factors are the most severe and which are the least important.

Perhaps counter-intuitively, I recommend fixing the less

important ones first. These will be relatively easy to tackle, and should build the confidence needed to deal with the bigger ones. For example, she could move to an area of town where she will be able to do the sports she likes. This should give her a moderately more positive outlook and also dilute her isolation, making her meet people, in turn perhaps finding friends and eventually confidants.

Medication
Bootstrapping, going from the least to the most severe. EXPERI-ENCE MINING and EPIPHANY RECOGNITION – build self-knowledge over time. MOCK SELF-INCRIMINATION – be the agent, not the victim. Like and dislike, building insights into strengths and weaknesses. Take advice responsibly as social nexus grows. Progressively build comfort zone.

Profile 2: Negative slash

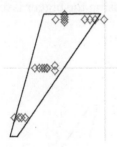

Description
As for *negative backslash*, with one difference: factors identified as fundamental detract less from happiness than those seen as less important.

Diagnosis
This person is likely to be severely unhappy in life. Everything in his life makes him unhappy, but not always for fundamental reasons. Indeed, it appears that factors considered less fundamental result in greater unhappiness than those seen as more

important. Example symptoms: Person would like to go travelling, but cannot find a travelling companion. Person would like to take up sports activities not available to him. Fundamental issues similar to those mentioned for profile 1.

Treatment

A person displaying this profile is only moderately better off than a negative backslash person. I would recommend fixing the simple issues first, as these tend to detract disproportionately from this person's happiness. So for example, go travelling alone and see whether you meet people on the way. Go on sporting holidays once a year or join a club to engage in sports activities during the weekend.

Medication

Self-knowledge. Explore why little things tend to make you more unhappy than the factors seen as fundamental. Insights gained may aid in addressing the bigger issues. Other medication as for profile 1.

Profile 3: Positive backslash

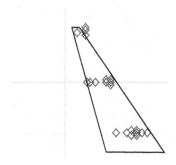

Description

All dots are in the area to the right of the vertical axis. All factors identified by the respondent in the construction of his HAPPINESS GRID *contribute* to overall happiness – none detract.

The profile is a *backslash*. Points to the north of the

horizontal line (factors that contribute to happiness least) are associated with points sitting high up on the vertical line (reasons for the contribution are regarded as fundamental). Equally, the respondent regards factors that contribute a lot to happiness as less important or superficial.

The backslash has a wide base. This means that the number of factors that contribute to happiness *materially* is higher than the number that contribute only *moderately*. Although this is the case, that higher number is associated with factors that are superficial rather than fundamental in nature.

Diagnosis
This person is likely to be very happy in life. Everything in life makes her happy, albeit mostly for superficial reasons. Example symptoms: Person loves shoes and has a large collection. Person loves chocolate and indulges (responsibly) on a regular basis. Person loves clothes, holidays, spa visits. Person enjoys the fact that her house, car, other possessions are the envy of the neighbourhood. Person draws confidence from the fact that she is financially secure.

Recommendation
A person who fits this type of profile is unlikely to require treatment. Arguably, if every factor in your life makes you happy, you are in a very good position indeed. However, the respondent may still pause and ask herself whether it would be desirable to shift the quality of this profile from happy for non-essential reasons to happy for fundamental reasons.

The answer to this question is by no means trivial or obvious. To help us answer it, I would like to offer you a short anecdote.

Recently, I crashed my car. I parked it in a car park and, when I got back to it, I pulled out straight into a low wall that somebody must have put there while I was away from the car. Or perhaps it was there in the first place and I never saw it. Regardless, the point is that I damaged my door and incurred cost and hassle to get it fixed. However, beyond the obvious inconvenience, the incident did not materially affect my overall happiness. The fact that it did not is consistent with my HAPPI-NESS GRID, in which the factor 'my car' shows up as moderately contributing to happiness as a superficial factor in my life.

Now think about how this same incident might affect a profile 3 individual. A profile 3 person derives a large amount of happiness from her car. Consequently, a relatively innocuous accident would have a big negative impact on her overall happiness. Of course, the factor 'car' is just an example. Shoes can be lost or they can break, spa visits can be spoiled, a new neighbour might refurbish his house in greater splendour than you. But a friend, as an example for a fundamental factor in life, will not simply disappear as a result of a casual coincidence. Of course, it is possible that a friend may tragically die or fall ill, but I would argue this is less likely to occur than everyday mishaps.

Speaking less abstractly, we all know the feeling that the world is coming down on you – the plumber did not fix the bath properly and needs to be called back in, the car needs servicing, the insurance company did not pay the claim so another tedious conversation with them is on the cards and so on. This does not happen every day but we all know days where these sorts of things just seem to happen all at once. Now imagine that your overall happiness in life depended on trivial things like that *never going wrong*. As soon as they do, your happiness is severely affected.

In short, if a person's happiness is generated for the most part by superficial factors, there is a significant risk that he or she may flicker between happiness and unhappiness from day to day. If a person's happiness is generated by more funda-mental factors, the chances are that it is less volatile, more resil-ient and hence provides a steadier foundation in life.

For this reason, I would suggest that, even if you are a profile 3 person, you are likely to receive benefits from trying to change that profile into a funnel. This is a profile that displays a good balance between essential and non-essential contributions to happiness and for this reason comes closest to the ideal of 'perfect' happiness.

Medication
EXPERIENCE MINING (to build self-knowledge). ABACUS and DICE TESTS (to find out what it is you really want). Like and dislike. EPIPHANY RECOGNITION (to note what matters in your life).

Spiralling into control

We have completed the HAPPINESS TEST. Apologies that I was not able to offer a simple multiple-choice test or a handy, ready-made happiness index measuring where we are on a scale of 1 to 10 (for example).

Happiness is an elusive concept and, as we have seen, it is affected by a large number of moving parts. These are difficult enough to pin down in isolation, but certainly trickier still when they are working together in complex and ever-changing dynamics.

But we have to start somewhere. I believe my HAPPINESS TEST may be a good place to start. By working through it, we can get a good first glimpse of the structure of our happiness as it is at the moment. We can then see what profile we would like to fit and we can observe the dots on the chart that are outside that profile.

Once we are there, we are ready to begin the journey. We need to develop or enhance self-knowledge. This is the key to everything else. As we do so we will encounter questions and challenges. Some we will be able to tackle with the methods I have described in the book and which have worked for me. Others may lie outside the scope of the methods presented in this book, and for those we will have to craft new methods.

After a while, we may feel that our attitude to life has changed somewhat. We may feel that in some aspects of our lives we have become more balanced. We may feel that in some issues we have found a more confident voice. We may feel that in others we place less importance on the expectations of others. If we feel that, we have come full circle and climbed the first level on the spiral staircase. If we feel that, we are ready for the next HAPPINESS TEST.

By working through it, we get renewed insight into the structure of our happiness. We can then see whether it has approached the profile we wanted it to be, and to what extent. We can observe the dots on the chart that are still outside that profile. We can identify a new target profile, or continue to work on the original one.

Once we are there, we are ready to continue the journey. We need to develop or enhance self-knowledge. This is the key to everything else. As we do so we will encounter questions and challenges. Some we will be able to tackle with the methods I have described in the book . . .

Are we there yet?

Well. You probably guessed what I am going to say. No, we are not. Nor will we ever be. The quest for happiness lasts a lifetime. Even those who can say that they have attained a high level of happiness are not there – life has a habit of redefining goalposts and then shifting them around when we are not looking.

Happiness will almost certainly change as we go through life. But we have the tools at our disposal to get happiness back if we lose it, or get to it if we are still looking.

We may never truly arrive. But we can make the journey as fulfilling, and as much fun, as possible.

That is kind of all I wanted to say.

Works cited

Pre-20th century

Al-Kafi, vol. 2. Translated by Muhammad Bin Yaqoub Al-Kulayni, www. hubeali.com/alkafivol2.

Aristotle. *The Nicomachean Ethics*. Translated by WD Ross, The Internet Classics Archive, http://classics.mit.edu/Aristotle/nicomachaen.html.

Babylonian Talmud. Tract Sabbath, www.jewishvirtuallibrary.org/tractate-shabbat.

Confucius. *Analects*. The Internet Classics Archive, http://classics.mit.edu/Confucius/analects.1.1.html.

Euclid. *Elements of Geometry*. Translated and edited by Richard Fitzpatrick, 2008, http://farside.ph.utexas.edu/Books/Euclid/Elements.pdf.

Kant, Immanuel. *Groundwork of the Metaphysics of Morals*. Translated and edited by Mary Gregor, Cambridge University Press 1997.

Kant, Immanuel. *Grundlegung zur Metaphysik der Sitten*. Felix Meiner Verlag 1999.

Kant, Immanuel. *Fundamental Principles of the Metaphysics of Morals*. Project Gutenberg 2004, www.gutenberg.org/ebooks/5682.

Pausanias. *Description of Greece*. Translated by WHS Jones, Theoi Texts Library, www.theoi.com/Text/Pausanias5A.html.

Plato, Phaedrus. Translated by Benjamin Jowett. The Internet Classics Archive, http://classics.mit.edu/phaedrus.html.

Seneca, *De Beneficiis*. Project Gutenberg, www.gutenberg.org/ebooks/3794.

The Bible. New International Version. Hodder & Stoughton 2005.

The Holy Qur'an. www.clearquran.com.

20th century to date

Betz, Hans Dieter. 'The Sermon on the Mount'. *Hermenia – A Critical and Historical Commentary on the Bible*. Fortress Press 1995.

Collins Dictionary of the English Language. Editors Urdang et al., Collins 1984.

Cox, Brian and Forshaw, Jeff. *Why does E=mc²?* Da Capo Press 2009.

Dihle, Albrecht. *Die Goldene Regel. Eine Einführung in die Geschichte der antiken und frühchristlichen Vulgärethik.* Vandenhoeck & Ruprecht 1962.

English, Ella. 'Family Feud'. *The Boston Globe*, 26th April 2006, www.boston.com.

'Golden Rule'. *Wikipedia*, https://en.wikipedia.org/wiki/Golden_Rule.

Handy, Charles B. *Understanding Organizations.* Penguin 1985.

Huxley, Aldous. *The Perennial Philosophy.* Georges Borchardt 1945.

Kellaway, Kate. 'No pain, no gain'. *The Observer*, 15th February 2004, www.guardian.co.uk.

Kelling, George and Coles, Catherine. *Fixing Broken Windows: Restoring Order and Reducing Crime in our Communities.* Touchstone 1996.

Koorsgaard, Christine M. 'Introduction'. In Kant, Immanuel. *Groundwork of the Metaphysics of Morals.* Translated and edited by Mary Gregor. Cambridge University Press 1997.

Kraft, Bernd and Schönecker, Dieter. 'Einleitung'. In Kant, Immanuel. *Grundlegung zur Metaphysik der Sitten,* Felix Meiner Verlag 1999.

Mehari, Senait G. *Feuerherz.* Knaur 2004.

Mehari, Senait. *Heart of Fire: From Child Soldier to Soul Singer.* Profile Books 2006.

Meier, John P. *A Marginal Jew. Rethinking the Historical Jesus.* Vol. IV: Law and Love. Yale University Press 2008.

National Society for the Prevention of Cruelty to Children (NSPCC), www.nspcc.org.uk.

Office for National Statistics. *Focus on Families.* ONS 2007.

Office for National Statistics. *Measuring National Well-being: Personal Well-being in the UK, 2014 to 2015.* ONS 2016.

Pelzer, Dave. *A Child Called 'It'.* Orion Books 1995.

Pelzer, Dave. *The Lost Boy.* Orion Books 1997.

Pelzer, Dave. *A Man Named Dave.* Orion Books 1999.

Prynn, Jonathan. 'City still hasn't grasped the nettle'. *Evening Standard*, 10th February 2012.

Rhinehart, Luke. *The Dice Man.* Harper Collins 1972.

Russell, Bertrand. *History of Western Philosophy.* Routledge 1946.

Shaw, George Bernard. 'Maxims for Revolutionists'. In *Man and Superman.* The University Press 1903.

Sullivan, Roger J. *An Introduction to Kant's Ethics.* Cambridge University Press 1994.

Thompson, Leigh and Hastie, R. 'Social Perception in Negotiation'. *Organizational Behaviour & Human Decision Processes*, vol. 47 (1990), pp. 98–123.

Wharburton, Nigel. *A Little History of Philosophy.* Yale University Press 2011.

Wilson, James Q and Kelling, George L. 'Broken Windows: The police and neighborhood safety'. *Atlantic Monthly*, vol. 249 (1982).

Acknowledgements

A few big **THANK YOU**s

I often see authors pay tribute for their debt of gratitude by saying that those to whom thanks is owed are too numerous to name. This is certainly true in my case as well, and to make matters worse I could not name everybody who contributed to this book even if I wanted to. The reason is that many of my friends and acquaintances contributed stories, directly or indirectly, and need to remain anonymous.

So my first big set of **THANKS** is due to all my friends who kindly permitted me to share often intimate details with you, merely to let me make some point I considered worth making. I also wish to thank all those with whom I now have less frequent contact, and those whom I only met briefly and in passing. All of you have provided me with life experiences that I was able to interpret in this book, and I would not have been able to do so had we not had that drink in the pub, that conversation in the cab or that brief chat at the airport bookshop.

More specific **THANK YOU**s are due to Tom and Aaron, my 'bestest' of friends. Thank you, Tom, for reading through the book and giving me invaluable advice and feedback. And we both know that I owe you a huge debt of gratitude for discussing the earthquake at dinner. Only a true friend would have done that.

Thank you, Aaron, for your moral support throughout this process. Your comments and observations on many parts of the text prompted me to think about the issues involved in more depth, with clear benefits to the discussion. I find it profoundly comforting that I can ask you any question and you will not misunderstand me.

Here's a THANK YOU to all of you who worked with me on the book. No doubt I will forget some, but special thanks go out to Isaac Tobin (www.isaactobin.com), who came up with a cracking cover design and was a joy to work with, Margaret Hunter (www.daisyeditorial.co.uk), whose suggestions on style made this book better, Georgina Aldridge at Clays, who was always there with invaluable advice, Fatimah Namdar (www. fatimahnamdar.com), who turned a day-long photo shoot into fun and games, Rebecca Souster (www.rebeccasouster.com) for excellent advice, and my friend Noel Ashton, who expertly designed my website.

But the biggest **THANK YOU** of all goes to Ursina. This THANK YOU is made up of so many THANK YOUs that I cannot list them all without adding hundreds more pages to this document. So here is just a selection. Thank you for urging me to write this book in the first place. Thank you for reading through all the chapters as you received them in instalments, and for giving me insightful, penetrating and constructive commentary. Thank you for believing in me. Thank you for . . . Oh? Enough? Really? Was that OK? Well then . . .

But joking aside, one thing that I have found out again in the process of writing this book is how important it is to have true friends. Friends who stand by you and like you for who you are. In the end, if you have that, I guess you are truly happy.